AND FINALLY . . . ?
The News From **ITN**

To the independence of television news

AND FINALLY . . .?

The News From **ITN**

RICHARD LINDLEY

POLITICO'S

First published in Great Britain 2005
by Politico's Publishing, an imprint of
Methuen Publishing Limited
215 Vauxhall Bridge Road
London SW1V 1EJ

A catalogue record for this book is available from the British Library.

ISBN 1 84275 067 4
Printed and bound in Great Britain by Creative Print and Design

CONTENTS

FOREWORD

ANDREW MARR, BBC POLITICAL EDITOR

This is a reporter's history in the very best sense. The good reporter sniffs out the controversy, homes in on the sensitive areas and leaves no word unminced, no vital phrase mumbled. Even in the internet age, television news is the medium used by most people to keep in touch with the world around them. It is a bastard art. Vaudeville jostles with heroism; the grease-paint sits beside the fat books of political reference. It is where showbiz and celebrity shake hands with economics, world affairs and science.

So, speaking of bastard artists. . . . For those of us at the BBC it may be a hard truth to acknowledge, but ITN virtually invented the modern news broadcast as it is now understood. When it first arrived in September 1955 this little platoon ruthlessly exposed the BBC's stuffy and picture-scared traditionalism. Then they did it again when *News at Ten* launched in 1967, with American-style newscasters and a half-hour bulletin. As Richard Lindley tells us, not everything went smoothly then or now. But without its louche congregation of whisky priests, ravine-faced foreign correspondents and booming, patriarchal editors the story of television news in Britain would be duller and briefer.

There are heroes here, men and women whose gutsy reporting in the field brought us stories of death and hope over the decades, and the behind-the-scenes executives who fought bitterly for ITN's independence from its commercial paymasters. There is Michael Nicholson, in the middle of the Biafran war, finding himself to his horror filming a soldier being executed in cold blood, and waiting for his turn. There is Peter Sissons, whose awful shooting during the same conflict and its agonising aftermath echoes so uncannily the plight of my BBC colleague Frank Gardner. There is Sandy Gall, whose relations with MI6 clearly worried Lindley, but whose Afghan reporting will be remembered for decades. At home, I would single out Mike Brunson as a great political editor. But behind them stood the great Geoffrey Cox, who had himself been a war correspondent during the Spanish Civil War, and whose leadership of ITN inspired literally hundreds of journalists; his successors Nigel Ryan, David Nicholas and Stewart Purvis, each of them fighting bitter battles over budgets and commercial strategy; and then the half-outsiders, like David Gordon and Alastair Burnet, who struggled to stop ITN's owners making idiots of it and of themselves . . . not always successfully.

Burnet, of course, was better known as a newscaster. For a relatively small operation, ITN has been responsible for some of the most familiar faces in television. Burnet was one, Sandy Gall another, Anna Ford certainly a third; today Sir Trevor, the great survivor, is rightly described as the nation's best-loved newsman. But even he has never had quite the impact of the brilliant, sometimes awful man whose life story sits irresistibly in the middle of this book. Reggie Bosanquet's father invented the cricket googly, and Reggie's wild, hilarious, ineffably sad and awesomely public life entertained and appalled the nation for many years. Richard Lindley's portrait of the rise and fall of Bosanquet is wrenching and compulsive. It is comedy and tragedy combined, a complicated story about drink, class, loneliness and what happens when you fall off the high-wire.

But what happens if and when ITN's *ITV News*, as we must learn to call it, falls off *its* wire? There is a challengingly elegaic note to the title chosen by Lindley, and for good reason. His book opens in a world where the BBC has no competitor. ITN had barely got going before its editor-in-chief is resigning because of its owners' narrow vision and determination to "reduce the cost of such news to the barest minimum." Crisis after crisis followed, the troughs between the broadcasting peaks, and no mistake worse than the catastrophic decision to kill off the old *News at Ten*.

Since then ITN has been cut to, and beyond, the bone. There are competitors, of course. Sky News's hot breath is on its neck. But a rolling news channel, however professional – and however heavily staffed by ex-ITN people – is not quite the same as a package-based news programme maker.

But for how long now will ITN survive? Lindley has a genuine scoop here in getting ITV's boss Charles Allen to admit that when contract time comes round again he will not be asking an independent ITN to do the news for him any more.

At the BBC, we are always watching the ITN lot. Sometimes we clap our hands to sweaty foreheads and groan – too much cheese, too much ham, boys, you're not selling pizza just yet. Sometimes we grit our teeth and curse – a scoop, or a brilliant swipe of interpretation we failed to get to ourselves. But the point is, we watch; and so do millions of viewers. If the end is nigh (and I hope it isn't) then Britain needs another lot of rumpled, ambitious, hyperactive and above all honest hacks to start again. And if so, they'll find this exhilarating book is a handbook as well as a history.

PREFACE

In January 1965, at his London home in Hyde Park Gate, Sir Winston Churchill lay dying; the long, eventful life of Britain's great wartime hero was at last drawing to a close. In a mini-cab outside, cold and uncomfortable, I tried to stay awake through the night. My job: to alert ITN, Independent Television News, to any signs of activity around Sir Winston's door and, if all remained quiet, to give political reporter Julian Havilland a chance to get some sleep before he returned in the morning to continue the vigil.

A year and a half before, the editor of ITN, plain Geoffrey Cox as he was then, had agreed to give me a job. 'I've seen your work,' he said, although because, until then, I had appeared on the television screen only in a 'God slot' programme called *Sunday Break* I found that hard to believe. 'But,' Mr Cox had continued, 'I don't have room for you at the moment. Get a bit more reporting experience and I'll send for you when I can.'

So when Southern Television offered me a contract (I later learned I had beaten a certain Michael Nicholson to the job) I took it. *Day by Day* was the local evening news programme and I contributed film reports, sometimes read the news and occasionally did studio interviews. Now, in a cold, dark January, I had been summoned to London, seconded to ITN to help out on a major national story. My contract with Southern was still running: as far as I knew I would soon return to my weekday base in Southampton. As morning broke I was relieved from my post and reported to my temporary headquarters at ITN, Television House in Kingsway.

Tentatively, I entered the busy newsroom, larger than any I had seen before. I recall lines of dark wooden tables covered with newspapers and typewriters, and greenish lino on the floor. Round the corner to my left I found a small, bright-eyed, sharp-tongued young woman slashing open the mail. This was the news-desk secretary, Amanda Griffin. Next to her, with a beard and an amiable grin of which I learned later to be wary, was her boss, the news editor Peter Cole.

'Looks like you're here, then,' he said, and so I was.

I spent the next eight years at ITN as a general reporter, very often on foreign assignments, before going away to work in current affairs for the BBC's *Panorama* and ITV's *This Week*. But I returned to ITN in the 1990s for another seven-year stretch, first to present the *ITN World News*, and then to make special reports for *News at Ten*.

I remain extremely proud to have worked for such a wonderful organisation as ITN, in the company of so many talented people – such very good companions.

R. L., December 2004

RESEARCH NOTE

ITN was never much of an organisation for paperwork. It has, however, kept most of the minutes of its board meetings and the associated papers, and I am most grateful to ITN chairman Mark Wood for giving me access to all but the most recent of them for this unofficial history.

For another, and sometimes more revealing, view of ITN's earliest days, I turned to records of the first regulator of commercial television, the Independent Television Authority. These files were in the care of the Independent Television Commission, the ITA's successor, until the ITC's own demise in 2003. For permission to study them I am indebted to the ITC's secretary Michael Redley, and its record-keeper Karen Firmin-Cooper. I am particularly grateful to the manager of the ITC's information office, Jan Kacperek, for unearthing the files at a time when the ITC's library was in the process of closing down, and for allowing me to make many visits there to read them. The ITC's newspaper cuttings about ITN have now been transferred to the library of the British Film Institute, where Wendy Thomas very kindly arranged for me to see them.

Other useful records have emerged in a more haphazard way from many different sources, but I owe a special debt, which I acknowledge in my text, to those who have previously written about their own time at ITN. The official history of Independent Television has proved a most reliable and informative guide to the changing television system in which ITN has operated, and I am particularly grateful to Paul Bonner who, with Lesley

Aston, has been responsible for the two most recent volumes. The two books written by Sir Geoffrey Cox, ITN's second editor, were indispensable to my understanding of ITN's genesis and development, as were various books written by the late Sir Robin Day, television's first and best interviewer, and by the late Aidan Crawley, ITN's remarkable first editor. I have found other books very helpful too, including those by Michael Brunson, ITN's former political editor; David Stanley, the chronicler of the *News at Ten*; producer David Phillips; and two reporters, Sandy Gall and Michael Nicholson.

At my publisher Politico's, Iain Dale, John Schwartz and Sean Magee have always been encouraging, and I am very pleased that my agent Andrew Lownie introduced me to them. I am lucky to have had the services of Barrie MacDonald, formerly the librarian of the ITC, as an indexer, as well as the wise legal advice of David Hooper. I gratefully acknowledge all the help and co-operation I have received from many people now at ITN, particularly Sophie Cohen, Sarah Christie and John Nolan. Helen Fairley has very kindly allowed me to use many of the memorable pictures that (as Helen Gane) she took of ITN at work in its early days.

For this book I have interviewed more than a hundred people. Each of those interviews I have found helpful, whether I have quoted them or not, but I am particularly grateful to all the surviving ITN editors who have, in more than one encounter, tried so patiently to explain to me the particular issues with which they had to deal – and, of course, why everything was fine leaving their hands. They are, in chronological order: Sir Geoffrey Cox, Nigel Ryan, Sir David Nicholas, Stewart Purvis and Richard Tait. The British Academy generously made me a research grant, which enabled me to have transcribed many of the interviews I carried out, work most professionally performed by Lucy Edyvean and Bryony Kinnear.

Finally I should like to thank the man who, more than any other, is now the guardian of ITN's history – Frank Miles, secretary of the ITN 1955 Club and editor of its newsletter. Throughout this project he has been an unfailing source of information and material, most generously devoting his time and energy to helping me get it right.

That said, this is not an official history, and I am conscious that although I have talked to and written about so many people I have missed out many more who have been important in ITN's half-century. To all of them I apologise. I can only hope that they, along with those to whom I have spoken, will nonetheless recognise in these pages some aspects of the ITN I have described.

INTRODUCTION

The big issue for ITN has always been this: what is it for?

Is it a news service provider, essentially owned by its most important customer, ITV, or is it an independent company, competing with others to sell television news and associated services worldwide?

That is the question that in ITN's history has been debated time and again at its boardroom table, a question that has, over the past fifty years, been tackled in quite different ways by those who have had charge of what in the beginning was called simply 'the news company'. Their attempts to answer the question have caused hopes to rise, only to be dashed; they have led to boardroom quarrels and dramatic resignations; they have brought the company to the brink of bankruptcy and the risk of extinction; they have resulted in profits, and more often in losses; they have meant either that ITN is worth a good deal or, on the contrary, virtually nothing at all. And still, fifty years on from its creation, the real nature of ITN in the future is undecided. Will it remain independent, or become a wholly owned subsidiary, or simply the news division of ITV? Will getting the news and making news programmes for broadcast remain its core business or will other activities – like exploiting its film and videotape archive – become more important? Will ITN continue to exist in some form, even adding to the reputation it has built up over the last fifty years, or is the time soon coming when it will have to say, 'And finally . . .'?

CHAPTER 1
FOR LOVE AND MONEY

It was Winston Churchill's return to power in 1951 that opened the way to commercial television, although it was some time before Churchill himself was won over to the idea. At first there was no great clamour for any new broadcaster to rival the BBC, just as there had been no clamour for electricity in the days of gas lighting. The fact was that the BBC had had 'a good war' and people were proud of it – or at least accepted the Corporation as an established and valued piece of the furniture of Britain.

BBC television had closed down during the Second World War lest the signal from its Crystal Palace transmitter should guide enemy bombers to their targets. But when hostilities were over, the television service reopened, and made slow but steady progress. By 1954 its transmission network covered 90 per cent of the population and it broadcast forty hours of television a week to some 4.5 million licence payers – and another half million freeloaders. But it was to be measured by more than just the number of viewers it attracted. As the television critic and commentator Peter Black later put it: 'In these early years of television and the last of the [broadcasting] monopoly, the BBC performed the priceless service of establishing standards, which the public accepted not simply because there was no choice but because it shared the BBC's view of television as an instrument of power and responsibility and wonder.'[1]

Television had received a tremendous boost in 1953 when it had covered the coronation of Queen Elizabeth II with distinction. Richard Dimbleby, a great wartime radio reporter, had risen to the occasion with an authoritative live commentary on the outside broadcast. Fifty-six per cent of the adult population, more than 20 million people, had watched the elaborate ceremonial in Westminster Abbey and the young Queen's happy progress through the streets of London.

American interest in the coronation had been intense and the television networks there had competed vigorously to be the first to show tele-recordings of the event. The result was nearly enough to snuff out the idea of commercial television in Britain. Reports came back across the Atlantic of how the solemn ceremony had sometimes been interrupted by US networks with sales messages from the programmes' sponsors in what seemed to the British, brought up on the advertisement-free BBC, the most irreverent and vulgar fashion. But the idea of a second television service to break the BBC's monopoly was gaining ground, fuelled as much by a love of liberty as by commercial ambition.

As far back as 1946 Sir Frederic Ogilvy, who had succeeded the founding father of the BBC Lord Reith as its director general, had, in his retirement, written to *The Times*: '. . . what is at stake is not a matter of politics but freedom.'[2] It was increasingly recognised that the case for monopoly was weak, and that competition might even be good for the BBC. Through the early fifties the case for and against commercial television was passionately argued in Parliament. Among the fears expressed was that news programmes would be biased because of powerful commercial pressures, and find themselves unable to report impartially – or at all – on matters in which shareholders had a financial interest.

Listening to these debates with a growing personal as well as professional interest was the lobby correspondent, later assistant editor, of the *News Chronicle*, Geoffrey Cox. It was here at Westminster that he first became aware of the possibilities a new television service might offer, and the issues that would have to be dealt with.

The lobby for commercial television had been given a great impetus by the efforts of one man, Norman Collins. A successful novelist (*London Belongs to Me*), and one of the relatively few people at the BBC who saw the real possibilities of television, he had been passed over for appointment to the new post of director of television in favour of a radio man,[3] and decided to leave. Geoffrey Cox, reporting the 1950 Conservative Party conference in Blackpool, remembers emerging from some debate to see the news vendors' placards announcing 'BBC Chief Resigns.'[4]

Prophesying that 'the future of television does not rest solely with the BBC' Collins now set about orchestrating a campaign to set up a rival system. Lord Simon, the BBC chairman, was later to say: 'If we hadn't fired Collins there would be no commercial television now.'

To refute the charge that this was all commercially driven, Collins tried to devise a television system that would, unlike the American market model, incorporate a mechanism that he thought would maintain programme standards. At a meeting in the Reform Club, he and his associates settled on the idea of a body that would effectively organise and police the new system as a defence against commercial barbarism – and political interference. It would be called the Independent Television Authority. While the system would be financed by advertising, direct sponsorship of programmes would be forbidden. Nowhere in the Bill that was eventually presented to the House did the word 'commercial' appear.

The puritan argument against commercial television was simple: that the greed of businessmen would inevitably lead to what we should call today a 'dumbing down' of standards that would debase the whole of British broadcasting. As Peter Black puts it: 'The puritans fought the Bill as a desperate attempt by a small group of Tory MPs, who had become the sharp point of a drive by advertising men, to wreck the traditions of British broadcasting as established by the monopoly under Lord Reith.' But the problem for these puritans was that to make their argument they had to admit that they did not trust the people to value quality television or want to watch it. This left them open to attack as patronising élitists who despised those who had elected them. Lord Simonds, the lord chancellor, thundered, 'Does Shakespeare live? Has that immortal voice been stilled? Shakespeare reigns. And why? Not because he has been proclaimed by the director general, the governors, the angels and archangels of the BBC, but because he is the chosen of the people who you so sadly and strongly distrust.'[5]

This argument, that those in favour of commercial television trusted the people while their opponents did not, was powerful and in the end decisive. The Broadcasting Act 1954 introduced a new television era, and with it a new television news service.

CHAPTER 2
'WONDERFULLY GOOD'

No doubt keen to add as much class as possible to this commercial enterprise, the government chose as the first chairman of the Independent Television Authority a man sometimes described – and not without justice – as 'the most cultivated man in Europe'. Sir Kenneth Clark, as he was then, was already serving the nation as director of the National Gallery and chairman of the Arts Council. Later he would go on to make for the BBC one of its most admired television series ever – *Civilisation* – and be created Lord Clark. As his director general at the ITA Clark decided on Sir Robert Fraser, whom he had met and liked during the war, a journalist turned civil servant currently in charge of the Central Office of Information.

It was Fraser who now devised the ITV system which was to last into the next century, in which the country would be divided up into fourteen geographical areas. Companies wishing to provide a television service in any area would have to convince the Authority that they had the necessary finance available and the ability to provide programmes of sufficient quality and quantity. The ITA first met at the beginning of August 1954 and at once advertised for 'contractors'.

All sorts of companies applied but only a very few were initially granted a contract, for it was clear that the new network could not be ready everywhere in the country for the launch of ITV in September the following year. After some shuffling, four companies emerged successful and began the frantic work of preparation. Associated Rediffusion was awarded the London weekday contract, and Granada the weekday in the North. ATV had London weekend and Midland weekday, while ABC took the North and Midland weekend.

But what about the news? How it should be provided and presented – and by whom – had not yet been decided.

'Dear Bob,' wrote Norman Collins to Sir Robert Fraser on 23 September 1954. 'Our next talk should be about the News. I have always felt that News covering and sifting should be in the hands of PA/Reuters, whereas the presentation must rest with the people who are running the Service. This, as you will realise every bit as well as I do, is a key subject. If you can stand it, I would like to suggest another evening session on it.'[1]

When the Authority met on 5 October 1954, members discussed the news in some detail. Chairman Sir Kenneth Clark said that 'he thought everyone would agree that it was necessary for the Authority to broadcast spoken up-to-the-minute news as well as newsreels'. In this he was following the BBC pattern in which 'newsreels' had become a firm feature of the television schedule, and indeed much better than the news bulletins, in which news items were read out by an unseen newsreader, usually illustrated by a still picture.

As director general, Fraser said he felt the ITV programme companies would be reluctant to provide the news themselves 'as they would be afraid of incurring charges of partiality. Some of them would of course have obvious political affiliations, which would make their position the more difficult.'

The idea of getting news agencies Reuters and the Press Association to produce the programmes was considered, but turned out to be a non-starter – Reuters' charter seemed to limit it to the straight provision of news rather than making news programmes. But there was another suggestion from one of the Authority's members, the film critic Dilys Powell: why should the Authority itself not provide the news for ITV? This possibility was allowed for in the Broadcasting Act, and indeed the government had agreed that, if necessary, money would be provided for the purpose. But it would clearly be a considerable undertaking for the Authority to set up and run. What was more, as the ITA's lawyers later advised,[2] it would only be permissible under the Act if the news could not be provided by the programme companies in some other satisfactory way. So there was a cool response to Dilys Powell's suggestion that the ITA should do the news:

> The chairman agreed that it could, but foresaw difficulties in providing the newsreel which would immediately follow the news, and which would require a large staff for a few minutes a day . . . The director general stressed that in his opinion both news and newsreels should be edited together by a group of professionals under an editor-in-chief responsible to a board in which the Authority, the programme contractors and possibly the three main political parties were represented.[3]

Further discussions with the companies took place and on 13 January 1955, in a memo headed 'The News Company', Fraser asked Clark to give his blessing to his latest plan so that, if the Authority approved, it could go forward:

> The four programme companies will collectively create a specialist subsidiary in which each will take a quarter share. The governing board will have eight members, two from each of the companies. The working head of the organisation – that is to say, the editor-in-chief – will be appointed only after consultation with the Authority and with its prior approval. If this approval is withdrawn, the appointment will lapse, and a new editor be found. The Authority will have the right to appoint a senior adviser to the company. I am given to understand that his advice would be welcome over the whole range of the news problem, but of course his real function will be to watch the operation of the news through the eyes of the Act.
>
> It was suggested by one or two of the companies that the Authority might care to be represented directly on the board. After discussion among them-selves, however, the companies felt that this could well saddle the Authority with an extensive and embarrassing responsibility, and they have dropped it as a proposal, substituting the suggestion of an adviser instead. It is perhaps a better one and could well prove, as you were pointing out to me, much more influential.[4]

So the shape of the News Company was agreed. All mention of representatives of the main political parties being on the board had been dropped. It would be a wholly owned subsidiary of the four companies that would take its news service, and these companies would supply its directors and chairman. It would be their creature. At the same time its performance would be closely monitored by a senior member of the ITA.

So who should be the editor-in-chief of the News Company? This was a delicate matter indeed. Following the furious debates in Parliament about commercial broadcasting, and at a time in British politics when divisions between left and right gaped wider than they do today, all political parties were waiting to pounce on a choice that suggested the new television channel's news would be biased, whether to right or left. The Authority was therefore looking for someone politically neutral. In the event, the businessmen of the new ITV came up with a clever choice – which the ITA hastened to endorse. Given that most of the concern expressed was whether the news would succumb to right-wing, commercial pressure, the programme companies put forward a name to which no one on the left could object. Fraser's ecstatic letter to his chairman is worth quoting in full:

> We are now formally asked by the four programme companies whether the appointment of Mr Aidan Crawley to the post of editor-in-chief of the news company would have the approval of the Authority. It is the unanimous wish of the four companies that he should be offered the position. I am privately given to understand that his nomination came from Associated Rediffusion. I have promised the companies that I will give them the Authority's reply on Tuesday afternoon after the Authority's meeting.
>
> For myself I regard the proposal as wonderfully good, although it is not in fact consistent with my first prescription that the occupant of the post must be entirely without political associations.
>
> Aidan Crawley sat in the 1945–1951 House of Commons as the Labour member for North Buckinghamshire. He lost his seat in that year. He was always a man of moderate opinion, and a member, if one can use these terms, of the Labour Right. At one time I knew him quite well. On grounds of personal character and integrity he is a fine choice. Since he lost his seat, I think he must have earned his living as a free-lance, very largely – as of course everyone will know – as a television B.B.C. speaker on public affairs.

In so far as an appointment could do it for us, I should have thought that his was the perfect answer to our initial problem. It is a wordless demonstration of the most vivid kind of the way in which the programme companies are approaching their responsibilities in this field, and it will seem to many to go a long way to make nonsense of much that was said of the baneful influence of the *Daily Mail* and Lord Kemsley. It is also, one hardly need say, quite a capture.[5]

CHAPTER 3
GENTLEMAN AMONG THE PLAYERS

Aidan Crawley was almost too good to be true – wonderful in every way, a truly impressive character from whatever angle you looked at him. His father had been chaplain to the Archbishop of York, and was a man of independent means: Crawley grew up in a typically well-to-do, upper middle class, pre-war household. There was nanny and the nursery-maid, the butler, the parlour-maid, the cook, the kitchen-maid, two housemaids and his mother's maid. Crawley did well at Harrow, where he won the top history scholarship to Trinity College, Oxford. The most promising cricketer of his generation, he played for Oxford University and for Kent.

Crawley moved in superior social circles and was well connected. 'He was not titled,' says his daughter Harriet, 'but some of his relations were. At Oxford several of his greatest friends were the sons of peers.' But Crawley was not a snob. 'He was genuinely interested in everybody whatever their circumstances . . . He seems to have been hugely liked – I can remember so many people coming to the house to see him – and he was always thought to be fair, not tricky; firm, not a trimmer. He was a tremendously active person – immensely fast at grasping new ideas. You had to think on your feet with him; and he liked clarity, getting the facts right.'

Crawley had all the social skills and graces. He played tennis very well, and danced beautifully. 'He was terrific fun – instinctive, full of feeling: I've never met a man with more natural abilities.' On top of all this he was more than six feet tall and extremely good-looking. This, says Harriet, he regarded as a disadvantage: 'He used to say, "For a man to be very good-looking is a bore: people don't take you seriously."'

Not for Crawley the anxious search for a potential employer at the end of university. Hardly had he begun to look for a job when, unsolicited, he received a letter from Esmond Harmsworth, the friend of a friend and son of Lord Rothermere, who offered him a job on the *Daily Mail*. There, Crawley learned the business of journalism, developed Labour sympathies, and travelled the world. After he left the newspaper, where he had grown increasingly unhappy with the appeasement policies of its proprietor, he spent six months in the Middle East making a documentary film about the history of the Holy Land. When war came he qualified as an RAF Hurricane pilot and, after an interlude attached to the Balkan Intelligence Service, was shot down in North Africa. Four years as a prisoner-of-war in Germany followed – with several unsuccessful escape attempts – before Crawley was back in Britain. In the post-war election of 1945 he was returned as a Labour MP for North Buckingham. Clearly a rising talent, he became a junior minister as under-secretary in the Air Ministry but lost his seat when the Conservatives returned to power in 1951.

Now Crawley built on the experience of documentary film-making he had gained before the war. With his wife Virginia Cowles (herself a distinguished war correspondent and writer), he was commissioned by the BBC (of course he knew its director of television, George Barnes) to make a series of fifty-minute programmes on newly independent India. They were to do their own filming. As ever, Crawley's contacts came up trumps. At dinner one night before they set off, Henry Ford himself promised them a car and driver for their travels in India; on their arrival in Delhi the British High Commissioner at once invited them to stay.

But the Crawleys socialised with a purpose, and their contacts helped them to explore a great deal of India until then unseen by most Britons. They filmed in a leper colony, investigated the caste system in the countryside's villages, and interviewed and were entertained to dinner by the prime minister Jawaharlal Nehru – who had of course also been at Harrow.

India's Challenge led on to regular work for Crawley on the BBC television *Viewfinder* programme, which covered many topics that would soon become the staple diet of a newly invigorated *Panorama*. There were interviews with politicians like King Faisal of Iraq and Éamon de Valera, the Irish prime minister, as well as investigations of British Railways and the National Health Service. Soon Crawley was a television star: 'The reviews of *Viewfinder* had been favourable,' he wrote later. 'Hyperbolic phrases like "the near-perfect screen reporter", or "the ace investigator of BBC television" outnumbered those who found me "depressing", "humourless", or "pedagogic".'[1]

It was just at this moment, in February 1955, that the 'contractors' of the newly formed independent television channel were urgently looking for the man to lead their news company. Crawley had all the right qualifications, and the press agreed: 'Mr Crawley chances his arm again – but he's used to it,' was the *Daily Herald*'s headline when Crawley's appointment was announced.

> For a prison-camp concert, Flight-Lieut. Aidan Crawley trained a bunch of tough RAF men, including Canadian lumberjacks, into a team of high-kicking dancers as skilled, if not as glamorous, as the TV Toppers. He will need the same resourcefulness, patience and tact, on a larger stage in his new job.
>
> Crawley, the man who has shown with his *Viewfinder* programmes that TV can be intelligent and top entertainment at the same time, has been made chief of the Independent Television Authority's news service.
>
> His job is to see that we get unbiased and objective news.
>
> A tough assignment! But Crawley is used to overcoming tough obstacles.[2]

By May Crawley felt it was time to tell the press something about what he was planning. There would be two evening news bulletins, one of eight and a half minutes at 7.05 p.m. and a second one of thirteen and a half minutes at 10.00 p.m. Though the report in the *Manchester Guardian* does not say so, the second half of the later and longer bulletin was planned as a newsreel – softer stories rather than hard news. Some of the advantages Independent Television News, as it was now called,[3] would enjoy over the BBC included the greater use of lightweight 16mm cameras, a studio in central London where guests could more easily be interviewed live, and a fast film-processing 'lab'. But it was noted that Crawley was reluctant to give financial details: 'A good many appointments had been made, he said, including those of several women on the editorial side, but matters of staff and budget would have to wait for final disposition until the budget had been finally settled.'[4]

Crawley had started work in March. His job: to create a television news service from scratch within six months that would be better than the BBC could offer.

CHAPTER 4
SIGNING ON

Inevitably it was to the Corporation that Crawley turned for some key members of his team. He was fortunate in his timing. Many of the BBC's best journalists were writhing restlessly under the iron constraints of Tahu Hole, editor of news, and longing to make a break for freedom. Men of talent and ambition saw ITN as an opportunity that must be grasped.

Hole's news empire, described by the future director general Hugh Carleton Green as 'the Kremlin of the BBC', was repressive in the extreme. The news was read off-screen by disembodied voices, visual illustration was minimal, journalistic enterprise frowned upon. Hole had brought to television news a habit honed in radio – as Arthur Clifford, by then a television news sub-editor, well remembered: 'I joined BBC Radio from Fleet Street in all innocence, thinking I must prove myself. Soon a big story came up: it was the British frigate *Amethyst*, held in the Yangtze river by the Chinese Communists.[1] I thought, I'll see if there's anything doing on this story. The Foreign Office News Department said, "Oh, very glad you rang, BBC, we're about to issue a statement in the next hour. The *Amethyst* has slipped anchor and is heading for the open sea; she's under Chinese shell fire but Commander Kerans sounds very confident and it's a wonderful thing. God save the King. Isn't that nice?" And I said, "It's terrific!" and somehow scrambled it into the one o'clock news.

'Fleet Street goes barmy – the phone calls came in from newspapers – "Where did you get this?" Anyway, a triumph for me, I thought. Summoned to Tahu Hole that afternoon and I, the young, newly joined sub-editor, was thinking, Wow, I've done pretty well. I wonder how big the raise will be. I wonder what he'll say? Walked into the presence of EN, (Editor, News, we always addressed people by job initials) and Tahu, this huge, brooding New Zealander, said, "Sit down, Mr Clifford," and I sat down and he said that I'd committed a mortal sin almost. It must never, never happen again. Hadn't I familiarised myself with the rules of BBC News objectivity – everything to be confirmed by three news agencies? What I did, it was a gross error, it must not be repeated. "My final words, Mr Clifford, are, on this occasion, I'm sure you'll draw a lesson from this episode. Your annual increment will not be withheld but I'll leave you with these words, Mr Clifford. Enthusiasm does not constitute journalistic ability." You could hear my heart sink. "Enthusiasm does not constitute journalistic ability." That was my first real experience of the old time traditional BBC news.'

Despondent, Clifford decided he'd have to go back to Fleet Street, and started looking for a job there. But Arthur Christiansen, legendary editor of the *Daily Express*, told him to hang on in television. Clifford recalls him saying: '"You're young enough to keep your options open, because what you're in now is the new journalism, this is the journalism of the future" – and then the grin – "but don't tell my people I said that." So I left feeling well pleased and then, back again, the anticlimax, back to Alexandra Palace,[2] and I soldiered on there until independent television appeared on the horizon, the first puff of smoke.'

But at ITN Aidan Crawley turned down Clifford's first job application: 'He said, "No, I don't want BBC Radio, ex-radio news people, or *News and Newsreel*. I want people with ideas, I want people with imagination." So then I sat down and wrote a long, proper application with a dummy bulletin.'

To make sure that his renewed application got Crawley's attention, Clifford enlisted the help of the intrepid John Cotter, a former BBC colleague already hired as ITN's new film manager: 'It was John Cotter who sidled along on the balcony outside the windows on the seventh floor of Ingersoll House in Kingsway to Aidan's office and found my application.

Aidan had a pile, John said, of applications on his desk. He fished mine out and dusted it off. Then he found some ropy-looking application and put that on top, dear old John, and mine was second.

'Aidan read it, he liked it, contacted me and then I was interviewed; and I trotted out a few ideas and he said, "I'm impressed by your enthusiasm and you've obviously got ideas that go far beyond, BBC bloody Radio news. I'll take you on as deputy news editor."'

As his director of operations, who would have the technical responsibility for getting ITN on the air, Aidan Crawley chose a man who had helped him establish a footing in BBC Television and who until recently had been in charge of the successful BBC *Newsreel*. Philip Dorté had already joined Associated Television, ATV, one of the new ITV contractors, but now he was seconded to assist Crawley. In April 1955 the two men made a hurried visit to the USA to learn what they could about a modern television-news operation, and make arrangements for access to foreign-news footage that ITN could not hope to provide for itself. At the first ITN board meeting on Tuesday, 17 May 1955,[3] Crawley, as editor-in-chief, reported: 'Columbia Broadcasting System [CBS], by the use of a developing machine specially made for them, were able to include in their bulletins news received thirty minutes before transmission.'

Crawley told the board that: '. . . he had signed an Agreement for one year from 1 September 1955 with CBS, for the supply of material from the United States of America, Canada, the rest of the American continent and the Far East in return for a payment of £10,000'.

But, of course, Crawley wanted ITN to produce as much of its own film material as possible. He needed cameramen, and first, a senior cameraman.

Cyril Page was old enough to have served in the Second World War; afterwards he'd worked on British feature films, like *The First Gentleman*, before joining the BBC. A day's freelance work for the Corporation, shooting the Boat Race at Putney, earned him five pounds and a year's contract, during which his filming assignments included the Interludes (like 'the potter's wheel'), which filled the gaps between programmes, and film inserts for *Café Continental*, *Candid Camera* (the car with no engine), and *What's My Line?*.

But Page was made for much more than a little light London filming. When war broke out in Korea, few cameramen were keen to go, but Page agreed. It was in an icy, dangerous Korea that his real talents, over and above his quick, effective camerawork, first shone. It would be wrong to say that Page was a spiv, but his ability to wheel and deal, to find a way, to make things happen, to raise morale in a dark hour and turn disaster into victory would prove invaluable to his colleagues and to ITN for the next thirty-one years.

Arriving in Tokyo, Page had found British troops thin on the ground. In any case they were, as usual, the junior partners in the war. He accredited himself instead to the Americans, got kitted-out in US uniform and equipped himself with two enormous aluminium suitcases, which he filled with bottles of whisky, bought at the American PX for a very reasonable price. Once he had arrived in Korea the Americans lent him a clapped-out Jeep and a trailer. Soon Page was in business, trading whisky for fur parkas that Canadian troops had brought with them, warm clothing which the frozen British, as badly equipped as ever, were grateful to be offered in return for all sorts of co-operation – including a driver for the Jeep.

Page went to Korea for a week and stayed for nine months. Following the tide of battle he got as far north as Pyongyang. Weather conditions were appalling: often he could only keep his Newman Sinclair camera going by warming it over a charcoal fire he lit in the Jeep's trailer.

By 1955, and home again, Cyril Page had made a considerable reputation for himself at the BBC. It was hinted to him that one day he might become head of Ealing Studios, so when Philip Dorté asked him to go to ITN he hesitated for a week before he signed up as senior cameraman, on £1,200 a year. His first, self-appointed, task, he says, was to intercept the other cameramen called for interview as they arrived at Ingersoll House, and warn each of them to insist on a salary of £1,000.

In Swansea, living at home after studying every aspect of the theatre at the National College of Music and Drama in Cardiff, a young Diana Edwards-Jones had been earning a modest living (£4 10s. a week) as an assistant stage manager for the Maudie Edwards Players. In 1955, excited by advertisements for stage managers at both the BBC and the new television company Associated Rediffusion she decided to seek her fortune in London. Rediffusion, said no, because she was a woman, but suggested she try ITN, which would soon be transmitting from the same building in a smaller studio. Fortified with Merrydown cider – she was living on the dole

– she assured her interviewers, James Bredin, a studio director, and Hilda Reynolds-Cooper, in charge of 'grams' and vision mixers, that she'd stage-managed at least a hundred plays and was perfectly qualified for a job about which she knew nothing.

'But I did know a bit about timing from the theatre,' says Diana. 'When you go to a matinée they always speak faster so they can have a bit of a rest afterwards before the next performance; and I used to shut the theatre bar after a minute and a half in the matinée interval so the cast could have a bit longer after the matinée and before the evening show. But also, you see, with rehearsals and everything . . . I knew all about setting a stage. The wicked thing I did, I told them I could type, and I hadn't a clue, so I went back home to Wales after the interview and had typing lessons – but I was still bloody awful.'

Diana was hired at ten pounds a week. To begin with, her main job was to type and sort out scripts, and arrange the collection of still photographs from agencies and newspapers.

As the launch date for ITV, and therefore ITN, approached, the nascent news team moved across Kingsway to its new home in Associated Rediffusion's Television House. In the lobby, waiting for the lift, Diana saw a dark-haired man in heavily framed spectacles headed in the same direction. 'He said, "What are you doing?", and I said, "Oh, I'm going to be a studio assistant. What are you going to do?", and he said, "I'm going to be a newscaster." I said, "Good God! Can't they do any better than that?"'

It was Robin Day.

Central to Aidan Crawley's concept of his news service was the idea of an in-vision newscaster. Not a newsreader, for that implied to him someone simply reading what others had written for him, but a newscaster who would bring his personality to bear on the business of conveying the news to the viewers in the most effective way. Crawley saw his newscasters not as pretty presenters, but as active participants in the process of gathering and editing the news. They would have the ability to make the stories written by the sub-editors their own, by putting them into their own words and, rather than sit idle until a newscast approached, would go out as reporters to bring back a story or an interview.

This was a revolution. The BBC had fought against its television news-readers appearing on screen at all, and even when at last they did, just three weeks before ITN went on air, they were still not at first identified. But as a popular presenter of documentaries, Crawley had recognised the powerful pull an on-screen newscaster might have on the public's attention.

As Robin Day later put it:

> The newscaster system was not just a publicity stunt, but hard journalistic common sense. The idea was that as the newscaster became known to viewers his professional grasp of his material, and his lively interest in it, would make the news more authoritative and entertaining . . . The newscaster must be clear and convincing. To that end, the newscaster must be himself. He must use his own style, his own words (unless quoting), and, when there is some fun in the news, his own sense of humour. That is what Aidan Crawley meant by injecting 'personality'.[4]

But where to find these newscasters, who must be both journalistic and charismatic?

In the middle of June Crawley told his board that

> great difficulty was being experienced in finding suitable candidates. Although a large number of candidates had been tested there were only two who could be considered suitable, Mr Geoffrey Cox of the *News Chronicle* and Mr John Bevan of the *Manchester Guardian*. Neither, however, was likely to come for less than £5,000 per annum. There was further discussion about the type of man necessary for the position. The board decided that before any appointment was made, they would like to see film of those candidates whom the editor-in-chief short listed.[5]

The search continued, and Crawley decided to cast his net wider than the newspapers. 'One hot afternoon in June 1955,' wrote Robin Day, 'the telephone rang in my small office on the second floor of Broadcasting House [BBC headquarters] where I was working as a producer of topical radio programmes.' A barrister friend of his had seen an advertisement for a newscaster pinned up in Gray's Inn that he thought might interest him. It read: 'Requirements: sound knowledge of current affairs, ability to think on feet, good presence . . . The work might appeal to a barrister thinking of giving up practice. The post would carry a good salary'.

To Robin Day this was almost too good to be true: the job description fitted him perfectly. He sent his secretary out for a cup of tea, then hastily typed a letter of application and enclosed his CV: 'Age 31. BBC Current Affairs producer. Various freelance broadcasts and articles. Served Royal Artillery 1943–47. Studied law at Oxford 1947–51. President of the Oxford Union Society 1950. Called to the Bar 1952. Practised until 1953. Press Officer with British Information Service in Washington 1953–54. Joined BBC Radio 1955.'

Day had got off to a good start in adult life, leading an Oxford Union debating team to America before he qualified as a barrister. But his legal career had fizzled out, and although he was now at the BBC he wasn't getting anywhere. In response to his application he was invited to an interview at ITN, then included in a short list. Eight candidates were to be screen-tested at television studios in Highbury on 22 July, and Crawley had invited members of the ITN board to watch, rather than see telerecordings later.[6] Day had been sent a summary of a day's news stories and told to re-write them in his own style, and put them in his preferred order. In the studio – he had fortified himself with a brandy at the Lyons tea-shop in Seven Sisters Road – he received a message from Aidan Crawley: 'I was to speak to the camera as if it were to a person sitting at home.'

After the test Crawley enquired: 'Could you get some lighter spectacles?'

Back at his BBC desk, Day received a cryptic telephone message: 'If you will come to see Mr Crawley tomorrow he will tell you something to your advantage.'

Later, Robin Day explained what his new editor wanted of him: 'The only requirements from Aidan Crawley were that the facts should be clear and that the style should try to combine the responsibility of the *Manchester Guardian* and the vigour of the *Daily Express*. This was aiming wide and high – typical of Aidan Crawley's approach. This tall, rugged man, with his jutting chin and warm, expansive manner, exuded energy and optimism.'[7]

The ITN board had watched the finalists in the newscaster competition and not all of them had liked the look of Robin Day. Sidney Bernstein, from Granada, had been particularly hostile. But Crawley made it clear that if the board wouldn't have Day they would have to do without *him*, and his will prevailed. Much more popular was his choice for the other lead newscaster.

Christopher Chataway's face and name were already nationally known: in the previous year as a long-distance runner he had taken the 5000-metres world record. Now he was working as a transport manager for a drinks company but nursing ambitions of making a different career. 'What I wanted to do,' says Chataway, 'was go into politics.[8] I needed to change my image as just an athlete, and learn something about something before I had a go at getting into the House. I had had offers to become a sports reporter, but then I saw the ITN advertisement and applied. I remember a basement in Hampstead where we were tried out. Henry Fairlie was one of us – he was the political commentator of the day – and there was an MI5 man there. We had to deliver a bulletin. The *Spectator* had a résumé of the week's news so I wrote and memorised something similar for this test. When I was offered the job I did ask two of my Oxford tutors what they thought . . . every so often then there were dismissive comments being made about ITV – by, for example, Randolph Churchill – but I don't remember agonising about it. Once I'd taken the decision I didn't worry about ITV being called cheapjack any more. ITN was so much more fun than working at Guinness. This was terrific!'

Aidan Crawley wanted to create a television news different from the dreary service offered by BBC Television, but he needed experienced people to make it work. It was all very well hiring newscasters whose skills were as yet untested because such a breed had not been seen before. But when it came to those who would produce the material the front-men would present to the public – the words and pictures – then Crawley needed professionals: sub-editors and cameramen. Though Crawley had worked as a journalist and made his own television documentaries, his knowledge of what would be needed in a television *news* operation was limited.

Says Arthur Clifford: 'The difficult part was trying to reconcile the Fleet Street types, and the old film newsreel types, and the radio news people like me who saw the possibilities of television news being something markedly different. All these disparate elements coming together produced chaos. Aidan was a great strategist but totally ignorant of the mechanics of running a newsroom . . . There was rank amateurism all around me. I'm no bloody genius but, though young in years, I was a thoroughly seasoned professional, and Aidan found himself leaning on me a bit. He said, "What's this I heard you talking about, Arthur, a copy taster?" I said, "Yes, it's a newsroom, Aidan, it's a big newsroom. We've got the tape machines, we need someone to look at the tapes. You need a copy taster," and I explained the copy taster's role. And Aidan said, "Well that sounds an extravagance". I said, "Aidan, you need a copy taster. Otherwise it'll be chaos. There'll be the f—g tape machine spilling out paper, and some aged tape man trying to keep track of it." He said, "Arthur, I thought the chaps could pick up their own." I said, "Aidan, it'll be absolute anarchy, it will be total chaos." He said, "But to pay a chap just to sort out the bits of paper?" "That's the copy taster's role," I said, "We've got to have a copy taster, and a chief sub-editor and sub-editors, and scriptwriters – we've got to get the mechanics of the news room right." I said, "It's like a jazz pianist, you know. You have to learn to play it straight, then you can improvise." "Oh, oh, all right, a copy taster then." But that's just an instance of the rank amateurism that one found when joining ITN.'

CHAPTER 5
THE WOODEN SQUARE

Time was short. Rehearsals began, but were less than realistic because the most important elements of equipment – the studio cameras, the control room, and the telecine machines, which would play the edited film into the news bulletins, had yet to be delivered, let alone installed. Full dummy runs began on 8 September 1955. By day an attempt was made to simulate the news-gathering operation. Reporters and cameramen would be dispatched to film and interview, then return with their stories to be written and subbed and their film footage to be edited. At the end of the day, all would gather in the newsroom to watch the result.

To give the onlookers an idea of how he might look within the confines of the television screen, one of the newscasters, sitting behind a desk, would address a pretend 'camera' through a large wooden picture frame. If the 'wooden O' (as the playwright described the Elizabethan theatre) was the setting for Shakespeare's plays, the 'wooden square' framed ITN's first attempts at a television news bulletin. With no telecine machines or studio monitors yet installed, the edited film sequences were simply projected on a blank wall beside the newscaster, and the commentary was read aloud over them.

Having their critical colleagues all around them looking on, the news-casters later admitted, was a far worse experience than the real thing turned out to be. Robin Day in particular was on edge: 'That went quite well, Robin', Aidan Crawley might say in his upper-middle-class voice, 'but I thought in the first item you sounded just a bit sorft.'

'I think you mean soft,' Day would snap back pettishly.

By most accounts, the rehearsals were rather depressing – there was even a suggestion that the ITA should be asked to postpone the opening of ITV. But as a former military man Aidan Crawley knew all about maintaining morale:

> One day I made everybody stay on for a few minutes after the bulletin rehearsal and gave them a pep talk. I well understood how bewildered they must feel that such an important operation should be so inadequately prepared, and I said so. I went on to explain the whole position in regard to equipment, to point out that ours was a comparatively simple operation and that it would be far worse if we were presenting a music-hall spectacular, which I gathered from the press was to be one of the features of the opening night, without being able to see what it looked like on a television monitor. I pooh-poohed the idea of postponement, saying that we had never been misled by our suppliers and I continued to believe in them. Finally, I promised them unlimited champagne after what I knew would be a spectacularly successful opening night. I was told afterwards that people had been cheered by what I said, and there was no further trouble.[1]

Behind the scenes, Crawley was more worried than he let on. On 7 September, just three weeks before ITV's opening night, he circulated an ITN paper to his board entitled 'State of Readiness':

> As the board will remember, it was stipulated very early in the proceedings that the News Company should have at least four weeks of dummy runs before going on air. Reluctantly the Editor-in-Chief accepted three weeks at a later date as the best that could be hoped for in the time that had been allowed the manufacturers to provide the machinery. It now seems possible that all that can be expected is TWO DAYS of full dummy runs. The reason for this is the failure of Pyes to deliver the telecine machines and television cameras . . . Remembering that many of the people who will be operating both the studio cameras and the telecines are inexperienced, it will be a

miracle if the programmes go through without technical fault. Nevertheless the News Company is quite prepared to crowd four weeks of rehearsal into a few days, and to take their chance on that if the board agrees, provided enough machinery really is in operation by September 20th.[2]

This produced a furious response from Pye,[3] who said that once their workmen at ITN heard about it they would all go on strike. Aidan Crawley replied soothingly that he was sure that Pye were 'doing their utmost at this moment' to deliver their equipment as soon as possible. Nevertheless, ITN's engineers and technicians were still installing and cementing in the telecine machines on the night before the first transmission.

CHAPTER 6

OPENING NIGHT – ON AIR

ITV began on Thursday 22 September 1955, at first in the London area only. After an outside broadcast showing the opulent opening ceremony at Guildhall there was light entertainment, drama and commercials. Then, at 10 p.m., a fast moving title sequence showing a can of newsfilm being rushed to ITN appeared on the screen, accompanied by a lively signature tune.[1] With a sweep of her arm, Diana Edwards-Jones, as floor manager, signalled to newscaster Christopher Chataway, and the first ITN bulletin was on the air, 'sandwiched', as James Thomas wrote in the *News Chronicle*, 'between an electric razor and a lemon pie'.

That first newscast was generally regarded as a success although, other than a report on a criminal trial still in progress at the Old Bailey, there was little to distinguish it from the BBC broadcast of that night. The general verdict of BBC news chiefs was that they did not have much to fear. Only the future director general Hugh Carleton Greene saw in that first ITN bulletin the beginning of a revolution in the way news was presented on television.[2]

When it came to the content of his bulletins what most excited Aidan Crawley was not the standard newsreel fare of statesmen arriving and departing, or predictable 'diary' items like a Shrove Tuesday pancake race, but sharp-eyed insights into the hot issues of the day, told in human terms that everybody could understand.

From the window of his study the Labour MP for Dartford, Norman Dodds, had been watching a gang of workmen in the road outside. Increasingly incensed at how long they seemed to be taking over the job, he kept a note of the time they spent actually working and how long they took over their tea breaks. His conclusion: that a decade after the Second World War had ended the British workman had become lazy. There was uproar when Dodds publicised his findings. Union leaders, politicians and the press – at home and overseas – joined in furious argument on the state of post-war Britain.

Arthur Clifford remembers grabbing the story as he scanned the papers in the ITN newsroom. 'I thought, here's a way of bringing ITN to life, of driving home the point that ITN is a new force in journalism. It's going to tell the news, project the news, in an entirely new way.' With a good deal of effort, Clifford persuaded the workmen to invite Dodds to join them for a mug of tea in their canvas roadside tent. The argy-bargy that followed between the portly, rather pompous Dodds and the foreman Percy Diamond – cheered on like some Alfred Doolittle by his mates – made for lively television, and it revealed a good deal about class, politics and the public's attitude to the unions. The item was skilfully top-and-tailed with pieces to camera by reporter Kenneth Allsop.

But here the conflicting attitudes to television news that had not yet been reconciled at ITN became apparent. The way the system worked meant that newsfilm, as soon as had been processed, was screened in the viewing theatre on the eighth floor, in the presence of the film editors, their shift leader and the chief sub. They would agree on the strength of the material and how long it was likely to run – not usually more than a minute and a half. Then it was handed over to an editor to cut as he saw fit. The reporter who had gone out on the story or the sub-editor in the newsroom on the first floor, who would be writing the commentary, had no part to play while the film-editing process was going on. Only when it was finished would anyone on the journalistic side climb the stairs or take the lift to the top of the building to see what was in the cut story, make a 'shot list', and return to the newsroom to write a commentary to fit.[3] Essentially, therefore, it was the film editors rather than the journalists who decided what was in the film stories that ITN news bulletins broadcast.

That had worked perfectly well in the rather simple-minded cinema newsreels, from which most of the film editors had come to ITN, but Aidan Crawley and the journalists he had recruited saw it differently: they wanted something sharper, more revealing, more informative than a superficial 'look at life' – however well-crafted.

As Arthur Clifford recalls it, the Dodds story developed into quite a battle within ITN: 'Bang, got the film back and I was delighted and relieved and thought, We'll really hit this one hard. Off it disappeared into the maw of the editing department upstairs. And then, a bit later, the script writer came down to the desk to see me and said, "Arthur, I think there's some trouble upstairs with the Norman Dodds story." I said, "Oh God, was the film fogged?" "No, no, no, but they say it's inconclusive." I roared up seven flights of stairs to the film editing department and whoever it was said, "We can't do anything with this. It's so inconclusive, they're just sort of arguing." And I said, "Look, I've gone to a lot of trouble to get this story. It's a new way of telling the news. It hasn't been done before in the context of a news bulletin. Big story. You people wouldn't understand it." Then I said to him, "I'm trying to keep my temper. Do you come to work in a bloody stage coach? Hold it where it is." Went down to see Aidan, and he said, "I gather you've been creating mayhem upstairs." I said, "Yeah, I have, Aidan, and this is why," and told him. And he said, "Well this is the kind of thing that we're bound to encounter. To them," he said, "it's an alien world. So we've just got to keep cool about it." Aidan and I then went upstairs and Aidan said, "Look, I've got an over-run on the late bulletin on this one and we can trail it at the start of the bulletin, and we can say, "At the end of this bulletin there'll be a special report on the story of Norman Dodds MP and the navvies in the tea tent." So you can stop worrying whether or not it's inconclusive, gentlemen. That is not your concern. Just give us a good five-minute film to get the flavour and the mood and the atmosphere of it."

'This was the birth pangs of ITN. It duly appeared on the screen, and the critics loved it. Bernard Levin weighed in: "Here at last," he said, "was pure television, television as it ought to be and yet might be. For five minutes, the screen looked in on life and came alive."[4]

'Well, briefly I was the toast of the town upstairs – "Look what the critics said!" But when people wrote about ITN afterwards they all talked about it as if we were a happy band of brothers, all thinking the same, believing the same, rowing in the same direction. But, behind the scenes, it was mayhem.'

But some people from a pre-television age were more than ready to start rowing in the same direction as Crawley and Clifford. Alfred Wilson had had a traditional start in the film industry – he'd been a page-boy at Gainsborough film studios before he went into film editing. His cutting room at Lime Grove was next door to the Gaumont British News unit, so he could see how they put their reel together. He had also worked at Alexandra Palace, where he dubbed BBC Television's *Newsreel*, adding the sounds that brought silent film alive. 'I learned how music should be used,' he says, 'so that it would never get in the way of dialogue or intrude in any way. That was to be very useful in the years to come.'

Wilson joined ITN as a dubbing editor a month before it went on air. 'I had to set about building both a sound effects and music library,' he says. 'I soon realised that the stories we were covering called for a far greater range of music than normal newsreels even at the BBC, and I learned from viewers' letters that they were more aware of music on television than they were in the cinema.' Wilson organised the 'ITN Choir', a gang of newsroom people who could be called on to come and record suitable shouts and thumps to simulate a punch-up, or sing and whistle old soldiers' songs to cover a story about a First World War anniversary. 'The Musicians' Union,' he says, 'would have been furious, if they'd known. Multi-skilling at ITN didn't come in in the eighties, it started right at the beginning.'

Wilson knew when to leave out as well as put in. 'I remember Alfie one weekend,' says Arthur Clifford. 'There was some story on gliding becoming more affordable to ordinary folk. There were some lovely pictures of gliding – a very soft, down the bulletin, weekend story. Normally a head of sound would have put over the glider some sort of "up we go, magnificent men in their flying machines" music, but Alfie said, "Cut all that out. I just want silence." And there was the intro, and the piece from the newscaster, and the glider took off and there was silence, and you were up there, you were gliding in magic silence, and Alfie said, "It's right, isn't it? That's the true beauty of flight." I said, "Alfie, if you were a blonde, I'd kiss you. That's terrific." He was a great head of sound.'

Within the newsroom itself there were also some journalistic attitudes imported from newspapers which were in conflict with the new world of television news. Television was highly regulated, with the ITA in charge of monitoring ITN to ensure 'due accuracy and impartiality', quite unlike the free-booting, untrammelled ways of Fleet Street. ITN's first news editor, Max Caulfield, a tough Irishman from the *Daily Express*, clearly felt no scruple in taking the occasional backhander. When ITN covered a motor-scooter show at Earl's Court he had a word with one of the exhibitors – and another with the film editor cutting the story. As a result, the news item as transmitted contained a good few shots of one particular manufacturer's product. A couple of days later ITN's receptionist reported to the news desk that a moped addressed to Max Caulfield had been delivered to reception. Apparently Caulfield saw nothing wrong in this – he protested that the moped had been offered to him on 'indefinite loan'.

But when Crawley heard about this dubious arrangement he was outraged. Conscious of the widespread worries that news programmes produced by commercial television would be corrupt, a soft target for commercial pressures, he felt that Caulfield, a senior member of staff, had acted with near-criminal irresponsibility. Max Caulfield was fired.

At a meeting of the board on 2 December, 'It was reported that the News editor, Mr. Max Caulfield, had placed himself in a position which necessitated the editor-in-chief requesting his resignation. This had been tendered in consideration of receipt of six months' salary[5] in lieu of notice.' Crawley's decision was confirmed by the directors, although he was told 'that in future the correct procedure would be to suspend the member of staff from duty pending a decision by the board.'

Arthur Clifford remembers, 'I had a telephone call from Aidan at home, and he said "It's Aidan here. Arthur, you're the new news editor. I've fired Max. We've got too many problems on our plate to be bothered with this kind of childish, irresponsible behaviour. I suggest you come in." I said, "Well, I'm just cutting the grass, Aidan." He said, "Well, you'd better leave it for now because there's a lot to be done, old boy, and I'm sure your good Beryl will understand." And that's how I became ITN's news editor.'

CHAPTER 7

ALMOST ALL OVER

Even before ITN was on the air, trouble was brewing. It was, as it has usually been ever since, a matter of money.

On 14 June 1955, three months before ITN went on the air, the directors discussed the estimated expenditure of £400,000 for the year ahead. 'The board considered that this figure was alarming and every endeavour should be made to get the operation done more cheaply . . . The editor-in-chief was asked to do all he could to see where economies could be effected . . .'[1]

The owners of ITN wanted to charge the programme companies a price for the news that would enable ITN to provide a good service. But, of course, those owners were also the broadcasters who wanted to pay as little as possible for the news bulletins they were buying, so they could contribute to as big a profit as possible for their own ITV companies.

So whenever the directors of ITN met they were wearing two hats. On the one hand they were pleased with, even proud of, what ITN was doing and wanted more money to make it even better. On the other they were trying to run the news company as cheaply as possible. Some companies and their representatives on the board rather liked wearing their ITN hat. Others preferred their own company's.

Overseeing this difficult relationship between ITN and the companies was the regulatory Authority in its successive forms: the Independent

Television Authority, the Independent Broadcasting Authority, the Independent Television Commission and, since December 2003, Ofcom.

During 1954 and early 1955 the ITA's preoccupation had been to select the contractors that would form the basis of the regional system devised by director general Sir Robert Fraser. In each of the fourteen regions the chosen companies would have exclusive rights to all the revenue from television advertising. The ITA had studied the American experience and concluded that 'If a television company held a monopoly of an advertising outlet there was no way in which the money could be prevented from climbing up the wall and pouring through the window.'[2] But not immediately. The ITA's calculations showed that at first there would be heavy losses, and that not until year four would the ITV companies begin to make those fat profits.

And so it proved. Despite the euphoria that surrounded the launch of ITV the companies were quickly in financial trouble, and looking for ways to save money. ITN became a tempting target, as it would again nearly half a century later.

After the original bidder had pulled out, the North and Midland weekend contract had gone to ABC Television. But now in the autumn of 1955 ABC balked both at joining the other three founding companies as owners of ITN, and at taking ITN's news service, until costs were greatly reduced. Sir Philip Warter, the company's chairman, wrote to Robert Fraser at the ITA:

> Having studied the matter in detail, my colleagues and I are appalled at the heavy, indeed reckless capital expenditure which is contemplated, some of which has already been incurred by the News Company . . .
>
> There is, in our view, no justification whatever for this grotesquely extravagant capital expenditure on equipment. Moreover, the weekly running costs are of an unwarrantably high order, quite out of relation to the results achieved.
>
> We have also had the benefit, since I.T.V. started in the London area, of seeing the results produced by the News Company. These are disappointing in the extreme, and serve to confirm our view that the present organisation of the News Company requires drastic overhaul with a view both to considerable reduction in expense, and improvement in quality.

We are, therefore, disinclined to participate in the News Company, as at present constituted. We believe we could prepare our own news items at much smaller cost and with much greater efficiency.

We hope to make a definite decision in a few days with regard to our membership of the I.T.N. . . .[3]

There was dismay at the ITA. In response Fraser wrote to Eric Fletcher, ABC's deputy chairman:

In the whole of the last year I do not think anything has happened – despite all the myriad of possible sources of anxiety – that has caused me any real distress. But I am now in this state of mind about the affairs of the News Company . . .

I have always felt that television must accept, and happily, a great responsibility in the field of public affairs, and particularly the responsibility of giving people each day a lively account of the significant events of the world in which they live. It should, in brief, give the news. More than this, it should present the news in such a way that it possesses what my chairman once called 'democratic value'. That is to say, the news should not consist of a featureless recitation, but be told or shown to the viewers in such a way as to be enlightening. If that is to happen, not only must the news programmes rest upon these principles, but they must be allowed whatever length and position in the programmes are necessary to let them do this democratic job. They must not be cut to headline length and they must not be relegated . . .

I think the News Company has gone quite a long way towards meeting these requirements. There was at one time great anxiety about how the news should be handled in the programmes. Those who were then most anxious are now most respectful. There is of course room for improvement, but what has so far been done – or so we all think at Prince's Gate[4] – is one of the very best things that independent television has done.[5]

The ITA endeavoured to persuade ABC to fall into line and join up to ITN by hinting that once they had, the Authority would show flexibility about the amount of expensive film material it would insist that ITN carried. But while this argument continued unresolved,[6] Fraser and his colleagues were angry to discover that ITV had already cut the early ITN evening bulletin from fifteen to seven minutes, and put back the later bulletin from 10.00 p.m. to 10.45 p.m. At a meeting of the ITA on 6 December the worried ITA chairman said that, while the views of Howard Thomas for ABC and Sidney Bernstein for Granada must command respect, the ITA had to worry about what ITN's editor-in-chief was going to do under this sort of pressure:

> Mr Crawley was . . . very unhappy about the present situation and it was important to find some way to keep him in his present post while at the same time meeting legitimate and well-founded criticisms. His resignation would be a serious blow to independent television.
>
> Miss [Dilys] Powell said that in her view the news film was amateurish but not at all on the wrong lines . . . Lord Layton[7] said that he was sure that the illustration of the news would survive and that it was the most difficult thing that the companies had so far had to do. Illustrated news was new to television in this country but it was the coming form of news; he very much hoped that ITN would not revert to the former style of the BBC's news bulletins after only nine weeks' experience . . .
>
> It was agreed that an attempt should be made to persuade the directors of ITN to let it have further time to develop its news service on present lines. Concluding the discussion the Chairman pointed out that the cost of ITN (£300,000 per annum) was less than that of the BBC's news service and much less than that of any American company.[8]

But at the very moment the companies were insisting on economies, Aidan Crawley was telling them that he needed more money to do the job he believed ITN had been set up to do: 'As was clearly understood at the time,' he told the ITN board, 'the original News Company budget was essentially based on guesswork. We have now been operating long enough to state categorically that the Company is not staffed for a 7-day operation on any programme schedule. In order to maintain 7-day working, key personnel are being strained to breaking point – two have already had to be absent from this cause and more absences are feared.'[9]

But ABC had still not joined ITN, and before they did, their managing director Howard Thomas was determined to achieve cuts in the ITN budget. He wrote to Tommy Trail, ITN's secretary: '. . . the scale of both capital expenditure and day to day expenditure envisaged by your company seems out of relation to what is required for the preparation of news items on Television ...'[10]

Now Crawley, harried by the companies while trying to run a news operation for them, began to lose his temper:

> The most important point which has not so far been addressed in the deliberations of the board is that a stable policy is essential NOW. Not only is it impossible for the Management to devote their energies to the improvement of the Company's product if the basis of the Company's existence is constantly called in question, but it will soon be impossible to retain staff. The staff are aware that we have so far been unable to make minor adjustments in salaries and establishment, which operation has shown necessary, and there is already a sense of frustration and uncertainty in the Company.
>
> In broad terms, therefore, it is recommended by the Management:
>
> 1. That the cost of the news operation be accepted as £1,050 per day, or £383,250 per annum. When three stations are operating this will mean that Programme Contractors are getting their news programmes for approximately £350 per day ...
> 2. That, within that figure, the Company be permitted to continue its operation without the necessity of reporting to the board the day-to-day staff and operational changes.[11]

The patrician Crawley was telling the penny-pinching commercial operators to get off his back – but they would not. On the contrary the argument intensified, with some directors wondering if film coverage was really necessary and whether brief news headlines could not simply be slipped in between programmes in place of proper scheduled bulletins. Crawley warned the board that if any of this came about he would resign. All the worst fears of those who suspected that commercial television would not provide high-quality news looked like being justified, but Crawley agreed that for the moment he would soldier on.

The crisis came at Christmas time. On 20 December the members of the ITA paid a visit to ITN in Television House to see the news operation for themselves. As the news company's fate hung in the balance there was a wonderful moment of farce. Crawley described it:

As I was leading our visitors out of the lift to go to the News Room, I noticed two men rolling about on the floor of the passage having a fight. It was so unusual a sight that I stopped to identify them. The only one I could see clearly was the man on top, Arthur Clifford, the News Editor, whom we were just about to visit.[12] I turned to my guests and said, 'At the moment the News Editor seems to be engaged in a rather heated argument with one of his staff. We will visit the sub-editors first.' By the time we had finished talking to the sub-editors Arthur was back at his desk and gave such a lively account of his job that his recent 'argument' was forgotten.[13]

It seems so indeed, for the next day the ITA chairman Sir Kenneth Clark wrote to Crawley to say how impressed the members had been with all they had seen at ITN. He continued: '. . . how glad and relieved I am to learn that, for the time being, your resignation is withdrawn. The news that it had been tendered was a very great shock to the Authority. They are entirely behind the News Company and I do hope that you will not take such a step again without having given me the opportunity of putting your difficulties to them.'[14]

The same day, the ITA's director general attended a special ITN board meeting at which he defined the ITA's attitude to the place of news on the growing network. First, Fraser insisted: 'The News Company has the complete and continued confidence of the Authority, which is more than content with the way in which the news has been edited and presented.' Second: 'While this remains the position, the Authority will as a matter of policy require the national news, as supplied by the News Company, to be included in the programmes of all future companies.' This meant that the ITV companies could no longer hope to go off and produce their own version of the national news. They could only do regional news bulletins.

Perhaps most importantly, the ITA had made up its mind about the amount of news that should be shown: 'On a programme output of fifty hours a week, the Authority would regard a total of twenty minutes a day as the minimum necessary to produce balanced programmes.'

It must have been a worrying Christmas for Crawley. From his home in Chester Square he sent a handwritten note to Clark:

My dear Kenneth, I should have answered your kind letter before Christmas. I really do appreciate your backing, and that of the Authority as a whole. It should enable this little company to be put on a really firm footing, and that is my aim in the discussions on policy for which I said I would stay on.

I don't want to mislead you, however, into thinking I am likely to stay for very long. I won't go into details but I will certainly come and see you to explain why.

Yours sincerely,

Aidan Crawley[15]

In its statement of 23 December the ITA had been firm on the amount of news it would require, and had insisted that there should be 'some element of film'. However, 'The Authority . . . did not think it would be unreasonable that the production, procurement and use of film should now be made the subject of careful review.' Prevented from turning ITN into a simple 'rip and read' headline news service the companies now took the other way they had been offered of cutting ITN down to size: taking an axe to its budget.

At a board meeting on 5 January 1956 new times and lengths of the bulletins were settled in accordance with the ITA's ruling, and it was agreed that they would be 'illustrated'. But the pure 'newsreel' elements that had been a feature at the end of the bulletins would cease. Since the 'newsreel' material was really no more than what was left over from the harder news in the early part of the bulletin, scrapping it would save little money. However, because they could say that the bulletins would in future just give the news, the board now felt able to discuss cuts of more than a third in the annual budget – from £350,000 to £200,000.[16] In what was clearly a vote of no confidence in the current management of ITN, a sub-committee would be set up to see how the money could best be saved.

This was too much for Crawley. At another special meeting of the ITN board on 15 January the secretary read out the editor-in-chief's letter of resignation:

I have been considering the last board meeting over the weekend and I am afraid that I have come to the conclusion that I can withhold my resignation no longer. I will not go into details that are old, but it is clear that the board has no intention whatever of meeting my views, and that our attitudes are too far apart to make it possible for me to continue.

To recapitulate very briefly, in my view the News Company has made a successful start and has reached a point where every effort should be made to expand both the sale of its products abroad and its use as a basis for other programmes connected with the news. The board, on the other hand, are determined not only to limit the scope of the News Company's operations to the narrowest conception of news, but to reduce the cost of such news to the barest minimum.

Not content with asking the management of the News Company to say what is the absolute minimum on which the new schedule of programmes can be produced, the board has appointed a committee of outsiders to examine the management's figures with a view to making further reductions. All this has been done at a time when not only the operations of the individual contractors are being expanded, but when, as you know, the B.B.C. is embarking on a vast programme of capital expenditure to extend its television news organisation in every region in the country. That I had already objected to such an investigation is a wholly minor matter except in so far as it shows a complete indifference on the part of the board to my views.

It was always clearly understood that if either I myself or the board were dissatisfied one with the other we were free to part. I cannot continue to discuss a policy with the whole basis of which I disagree and I must ask the board to accept as final my decision to resign, the resignation to take effect at the end of March.[17]

The board thought Crawley's resignation 'very regrettable', and Sir Robert Fraser for the ITA agreed. But Crawley was adamant, saying only that to help ITN establish itself he would stay on until May, or until his successor was appointed. Crawley was thanked for his services to ITN and told he could keep the television set with which he had been supplied.

Fed up with the way the companies had treated him, Crawley had come to the conclusion that these commercial operators were not fit to be in charge of the News Company. In a statement on 15 January he explained his decision to quit:

> The main reason for my resignation from Independent Television News is my conviction that a board composed of representatives of contractors who differ so widely in their outlook towards television is incapable of maintaining a consistent policy towards the news. In my view the only way to ensure that news is properly handled, at least until all the main contractors

are properly established, is for the Independent Television Authority to take over the company.[18]

The ITA's chairman, Sir Kenneth Clark, agreed, and went to see the post-master-general, Dr Charles Hill, to ask for more government funds to be made available. This possibility had been provided for in the Broadcasting Act if it proved necessary to ensure that there were 'balancing' (i.e., public service) programmes in the schedule. Clark's idea was that the Authority would run ITN on a temporary basis, bypassing the ITN board and using the extra money to top up what the companies were paying ITN. But Hill said no, they would have to make the system work as it was.

During the battle for his budget Crawley had at times angrily accused the ITA – and Fraser in particular – of not giving him sufficient support. Once he had resigned, good relations were restored. 'You know my feelings about it so well,' wrote Fraser to Crawley, 'that I suppose I need not put them into writing, yet I feel I must tell you with what profound and always increasing admiration I watched your handling of the News Company.'[19]

Crawley responded warmly:

> My dear Bob, How particularly generous of you, because I attacked you pretty hard when I felt the Authority was letting us down. That apart, I have enormously enjoyed working with you and am grateful for both the support and the criticisms you have made. I am sure the News Company will prosper if the contractors will let it. It has been a fascinating and rewarding experience.
>
> Yours ever, Aidan.[20]

So ended the first era in ITN's life. The owners had so circumscribed their captain's ability to sail his ship as he saw fit, on the terms he believed had been agreed, that he had resigned his commission. Those who had been appointed to see that the ship was well found and properly provisioned had failed to do enough to prevent his departure. Now this craft, which carried with it the hopes of all who had wanted ITV to be more than just *Double Your Money*, was facing a very difficult voyage. Its course was unclear, the weather worsening and, with no prospect of better pay or conditions, the crew were restless, morale sinking. It would take a new captain of skill and determination to negotiate the hazards facing him, and bring the ship safe through.

CHAPTER 8
THE OTHER
NEW ZEALANDER

On 22 June 1956 the chairman of the Conservative Party, Oliver Poole, sent a letter to 10 Downing Street. 'Prime Minister,' he wrote, 'You told me at luncheon yesterday that an approach had been made by Independent Television News to the Conservative Party asking us to make suggestions for a replacement for Aidan Crawley but that no reply had been given.'[1] It seems from Poole's letter that Norman Collins, as current chairman of ITN, had indeed contacted two senior Conservatives with a view to finding a Tory editor to replace Crawley, but that they had failed to pass on his message to Conservative Central Office. Now it was too late. The Tories had missed their chance: the decision had been made. To those in the know, it was not a surprising choice.

They were both New Zealanders, but in 1956 the two editors of television news in Britain, at the BBC and at ITN, were otherwise very different. At the Corporation Tahu Hole was tall, sepulchral, and determined that television news should remain as much like radio as possible. At ITN was a small, precise man determined to develop what Aidan Crawley had begun and provide quality popular news for the mass television audience. His name was Geoffrey Cox.

When he joined ITN as its editor Cox had fifteen years of national newspaper work behind him. From Oxford, where he had been a Rhodes Scholar, he had gone to work for the *News Chronicle*. Eighteen months later he had had a lucky break. With the Spanish Civil War reaching a climax and the Fascist rebel forces of General Franco advancing on Madrid, the *Chronicle* wanted their own man in the capital. But any British journalist there, if he survived the horrors of civil war, and Madrid fell, was likely to be arrested and unable to get out, perhaps for some considerable time. The *Chronicle* could not afford to have its star reporters out of action for long, but the youthful Geoffrey Cox was expendable: he found himself one of only two correspondents in Madrid when the Republican government abandoned it to Franco. Cox rose to the occasion, and for days at a time his reports led the paper.

Later, at the *Daily Express*, Cox was their man in Vienna as Austria and Germany joined forces in the Anschluss, and in Paris as the Second World War began. Back in England he decided to fight the war rather than cover it. As an infantry officer he came unscathed through campaigns in Greece, Crete and Libya, and was made chief intelligence officer to the 2nd New Zealand Division. Sent to Washington as first secretary to the New Zealand legation he represented his country at meetings of the Pacific War Council, headed by President Roosevelt. Then, in 1944, Cox returned to the army and his intelligence job with the New Zealanders as they fought their way across Italy, from Cassino to Trieste.

Back in Fleet Street after the war, his promised promotion to a senior job at the *News Chronicle* was slow in coming. But Cox used his time as the paper's lobby correspondent to get to know a new generation of post-war politicians, and in 1954 he was made an assistant editor. That experience would be helpful to him when he applied to become ITN's editor, but even more valuable was what he had learned about television.

At the BBC, that great discoverer of talent Grace Wyndham Goldie had begun to hire Cox from time to time as a political expert for television programmes like *Press Conference*, in which, along with another journalist, he would interview leading figures of the day like Aneurin Bevan or the Roman Catholic Bishop Heenan. In the autumn of 1955 he was asked to report the Labour and Conservative party conferences for the BBC – the first time they had been covered by television.

Cox experienced for himself the way television worked and how, at its best, it could engage a mass audience. In his biography he vividly evokes the sense of drama, the feel of 'putting on a show', that the best television broadcasts capture. And he learned about the pressures on performers who had to put across to the viewer material produced by many different hands:

> The report of the last day of the Conservative Conference, a Saturday, was scheduled to go out at the peak time of 7.30 p.m. There had been an exciting atmosphere of show business about the Lime Grove studios that evening. For this occasion I had even been allotted a dressing room. Father Grove of The *Grove Family*, the soap opera of the day, had the room to one side of me; Glyn Daniel of *Animal, Vegetable and Mineral* was on the other side. There was a healthy flow of adrenaline in my veins when I walked across the wide studio floor to take my place at the desk, ready for transmission.
>
> I needed it. For suddenly, alone under the lights in the centre of this huge studio, I realised as never before how much the effectiveness of the next half-hour depended on me, and on me alone. In the unlit half of the studio I could see the gleaming dresses of the girls and the white evening shirts of the men of the cast of the next programme, *Café Continental*. As I waited for the Studio Manager, earphones on head, to swing down his arm to cue me, I was aware of families settling down in their millions across the country in front of their sets, and I felt very much on my own. But the gods were with me and I found myself suddenly relaxed, alert, authoritative. By the time I had finished – and how short that time seemed – I knew that I had done not only a good, but a very good broadcast. As I hurried off the set a murmur of approval arose from the *Café Continental* extras, and the Floor Manager gave me an enthusiastic thumbs-up sign.
>
> That experience was, for me, irreplaceable. For I had learnt, isolated under those lights, the responsibility which falls on any performer who faces the camera alone. Later when I had to deal, not only with newscasters and inter-viewers, but with restive backroom journalists impatient with the way the front men were handling their copy or their ideas, I drew on the knowledge I had gained that Saturday evening.[2]

CHAPTER 9
'AWAY WE GO AGAIN'

While he was sitting though the months of debate on the Broadcasting Bill as a lobby correspondent, Geoffrey Cox had decided he wanted to be involved in television news. Shrewdly he went to see Norman Collins, ITV's founding father, and obtained Collins's endorsement for himself as the editor of the news company when the moment came to choose one. But when it did, Aidan Crawley's star quality, and the name he had already won for himself as a leading television broadcaster, meant that Cox did not get the job – it was not even advertised.

At that moment Cox felt that his hopes of moving into television news were lost: 'Absolutely, I mean, I didn't disagree with the appointment of Aidan. Aidan had more guns, and bigger, than I did. And he was a bloody good broadcaster. But I thought, He hasn't got the real gritty of news in him. If Aidan had had any sense he'd have got me in to do the hard work, and he'd have had a most glamorous time! But Aidan wasn't that sort of chap, to give him the respect he's due.'

Would Cox have gone to ITN as Crawley's deputy? 'Oh, yes. But I wasn't going to apply for it, and to begin with he showed no signs that he wanted a deputy.'

Before ITV opened up, Crawley asked Cox to do a screen test along with other hopefuls, which went well. But Cox demurred: 'The real reason I didn't take it on was that I'd four children to bring up and educate, and I wasn't prepared to meet the school bills with the knowledge that if I didn't have a good night's sleep I would make a mess of it . . . I wasn't prepared to risk it. My wife was quite prepared to take the risk but I thought, I'm an erratic sleeper – although I slept very well right throughout my ITN time as I did throughout the war – and I was frightened. Secondly, by this time I'd had had enough of having to earn my living by what I wrote or by what I did on the box. I wanted to become an executive. I thought it was a much safer job.'

When Crawley resigned only four months after ITN had gone on the air Cox was a clear contender for his job. But others put in for it, including a youthful Ludovic Kennedy, who was then presenting Rediffusion's arts programme, *Sunday Afternoon*, and (a more serious competitor) Kenneth Adam, a senior manager at the BBC.[1]

On the eve of his appearance before the ITN selection board Cox sent them a letter that crisply summarised his qualifications. It concluded: 'If I am selected as Editor-in-Chief of the Independent Television News Service I would propose to continue the present basic structure of the programmes, though there are some modifications which I would like to introduce.'[2]

When the selection board considered the candidates, all except the general manager of Rediffusion, Captain Thomas Brownrigg, DSO, RN (retired), were in agreement. As Sir Robert Fraser at the ITA wrote to his chairman Sir Kenneth Clark:

> Well, we all met at Golden Square[3] last night to choose the editor, and it was a walkover, really, because everybody except Tom Brownrigg thought Geoffrey Cox easily the best, and he will be offered the job. I said I was quite sure the Authority would regard the appointment as acceptable.
>
> It was a pleasant occasion – it really is remarkable how rapidly things have settled in the News Company. It seems an utterly different sort of thing, friendly, clear-headed, kind hearted and stable. . . I think most of us felt that if either Geoffrey or Kenneth withdrew, we would quite happily appoint the other. However, there was, as I say, an emphatic and unanimous preference, save on the part of Tom, for Geoffrey . . .
>
> One of the things I began to feel during the interviews was that Geoffrey would really run the thing a good deal better, and that our two boys,

Christopher [Chataway] and Robin [Day], would address their prayers to him more respectfully than they might to Kenneth. Anyway, there we are, and away we go again, and all looks quite well.[4]

Shortly afterwards Cox was invited to lunch by a somewhat grumpy Brownrigg. They got on to a better footing as ex-servicemen when Cox challenged the captain's assertion that the Navy should never have risked its ships to take off the New Zealand troops when Crete fell to the German airborne attack in 1941. Cox rejected the salary he was offered – £4,000 – and boldly held out for more. He knew that Crawley had been paid £5,000 and, not surprisingly, wanted no less for himself. 'I was absolutely terrified of losing this opportunity,' he says now. I told Brownrigg, "I want this job, I'm made for this job, but if I don't get paid enough the rate for all the other jobs will be downgraded too, and you won't get good men."' At Cox's insistence, Brownrigg went back to the board and, on top of the £4,000, Cox was now offered a 'top-hat' pension and a car. 'I later discovered the reason for Brownrigg's stinginess,' he says. 'As general manager of Rediffusion he was paid £5,000 himself, and he couldn't bear the thought of the editor of ITN getting the same.' After a year in the job Cox's salary was increased to £5,000.

On becoming editor of ITN[5] Cox agreed to a budget that Crawley had decided was impossibly small. 'I bought it because those were the terms of having the job,' he says, 'but I knew it wouldn't work. I didn't think ahead at all. I thought, I'll get by somehow or other, and we did, by cutting costs to the absolute limit. We relied on our own film; we only had, I think, three or four sound cameras. We had to make do with silent coverage. And, somehow or other, I got us through. One of the conditions laid down was that I didn't have a deputy as Aidan had decided to have. It was a small saving, but it helped, and I got through.'

One of the immediate causes of Crawley's resignation had been the appointment of a sub-committee from outside ITN's own management to identify savings in what the contractors suspected were profligate working practices in the News Company. In the newsroom Arthur Clifford was not best pleased. 'This portly figure came in and Aidan said, "Just to introduce him before you get started, Arthur, this is Mr Charles Eade, editor of the *Sunday Dispatc,h*, and he left the two of us together. Charles Eade said,

"Come on, we want to make a go of this," and I said, "I don't hold it against you." I liked the guy. And he said, "What time do your news desk people start to come on?" I said, "Sorry, Mr Eade." He said, "Come on, don't be clever-clever." I said, "I'm not, but what did you say?" He said, "I simply asked what time your news desk people start to come on." I said, "No one starts to come on at any time except me. I do it on my own." He said, "What? And you're in charge of input for a national news programme, seven days a week?" I said, "Yes." And he said, "You're the sole occupant of the news input desk?" And I said, "Yes." And he said, "Christ, OK.'"

Not surprisingly, after two and half weeks of watching Clifford at work – he started at 7.30 a.m. – Charles Eade reported that to cut ITN's budget any further would be to risk disaster. As he succinctly put it: 'The news operation was economically performed, and no changes are proposed.'

In a similar investigation of the control room and studio operation later in the year a Mr Marsden from ATV reported that:

> Broadly speaking, if one considers the end-product of ITN's activities and considers the relative cost of what the BBC produces one is faced with the striking fact that ITN is, by generally accepted standards, fantastically efficient . . . While it is true to say that economies can be made in ITN's operation, I must make an emphatic plea that whatever changes you consider should be made be approached most delicately and carefully on a long-term basis. ITN's whole character and personality is the secret of its success and I am convinced that the economy achieved by eliminating one or two operational personnel would be more than offset by the destruction of the high-morale which exists and is embodied in the vitality and personality of the ITN broadcasts.[6]

Staff morale was very much in the mind of the new editor. Even before he had taken over from Crawley on 14 May 1956 Geoffrey Cox had become worried that key staff were leaving ITN. The deputy editor, Richard Goold-Adams, had resigned with Crawley and had not been replaced. When Cox took Christopher Chataway to lunch at the Garrick Club to tell him about his plans for ITN he was aghast to learn that his star newscaster was also leaving – worse, to go to the BBC.[7] Now news editor Arthur Clifford, worried about ITN's future, told Cox that he, too, had given in his notice some months previously. 'Three months after I'd got the job, Arthur came to see me one evening and said, with great embarrassment "I'm sorry but I'm going tomorrow." And I said, "Arthur, you can't." He said, "Well, the BBC have offered me a job as chief sub at Bush House. They gave me three months', grace, and the three months expire tomorrow and I've got to keep to it." And I said, "Arthur, you can't go because you've got to give *me* three months' notice." And he said, "You wouldn't do that to me, Geoffrey, I mean, you couldn't." And I said, "Well, I've got to think," and I could see disaster staring me in the face, because Arthur had the flair that was keeping us going. I thought, It's going to be absolute hell if he goes. So I took Arthur out on Hampstead Heath and I talked him into staying, which he did.'

The fact was that morale at ITN at this time was up and down like a ship in a storm. People didn't know whether to jump off or hold on in the hope that the gale would pass. No wonder that, as ITN's owners tried to force down the company's costs, Cox told the board:

A decision on the budget at this stage would be of the greatest value editorially, as well as administratively. The staff has inevitably had, during this formative year, periods of uncertainty about their jobs . . . The dismissals which will follow from the budget will undoubtedly come as a further blow to morale, particularly as they must take place at a moment when the work of the Company has received much favourable publicity . . . Much of the vitality and sparkle of the ITN bulletins has sprung from the extent to which the staff have felt able in recent months to get on with their work without looking continually to see if the posts they hold are going to survive . . . I am most anxious to preserve this spirit intact through this period of change.[8]

To hold on to staff he considered vital to ITN's future, Cox had to be ingenious. He had agreed that to save money there should be a reduction in the dubbing of film stories: instead of having commentary and 'natural sound' or 'F/X' (sound effects) mixed together before transmission in the usual way, more stories would be mixed live on air. The results would be more hit and miss, but the services of one dubbing editor could be dispensed with at a saving of £1,100 a year.

The man fingered for firing was Alfred Wilson. 'Soon after I'd taken over,' recalls Cox, 'Norman Collins – he was chairman at the time – said,

"What about this chap Wilson? When are you laying him off?" and I said, "Well, I've got it in train"; but I thought, If I lay him off, the effect on most staff will be catastrophic. They'll think, We've got an editor who won't stand up for us. And then the good men I wanted to keep would have gone. I knew that I had to keep Alfie, so, by one way or another, I hid him. His salary didn't appear, he wasn't on the list, I paid it out of freelance fees, and we got through to the autumn, and suddenly in the autumn the oil started to gush and the advertising rolled in and the companies had money. In those early days, they were always stingy about spending at ITN, but I got enough to save dear Alfie.'

Cox 'hung on' just long enough. On 14 September 1956 he submitted his budget for the following year. Some economies had already been conceded by his predecessor Crawley, including reducing the use of foreign stringer (freelance) cameramen and 'special contributors', and cutting the cost of the contract for studio graphics. Cox had made other savings too, in the acquisition of a new and cheaper teleprompter system for the newscasters; a reduction in the use of film and magnetic tape, and by renegotiating the contract for the studio video cameras. But he strongly resisted savings proposed by the independent sub-committee which would have meant – among other things – sacking two 'silent' cameramen and two film editors. He concluded: 'The total of the new budget, as submitted on the attached schedules, is £348,680. This represents a saving £16,320 a year over the rate of expenditure which has prevailed until now, or a saving of £11,225 a year over the budget drawn up on 1 January 1956.'

Cox's determination and tenacity prevailed. At the beginning of November the board not only agreed to his proposed budget but accepted the addition of a figure to deal with a few essential salary increases and provide a small sum for contingencies. ITN ended up with £365,000 for the coming year – a thousand pounds a day. The board resolved that, 'Within that figure the Management be given freedom to operate.'[9]

It was a small enough income for a national television news company, but sufficient to let ITN live. And Cox was determined to live within it. 'I did take great pleasure in staying within budget, running a tight ship. When the advertising money began to come into ITV I ought to have fought for more of it to come to ITN – I didn't get enough of it. But after all I had been put in because the previous chap wouldn't toe the line, and it's chastening to know that your predecessor got the sack for overspending: it tends to make you pretty cautious yourself.'

There was a further battle that Cox had to win before ITN could hope to thrive. The ITA might have stood firm when it came to the quantity of news that the companies must take from ITN – a minimum of twenty minutes – but it had been silent about when that news should be transmitted. Now the ITV companies proposed a summer schedule for 1957 that, Cox told his board, 'may damage ITN seriously and result in a lowering of the quality of bulletins, and perhaps a loss of key staff . . . I realise fully the commercial considerations which have led to the proposed programme times. On the other hand, the quality of ITN bulletins is not without its commercial value, and I would therefore ask the board to consider, before the present schedules are brought into operation, whether some alternative times cannot be found.'[10]

At the ITA deputy director general Bernard Sendall wrote to his boss Sir Robert Fraser:

> Geoffrey Cox is terribly anxious about new developments in regard to the timing of late news bulletins. These will come to a head at the next meeting of the News Company. It seems that there is a move to defer the late night news bulletin during the summer at weekends to 00.15 on Saturdays and midnight on Sundays.
>
> Geoffrey is contesting this on the argument that it will so dishearten his staff as to endanger the quality of their output. At the same time he is counter-attacking by saying that it should now be possible to place the news at 10 p.m. Mondays to Fridays and 11 p.m. Saturdays and Sundays without any serious danger to the precious ratings.
>
> It looks as if we may have to intervene in this argument. It would be ludicrous to countenance the presentation of full ITN bulletins at midnight or later, leaving a gap of more than six hours between the early bulletin and the late one. When the Authority laid down its twenty minutes of news rule, it came very near to making provisos about the timing of the bulletins, and certainly it would have done so if it had ever thought that the main evening bulletin would be timed for a later hour than 10.45 p.m.[11]

Fraser replied saying that since the weekday position, with the late news at 10.46 p.m. now standard throughout the network, was so satisfactory, it was going to be difficult to argue with the companies over the weekend timings: 'I told Howard Thomas and Norman Collins that I think the Authority will prove very cold about these proposed weekend changes, yet I honestly do not feel it is possible to find grave fault in them, the whole weekly position being taken as a background.'[12]

But after more skirmishing, and a degree of support from the ITA, Cox had his way on the transmission times of the bulletins. Early in April 'it was agreed that the weekend contractors would consider a proposal that the main bulletin should be at 6 p.m. and the subsidiary bulletin(s) during the evening and not at the end of the transmissions.'[13] By the end of the month this proposal had been confirmed. As Fraser wrote to Tommy Trail, ITN's company secretary, the weekend timings were now 'a great improvement on what was first suggested', which had looked like 'something the cat brought in.'[14] For the first time ITN had five-minute weekend bulletins in peak time. Under its new editor, the news company was consolidating its position in the ITV network, and its bulletins in the ITV schedule.

CHAPTER 10

SOMETHING NEW IN NEWS

Nothing so demonstrates the bold new approach of ITN to the television news as what happened on the night following Aidan Crawley's resignation.

Robin Day had not been enjoying himself as ITN's second newscaster; he knew he was unpopular both with ITN's directors and with his colleagues, some of whom had even petitioned Crawley for his removal. 'He was a troubled Robin Day at the dawn of his television career,' says Arthur Clifford, 'wondering, worrying, doubtful, pretty depressed at times because he knew that he attracted so much criticism, so much sheer dislike in some quarters. Robin never resented Chris Chataway's success. He said, "I think he deserves all the popularity he's getting; I just wish I could have some of it, because they don't like me."'

After the early bulletin, which he usually presented, was over, Day sometimes invited Clifford to his flat off Church Street in Kensington. There, glass in hand, he would play records of Churchill's most famous wartime speeches, declaiming along with the great man that 'this was their finest hour', in an effort to cheer himself up.

As with Churchill, difficulty and disaster brought out the best in Day. When Aidan Crawley resigned, the future of ITN itself looked in doubt. Day suggested to Crawley that the only way to deal with the immediate crisis was for him to conduct an interview in that night's late bulletin with the chairman of the Independent Television Authority, Sir Kenneth Clark. To his surprise, both Crawley and Clark agreed:

> It was a crucial moment for me and for the staff of ITN. My colleagues – those on duty at TV House, and those at home – would be watching anxiously. It was Aidan Crawley's vision of ITN's future that had led many of them to join. Was the news company for which they had such high hopes on the brink of extinction? Would a lot of them be sacked? Were they to be denied the chance of building up ITN for effective competition with BBC News?[1]

Day's questions that night were tough and uncompromising, in the style for which he was soon to become so well known: did Clark agree that news was not getting the support the ITA should be giving it? Was the ITA being weak-kneed in the face of the commercial network? Clark dodged some of the questions and said that he understood ITV's need to capture an audience before it could 'build up to a higher level'. But, he said, 'a full and responsible news service of at least twenty minutes a day is absolutely essential'.

The interview was the first Day had ever done live – and it brought him, he said, his first favourable press notice: 'A dramatic end to the evening's viewing,' wrote Kendall McDonald in the next day's *Evening News*. It also won him the respect of his colleagues: 'The questions I had put were the questions they had been asking and which they never dreamed would be asked on TV,' said Day. Altogether it had been a remarkable piece of television, which did much for the reputations of both Robin Day and ITN.

With Chataway gone Cox knew he had to keep Robin Day at ITN, and was quick to see the attraction of the new kind of interviewing Day had to offer: 'I'd done enough interviewing myself in the House of Commons,' he says, 'but it never entered my mind to be tough with people. I mean I wanted the information, I wasn't engaged in doing this in front of the public; but when I got in there at ITN I suddenly realised that Robin was doing this in a way which made it very good television as well. So I backed him to the hilt, and Robin, of course, appreciated this.' Was it his training as a barrister that made Robin Day's style? 'No, I think he was just a natural enquirer. People felt he was a very aggressive fellow; he was, not in putting himself across but in getting at the news. And that's what I respected about him.'

Rightly remembered is Robin Day's interview with Gamal Abdel Nasser, some six months after the Egyptian president's nationalisation of the Suez Canal and the consequent invasion by British forces. The situation was still tense: soldiers and civilians had died; diplomatic relations had not yet been restored; two British subjects were on trial in Egypt charged with spying. Arranged in great secrecy, with the help of a maverick Tory MP friendly to Nasser and the Indian High Commission, the interview was a major test for Day and Cox. ITN did not tell either the Foreign Office or the ITA until it was too late to stop the project going ahead. But was the youthful ITN now mature enough to handle a subject that had aroused such fierce political passions in Britain? Could little ITN really tackle a subject that had only recently led to the most vitriolic exchanges between the government and the mighty BBC?

'I remember I was at home in Hampstead', says Cox, 'when news came through that the two British men had been sentenced to death in Egypt for spying; and Robin and his crew were already on their way to Cairo. I was aghast. I thought, If I cancel the interview Nasser may take offence and bump these chaps off; and if I don't cancel it I may find myself accused of letting Robin shake hands with a murderer. So I went off and played a round of golf with John Cotter [ITN film manager] in Highgate. And early next morning one of the subs from the ITN newsroom rang me to say the two men had been reprieved. So we went ahead.'

'Sitting in the garden of his Cairo home,' wrote James Cameron in the *News Chronicle,*[2] 'President Nasser leaned forward last night into British television screens.' For some reason the technical quality of the filmed interview was poor: it had to be introduced with a phrase like 'filmed in the harsh Egyptian sunlight' to account for it. But that was no matter. Day's clear and insistent questioning of the Egyptian president rose above such technicalities. 'Is it right that you now accept the permanent existence of Israel as an independent sovereign state?' he asked. 'Well, you know, you are jumping to conclusions,' Nasser replied. 'No,' said Day. 'I am asking a question.'

In the course of the interview, wrote Cameron, '[Nasser] became lost in the sort of tangled casuistry that passes for fair comment among diplomats, but looks like blotting paper when exposed to common sense'.

Day and ITN had passed every possible test. They had gained an exclusive interview with a figure whose opinions were of great importance to Britain; far from making relations between Britain and Egypt worse the interview had probably improved them; it had added greatly to ITN's reputation for handling important subjects in an intelligent, effective way; and it had helped cement the bonds between the ITA and ITN, which had nearly come undone during the news company's first months.

At the ITA Bernard Sendall wrote to Geoffrey Cox:

> I would like, if I may, to congratulate you, Robin Day and all concerned on last night's interview with Nasser. I found it utterly absorbing and I was lost in admiration of the skill with which it was conducted.
>
> To my mind there is no greater service that television can do than bring the statesmen of the world into people's homes in this way. I do not think anybody who saw last night's interview could fail to find himself better able in future to form an opinion about Nasser's policies.[3]

Cox sent a handwritten note to Sendall's boss, Sir Robert Fraser:

> Now that Nasser is safely in the bag – and also safely let out of the bag – I would like to thank you for your constant support during the time I was planning the interview. It involved the double risk of being politically dangerous and also of getting mixed up with the spy trial, and the decisions were as a result not easy. I was immensely encouraged and strengthened at the critical stage by your steady backing, which was a vital element in maintaining our momentum when the prey nearly got away from us.[4]

Robin Day became notorious among his colleagues for the careful, almost obsessive preparation of his interviews. 'If I ask him this and he says that, how shall I follow up?' he would ponder. Pressing his producer, or another member of the team, to stand in for his interviewee, he would try to judge the likely effect of his questions by practising on them his forthcoming interrogation. Day's approach was highly sophisticated, but he soon recognised how important it was on television to keep the questions simple. It didn't necessarily matter – particularly in television news – that a reporter might arrive to conduct an interview little better informed than the viewer:

'His freshness to the subject will ensure straightforward questions. However much he gets to know about his subject he should not approach it as an expert. The good television reporter should see himself as the representative of the ordinary viewer. He should not over-estimate the viewer's interest, but he should not under-estimate his intelligence.'[5] Absolutely right.

ITN rapidly developed an interviewing style that was short, sharp and to the point. There was no messing about because there was no time for it in television news. Day quotes his editor, Geoffrey Cox: '. . . the television journalist is forced to go to the point at once, as bluntly and curtly as is practicable. His questions must also be designed to produce compact answers. In this sense he has to be sub-editing his final story as he goes along, for although film can be cut, it cannot be compressed.'[6]

At ITN Robin Day conducted many more memorable interviews, some of them in a separate ITN series entitled *Tell the People*. It was in one of those broadcasts that he interviewed Harold Macmillan, the prime minister. Political commentators were aghast at the way Day asked Macmillan whether he still backed his much-criticised foreign secretary Selwyn Lloyd. This was the first time such a question had been put to the most senior member of the government on television, and the interview was, as Derek Marks described it in the *Daily Express*, 'the most vigorous cross-examination a prime minister has been subjected to in public.'[7] Its importance to ITN was that it showed the potential of television to overtake the written press as the main source of news for most people. As the columnist Pendennis put it in the *Observer*: 'Will the television screen begin to by-pass the House of Commons, or even (dread thought) the Press? This is the kind of question that has been sending a shiver down what's left of Fleet Street's spine.'[8]

At ITN Robin Day was not just the studio-bound interviewer and presenter of his later BBC career. Frequently he showed that he could take an Arthur Clifford idea, however unpromising, and make it his own in true ITN style. Dispatched to interview the Japanese foreign minister, for no very obvious reason other than that the man was in Britain, Day discovered from the cuttings that British industry was furious with the Japanese for blatant pirating of British products. In his interview with Mr Fujiyama, Day produced two packets of ball bearings, virtually indistinguishable but one a Japanese imitation, and asked what Japan was going to do about this piracy. British officialdom was furious, and Day was accused of 'treachery', but he had made a serious point briefly, effectively and perfectly politely. Despite protests from the Foreign Office his interview ran on the *ITN News* and itself made news in the next day's papers.

A serious political journalist, Day was quite capable of making something memorable even from what we have learned to call a 'photo opportunity'. In 1956 Marilyn Monroe was in London, with her new husband Arthur Miller, to film *The Prince and the Showgirl* with Laurence Olivier. Day liked the idea of interviewing her, but he was considerably put out to discover that while Marilyn could be filmed talking to him after her press conference, as if she was being interviewed, no sound recording would be permitted. As he wrote later: 'The assignment was not one for which a political interviewer was suited.' Arthur Clifford suggested presenting her with a big bunch of flowers. Day grumpily replied that he was 'not a bloody florist', but on his way to the hotel where filming was to take place he refined Clifford's idea into a more stylish gesture. 'My romantic and imaginative nature found a brilliant solution. I bought a lovely red rose from the florist in the Savoy Hotel foyer. I sat down in front of Marilyn. The cameras began to roll. I removed the rose from my button-hole and presented it to her in a courtly manner.'[9] As Monroe held the rose, not quite sure what to do with it, Laurence Olivier intervened to enquire with mock asperity what Day meant by this gesture. 'Adoration' he would like to have said, but 'Admiration' he stammered.

> Feeling a little out of my depth, I rose to leave the presence. But then from the assembled mob of cameramen, whom I had totally forgotten, came a great yell: 'Give it to 'er again, Robin. The rose – give it to 'er again, will you?' The momentary magic was rudely shattered. I presented that red rose to Marilyn at least three more times. She never did know where to put it. But it gave me something to do with my hands.

Day had now been joined as a newscaster by Ludovic Kennedy. Clever, creative and entertaining, 'Ludo' was somewhat in the Aidan Crawley mould. Like him, he had married a woman who had made a great success of her own career. His wife was Moira Shearer, the ballerina and star of the film *The Red Shoes*. Kennedy was beginning to make his name as a writer, but in 1955, when ITV began, he had become presenter of the Profile spot in a programme called *Sunday Afternoon*, produced in London by ATV. When Crawley resigned as editor of ITN in early 1956, Ludo had been quick to write[10] asking if his own name could be 'borne in mind' as Crawley's successor. He had not been seriously considered, but because his Profile series was ending he immediately applied again, this time for a job as newscaster. He was interviewed and given a test on a Wednesday, then found himself newscasting the following Monday because Robin Day had 'flu. It all happened in the interim after Crawley had resigned but before Cox had taken over, so before Crawley offered Kennedy a permanent job he checked with his successor. 'And I said "yes,"' Cox recalls. 'And I thought, He's probably not the right man because he's a feature writer, he's not a hard news man, but in fact he did the news superbly. Initially I was worried that his old Etonian accent might jar with our mass audience, but I was quite wrong about that. He was immediately accepted – there was no sense of class consciousness about him at all.'

'A new face for the news,' wrote Kenneth McDonald in the *Evening News*, 'and I don't think I am sticking my neck out very far if I forecast that he will prove just as popular with viewers as Chataway and Day.'[11] As a newscaster, it was Ludovic Kennedy's great skill to create just the right tone for every story he had to read. One night Arthur Clifford noticed that the death of Violet Lorraine – well known for a song she had sung during the First World War – had just been announced. Rather than mark the event with a line or two over a still, Clifford found an original recording of the song and a wind-up gramophone with a horn. At the end of the bulletin Kennedy announced Violet Lorraine's death, and reminded the viewers that her song had been the last that many young men had heard; it summoned up the nation's memory of the Great War. Then he walked over to the gramophone, wound it up, switched it on and went back to his newscaster's desk where he sat listening as Violet Lorraine sang 'If You Were The Only Girl In The World.' 'We let her sing on over the credits instead of the normal closing music,' says Arthur Clifford, 'and at the end Ludo looked up at the viewers and just said, "Goodnight." It was quite beautiful; it made my evening. Afterwards, so many people were ringing up we all had to help take the calls. I talked to a lady who said, "It's about Violet Lorraine. I watched with my husband. He was one of those who came back, who survived, and we listened to it together and I wept, and it meant so much to us and brought back all those memories. God bless ITN.'"

In January 1957 Geoffrey Cox sent a paper to the board about Robin Day and Ludovic Kennedy, whose current contracts were soon to expire. Because of the reporting as well as newscasting that Day was doing for ITN he was working harder than Kennedy for the same money, and Cox wanted to put right this anomaly. In addition, Day was interested in other work of a feature kind, which worried Cox. In his opinion: 'The essential need from the News Company's point of view at this moment is to retain during the next twelve months both the main newscasters as newscasters, to provide time for building up reinforcements of comparable calibre.' The editor now proposed to offer a basic payment to both men of £2,000 a year for three days' newscasting each week. On top of that he suggested that Kennedy should be paid another £250 for one extra day a week as a newscaster, and Robin Day an extra £500 to work either as a parliamentary correspondent or in special programmes (which ITN would control) for another two days a week. The board appears to have agreed these fees.[12]

By training and instinct a Fleet Street journalist, Geoffrey Cox was very appreciative of what Crawley had done to hire people for this new medium of television news. 'He left me a bloody good staff, marvellous, those early people. And I wouldn't have been able to select them myself because half of them had never done any journalism at all. I mean, people like Ludovic Kennedy, Lynne Reid Banks, Reggie Bosanquet . . . '

Lynne Reid Banks had been a repertory actress who had taken up writing. Her play *It Never Rains* was broadcast in BBC Radio's Sunday Play slot on Easter Sunday in 1954 but, she says, was not particularly well received. 'It never rains but it bores,' said an unkind critic. Undeterred, she continued to write, but, to earn her living, she took a job with a magazine that did listings for and features about the new television channel. Briefed by her editor that ITV's news operation was going to be something different, she went to interview Aidan Crawley: 'He was an extremely handsome man, looking at me across the desk. I didn't know anything about television news, but he began telling me about how it would be newscasters not newsreaders, and that he would employ women – not, of course, to read the news, but as reporters. After a while it seemed as if the balance of the interview was shifting. He was asking more questions than me, such as "Where have you been? What have you done?" Then, "I'm busy," he said to me. "I get inundated. Are you interviewing me or am I interviewing you?" "Definitely you are interviewing me if there's a chance of a job," I said. I had to memorise an eight-minute broadcast for my test; I had to get stories from the paper and speak them to camera. Aidan said there would always be a funny little end-piece and I found one in the *Daily Mirror*. In the studio I looked at the camera: it was like some great beast shifting its bulk. While I was reading a story the telephone on the desk rang, and a voice said, "Someone has just sent a bomb through the post to the prime minister." I had a vision of this bomb coming in like a Christmas pudding on a plate. Then James Bredin[13] appeared smirking. Later, ITN phoned and said, "You've got the job."'

As a reporter Reid Banks found ITN, 'Fizzing with innovation. Aidan wanted us to be more populist than the BBC, to be noticed, to be more flexible, more public-friendly, so we pioneered vox-pops. People had never seen the like of it before. The public always loved us, but above all Aidan wanted us to be respected, because the television companies had no respect for us. We had just a couple of dispatch riders run off their little wheels – we were always the poor relation. Aidan was furious we were not getting the recognition we needed from our bosses.'

She found that vox-pops – stopping people in the street for a comment on some topic in the news – were tricky for a woman reporter: 'Most people assumed you were soliciting. Male reporters got more money because they did the tough stuff. I knew I was pioneering, that no one had done it before, but at the same time I knew I was not on a par with men: I was something of a decoration.' Suddenly assigned to cover a plane crash because no other reporters were available, she remembers being told by news editor Arthur Clifford, 'I want you to stand there with all the bodies and bits around you and let your real feelings come through. Don't try to do it like the men.'[14]

After she had reported for more than three years, Reid Banks was taken off the road and brought back into the newsroom. She feels her interview with Paul Robeson, the American singer with Communist sympathies, might have been to blame. Robeson had just returned from visiting the Soviet Union and Reid Banks had been told by his minders not to put political questions to him. Undeterred, she had asked him what

Communism looked like close up. Apparently there were complaints from Robeson's team, although it was obviously the right question to ask.

Indeed, she received a rare 'herogram' from her editor – now Geoffrey Cox. 'You did us proud last night,' wrote Cox, 'in your interview with Robeson. Your return to the attack after his attempt to rule out of order any questions about his Communist leanings was most effective – and courageous. It sounded just the right note in our third birthday bulletin. Thank you.'

Whatever the reason for her recall to Television House, Reid Banks felt it a sign of failure. But she had the last laugh on ITN when the novel she had been working on in idle moments in the newsroom was published. *The L-Shaped Room* was a sensational bestseller and, reading the papers, her colleagues discovered that she had sold the film rights for more than £20,000. Soon afterwards Reid Banks left ITN to marry and live on a kibbutz in Israel. Later she became a highly successful full-time writer – mostly of books for children.

Lynne Reid Banks was ITN's pioneer woman reporter, and Barbara Mandell its first woman newscaster – indeed the first female newscaster in Britain. An experienced broadcaster from South Africa, she presented the afternoon bulletin. This was quite something, another example of ITN's determination to be out in front of the boring BBC. 'I thought how wonderful it was for Barbara to read the news,' says Reid Banks. 'I read it once myself – they must have been desperate, it just wasn't done. It was always said that a woman reading the news would just not have the necessary gravitas.' That was certainly not true in Mandell's case. But in that first frantic economy drive her daytime newscast was hacked out of the schedule, and she joined the other reporters and scriptwriters, although she continued to present some weekend news bulletins.

One of Barbara Mandell's most effective reports focused on what had become known as the 'Heartbreak Special', the night train carrying young British emigrants to Liverpool where they would take passage for Canada, hopeful of making a better life there than Britain could offer. On the platform parents said goodbye to children whom they knew they might never see again. Stan Crockett, Mandell's cameraman on the assignment, was one of ITN's toughest and roughest, but together they came back with a human story that stuck in viewers' minds. 'The story they'd remember that night, looking back, it wouldn't have been student riots in Seoul or something,' says Arthur Clifford, 'it would have been those people trying to bite back, fight back their tears on a station platform, saying goodbye to younger ones who they would never, never see again; and even that thug Crocket came back and said, "I felt like piping my eye a bit, mate." And I said to John Cotter, "To hear Stan say that, John!" He said, "Well, don't keep on about it, Arthur, I know it was a good story."'

Down at the end of the subs table George Ffitch had caught Clifford's eye as someone who might make a reporter. A grammar-school boy from Dagenham, he was one of that select band thought clever enough to learn Russian during National Service. Indeed, he was intensely bright, with a bearing, as Geoffrey Cox noted, at the same time pugnacious and cheerful.[15] Ffitch proved a master of the sharp question and the incisive commentary and, like other ITN reporters, he was no respecter of persons.

Much later, at a Labour Party Conference, he was waiting to interview Harold Wilson. The prime minister arrived with a stye in his eye. While makeup and lighting people gathered round to minimise the problem, Wilson's aide told Ffitch that the PM wanted no questions about the imminent announcement of the election date. On air, Ffitch's first question was 'Mr. Wilson, when you are worried you sometimes get a stye in your eye. How is your eye tonight?' He followed up with 'When will you go to the country?'

'George was tough and acerbic and could be withering, very laconic,' says Clifford. 'He could be intolerant of people of lesser intelligence and so on. For all that, he was a terrific reporter, and became a close friend. He was absolutely straight up and down. There was no hidden side to George; he was just a natural journalist, and there's never been a more incisive inter-viewer than George Ffitch on political and industrial stories.' Appropriately, Ffitch became industrial, then political correspondent at ITN, where his own left-wing politics illuminated but never otherwise affected his reporting. There were plenty of angry red faces at the annual Communist Party conference in 1956 when Ffitch asked the delegates pointedly whether they agreed with Khruschev's recent denunciation of Stalin – and, if so, why they hadn't disowned the Soviet tyrant earlier.

But Ffitch's politics caused him some personal problems. Shortly after the Soviet invasion and occupation of Hungary in 1956, Ffitch summoned an engineer to repair his television set at home. On observing the portrait of Lenin in pride of place on Ffitch's wall the man took apart the TV set before revealing that he was a Hungarian refugee. He then packed up his tools and departed, leaving Ffitch to pick up the pieces.

Ffitch was later to contribute effectively to many of ITN's special election and budget programmes and held important posts at *The Economist* and the *Daily Express*. In 1979 he became managing director of the London Broadcasting Company and Independent Radio News, ITN's venture into commercial radio.

And then there was Reggie, Reginald Bosanquet. A founder member of the ITN repertory company, Reggie played his part in ITN's history with unforgettable panache. Later, he would become famous – and infamous – as a newscaster, but it is sometimes forgotten what a very good reporter he was. He had endured a miserable childhood with stoicism. His father was a man of independent means and a notable cricketer, the inventor of the googly, who turned out at Lords for the Gentlemen of England against the Players. But he had not been impressed when his son was born paralysed down one side: 'It would have been better if he hadn't lived,' Bosanquet was told his father had remarked. That early physical setback did not prove crippling, but he was left with a slight lack of co-ordination on the left side – and the trademark lopsided grin. Both his parents died while he still very young and the relationship of the young orphan with his guardian was unhappy. During the war he was sent to Canada – he remembered being deloused on his arrival there. It was not an auspicious start in life.

In 1944, back in Britain, Bosanquet was sent to Winchester, then won a scholarship to Oxford. There he met Karin Lund, half Russian, half Norwegian, who was at Somerville. 'His knowledge and intellect impressed me so much,' she says. 'Reggie had a wonderfully wide intellect, and he used it. He opened my eyes to a whole lot of things. At Oxford he really did spend quite a lot of the time just studying.' They married in April 1955 while Bosanquet was in his final year of university and thinking about a career. Through friends, he was introduced to Sir Kenneth Clark, and Aidan Crawley, who offered him a job at ITN. 'I want to be a television star,' Bosanquet recalled telling him. 'I don't know about that,' Crawley replied, with a kindly smile, 'but you can be a television tea boy.'[16] So Bosanquet joined ITN straight from university, setting up home with his new wife in a small flat in London's Regent's Park.

Bosanquet described himself as a typical Leo: aggressive, selfish and affectionate – a pretty good self-assessment, though he might have added exasperating and lovable. At first a very junior sub-editor, he badgered Arthur Clifford until he was promoted to reporting. 'He loved being on-screen,' says Karin. 'We had an old high-backed armchair, and Reggie would stand behind it so that I could see just the top half of him, and practise talking to the television audience by reading the newspaper to me. He realised that being chosen by Aidan Crawley was the best possible reason for him to have confidence in himself.'

'Reggie, like most of us flawed human beings, had a good side and a bad side,' Clifford recalls. 'He could be wonderfully generous and open-hearted. At other times, he was a tricky, awkward cuss who had to be bullied. I'm not saying Reggie ever wilfully disobeyed me when I was news editor, but I had to treat him as if I was his headmaster. Every other reporter did, without question, everything I asked of them. In Reggie's case, while for the most part he responded with alacrity and with great efficiency to whatever stories I put him on, there were times when he'd question and challenge, I had to say "Whether you want to do the bloody story or not, Reggie, there's a missing python in bloody Clapham, go and find it, and put it round your neck. If you don't like it, you can seek work elsewhere." And he said, "You're not fun any more," and I said, "I'm not trying to be fun, Reggie, I just want to get this story covered." He could be mean and generous, truculent and tremendously co-operative by turn. I had a lot of time for him but I suppose, adopting headmasterly tones, I could say "A difficult young man."'

A scriptwriter colleague, Sue Tinson, agrees: 'Reggie would sit there making paper darts and firing them out of the window into Kingsway,' she says. 'He was like the little girl with the curl: when he was good he was very, very good, and when he was bad he was horrid. But he was charming and usually nice to me – though I think I was one of the few women in the office who didn't have an affair with him.'

Perhaps it was because of the many blows Bosanquet had taken in childhood that he proved a tough interviewer. He was never deterred by a brush-off, or content with weasel words, whether interviewing Archbishop Makarios trying to deny his links with terrorism or clambering on to a platform in front of angry, on-strike boilermakers to interrogate their leader, Ted Hill. 'Reggie was fearless,' says Clifford. He would take on the toughest politicians, the most awkward subjects, international figures, and he'd question them without fear and without favour. And I thought that was Reggie's great strength. Because he was the handsome, womanising Reggie, and all the rest of it, people forgot his great value as a natural television reporter.'

As 1956 drew to an end, and the fortunes of the ITV companies began to look a little rosier, modest pay rises for some of the reporters were approved. For example:

Reggie Bosanquet went up from £928 to £1,050;
Lynne Reid Banks went up from £750 to £850;
Barbara Mandell went up from £1,000 to £1,050.[17]

Fundamental to a television news service that was more than just a newscaster monologue were the cameramen. Cyril Page, senior cameraman, and John Cotter, film manager, who assigned the crews in the most cost-effective way, had come from the BBC. But virtually all of the other cameramen and film sound recordists at ITN were recruited from cinema newsreels. These men could see that their big-screen business was now running through its last reel, while television offered them another opening, another show.

They brought with them great strengths and some drawbacks. Geoffrey Cox, a physically small man, recalls the impression they made on him when he met his camera teams for the first time: 'As one huge, quietly aggressive man after another filed in I felt I was in the All Blacks' changing room before an international.' They were tough characters, veterans of good-humoured but ruthless turf wars between the different newsreels, where choice camera positions were fought over and all sorts of skulduggery practised to ensure that one cameraman's newsfilm got safely into the 'bath', the processing laboratory, on time while his rival's somehow did not. This was invaluable experience for those engaged in a virginal operation like ITN's, where some of the reporters were not trained journalists at all, but real innocents abroad. The cameramen and their sound-recordists proved adept at everything, from talking their way past recalcitrant customs officers to finding a drink in the middle of a battlefield. Best of all, in my own experience at least, they were brave: lions sometimes led by donkeys, men who, however rude and sometimes unkind they might be to an inexperienced reporter, would usually do their best to cover the action, whatever the personal danger.

But there were some drawbacks to them. To start with, their tough union agreement with ITN gave them the title of 'cameraman/director'. This meant that they often felt they should be 'calling the shots', or at least insisting on the lunch-breaks and ten-hour rest periods to which they were entitled, but which did sometimes interfere with covering the news effectively. And, because their basic pay was supplemented with overtime, they were usually much better off than the reporters they worked with. Needless to say, these were not insuperable problems, if camera crew and reporter had some respect for each other. If the reporter could get his crew to the right place at the right time, and if the crew could shoot the action or the interview so that the snaps came out, both sides were content. Like a young second lieutenant grateful for the experience of his grizzled platoon sergeant to help him through until he'd learned a bit about soldiering, many a tyro reporter knew he was lucky to have a seasoned cameraman to tell him what to do next – even if the suggestion was sometimes rather rude.

But the cameramen were being asked to change the habits of a working lifetime – to 'hand hold', to pick up their cameras and walk with them while filming. Most of their newsreel assignments had been to cover predictable events: a Christmas Day swim in the Serpentine, a Remembrance Day parade, Ascot, a Test match. Cameramen put up their big heavy 35mm film cameras on equally heavy tripods in the best position they could find and waited for the largely predictable action to come to them. If that wasn't possible, they took lighter, silent cameras, with a mere 100 feet – two and a half minutes – of film, and shot the scene 'mute'.

But in America Aidan Crawley had seen the way in which, for better, livelier, cheaper film coverage, the television networks were turning to what was then thought of as amateur 16mm equipment – half the size of cinema film. CineVoice cameras, converted to take 400-foot film magazines, could record ten minutes' worth of pictures and sound. They were light enough for a strong cameraman to carry on a brace resting on his shoulder and sticking out in front of him, with the viewfinder at just about eye level. He would be linked to his sound-recordist by cable. From him, another cable led to the microphone, which would be in the hands of the reporter as he fought to get it under the chin of his 'doorstep' interviewee. For the first time these cameramen were being asked to get close up to the heart of the action, not stand aloof.

In the beginning at ITN most of the pictures were shot silent and screened with sound effects added back at base. Even when a sound crew was assigned, its primary purpose was to shoot an interview to accompany the 'silent' story, before hurrying off to do the same thing elsewhere. Geoffrey Cox vividly described the moment, when he realised how much more effective 'natural sound' coverage could be.

In July 1956 a strike at the Austin plant at Longbridge looked as if it might turn nasty. ITN had sent a sound crew, with John Hartley as reporter, Stan Crockett as cameraman and Bill Best as sound-recordist. They were preparing to film interviews on the edge of the crowd when a lorry tried to force a way through the pickets; scuffles broke out and mounted police moved in.

> Hartley, Crockett and Best, held together by the quarter-inch insulated cable which linked the microphone to the camera, thrust their way through the crowd towards the scene of action. John Hartley moved in front, holding out the microphone to pick up the sound as the mounted police reached the crowd around the lorry. Struggling to keep up with him, Crockett filmed the scene from the sound camera on his shoulder.

> When we viewed the film that evening I knew we had something special. The clatter of horses' hooves, the half bantering, half menacing shouts of the pickets – for we were a long way then from the grim visages of flying squads of secondary pickets – the curt orders of the police, the roar of the lorry engine revving up, the clang as the factory gates shut behind it all gave not only vividness but authority to the story . . . In those few minutes Hartley, Crockett and Best had carried the coverage of news on television in Britain a major step forward. Though our chances of using the technique were for many months ahead to be limited by a shortage of cameras, the shooting of natural sound to accompany action film was now established as a key element of the new journalism.[18]

Some cameramen were quicker than others to pick up this new way of working. Others had to be cajoled into taking their cameras off the tripod, putting them on their shoulders and getting in amongst the action to record more dramatic pictures and the sound that went with them. But that was the way forward on television.

Despite that, it was two cameramen shooting silent who made the most important contributions to ITN's reputation in its first years of operation. In late October 1956, just as the Suez situation became critical, the Hungarians rose in revolt against their Communist rulers. ITN's Martin Gray, who had had considerable experience as a cameraman in the Second World War, was dispatched to Vienna with orders to try to get to the Hungarian capital across the border. Eventually he found an unguarded crossing point and drove the two hundred miles to Budapest. There he filmed for an hour or two, then drove back to ship his film from Vienna to London. He snatched a few hours' sleep, then set off again for Budapest. This was to be his exhausting schedule for the next few days. As Geoffrey Cox recalled,

> Despite these pressures, Gray's coverage was admirably shot. Here for the first time were the students and workers of the new Militia, their shoulders draped with bandoleers, rifles and machine guns in hand, patrolling the streets of their liberated capital. Huge Soviet metal stars were hauled from the front of Communist headquarters; a statue of Stalin was toppled from its pedestal and smashed. One gripping sequence showed secret police of the old regime, curiously young, with lank, dishevelled hair, their faces white with terror, being escorted at rifle point from their headquarters. In another a frenzied crowd dug away at rubble barring the entrance to a building where other police agents were still holding out. Here indeed was television news fulfilling its role, catching a moment of history in the making.[19]

Then the Russians invaded to crush the revolt. Hurrying back to the border in filthy weather, before he could be trapped along with his latest batch of film, Gray met a column of T34 tanks pounding towards him. 'Through the windscreen, with the wipers clearing a cone of vision through the rain, Martin Gray filmed these tanks, so securing one of the classic film stories of the crushing of the Hungarian revolution.'[20]

Gray had been the only British cameraman to get pictures out of Budapest during the uprising. For the infant ITN it was a most effective demonstration that 'the News Company' was up to the job it had been given.

While Martin Gray had been covering the Russian invasion of Hungary, Cyril Page had been with British forces as they invaded Egypt. He had been sent as a silent cameraman because ITN could not afford a sound crew, even on a story as momentous as this. Waiting with the rest of the media in Cyprus, Page had won the draw to go as pool cameraman with the invasion fleet. A polite young sub-lieutenant called Michael Parkinson (yes, the future television host) offered to kit him out with British military uniform, but Page replied that he preferred to stick with the American gear he had worn in the Korean war.

Once ashore at Port Said Page liberated a lemon-yellow Chrysler convertible from a car showroom, together with a quantity of bottled gas that he instinctively felt might come in useful for trades of various kinds. Now mobile, he roamed the town, where fighting had only just ended, to film bomb damage and the bodies still lying in the streets. At the nearby airfield captured by the British he found a plane about to take off for Cyprus and got his film aboard. Next day it turned up at the War Office in London, which, amazingly, handed it over to ITN without comment. The 'dope sheets', the notes a cameraman writes to explain the pictures he has taken, had been lost, so neither ITN nor the BBC knew that the film was 'pool' and should have been available to them both. As a result ITN had a scoop, exclusive coverage of the biggest story of the year. It made the most of it, and Page's silent material ran as a seven-minute story on that night's bulletin. It provided vivid visual evidence to inform the furious debate about Suez that was now dividing the country.

Page went on filming and was there with the British Land Forces commander, General Sir Hugh Stockwell, when he received prime minister Anthony Eden's reluctant order to halt the British advance. Stockwell was clearly amused by the sight of Page stylishly covering the Canal Zone in his yellow Chrysler and by the idea of a cameraman working in a theatre of war for the new television channel funded largely by soap-powder commercials: he promptly christened Page 'Omo'.

Geoffrey Cox had now found an ingenious way to get a soundman and reporter to the Canal Zone without paying. The government's Central

Office of Information flew them out for nothing, in return for some film that would counter allegations of widespread and wanton destruction of civilian property. Cox insists there was no impropriety in this since film shot for the COI would not be used by ITN – and, of course, it did mean that Robin Day was now in Egypt and able to report the somewhat ignominious hand-over by British troops to Danish soldiers of the United Nations – which can plausibly be seen as marking the end of the British Empire.

As a Korean war veteran Cyril Page was entirely at home in this war-torn environment. He was, as he says, 'wheeling and dealing a bit', and before the crew left for home, he organised a handsome party for his colleagues and contacts in a luxurious flat that had been abandoned by its Egyptian owners. The Navy came ashore with lots of food, a bevy of nurses and a pianist, and General Stockwell made an appearance – he was amazed by the extent of the spread Page had organised. 'This bloke could have bought Suez,' he told Cox later, but ITN's editor was not quite so impressed with Page's social and entrepreneurial skills. He proved extremely stuffy about approving Page's twenty-pound Suez expenses claim – though he eventually did so.

As an ITN cameraman Cyril Page had made a good friend and contact in General Stockwell. As Cox relates: 'Fifteen years later the dignitaries waiting in the courtyard of Caernarvon Castle for the arrival of Prince Charles for his investiture as Prince of Wales were not a little surprised to see a figure in the full dress uniform of a field marshall rise from their midst and greet a passing cameraman with a cry of "Omo – Omo, my dear fellow, how are you?"'[21]

Cox had always been concerned that although the breezy, entertaining ITN style his predecessor Aidan Crawley had pioneered had proved popular with ITV's viewers it would not necessarily hold them for more important stories. He feared – and it was a concern that his successors shared – that when some issue arose that affected the nation's vital interests, they would switch to the broadcaster that had seen them safely through the Second World War – the BBC. But when the figures were in, it transpired that a majority of viewers had chosen to stay with ITN throughout the crises of Suez and Hungary: 55 per cent had watched ITN's main bulletin rather than the BBC's. This was a tremendous achievement, a demonstration that ITN was more than the cheeky chappy of television news, confirmation of its place as a worthy – as well as livelier – alternative to the BBC.

In September 1957 Cox led ITN's second birthday celebrations. 'Since ITN has been the one consistently successful branch of commercial television, those in charge have good reason to be pleased with themselves,' wrote Bernard Levin, who was usually a severe critic of ITV. 'And so they are; but Mr Cox made it clear that they were not planning to bask idly in the sun of critical approval. Reviewing the two years' work of ITN he said that the two biggest news stories which had strained the ITN resources to their limits had been Suez and Hungary; the organisation had come through that test successfully, and Mr Cox seemed confident that nothing worse could now happen to it.'[22]

Two years in, ITN had recovered from its post-natal problems, climbed out of its pram and started to walk.

CHAPTER 11
BIG IDEAS –
TWO FOR THE PRICE OF ONE

Hardly had ITN set out than it began to have ideas about expansion, about doing more than just the news for ITV. There were several reasons for this ambition, and the first was the editor's concern that unless he could offer his newscasters, reporters and producers more than just the opportunity to work on the relatively short news bulletins the best of them would grow bored and leave.

Geoffrey Cox had been shaken to discover, even before he took over, that Christopher Chataway was about to leave ITN and join the BBC. Chataway was not being disloyal to an organisation that had made him a television star: he had accepted Aidan Crawley's offer of a job on the basis that ITN would soon be producing a weekly current-affairs programme in which he would be involved as a political interviewer. But first came the budget cuts, when all attention was focused on survival, and then a change of plan. The ITA still wanted a current-affairs programme but when ITV started to become profitable, it saw no reason why the programme companies should not fund it themselves, rather than expect ITN to do so. The Authority wanted the companies, as well as ITN, to add more serious 'balancing' programmes to their light entertainment and soap-opera schedules. And indeed, now that the companies did have money they preferred to spend it on their own efforts rather than give it to ITN. They might be proud of ITN's success, but they were jealous too. Understandably they wanted to get full credit themselves for any money they put into 'balancing' programmes, rather than allowing ITN to claim it.

Hanging on to good staff was important for ITN, but the main argument for expansion that ITN put to the companies was more basic, calculated to appeal to their desire to keep ITN's costs down. As an ITN paper circulated at the beginning of 1956 had already argued:

> The organisation of the News Company makes it a good basis for programmes on current affairs, sport and perhaps, later, outside broadcasts. The News Company could handle programmes of this nature more cheaply than individual contractors, since the nucleus of the required staff and equipment (other than O.B. equipment) already exists. Much attention has been devoted to the reduction of operating costs, whereas the right policy might be to place more emphasis on the earning capacity of existing staff and equipment.[1]

The first real opportunity for expansion occurred early in 1957 when – in response to the pleading of the programme companies – the government abolished what was known as the 'toddlers' truce', the period between six and seven when no television broadcasting – and, of course, no advertising – was allowed. Having won the argument, the companies found themselves just as unprepared to fill the slot as they would turn out to be decades later when they got rid of *News at Ten*. Short of material, they turned to ITN to help fill the gap, and Geoffrey Cox accepted a request from Associated Rediffusion to provide it with a weekly current-affairs series called *Roving Report*. The ITN directors ticked him off – he was not to accept further commissions of this kind again without first getting their approval[2] – but nonetheless they went along with the idea.

The cost of each *Roving Report* was to be kept very low. Its budget, as the series began in the spring of 1957, was just £800 per programme. This included a cost of £42 for the producer, £37 for Robin Day as reporter, travel and expenses of £300 and a notional 'profit' of £50. Though ITN was at this time seen as a non-profit-making news provider to the ITV companies, it was felt that additional enterprises should bring in more money than ITN spent making them.

In fact, the first *Roving Report*[3] cost ITN more than twice what the companies had agreed to pay for it. Geoffrey Cox had seized on the meeting between prime minister Harold Macmillan and president Eisenhower in Bermuda – the first such British/American summit since the Suez fiasco – as his cue. Determined to make a splash, he sent Robin Day to the USA to test American attitudes to Britain, and the strength of the 'special relationship'. Breaking all the strict rules about ensuring impartiality, he persuaded BOAC to carry the crew free to New York in return for generous on-air coverage of the airline. Then, in a frantic schedule of filming in Washington and New York, Day interviewed Senator Hubert Humphrey as they travelled on the little underground train that connects the Capitol with Senate offices, talked to ordinary Americans in Grand Central Station and at the top of the Empire State Building, and out-interviewed Mike Wallace, then regarded as the rudest television interviewer in America. Finally, coached in London by news editor and amateur boxer Arthur Clifford, Day ducked through the ropes during a training session to throw a few questions to the boxer Sugar Ray Robinson, in true Damon Runyon style.

This first programme was a success, but the question was, what should follow that? To protect their own current-affairs programmes the companies had insisted that *Roving Report* deal with foreign subjects, which would always be more expensive than domestic coverage, and the budget was too small. Cox's producers continued to wheel and deal shamelessly for free flights in return for including shots of the airline's planes in the programme – quite against the spirit and letter of the Television Act.

Michael Barsley, a lively and inventive producer, was instrumental in getting *Roving Report*'s first thirteen-week series off to a good start. He had previously helped rescue the BBC's *Panorama* programme when, in its early days, it looked like going under. But in 1955 *Panorama* had been transformed into a much harder-hitting, newsier programme under Michael Peacock, and Barsley was out of a job. Cox recognised his 'daring, if at times zany mind' and hired him for *Roving Report*. 'Barsley brought to the programme,' Cox wrote, 'not only an unquenchable, quirky zest, but a capacity to write clear, stylish, often witty English, which gave the commentaries distinction and sophistication.'[4]

Roving Report's main film editor was Brian Lewis. Unlike most of his colleagues in the department, he had come to ITN from editing feature films rather than newsreels. He was keen to bring more sophisticated techniques to the half-hour film he was cutting than was normal with daily news items, yet at the same time he was still able to work at the speed a news feature like *Roving Report* required. His young assistant was John Boorman, later to become a noted feature film director: 'I could see that the cutting-edge work was being done by Brian Lewis. I campaigned to become his assistant,' wrote Boorman. 'He was small, neat and compact, shy and inarticulate, but behind his thick, rimless glasses his eyes were ferocious with intent. He saw himself as an artisan, an NCO, but I recognised an artist.'[5]

Roving Report became popular. Its first programme, at a time when only three ITV stations were on the air, was seen in over a million homes by 32 per cent of the total television audience. By February 1958 it was being watched in well over 2.5 million homes and had achieved an average rating of more than 40 per cent. At the fourth annual general meeting of ITN[6] Captain Brownrigg reported that in the autumn of 1959 it had had the highest rating of any current-affairs programme screened between 6 and 7 p.m. on weekdays: 'The *Roving Report*s had been deliberately varied from programmes of a definitely political character, such as those on Yugoslavia, Egypt and Kenya, to programmes with a strong human-interest slant, such as those on the Left Bank of Paris, and on a coach tour of Europe.'

Roving Report, in its various guises, endured for a decade on ITV, but in its early years it was essentially a device for spreading the cost of sending ITN's own crews abroad. The idea was that a camera crew covering an overseas news event would shoot extra material which, with re-cut news stories, would be edited to make a half-hour *Roving Report*, or a substantial part of it. Alternatively, when the action was over, the crew might stay on for a few days to make an original 'Rover' on some other topic in the same place. As the editor explained to the board in 1960, it was a very cost-effective system. Under the heading 'Sending Our Cameramen Abroad' Geoffrey Cox reported: 'We have done this on nine or ten major news stories over the past two years. This gives us excellent coverage, but is costly, and in practice can only be afforded if we interlock bulletin coverage with *Roving Report*. For instance, we got excellent coverage of

Princess Margaret in the West Indies at reasonable cost by doing a *Roving Report* at the same time. The existence of *Roving Report* has been of very great assistance to the bulletin in this way.'[7] As another example, ITN sent Reginald Bosanquet and a crew to Kenya to report on moves towards independence, paying their way with *Roving Report*s on game parks and the Masai tribesmen.

But convenient and cost-effective though it might be, it was not necessarily the best way to run a weekly news programme. Just because there was a good news story somewhere did not mean that there was necessarily a strong *Roving Report* there too. Sometimes these programmes were simply travelogues, and sometimes rather feeble ones, lacking any news value. Over the years, criticism from the companies – which of course wanted scintillating programmes at minimal cost – grew.

In March 1964 Sir Robert Fraser wrote to Bernard Sendall, his ITA deputy: 'Captain Brownrigg tells me that resistance is growing among the companies towards the kind of ITN activity represented by *Roving Report*.' Brownrigg had told him that while the companies were generally supportive of ITN when it suggested more late-night news, or wanted to produce programmes for big events like a general election, they did not want it to stray beyond that:

> As for the *Roving Report* type of activity, he said that he thought it logically difficult to defend as an ITN rather than a programme company responsibility. There seemed to him almost nothing in the argument that ITN found it easier to attract and retain staff if they could be given opportunities in such programmes, for in fact the *Roving Report* team was now self-contained and specialised.[8]

On examination it appeared that out of the twenty-six most recent programmes only ten had been 'political': for example, the Arab summit conference, the crisis in the Dutch royal family, Cyprus, and UN withdrawal from the Congo. The remainder were described as 'miscellaneous', and included three programmes which were definitely travelogues, of Madeira, Tunis and Crete. There had also been an anniversary programme with extracts from notable programmes over the previous seven years.

In April Sendall reported to Fraser: 'With reference to the attached list, McMillan and Windlesham[9] launched into a pretty strong attack on *Roving Report* at our programme meeting with them yesterday. The burden of their criticism was that it was a rag-bag and had simply not made any advances of any sort over the years in style or technique.'[10] 'I must say', added Sendall in a handwritten note, 'it does look a bit of a rag-bag.'

Geoffrey Cox admitted *Roving Report*'s shortcomings to the ITN board but blamed the companies for its failings: '*Roving Report* is not properly networked at the same time. . . It is not financed to do hard news every week and has to present, as a result, a proportion of softer travelogue material. This has given the programme an inconsistent character, and weakened it as a medium for news reporting.'[11]

The programme was renamed *ITN Reports*, given more money and ordered to focus more sharply on the news, at home as well as abroad, but the complaints continued. In early 1965 Sendall wrote to Fraser:

> I have just been at the receiving end of a (for him) strongly worded onslaught from Cecil Bernstein against *ITN Reports*. He referred in particular to last Wednesday's edition which, according to him, related in the main to ex-Queen Soraya's presence at a première in Milan of her film and, as to the remaining part of the time, to Persia generally, on film which appeared to have come from petroleum company sources. He said that Granada alone was paying £750 for *ITN Reports* and that it simply was not worth it. Any company could fill the time to better advantage from its own resources.

Sendall suggested the ITA should have a viewing session, adding: 'It will not escape you that the Authority's prestige with the companies is very much involved over this range of ITN output, for we have taken a stronger line over the networking of it than over any other class of output.'[12]

Geoffrey Cox rather liked good travelogues, but he could see trouble coming from those who didn't. In a letter to the ITA he tried to answer the criticisms. First, he insisted, a half-hour weekly news feature *did* help attract good people to work at ITN. The news bulletins might provide fulfilling work for newscasters 'but not for those on whom we rely for the individuality and flair essential to give a programme character – the reporters and producers (or, as now is most common, the reporter/producer). This is particularly true of foreign correspondents and specialists. Peter Woods has put a new dimension into bulletin coverage from America; he would not have joined us had we not been able to offer him *Roving Report* . . .'

Second, said Cox, there were enough stories around each week that justified reporting at length. He gave some examples from the previous three months, including the mercenaries and Stanleyville in the Congo, the 'gnomes' of Zurich, interviewed by Alastair Burnet, the background to IRA violence, and the Vietnamese war from the Vietcong side.

But, he conceded, '*ITN Reports* has not done this job adequately. The task of covering three or four major stories a week in depth has proved more exacting than we anticipated . . . So far the result has been patchy, but I would urge that the good patches have been good enough to merit a further period of trial before a final decision is made.'

Cox got his three months' trial and the programme continued after that. Indeed, I may have benefited from the renewed effort ITN was now putting in to make *Roving Report* work. I had been working at ITN for less than a year when I was given a fascinating commission – just the sort of thing that Geoffrey Cox argued made television journalists want to work at ITN. It was also a story idea that fitted neatly with what he thought *Roving Report* had often been good at – a superior sort of travelogue.

Some years before, in 1961, there had been a volcanic eruption on the most remote inhabited island in the world, the British dependency Tristan da Cunha. From their home in the middle of the Atlantic, half-way between South Africa and South America, all 268 islanders had been evacuated to Britain. There, living as a group near Southampton, they had been made welcome. Some of the islanders had come to enjoy life in the modern world, but many hankered after Tristan. Two years later, when the volcano showed no further signs of giving trouble, all but fourteen went home to the simpler life they had previously known. The idea was for *Roving Report* to go and see how they were getting on. Did they regret going back? How had their brief sojourn in mid-twentieth century Britain affected them?

It was quite an undertaking to get ITN to Tristan da Cunha – proof, perhaps, of the effort Cox was making to improve the programme's quality with original material and stories done for their own sake, not merely as makeweight sideshows to news coverage. Twice a year a South African government survey ship, the *RSA*, based in Cape Town made the 2,778-kilometre voyage to the island with supplies; I was to make the voyage and film for a few days while the cargo was unloaded. Then we would steam back to Cape Town. An ITN crew would have been expensive, both in terms of travel and the time the story would inevitably take, so I was to work with a freelance team based in South Africa. The use of foreign crews was a frequent money-saving device, which often meant reporters working with people whose camera equipment and filming techniques were equally out of date, but I was very lucky. Ernie Christie was my cameraman, one of the best any reporter could hope to work with. Peter Hawthorne, Ernie's 'soundman', was in fact a news and features journalist. He would write his own story of our trip, and Christie would take still pictures for him when he wasn't shooting film for ITN. On this occasion the absence of a fully qualified soundman did not matter since we would not be working in difficult conditions – under fire or in the middle of a riot. No doubt Christie had struck some complicated financial deal with ITN that suited all parties.

The voyage to Tristan da Cunha, as the *RSA* heaved and pitched its stomach-churning way through the 'Roaring Forties' took eight long days, but once we were ashore the assignment went well. Although the islanders were generally shy, a sufficient number were happy to talk about the way they lived and why they had wanted to return to Tristan. It was a close-knit community, founded by a Scottish army corporal who had been stationed there in the early nineteenth century amid fears of a French attempt to free Napoleon from his island prison on St Helena. Although a few shipwrecked sailors had arrived since then there were still only six family names among the islanders. They lived on fish, potatoes and what they earned from catching and canning crawfish – self-sufficient but for some small capital projects that needed modest help from the British taxpayer. But their time in England had unsettled them, the younger people in particular. In the year following our visit, thirty-five left the island for good.

There was no harbour in which to unload the ship that had brought us: everything had to be taken ashore in the islanders' longboats. Each morning, as we prepared for another day's filming, we looked anxiously out to sea, fearful that the *RSA* had pulled up its anchor and sailed for home, leaving us marooned for the next six months. And, indeed, one morning the ship had gone. We were in agony until we learned that she had taken shelter from a storm on the other side of the island.

I had felt that in sending me to Tristan da Cunha for this half-hour *Roving Report* Geoffrey Cox must have had some confidence in me. Now I realised that I had been chosen because I had only recently joined the company and was paid a rather modest sum: it would not be much loss to ITN if I did get stuck on the island. Like Geoffrey Cox years before, as the *News Chronicle*'s man in Madrid, I was expendable.

However interesting it was to see what had happened to the islanders of Tristan da Cunha after they returned home, it was difficult to argue that this *Roving Report* was strongly related to the news. It was the kind of thing the network would have regarded as too far from what ITN should be doing.

There were, of course, more urgent stories that were covered. The Beatles were always news, and when they went to the United States in 1966 for their second American tour ITN decided that *Roving Report* should go too. This time there was a specific news peg: John Lennon's casual remark that the group was now probably more popular than Jesus Christ had not gone down well in America, particularly in the Deep South. *Roving Report*'s film was entitled *The Beatles in the Bible Belt*. Filming in Birmingham, Alabama, was interesting, and I realised for the first time the gulf that exists between two peoples who share the same language. 'London?' said the waitress who had asked me where I came from. 'Isn't that where they speak French?'

Outside the auditorium where the Beatles were to perform, young people paraded with placards that urged a boycott of these British 'Communists'; at the radio station the DJ explained why he was refusing to play Beatles records, even though they were top of the pops; in the record shop teenagers explained why they were buying them; and the Grand Wizard of the Ku Klux Klan (a contact of the American cameraman) explained why they were the work of Satan.

In the middle of the night there was a tense three-way telephone conversation as, with ITN's deputy editor David Nicholas in one ear and Brian Epstein, the Beatles' manager, in the other, I tried to negotiate how many seconds of their concert we could use in *Roving Report* without incurring some prohibitive fee. In the end the fans screamed, the Beatles played – not that we could hear much of them – and these Liverpool lads whose off-hand remark had caused such a storm in the States gave us a good-humoured interview in their dressing room. For once, back in the ITN viewing theatre, I didn't mind watching the rushes.

Even when it worked, Geoffrey Cox was not satisfied with a weekly news feature like *Roving Report* or *ITN Reports*, as the programme became. He decided that a late-night 'Part Two' to the weekday evening news was wanted. In 1963 a paper prepared for the ITN board by a sub-committee argued that because of limited air-time the news was not being covered properly:

> If ITN is assigned a clear responsibility for giving a full and efficient news service of national and international news, it should provide in addition to the daily news bulletins and special programmes on big news events like the Profumo debate, a news in depth programme each weekday evening fifteen minutes in length, not later than 11 p.m. but preferably at 10.45 p.m.[13]

Since 1961 an ITN programme called *Dateline* – initially *Dateline London* – had been broadcast in the London area. It was a fifteen-minute programme that analysed the day's top story, and from the start it attracted many talented people to work on it, not least the urbane, laconic Brian Wenham, who subsequently rose high in the BBC hierarchy to become controller of BBC2, and the able, intellectual John Whale, who became ITN's Washington correspondent. A Friday edition – *Dateline Westminster* – covered political developments when Parliament was sitting.

In 1964 Cox tried to persuade the rest of the network to take *Dateline*, but the ITA let him down. Certainly the Authority wanted the companies to broadcast a programme that would analyse the day's news, but not at the expense of the 'regionalism' which the ITA had always held dear. It was decided that while the companies could show *Dateline*, they could if they preferred produce their own news-analysis programmes. For Cox, this was a serious setback for ITN. As he wrote later: 'The battle for the two-tiered bulletin had been lost. The outcome was a patchwork, with some companies taking the ITN late programme, others doing their own, and yet others taking ITN's irregularly – and almost all of them transmitting it deep in the night . . .'[14]

It was indeed an unsatisfactory situation for ITN, which so much wanted to expand with more and deeper coverage of the news. But ITV was unwilling to see it happen, to let ITN become a bigger player within the network. Cox felt that there must be a better way to proceed.

As early as April 1964 he was advocating a more radical approach that, rather than fiddle around with spin-off programmes, would give ITN real scope to expand and improve its mainstream news coverage. 'I believe,' he wrote, 'the better course would be to strike out on the new line offered by the half-hour news.' This, he said, would give ITN the opportunity to become dominant in providing Britain's television news. 'We are going to have to face greatly intensified competition in news from the BBC, as the increased outlets on BBC2 enable them to put more news on the air. It is nevertheless possible, if we adopt an attacking rather than a defensive policy, to establish firmly in the public mind the impression that for news of all kinds Independent Television is best.'[15]

At first the companies paid scant attention to his suggestion. In June 1964 the Network Planning Committee discussed his proposal and turned it down flat: 'A half-hour news at 9 p.m., or indeed at any other time, was not considered practicable at present.' But Cox didn't give up. He was now convinced that the way forward was to put ITN's effort into a half-hour bulletin, rather than struggle to convince the network of the value of *ITN Reports* and *Dateline*.

CHAPTER 12

JEWEL IN THE CROWN – THE *NEWS AT TEN*

In March 1965 Geoffrey Cox wrote a tactful, cautious letter to Sir Robert Fraser:

> I have been thinking very hard over all you said last week, and on the main issue of ITN's functions I wonder whether in fact your thoughts and mine are not tending in the same direction – to a policy of ITN's activities being concentrated in a substantially longer daily bulletin. I do not make this point in any lobbying sense. I realise that the time is not ripe for a half-hour bulletin, and may not become ripe until there are longer broadcasting hours. As you know I have not pushed this view at all strenuously with the NPC [Network Programme Committee] at this stage. It is a view which I first formed last summer largely as an intellectual exercise, but which since then has been constantly reinforced by experience.[1]

If he could persuade the Authority, under its new chairman Lord Hill, to support him, Cox knew that his best chance of getting a half-hour news would come in 1967, when the companies had to get their contracts renewed by the ITA. So in the year before those decisions were to be taken

– also the year in which he was knighted – he stepped up his efforts. At first Hill, though friendly to the idea, was not encouraging. Over dinner at the Reform Club he told Cox plainly that the Authority could not overrule the combined weight of the companies if they remained adamantly against the idea of a half-hour news. 'I said to him,' says Sir Geoffrey, "Look, Chairman of the Authority, please rule that this should be done even if only for a trial period." He said, "Geoffrey, I can't do that, it's not in my power." It was in his power, but he wasn't going to do it. Charlie kept in with the powers that be, the companies, very skilfully. And he said, "If you can split the companies, I'll make a ruling between them – if you line up some companies . . . " and I said, "I can't. Nobody's going to back us."'

So discouraging was Hill that Cox, driving home to Hampstead from the Reform Club that night, decided that he would have to leave ITN to join one of the consortiums bidding for the new regional franchises. His hopes of a half-hour news seemed unlikely to be realised.

However, early in 1966 the ITA held one of their regular consultations, this one to chart ITV's way ahead in news and current affairs. To the Authority's Robert Fraser and to Geoffrey Cox it seemed pointless, even counter-productive, to raise the half-hour news issue, but among those who spoke was the former political editor of ITN who had subsequently become editor of *The Economist*, Alastair Burnet. He had already been sounded out by Lord Hill, who had asked him if he was in favour of a half-hour news. 'Certainly. Long overdue,' Burnet had replied. Now, at the consultation, and to Cox's consternation, he seized the moment to argue for it. The consultation reported: 'Many effective forms of news presentation needed time if their impact was to be felt . . . Mr Burnet was confident that such a programme, if introduced by ITV first, would give the network a considerable competitive edge over the BBC . . . He thought the most suitable time would be somewhere between 10.00 and 10.45 p.m., any later would be unsuitable.'[2] Burnet remembers observing Lord Hill turn to his director general Fraser and mutter, 'Do you hear?'

Now that the issue had been publicly raised Sir Geoffrey Cox took every opportunity to make the case for a longer news programme. First, he said, television had now become the public's main source of news – as research commissioned by ITN had shown. Second, more material was available more rapidly. Third, a longer slot would make for good programmes. A trial, he said, was essential, the only way a half-hour news could be properly tested. With the support of ITN's chairman, James Coltart from Scottish Television, he was authorised to produce some pilot programmes.

In September, ITA officials and Cox had a look at the first. 'We really came to the conclusion – all of us', wrote deputy director general Bernard Sendall, 'that little would be achieved by trying to acquire a more regular and earlier slotting of *Dateline* over the network, and that the time was ripe for pushing forward discussions about the possibility of a half-hour news bulletin on the five weekdays at around 10 o'clock.'[3]

The ITA was increasingly convinced that the time for a half-hour news had come, and the relative weakness of ITV's schedules at the time gave the Authority the chance to insist on a shake-up in which the half-hour news would become the fixed point in the evening. At the beginning of 1967, in a paper entitled 'A New Look', Sir Robert Fraser wrote:

> I have been brooding over the programme problem. I have been trying to compose the Authority's desire somehow to depart from what now is, Cecil's [Bernstein's] desire for system, Howard's [Thomas's] desire for 'big' programmes, and Geoffrey's desire for a long news programme. Now if we could get a half-hour news, and it became as well known as Huntley-Brinkley [of America's NBC] or Cronkite [CBS], we would have a new big programme, and that would please the Authority, and Howard and Geoffrey. I think it must be either 6 p.m. or 10 p.m.[4]

Things were moving forward, but there were still some hitches.

'At last Wednesday's meeting of the board,' wrote Fraser on 6 January to his deputy Bernard Sendall, 'Geoffrey showed a new half-hour news bulletin. It was well done, but it was not very well received. No one seemed to think it held the attention sufficiently.' The problem seemed to be that the pilot was simply an ordinary news bulletin with extra stories added to it. Cox was told to come up with something better.

But on the principle of the thing the Authority had now made up its mind. When the ITN board met on 8 March 1967 it was told that the ITA would now require a longer news programme at 10 p.m., and after discussion it was agreed that it should run at twenty-six and a half minutes. To help pay for it, *Reporting '67* (a renamed *Roving Report/ITN Reports*) and *Dateline* would be scrapped, which would save £171,000 and £67,000 respectively. In addition a longer news programme would bring ITN an additional £37,750 from the network; in all, a total of £275,000. It was proposed that the new programme should run for a three-month trial period through the summer; the additional money should mean that there was no need to rebudget the bulletin costs for the last three months of the financial year, which would end on 30 September. Clearly the ITA was worried that the companies might be reluctant to fund the new programme adequately. It was only an experiment and no doubt some would not mind if it failed.

At ITN Cox sent an excited memo to 'all staff':

> I am very glad to be able to announce that it is probable that from July 3rd onwards, for a trial period of three months, the 8.55 p.m. bulletin on week nights will be replaced by a half-hour news programme at 10 p.m. . . . . This is not only the biggest opportunity which has ever come to ITN, but the biggest opportunity any organisation in British television has had to show that news can be made into full programmes, rather than bulletins. I am confident we can seize this chance, and bring about a further revolution in news presentation on the British air.[5]

Now that the experiment had been agreed on, the ITA was keen to make sure it worked. The director general came close to trying to edit the programme himself:

> Sir Robert Fraser said that the introduction of a half-hour news at 10 p.m. was the most important development for ITN and he felt that no expense should be spared in getting the programme right before it went on the air. The programme must have a recognisable character, just as the more popular newspapers had. He hoped that the Editor would see it as a 'people's news programme' and that the change of time and length would not mean that it would set out to appeal to a different audience to that of the present main bulletin. The programme should be heavily illustrated with still pictures and film. He felt that interviews should not be used as a means of explaining routine news items but should rather feature important people in the news. The key personality would be all important and he hoped that the three-

month trial period would be used to develop someone who could present the programme on five nights a week. The title of the programme would be equally important.[6]

Two further obstacles had still to be overcome. First was the middle break. The companies were adamant that they stood to lose a great deal of money if there were no advertisements in the middle of the news; ATV, for instance, estimated that having no break might cost its company £300,000 a year. Cox was happy to include one; he saw how useful the producer of a half-hour programme would find it to have a couple of minutes roughly half-way through to sort out problems and re-arrange stories in the second half; and he also thought it would give viewers a chance to take in what they had seen and heard, and then 'turn the page' into Part Two. At ITN, the National Union of Journalists saw it differently: as a nasty commercial intrusion on the purity of the news. 'Once the commercial boys are in,' said the father-of-the-chapel Iain Redpath, 'they will be in for five hundred years . . . We think this is the beginning of something much worse. I do not think there is room for compromise here.'[7] But compromise there was. It was agreed that since this was only a three-month experiment the programme would, to begin with at least, have a commercial break. It was never seriously queried again.

The other issue was the title of the programme and, related to that, the 'key personality' who would present it. ITN board members had urged Cox to look to the regions for the right person. The ITA, though, took the view that only the most high-powered of presenters, a national figure, would be able to establish the new format with impact sufficient to make it a fixture. Cox did not altogether agree with that – he thought programmes could grow their own successful newscasters – but he knew that now was not the right moment to fall out with the ITA. So the final choice was Alastair Burnet, an outstanding journalist who had already proved himself at ITN to be a broadcaster of great authority. The only problem was that Burnet was otherwise engaged as editor of *The Economist*. 'I went to Alastair,' says Sir Geoffrey Cox, 'and I said, "Look, this is the situation. Won't you come back to us?" He said, "No, but I'll come back for three months," and, of course, that got us under way. I had my star.'

So it was agreed that for three days a week, during this experimental period only, Burnet would combine his day job as editor of *The Economist*

– no mean responsibility in itself – with the lead role as newscaster of . . . what? Should it be *Alastair Burnet with the News*, or The *News at Ten with Alastair Burnet?* The companies were hostile to any mention of a time, since they didn't want to be tied to 10 p.m. for ever. Robert Fraser sent to John McMillan, at Rediffusion, a rather artful response to this concern: 'If the argument was that *THE NEWS AT TEN* would be initially useful to establish the new time in people's minds then I suppose I would not mind much if it were used for a start and then dropped when it had served its purpose.'[8] It was not 'dropped' for another thirty-two years.

Soon after the half-hour programme had been agreed, Cox sent two of his senior men to New York to see how the Americans coped with a news of that length. Nigel Ryan had been editing *Reporting '67*, while David Phillips had been producing the 8.55 p.m. evening news, both about to disappear to make way for *News at Ten*. 'It was a wonderful trip,' says Phillips, 'very instructive and fun – from the moment we landed on the Pan Am helicopter pad[9] and dived into the bar immediately beneath, where Nigel declared, "We're in Manhattan, let's order Manhattans!" Geoffrey Cox says that we came back from the States convinced that the key to the success of *News at Ten* lay in covering the news with integrated news packages – film stories for which the reporters had written and recorded their own commentary. Well, we'd *gone* there convinced of that. Nigel and I had both suffered long enough the frustrations of producing shows without reporters being able to stamp their authority on their packages. What the US nets would show was whether there were any production difficulties we should be aware of. There were not, and we were able to trumpet the fact on our return.'

In his report to Cox, Phillips said,

> After studying the half-hour bulletins transmitted by the three American networks and examining their newsroom organisation I am convinced that not only will ITN take the half-hour bulletin in its stride, but will produce a better, more varied and flexible show than either CBS, NBC or ABC . . . What the Americans have done is simply increase the number of stories in their bulletins. They have not come up with a new style, a new approach. ITN – not hidebound in its news philosophy nor hampered by so many commercials – can present a fresh-looking programme each night. One that lets the news dictate the formula.

Following a reorganisation of the newsroom team, *News at Ten* went on air for the first time on 3 July 1967, with Alastair Burnet as its leading news-caster and Andrew Gardner in support.

It was a sweaty business. ITN's studio, at the top of Television House, was far too small for the studio format devised for the new programme in which two newscasters would take the strain of delivering the half-hour programme. Behind the long curved desk at which they sat was a screen on which moving pictures, rather than just stills, could be shown, so that the newscasters could be more closely integrated with the film reports they were introducing. There was no room in the studio for the machine that made this happen; it had to be installed in the scene dock behind, its pictures beamed via a mirror round the corner into the studio. And because the ceiling was very low – just over ten feet – the studio lights sent temperatures soaring so high that by the end of rehearsal, even before they came on air, newscasters, production assistants and cameramen alike were dripping with perspiration. In a temporary solution that was typical of ITN's pragmatic approach, trays of ice were brought into the studio and cold air blown off them with the aid of electric fans.

The title music, 'Arabesque', by Johnny Pearson, was a late decision. 'During rehearsals,' says dubbing editor Alfred Wilson, 'the theme nearly bit the dust. There were many complaints from women that the sound was too shrill and ear-shattering. I got a composer to write and record another idea and at the same time tried to see if we could salvage the chosen piece. It had been recorded abroad on what was then the new four-track one-inch tape machine. There weren't many of them in Britain but we did finally find one and we remixed the sound to take out the harshness.'

As for the 'bongs', during early rehearsals with the new title sequence a sound-mixer had inadvertently brought up the sound of Big Ben striking the hour just as newscaster Andrew Gardner was trying out his opening lines – 'The *Torrey Canyon* is bombed; more border raids around Gaza; trade figures worsen' – and so on. In the gallery Diana Edwards-Jones, by now promoted to studio director, suddenly saw that a short headline could be fitted between the bongs to good effect. As Sir Geoffrey Cox recalled, 'It worked admirably. I was listening on the monitor set in my office, and the outcome seemed so exactly right that I sprinted up the stairs to the control room and agreed the pattern then and there . . . One of the enduring hallmarks of *News at Ten* had come into being.'[10]

At the end of the first programme Alastair Burnet told the viewers: 'Our aim is to bring you every weekday evening a half-hour news in depth, at a peak viewing hour, a new venture in British television. For television itself is now better equipped to cover the world's news than it was when the old, short news bulletin was devised. We know it means asking you to develop a new viewing habit at ten o'clock every evening, but we mean to make it worth your while.'

But for the first few nights *News at Ten* was, frankly, a disappointment. Launched in the middle of the summer, when news always seems harder to come by and fewer people are interested in watching, it was bound to be difficult to make an impact. But that first *News at Ten* seemed to have nothing exciting to report. A strike of freight services on the railways had been called off; after the fighting of the previous month, nothing was happening in the Middle East; at Westminster a bill to legalise homosexual practices was making its way through Parliament. Worse than that, the programme was dull and stiff: ITN's producers seemed to have no clear idea of what it should be doing. 'The first night it was a bloody poor programme,' Sir Geoffrey admits. 'There was no news and we were trying to make it look different. By Wednesday I knew it was a mistake.'

Overwhelmed by advice from the companies, the ITA and Fleet Street wiseacres, Cox had tried too hard to make his *News at Ten* completely different from what had gone before. He now realised that the extra time should be used not to cram in more stories but simply to let worthwhile stories run longer, the better to explain their meaning.

'I decided the only thing to do was to go back to doing a straight ITN bulletin. At the Wednesday morning conference I said "What I want tonight is an old fashioned ITN bulletin writ large," and we were away. It was the right formula, because it was news, and news was what mattered.'

Fine, if there is news. Difficult, if there is not.

The film list on the third day of the *News at Ten* looked as thin as it had on the previous two, but late in the morning a shipment arrived in the building from an ITN reporter more likely to whip up a storm than any other. In Aden, then still a British possession, the British Army was trying to deal with rampant Arab nationalism and insurrection. In a dawn raid designed to assert their authority, the Argyll and Sutherland Highlanders had taken their armoured cars into the deeply hostile Crater district. Reporter Alan Hart and his Kenyan cameraman Mohinder Dhillon had been with them, covering the action as it happened.

As he watched the rushes in the viewing theatre Cox was relieved and jubilant:

> They gave us a report which had almost the impact of live coverage as they captured not only the scene of the action, but also the sound of the clipped orders, the sudden bursts of firing, the shouts in Arabic and Glaswegian as the patrols seized crouching gunmen. The boyish figure of the Argylls' commander, Colonel Mitchell – Mad Mitch – who directed the action, spoke to Hart in the midst of the shuttered streets as this no-go area was brought back under British rule. We let the story run for every second it was worth, cutting it to six minutes twenty-four seconds – an unprecedented length for a story in a regular news bulletin . . . It transformed the night's programme. It was for this that we had sought the extra time, to enable us to use television to tell the news as only television can do, and we had done so with clarity and verve.[11]

The critics did not yet agree. In a review of *News at Ten* typical of many others, Milton Shulman in the London *Evening Standard* wrote: 'ITN had neither the personnel nor the resources to produce a news programme commensurate with their hopes and ambitions.' In other words ITN was not up to it. In the *Spectator* Stuart Hood, a former editor of BBC News, expressed 'a keen sense of disappointment'. This was dispiriting, and Cox saw that *News at Ten* might yet fail. But the second week of the 'experiment' gave him another opportunity to demonstrate what the longer programme could do with a good story.

On the far side of America, the ballet dancers Margot Fonteyn and Rudolf Nureyev had been arrested by the San Francisco drugs squad at a hippie party. ITN established that ABC had good coverage of the couple being ignominiously booked at the Hyattsville precinct police station. Rather than wait for the film to arrive by plane for use the following night, when the story would have been well aired in the British press, Cox took the decision to pay whatever it took to get it to ITN in time for that night's *News at Ten*. The film was fed by land line from San Francisco to New York and then by satellite to London. It was horrendously expensive. Cox wrote later:

> By all our previous standards, the costs – between £5,000 and £7,000 – were prohibitive. But with the fate of the new programme still in the balance, I agreed to the money being paid. The result outdid our expectations. Here was the stuff of innumerable American crime serials in real life. In a crowded office, against a background of metal filing cabinets and of desk tops littered with documents and paper coffee cups, a short-sleeved detective asked, 'Noo-ray-eff? Say, how do you spell a name like that? N like Nobody, U like United States . . . ?' whilst a cool but concerned Margot Fonteyn waited to be questioned in her turn. John Whale [ITN's US correspondent] provided good clear commentary. We had it entirely to ourselves. All the BBC could muster was a series of still pictures.

The story transformed what until then had looked like being another rather dull programme.

The next day, 12 July, Cox was telephoned by John McMillan, general manager of Rediffusion. Whatever the television critics might have said, the viewers – those at least who were not away on holiday – liked the *News at Ten*. In the first week all five editions had been among the top twenty television programmes, and two in the top ten. As Cox wrote, 'Far from diminishing the audience later in the evening we had strengthened it. In programme-making terms, this was a striking success. I knew that we had won only the opening round in a long contest. We had not yet secured a permanent grip on this segment of viewing time. But we had won the chance to continue the experiment.'[12]

When Cox wrote again to 'all staff' it was in positively Churchillian tones:

> I am glad to announce that the Network Planning Committee has decided that *News at Ten* will be continued in the schedules after the present three-month experimental period ends on September 30th. This means that we have won the first battle decisively, though we must keep in mind the fact that there is a long struggle ahead. To have established a half-hour news in peak viewing time is the biggest achievement in television news in the country since ITN first came on the screen.[13]

With a slightly colder eye, the ITA's head of research, Dr I. R. Haldane, made his own study of *News at Ten*'s performance over its first three weeks. As was only to be expected, the audience at 10 p.m. was slightly smaller than it had been at the earlier transmission time of 8.55 p.m., but *News at Ten* was getting a bigger *share* of the audience than the earlier bulletin had done. And it was proving at least as successful in holding its audience as the various programmes it had replaced. Perhaps best of all, first indications were that viewers liked the programme: there was 'real and positive audience appreciation of *News at Ten*, far in advance of the previous ITN 20.55 news bulletin.'[14]

By October Dr Haldane could write even more confidently: 'I am glad to observe that 69 per cent think ITV give as good or better a news service than the BBC . . . I wonder why some people are still apparently intent on "knocking" *News at Ten*? All the evidence suggests that it is one of the few real programme successes which ITV has produced over the past year.'[15]

The ITA certainly did have to deal with some knockers from the programme companies. Michael Peacock, now managing director of London Weekend Television, wrote to Sir Robert Fraser:

> . . . the *News at Ten* really is a problem. It's too long, forcing ITN to include soft feature material which they are professionally ill-equipped to produce. It's too late: by 10 o'clock most of us have seen or heard the news at least once before. And a fixed schedule placing makes it very difficult to plan weekday evenings that have a proper balance, and which, at the same time, 'work' in schedule terms.[16]

Fraser replied sharply: '. . . the fact remains that, after six months, *News at Ten* remains a perfectly sturdy and respectable programme, well appreciated by the ITV audience. With other important areas of programme weakness howling at us, it seems to me a bit of a pity that *News at Ten* could come to be regarded as one of the things that most needs to be put right.'[17]

When he faced further flak from the programme companies at their Programme Policy Committee in early 1968, he was forthright, adamant that the *News at Ten* experiment should continue for a full year at least:

> The Director General emphasised that the evidence demonstrated clearly that *News at Ten* was a successful programme in its own right; properly

handled it was therefore more likely to strengthen than weaken the evening schedule. The programme had established itself with the audience more quickly than had been expected. It was still improving. He was convinced that the half-hour bulletin was the format of the future.[18]

Fraser made it plain that while there was nothing sacrosanct about a 10 p.m. slot for the main *ITN News*, the companies had better come up with a solution as good or better if they wanted to move it. That, of course, was what, three decades later, Fraser's successors at the ITC claimed that they, too, had insisted on when *News at Ten*'s future again came under serious, and ultimately fatal threat.

News at Ten soon became a fixture in the ITV schedule. As the value of its centre break in terms of advertising revenue was recognised, the companies relaxed their opposition. They came to appreciate *News at Ten* not just as a nice little earner in itself but as a programme that had helped drag ITV up-market and added value to the whole network. Together, Granada's *Coronation Street* and ITN's *News at Ten* were the two constants in the schedule that gave the ITV network its special character, its reputation for popular quality television. Even that ultimate showman Lew Grade, president of ATV, later admitted to a parliamentary select committee, 'I resisted *News at Ten* and I was wrong.'[19]

On 3 July 1968, exactly a year after the start of 'the experiment', the ITN board was told that of 255 editions of *News at Ten* 180 had been in the top twenty, and 67 of them in the top ten. It was a palpable hit, and the source of news for more people than any other outlet in the country.[20] Another year on and, three times in the course of a few weeks, *News at Ten* was number one in the ratings – the most popular programme on television. As ITN's editor said proudly to the *Daily Mirror*, 'We have become the most successful serial on the air.'[21]

CHAPTER 13
THE SECRET OF SUCCESS

From the beginning, ITN had always recognised the importance of its reporters, and sent them out with a directive to report in vision – to put themselves on the screen – whenever possible. Few reporters needed urging to get themselves on the box. On arriving at the location they would knock off an interview, record their PTC, or 'piece to camera', then rush off on another assignment. But that, on the whole, was the extent of their involvement. They might point the cameraman in the right direction, they might phone in some information about what was happening on the ground but, generally speaking, they had little input to the story as it appeared on the screen.

Once their film footage had been processed it would be viewed – in negative – in the ITN viewing theatre, then given to a film editor to cut. While the output editor – who was responsible for that particular news bulletin – would select from the interviews the bits of 'sync' he wanted, it was the film editor who would cut the pictures as he saw fit. When he had finished, a scriptwriter from the newsroom would sit with him to take a 'shot list', noting the content and length of each shot, then go away to write a commentary, largely based on news agency material, to match the pictures. Then, sometimes recorded but often 'live', a 'voice' would read the commentary – each paragraph cued with a tap on the shoulder by the scriptwriter as the film appeared on the screen.

Thinking about it now, it was a curious way to produce a television news story. It denied the reporter who had been on the spot any hand in shaping the end result, and it divided the editing/scriptwriting roles to give authority not to the journalists in the newsroom but to the film editors upstairs, who might have had no more than the vaguest idea of what the story was about.

Under this system the film editors, members of the powerful ACTT, the Association of Cinematograph and Television Technicians, were always ready to assert their dominance, as scriptwriter Frank Miles vividly remembers: 'You were not allowed to touch anything that the film editor touched. I was sitting at the Steenbeck[1] once and the tea trolley came. And this guy got up and went to get a cup of tea, leaving the film running. And I was sitting there making my notes, and the film came to an end, and it was going "flip, flip, flip, flip, flip" as the reel went round, so I pushed the switch to "stop". He came back in with his cup of tea and he said "Who stopped that machine?" I said, "Oh, it just came to the end." "Who – who touched that switch?" I said, "Well, I just —" "Right! All out!" And they called a meeting in the preview theatre and said they were all going on strike. And I said, "Look, please, please, I'm very sorry . . . " And they forced me to make an apology in front of all of them and to promise that I would never ever touch equipment again! Would you believe? This was the strength of the ACTT.'

Over and above the union issue, any film editor could make life difficult for a scriptwriter like Frank Miles. 'The pressure was often enormous to get the script ready in time,' he says. 'But one particular film editor I can think of, when he'd come to the end of his edit, used to shot-list it backwards. He would give you the length of the last scene in feet first, while he was rewinding the thing. He would never do it any other way, and that was terrible, because you had all sorts of mathematical things which you then had to calculate. You carried around a conversion chart of feet and seconds so you could translate it into seconds and then write the script accordingly – three words a second.'

While bulletins remained relatively short and individual news stories correspondingly brief, this odd way of working, with film editors dominant and reporters uninvolved in the editing and writing of their stories, didn't seem to matter much. The system endured almost until the end of Sir

Geoffrey Cox's time as editor of ITN. But as the bulletins grew in length, and particularly when the half-hour *News at Ten* arrived in the summer of 1967, the need for a better way of doing things became very obvious. Decisions about the shape of a story that might run several minutes could no longer be left to a film editor.

During the Six Day War in the Middle East – just before the start of *News at Ten* – reporter John Edwards had repeatedly shown how effective it could be if, in addition to his interviews and PTCs, the reporter wrote his own commentary to the rest of the film his team had shot. The reporter, after all, was the one who had been there: he was clearly best placed to tell that particular story. Out on the road, in the middle of an exchange of fire, he might not know much about the big picture, what the world's statesmen were doing or saying about some top story, but he was the absolute authority on the microcosm, what he and his crew had been able to cover. Edwards had been prerecording his commentaries in the field for some considerable time – indeed, he had successfully done so for half-hour *Roving Report*s. Now, somewhat to their irritation, his reporter colleagues were summoned to an ITN seminar – organised by David Phillips – in which they were forced to compare an excellent report Edwards had sent back from Israel with their own less adequate efforts – and learn how it should be done.

Most reporters had already used this technique from time to time, but now it became routine. What the Phillips seminar had conclusively demonstrated was how effective a 'reporter package' could be. When it worked well it gave a reporter a much greater say in the shape of the story that appeared on the screen; and because it brought a new authenticity to each report, the bulletin as a whole gained greater authority.

It was hard work, particularly if the crew were filming abroad; it meant that now, instead of slumping exhausted at the end of a long day's work, or heading for the bar as soon as they had got their film on its way to ITN, reporters had to sit down at their typewriters and bash out a script to accompany the material their crew had shot. The film was tightly sealed in a couple of cans, unprocessed and unviewable, so the reporter, having talked to his crew about it, had to guess which shots would work well and the order in which they would best tell the story. Then, again guessing the strength of the piece and the length it might run in the bulletin, he would write commentary to fit the pictures and explain them. Finally, against the clock as the time of the last flight to London approached, the soundman would record the reporter reading his commentary. The camera was used as a tape-recorder and the commentary recorded on the magnetic stripe that ran down the edge of the 16mm film that ITN used. This saved time: when the film arrived in London the bit with the recorded commentary on it could be put straight on to an editing machine alongside the picture, rather than first having to be transferred from magnetic tape.

Under this system, the film editors now had a commentary track as a guide to the shape of the story and a clear indication of the pictures they should try to use. The reporter was now 'calling the shots' with his script, rather than the film editor choosing whatever pictures he thought looked good, long before a scriptwriter got near them.

That, of course, was the theory. In practice the system rarely worked perfectly. Perhaps some of the pictures the reporter had hoped would feature prominently turned out to be no good, or the piece might have to be so truncated to make room for better stories that whatever bits of commentary remained made little sense: prerecorded commentaries can be cut, but not sub-edited like a newspaper article. But the principle was right. It left sub-editors in London to decide on the headline-news developments in any particular story and write them for the newscaster to read; and it gave the reporter on the ground a much better chance of reporting effectively and accurately what he had seen and heard.

It was just before the start of *News at Ten* that Nigel Ryan and David Phillips had come back from their trip to New York determined that the old system of viewing rushes, then handing them to a film editor to cut the story as he thought best, must end. 'ITN has a team of film editors as fast as any American network unit and probably faster,' Phillips reported to Sir Geoffrey Cox. '[With some new equipment] they would be a formidable unit when cutting major stories close to the clock. But the administrative system built up around the ritual of the rushes run in the preview theatre must be broken down. The responsibility for the finished product – the news and film judgement it expresses – must rest on one man: the output editor (film) who in turn is responsible only to the executive producer.'[2]

Of course, it would be quite wrong to suggest that film editors through ITN's early years were collectively some sort of sinister fifth column, saboteurs out to destroy the noble efforts of the journalists at ITN. It was the system that was wrong. Indeed, once it had been recognised the journalists – particularly the reporters who had been at the scene – should take the lead in deciding what their story really was, the film editors came into their own. Now they were free to concentrate on making the best of the material they were given to tell the reporter's story in the most effective way.

To begin with their work was done back at base when a film shipment arrived from Westminster or Watford, or via plane and ITN dispatch rider from some faraway foreign field. But at the same time that 'reporter packages' were being developed so was satellite technology. Soon, television stations in major cities around the world were equipped to satellite a 'cut story' to London. Rather than rely on an untried and overworked local film editor, ITN soon took to sending its own man.

One of the best of these travelling editors was Leo Rosenberg. However late film might emerge from processing, however difficult the story, Leo's white-gloved fingers deftly constructed an effective package at the fastest possible speed. Time and again, without Leo, stories would never have 'made the gate' of the telecine machine, and so would have missed the satellite booking and the bulletin they were intended for. David Phillips recalled a typical example. All through the Indo-Pakistan war in 1971 an ITN team had been bottled up in Dacca, in East Pakistan, with no commercial flights on which to get their film out. They could shoot, but not ship, a most unpleasant condition for any television team to be in, akin to severe constipation. At one stage they had taken the risk of putting material aboard a Pakistan military plane heading for Rangoon, but on arrival their film had been impounded, not to be released until long after hostilities were over. Now, as the forces of Pakistan surrendered and the war came to an end, there was another opportunity to fly film out, this time with a planeload of civilian refugees. Determined to beat the BBC, ITN sent producer Phillips, with film editor Rosenberg, to Bangkok, where there were satellite facilities. The idea was to cut the story there and satellite it to London – ITN guessed that the BBC would not have thought of doing the same thing. And so it proved.

In Bangkok, waiting for the film, Rosenberg found a small chemist's shop he decided could handle the film processing and provide a bench on which he could set up his simple editing equipment. He was travelling light, with just his cotton editing gloves, a small synchroniser to keep sound and picture together and a Sellotape joiner – it all fitted into a BOAC airline holdall. After two days' wait, the news came that the film was out – but that the plane carrying it was headed not for Bangkok but for Singapore. Phillips and Rosenberg flew there, banged on hotel doors until they found the passenger who had hand-carried the film, and flew back with it to Bangkok. Says Phillips: 'The edit went well, and at Bangkok TV we had it all laced up and ready for our short allotted time slot on the satellite. On cue, we started to roll, but as the film ran the telecine machine began jerking – and a film join looked as if it was about to break. If it did, that was the end of this satellite transmission. Instantly, Leo had the film in his hands to smooth out the jerks and guide it gently through the telecine. It hiccuped through the gate, and the package was safely home at ITN in London.'

Phillips and Rosenberg flew back to Britain, but a week later Rosenberg was back in Bangkok for a similar operation. This time he came alone. With Leo Rosenberg, as Phillips said, who needed a producer?

Under Sir Geoffrey Cox's successor Nigel Ryan, who took over as editor in 1968, the reporter package quickly became the norm, and its introduction was helped by the move ITN made to new headquarters, in Wells Street, near Oxford Circus. Where once the film editors had worked upstairs in their own world, on a different floor from the scriptwriters, they were now right next to them, their individual cutting rooms arranged round the edge of the newsroom. Ryan deserved much of the credit for this new layout. He had seen the system working well at CBS, during his visit to America, and decided that it would contribute to improving the quality of ITN's journalism. It did.

CHAPTER 14
THE REPORTERS –
EARLY INTELLIGENCE

ITN was, at bottom and at its best, a relatively straightforward organisation. Its job was to report the national and international news. Theirs not to reason why or even how, so much as to report the 'what': what had happened; where and when; how big or small. To investigate, to comment, to speculate – these were not activities that ITN, or its owners, the programme companies, thought should be given a very high priority: they were more properly the business of the network's current affairs programmes. When editor Nigel Ryan tried later to wade into that territory he found it difficult to get through the barbed wire and establish any significant beachhead.

But if ITN's task was fundamentally the simple one of bringing people the news that is not to say that its reporters were all simple-minded newshounds. In the early days in particular, Geoffrey Cox had hired people who were not just go-getting action men but highly intelligent, thoughtful journalists. Before they moved on they contributed greatly to ITN's reputation for covering serious news stories.

Take, for example, John Whale. After Winchester and Oxford, he had wanted to become an actor and playwright. In Paris, gathering material for the dramas he hoped to write, he began working for the English section of French Radio and found that he could broadcast. In London, he impressed Geoffrey Cox and got a job at ITN. Interested in politics, he worked on *Dateline* and as ITN lobby correspondent. His reports often contained the most entertaining, even outrageous remarks but, delivering them in owlish glasses and a deadpan manner, he escaped his editor's censure. His junior colleague at the time, Julian Havilland, recalls Whale's reporting of a debate in which the prime minister, Harold Wilson, had publicly rebuked his own commonwealth secretary. 'John, in a gem of a report, described how "the prime minister had pulled the rug from under Arthur Bottomley's elephantine feet".' Cox was not best pleased with this, but in the end it was not so much 'colour' that he deplored as any hint of partiality; and there John Whale was guiltless.

Later, Whale was to go to America as ITN's first Washington corre-spondent, where he covered the 1968 presidential election campaign. His last service to ITN was to report the absurd British expedition to retake control of Anguilla, a little Caribbean island that had decided to throw off the colonial yoke. My crew and I had been sent with the Army to go ashore in what the briefing officer warned solemnly was expected to be an opposed landing. Whale and his team were already on the island, at the receiving end of this mighty military invasion.

Just before dawn the British force, nervous fingers on triggers, set off in landing craft as if for another D-Day. As the boats neared the shore in the darkness they were met with a blaze of flashes – but, strangely, not the sound of gunfire. Just as he was about to order 'open fire' in return, the landing-force commander realised that he was being met by Fleet Street's finest photographers and their flashguns, rather than heavily armed islanders.

Julian Havilland recalls John Whale's report of all this for ITN: 'At last the onshore camera picked up the approaching invasion fleet. Tension grew. Soon in the leading assault craft two or three figures could be made out. John's tone began to suggest that a show of controlled excitement, without taint of vulgar animation, might be appropriate. "And there, I think, yes, no doubt of it – there in the leading boat is Richard Lindley and an ITN crew." The voice grew solemn again as he signed off: "So now, in these pictures, you have the full measure of the bloodiness of this conflict."'

Whale's tongue-in-cheek report was the perfect put-down to an absurd political gesture by the Wilson government. As Havilland rightly concluded: 'As a corrective to the vaingloriousness of politicians it was exactly what the British public needed to hear. It was John's last utterance for ITN and, to my mind, exactly right.'

John Whale was never less than an excellent ITN reporter, with a deep understanding of the stories he covered, but he came to the conclusion that television was an unsatisfactory medium for conveying anything more than the superficial meaning of news. Because it was driven by the need for pictures, he felt, television would always find it hard to handle ideas. In that medium ideas had to be represented by people, and so viewers would respond not to the ideas but to the people who presented them. That, he thought, was not a satisfactory basis on which viewers should make political judgements. He expanded on these ideas in his book, *The Half-Shut Eye*.[1] He also became concerned that television was increasingly driven by numbers, the sheer size of the viewing audience. More and more, he felt, it was the wishes and taste of the least-educated section of the population that were coming to dominate; and that television news – and television generally – was contributing less and less to public understanding. Eventually he decided that he would have a better chance of communicating the meaning of events if he wrote about them, rather than try to deal with them on television, and he went to work for Harold Evans at the *Sunday Times*.

John Whale's intelligent reporting of complicated subjects was of great value to ITN in its early days, when it was trying to establish its credibility as more than just another bit of ITV entertainment between the commercials. He recalls going to see Geoffrey Cox in 1966 when, after ten years in the job, ITN's editor had just been knighted: 'I went to congratulate Geoffrey, and I was touched to see his eyes glisten and to think that I'd had something to do with helping him get this award.' He was right to think so.

Working as a lobby correspondent John Whale had been mightily impressed with his immediate boss, ITN's political editor Alastair Burnet. In 1963 Burnet had been recruited from *The Economist* where, as assistant editor, he had been writing leaders, to replace Ian Trethowan, off to fame and fortune at the BBC. This was the first but not the last time that Burnet would work for ITN. Says Sir Geoffrey Cox: 'Alastair was a gigantic find as far as I was concerned. I was desperate to find a newscaster, and Alastair had written a paragraph on slums in Glasgow in which he said "In the rest of the world good housing degenerates into slums. In Glasgow they build slums from the start." I thought, Anybody who can write like that! I found out who had written it, and my deputy Ian Trethowan and I took him to lunch at the Garrick. And when I met him, I wasn't at all sure if Alastair had it, but Ian said, "No, no, that's our chap." Alastair is a man of nerve and also a rather vain man. He was prepared, I think, to become a star. So he joined, and I respect his nerve for this, because being the assistant editor of *The Economist* was really something. He stayed with us until he was offered the editorship of *The Economist* and I backed him for that.'

'For me,' says John Whale, 'Alastair is the ablest person ITN has ever had on its strength. I first realised just *how* able during ITN's coverage of the 1964 election results, which he anchored. I was holding down an outside broadcast at Transport House, Labour headquarters. Anxious not to miss my cue I had Alastair's voice in my ear for hours on end. It was a revelation to me, a new kind of broadcasting. He was never at a loss – for a candidate's background, for local history, for the meaning of a result, for an apt question, for a joke. He was articulate, graceful, fair. As a sustained achievement it was astonishing. I also found him personally winning. The two years I spent as his number two in the lobby were two of the happiest of my working life. When he left to edit *The Economist* I was bitterly sad, even though I inherited his job.'

Burnet went back to *The Economist* after only two years at ITN, but he soon returned – at least on a part-time basis – to launch *News at Ten* in 1967. Later on still he would play a major part backstage, in the ITN boardroom, as well as in front of the studio camera.

In South Africa, working on a newspaper in Bloemfontein, Julian Havilland had learned to speak Afrikaans. It was not something that proved particularly useful at ITN in London, but he had other talents. He was, says another political correspondent, David Rose, someone who disproved the idea that nice people cannot be good reporters. But Havilland had one failing: he was perpetually, infuriatingly, in danger of missing his studio spot in the bulletin because he had cut things too fine. 'Yet,' says Rose, 'he couldn't even cut some boring taxi driver short when he was already overdue in the studio. He was just too polite.'

After some years as a general reporter Julian Havilland followed John Whale to Westminster as ITN's chief lobby correspondent. There he learned to resist the insistent demands of news editor Don Horobin that he follow up what sometimes seemed to him trivial stories. 'For Don Horobin,' says Havilland, 'it was the *Daily Mail* that set ITN's agenda. My view was that at ITN we must be at least as responsible and accurate as the BBC, without being so damned boring. But after a year or two I found I could tell Don, "I'm not going to do it, the story's not right." The trouble was that the more you were pinned down working on duff stories, the less time you had to prepare what Geoffrey Cox called "seed beds". To find out what was really going on you needed to put yourself in the way of ministers. That was so valuable that you didn't want to have to chase some of Don's stories.'

At Westminster Havilland used his time well on behalf of ITN. Says David Rose, 'I remember walking through the Palace of Westminster with Julian one morning. Three cabinet ministers – Lord Carrington, Jim Prior and Francis Pym all in turn stopped to talk to him – they took the initiative. At ITN Don Horobin liked to keep reporters running scared, so it was nice to go to the ITN office at Westminster and work with someone polite like Julian who had the clout to face up to the news desk.'

Perhaps it is inevitable that reporters who cover the more complicated stories, in politics particularly, eventually find the constraints of television too great for them. There are not, after all, many pictures to be had in stories from Westminster, and before the televising of the Commons began in 1989 there were even fewer. Polite, intelligent and sophisticated, reluctant to over-simplify, Julian Havilland, like John Whale, in the end abandoned television; he went back to newspapers, as political editor of *The Times*.

These 'thoughtful men', as David Rose rightly calls them, were a loss to ITN; they had boosted its reputation for serious reporting, and had proved that you can be a good reporter and a nice person too. But when it comes to hard news, nice guys do tend to finish last. Last was not where Alan Hart ever wanted to be.

A Bit of Rough

'From the age of seven I had wanted to be only one thing, and that was a reporter. My father was a very strict disciplinarian but provided I had my shoes cleaned for inspection by six thirty every schoolday evening, clean enough for him to see his face in the toecap, I was allowed a privilege, and that was to listen to one radio programme of my choice, which happened to be *Dick Barton – Special Agent*. Then as a family we sat down for the next fifteen minutes to listen to the old-fashioned *Radio Newsreel*, which I still think was almost the best radio journalism of its kind because it was three or four minutes of the world news straight, no comment or interpretation, and then over to reporters for background. And it was my habit, as soon as *Radio Newsreel* was off the air, to rush upstairs to my bedroom and grab a hairbrush as a microphone and pretend to be the BBC's correspondent. So I think it's fair to say that I started to become engaged with the idea of reporting the world when I was seven.'

Hart was always a restless figure. After grammar school, at the early age of seventeen, he took a job as manager of a tea and tobacco estate in Nyasaland. No sooner had he arrived in Africa than he abandoned estate management for a job reporting on the local paper. Independence was coming, the forces of black nationalism clashing with the colonial power, and British papers wanted a stringer on the spot to file for them. Hart soon learned some basic journalistic skills. There were just two reporters on the paper. 'We had a marvellous system,' he says. 'We only got paid a few pounds for every column inch, but we charged so many newspapers the same set of expenses, on the basis that editors didn't talk to editors about cost funds, that we began to earn a lot of money. I had a delightful time. I learned my journalism there, and I wasn't covering Paris – society weddings and funerals – I was reporting white resistance to the rising tide of majority rule. So it was politics right from the very beginning.'

But Nyasaland became increasingly dangerous. Hart, with a young Belgian wife and a baby, slept with a gun beside the bed. His car was fire-bombed. Soon an unflattering profile of Dr Banda, the nationalist leader, which he had been commissioned to write by the *Daily Telegraph*, got him fired from the *Nyasa Times*. Back in London he was taken on the staff by the *Telegraph* but, given little to do, quickly became bored. 'I went and knocked on foreign editor Ricky Marsh's door, and I said, "I can't take this." He said "Alan, you've got to go into television. And the reason is you can't spell and you're a pain to editors. Go into ITN." I said, "Well, I haven't a clue about anybody at ITN." He said, "Well, one of the guys there is an ex-*Telegraph* man, David Nicholas, but he doesn't call the shots at the moment. It's Geoffrey Cox." So I said, "How do I get to Geoffrey Cox?" He said, "Well, just go and bloody phone him! But don't phone from the newsroom here, 'cos there'll be a bloody stampede!" So I walked out of the *Telegraph* newsroom, and from the first phone box past the *Telegraph* building I rang and said, "Can I speak to the editor's secretary?" And I delivered my six sentences staccato: "You don't know me. I'm Alan Hart. I'm just out of Africa. I'm only young, but I'm bloody good. Could I have an interview?" And there was a silence, and she said, "Hang on." And there was another silence. And a voice said, "Geoffrey Cox." He'd been given the six sentences, and Geoffrey said, "Where are you, Alan?" I said, "Outside the *Telegraph*." He said, "You're only just round the corner. What time is it now? Five to four? Oh, you'll be here in five minutes." So I was shown in. And he drew in Denis Thomas, who was then the deputy editor, and the bastards quizzed me for the best part of two hours! And a few days later I got a letter saying, "We are prepared to start by employing you as a trainee scriptwriter."'

This first job at ITN didn't work out. Hart was impatient to become a reporter. Cox told him, in effect, to go and get some experience at someone else's expense first. He would contact him in a year's time. In Southampton, working for the BBC, both radio and television, Hart did his damnedest to get his regional stories on to the national bulletins, and often succeeded: 'Almost a year to the day Geoffrey wrote to me and said, "Come and join us – as a reporter."'

Back at ITN – it was 1962 – Hart remembers his editor giving him two pieces of advice. 'He said, "You're about to start travelling the world, and you'll be dealing with kings and presidents and prime ministers and whatnot. You must remember, whoever these people are, they are the most lonely people in the world. They're surrounded by fools and sycophants and flatterers of all kinds, so they can never actually have an honest conversation with anyone around them. And they're crying out for honest conversation." And I really read, marked and learned that. After a while I could metaphorically put my feet on Golda Meir's desk, or King Hussein's desk, and quite a few others I could name, and they would talk to me as though I was their best friend, in a way that they could not talk to their own advisers. And that was why I had a terrific relationship with the leaders, often on totally opposite sides of conflicts.

'But the second thing Geoffrey said to me was this. He said, "Alan, you must understand our mission. Television news by definition is more important now than newspapers, because it's from the television news that most people take their world view. Our job is to sustain democracy, to keep it alive." And this has been my pet theme since then. Democracy cannot exist unless the people of all nations have enough information to be able to make an informed judgement, and that's the simple truth. Democracy doesn't exist just because we vote for the least of two or three evils every four years! It's about people having a minimum amount of information. And that was Geoffrey's sort of editorial guidance to me: to understand the role of we television people.'

Whatever doubts he might have had about his ability to live up to this role, Hart kept quiet about. In public he had a disarming belief in himself that sometimes left his colleagues open-mouthed. 'I think it was once said,' he recalls, 'that there were two reporters who changed the face of broadcasting: one was Robin Day for his interviewing – Robin is rightly credited with pioneering the challenging kind of interview – and it has been said that Alan Hart pioneered the all-action style of reporting that actually added quite significantly to ITN's ratings in those days.'

Hart's reporter colleagues studied their rival's technique with awe and admiration – and some scepticism, too. As Michael Nicholson remarks: 'It was a bit bizarre at times and OTT, but we all learned from Alan . . . I mean, dodging the bullets, nobody did it better. I remember watching Alan's report from Aden when he was under fire. There he was on his belly, pulling himself along the way soldiers do with their elbows, under this enormous crack of machine-gun fire. You think, My God! I wonder if I'll be able to do something like that? This guy's just unbelievable! But at the back of my mind my subconscious, even though I was new to TV, kept saying, "Yes, but there's something wrong there". And I didn't know what it was until later I met his Sikh cameraman, Mohinder Dhillon. Of course, Alan was doing his stuff looking *up* at his cameraman, who was sitting up, with the camera to his eye on a shoulder brace. So if Mohinder could sit upright was there really any reason why Alan had to be crawling on his belly? But that's the kind of guy he was. And of course we all imitated him to some extent in the years that followed.'

Certainly Hart's 'action report' from Aden in 1967, as the Argyll and Sutherland Highlanders swept into the hostile Crater district, had lifted the first few dull days of *News at Ten* and turned them into something worth watching. Earlier that same year, in Israel for the Six Day War, Alan was the first British television reporter to reach the Suez Canal in the wake of the lightning Israeli advance through Sinai, driving night and day past still-smouldering tanks, decomposing bodies and long lines of Egyptian prisoners-of-war. As Hart remembers it, 'In one fabulous sequence, hundreds of them surrendered to our camera; but the greatest shot of all was the thousands of boots taken off them and making a chain right to the horizon.'

Alan Hart's technique was to be in the middle of the action, hot, sweaty, hands-on. He wanted you to experience what he was going through as he reported the events of which he had made himself a part. This was the antithesis of the cool, calm, dispassionate reporting of an earlier gener-ation. It was not about standing back, in the way John Whale might have done, as an observer of the scene, but of plunging in among the action. The difficulty in taking that course is in keeping your head when all about you are losing theirs, but Hart was good at that. His involvement meant that he often knew more about what was happening on the ground than many of those who stood back.

Now that there was a half-hour *News at Ten* Hart grabbed the chance to make longer and more exciting 'action reports'. As the Congo finally collapsed in chaos, white mercenaries, led by 'Black' Jean Schramme, went in to extricate the nuns and other white civilians who were now in great danger. It was news editor Don Horobin's idea that Hart and his camera crew, Len Dudley and Barry Martin, should go in too. 'I was absolutely terrified,' says Hart. 'In Nairobi we were warned how dangerous it would be – we were told to hide our money in our socks.' Crossing the border at Bukavu the team had not gone far into the Congo when they were arrested by armed Congolese police. 'One had a cannibal's tooth, a rather pointed tooth, around his neck. They put us in this room in a church and insisted we play Russian roulette with them. I remember one of them sat at the piano playing Christmas carols. Thinking we'd had it, we all wrote last letters home to our wives. I asked to see the British consul but was told all the whites had fled. After six or seven hours of this there was a sudden crash of gunfire. In an instant our police guards tore off their uniforms and threw down their weapons, and we legged it back to the border.' There Hart and his team set up their camera and filmed as refugees, including their former captors, streamed over the bridge, seeking sanctuary in Rwanda.

Then, caught in a vivid piece of filming, came the mercenaries. Geoffrey Cox describes the impression Hart's film story made: 'The camera picked up the mercenaries, in single file on the jungle edge, their torsos looped with belts of ammunition, heavy automatic weapons in hand, as they skirmished their way towards the frontier. "Here come the mercenaries, with Black Schramme's battalion leading," commented Hart, in the exact style of an outside broadcast. It provided a report of such impact that we decided to run it for thirteen minutes – as long as the whole mid-evening bulletin had been a year earlier. "These are the rare moments which electrify the electronic embalmer," wrote Maurice Wiggin [of the *Sunday Times*].'[2]

'Maurice Wiggin actually, at a very early point in my ITN career, put his finger on it,' says Hart. 'He spent almost a whole column on ITN and me. And he said, "What is remarkable about Alan Hart, he actually takes people out of their armchair and to the location where he's at. And he involves them."'

Hart understood his audience, and how to reach them. 'As far as I was concerned I was broadcasting to my mum in her council house. I was never intimidated by looking at the camera because I didn't see five, ten, twenty million people. I saw my mum. And I quickly developed – purely by luck, not really by judgement – an instinct for knowing what would excite people; and it happened in Biafra.'

In Nigeria the Ibo, one of the three main tribal groups, had broken away from the rest of an uneasy federation and set up their own state, Biafra. Control of the country's oil-producing region was the real issue. Educated by Irish missionaries, the Ibo were sophisticated and resourceful, but as the Nigerian federal army – with British support – slowly advanced to put down the rebellion the Ibo began to starve. It was Alan Hart who discovered what was really happening in Biafra, and made it a lead story.

'We came across the starvation in Biafra quite by chance. The crew and I were in a jeep and we just left the path a bit and we came across a little village, with huts all round a square, and in this square were about ninety to a hundred kids. And it was the first time since the end of the Second World War that anybody had ever seen anything like Belsen. They had these grotesquely swollen bodies, but their necks were almost breaking because they were so thin, and a baby of one looked as though he was ninety-nine. I think there is one thing worse than a dead body, and that's an alive body, and particularly when it's a child who is clearly somewhere between nought and six months or a year, and they have this wizened, accusing, haunting face which makes them look to be a hundred. I never had too many problems in my travels with death and dead bodies and the smell. I found it enormously difficult to cope with the living dead.

'I said to the crew, "There's only one way we must start this report, whatever we make of it. Give me the microphone, give me a long lead, and I want you to start this film report with a wide shot of this whole scene. I'm going to walk round the far side, and when I'm in place you'll start your shot, wide, and you'll zoom slowly in to my face. Because," I said, "I want the viewers to feel what I'm feeling." And God bless them, my voice broke with the emotion of it – I wasn't acting and they knew it – they kept running.'

Hart is sure it was the reporter involvement in the story that gave it impact: 'Viewers, of course, would have been moved for half a minute or so without my being there; but when all is said these were "black people miles away somewhere". Seeing their reporter coming to terms with it and being moved, I think that was the identification. And the evidence is that – it's a long time since I was in television – if I walk down the street now, it doesn't matter whether it's here or Yorkshire, and even abroad, people of our generation will sometimes do a double-take and say, "Didn't you used to be Alan Hart?" And I smile and say, "Well, actually I still am!" And then they immediately say, "I remember you sitting on a tank in Aden, I remember you in Biafra, I remember this from Vietnam," and all that proves is that we made an enormous impact on viewers. And I think the reason why ITN was so bloody good – and I say ITN meaning all of us – was because we were the pioneers. We were making the rules, setting the standards.'

Some days later, after filming his Biafra story, hand-carrying his film because there was no way to ship it out, Hart finally got back to London. But he arrived too late in the day to edit his material for that night's *News at Ten*. 'I was summoned straight up to Nigel Ryan, and he said, "Tell me in one sentence what it is." And I said, "Belsen."' That night Hart did a short studio spot promising a full report the following evening. Early next morning they viewed the rushes.

'Wonderfully good.' ITN's first editor, Aidan Crawley, 1956. (Courtesy of Harriet Crawley.)

Rough, tough and invincible. Sound recordist John Collings and ITN founding member cameraman Stan Crockett, 1956. (Courtesy of ITN.)

'Journey into Sunshine'. But for much of this Roving Report in the south of France reporter Lynne Reid Banks, news editor Arthur Clifford and cameraman Len Dudley were not on speaking terms, 1958. (Courtesy of Lynne Reid Banks.)

Film assistant George Butlin and film editor Alfred Wilson working on Roving Report, mid 1960's. (Courtesy of ITN.)

Sound recordist Hugh Thomson, cameraman Alan Downes and reporter Alan Hart in the Gulf of Aqaba, shortly before the Six Day War, 1967. (Courtesy of Alan Hart.)

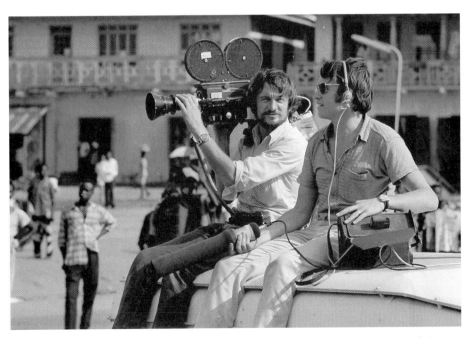

A new generation. Cameraman Jon Lane and sound recordist Bob Hammond, in former Biafra, Nigeria, 1970. (Courtesy of Richard Lindley.)

Setting sail for Tristan da Cunha. 'Sound recordist' Peter Hawthorne and freelance cameraman Ernie Christie in Cape Town harbour, 1965. (Courtesy of ITN.)

Freelance cameraman Mohinder Dhillon films the Argyll and Sutherland Highlanders in Aden, 1967. (Courtesy of Africapix.)

News editor Don Horobin, with (left to right) newscaster Alastair Burnet, chief sub-editor Alan Hankinson, and programme editor Antony Rouse, late 1960's. (Courtesy of Helen Gane.)

Reporter Richard Lindley, cameraman Cyril Page, and sound recordist Archie Howell invade Anguilla, 1969.

(Courtesy of Cyril Page.)

Editor Geoffrey Cox and his deputy David Nicholas, mid 1960s. (Courtesy of Helen Gane.)

The News at Ten top team. Studio director Diana Edwards-Jones, deputy editor of ITN David Nicholas, newscasters Alastair Burnet and Andrew Gardner, and interviewer George Ffitch, 1967. (Courtesy of ITN.)

Newscasters Andrew Gardner and Reggie Bosanquet in ITN's home from home, the Green Man, 1968. (Courtesy of ITN.)

Editor-to-be Nigel Ryan enjoying the hospitality of newscaster Reggie Bosanquet at Tidebrook Manor, 1967. (Courtesy of Delilah Bosanquet.)

Science editor Peter Fairley and Paul Haney, the 'voice of NASA', celebrate with a mock-up space helmet after the Apollo XI programme, 1969. (Courtesy of ITN.)

The Apollo XIV programme. Production assistant Jane Burdett operates the caption generator 'Chiron', the successor to 'Titlefile', on Frank Miles's cue, 1971. (Courtesy of ITN.)

'Nobody had ever seen television pictures like these before. And as the viewing went on people were coming in from everywhere – the tea ladies, Rediffusion people, the cleaners, and everybody was crying. Anyway, we put together a long cut. Nigel was summoned and we said, "Nigel, we've got a dreadful problem. We think it's terrific, but it's bloody nearly twenty-seven minutes." And he looked at it in stony silence, didn't utter a word as this report went on. The lights came on, and he leaned back and he was doing calculations. And he said, "I don't want you to cut a frame. That means we've only got two minutes for the rest of the world and the domestic news." And that's what we did.'

With his first Biafra story Hart had a major television scoop. For months the situation in Biafra remained near the top of everybody's running order. Hart had made it a big story by letting the audience see him there, among the starving children, reacting to their pitiable condition. But, as he admits, he went further: 'I became emotionally committed. But *what* I became emotionally committed to – and I think it's no bad thing for a journalist – was justice. I see no reason why journalism should not be on the side of justice.'

Fair enough. But the first job of the reporter is to give the facts: it is for others to take up the fight for justice. Starvation in Biafra was terrible, and Alan Hart made it known in a series of powerful reports that spurred many people to respond. But, as he admits, he became so involved in the story that it turned into something of a crusade. And that is the point at which impartial reporting becomes difficult.

Of course there was a downside to Hart's success: he left other ITN reporters jealous and resentful – sometimes with good reason. He was not about to brook opposition from his own side, let alone the BBC. For instance, ITN had signed up the first men – John Ridgeway and Chay Blyth – ever to try to row across the Atlantic from the USA. As they neared the Irish coast Hart set out to sea, with the two men's wives, to meet them. Unfortunately a gale came up and he failed to find the oarsmen. Instead it was my camera crew and I who were there to greet them as they came triumphantly ashore. It was a great television moment, and the two men agreed they would give me their first interview in the morning after a good night's sleep. Suddenly there was a loud rushing noise, and Hart arrived, late, but finally there, with the men's wives in tow, and determined that this would be his story. No prizes for guessing who ended up doing the big interview the following morning.

Alan Hart was one of ITN's most talented reporters, but he came at a price. He spent the company's money freely in pursuit of the big story. But the fact was that any story from Hart was likely to be worth it, likely to light up the newsroom, bring a bulletin to life and raise morale all round. Because of that his many extravagances on the road were forgiven – all the planes he hired, the generals he entertained, the grand hotels in which he and his crews stayed – at least he spent, not pocketed the money. When he left to go to BBC's *Panorama* he was presented with a leaving card in the shape of an ITN expenses form ('Dinner to 1st Nigerian Division – £4,000'), and they waved him goodbye to the strains of 'Big Spender'.

The Whispering Giant

'The two big days, I suppose, were the Munich Olympics and Bloody Sunday.'

He is today a prolific and very successful novelist, one of the few whose books sell in supermarkets as well as superior bookshops, books that are serialised, condensed, translated; their plots concerned with political violence and terror. And they had their origin in Gerald Seymour's time as an ITN reporter.

Geoffrey Cox, a small man himself, rather liked tall men about him. He would usually make them sit down in his office while he walked about, jingling the coins in his pockets. Seymour, known as 'the whispering giant' because of his height and conspiratorial mutter, fitted the ITN bill even better because of the reputation he had built up at University College, London, as a cricketer: 'I bowl leg breaks and googlies,' he told ITN's editor at his job interview. 'Geoffrey kept crumpling paper up in a ball and throwing it across the room. "Show me how you bowl your googlies," he said, so I did. What I didn't know was that ITN had just lost its annual cricket match with the BBC; Geoffrey wanted a bowler, and offered me a job as a reporter. I'm afraid that in the match the following year I was put on to bowl but, in spite of some near misses, got none for forty-six. I was taken off after four overs.'

Seymour was completely without experience as a reporter: 'On my eighth day at ITN, in August 1963, the Great Train Robbery happened. I was sent to the City to get some interview or other and I remember that the camera crew had to write my questions for me on the way there. From nothing and nowhere you were suddenly an eye-witness for the nation. Reporters were probably the most unprofessional part of the operation, but Geoffrey was prepared to back his hunches over people. Later, when I started doing some newscasting, I was still pretty young and quite consumed with fear: I'd had no training with the teleprompter, no coaching at all – but there was a lot of goodwill. Geoffrey said to me: "Gerry, you're waving your head about. I'd like you to think less of Cassius Clay and more of Sonny Liston." That was exactly it.'

Some talented people didn't make it as an ITN reporter: Sheridan Morley went off to make a career as a theatre critic and biographer; Richard Whiteley to become a local television hero and the famous presenter of *Countdown*; but Seymour prospered. By 1972 he was much travelled and highly experienced and, like many of his colleagues, well accustomed to spending two weeks every couple of months in Northern Ireland, as the 'troubles' came to a head.

'Northern Ireland was the best training ground for reporters, because there was no room for the adjectives and adverbs,' says Seymour. 'There was also no room for cowardice: just because you were in the middle of a big hostile Republican crowd, you couldn't say something sweet about them just so they'd think you a good chap. You couldn't do that, because the next day you would be walking up the Shankhill Road with an equally hostile Protestant crowd who had all seen your transmission the night before. But I think that reporting Northern Ireland taught you to be very spare with words, and really let pictures speak for themselves.'

Protests at the British government's internment policy had been building up. On the last weekend in January a civil-rights march was planned in Londonderry. Twenty thousand were expected on the streets. 'I'd said, "I want another crew, a back-up crew,"' says Seymour. 'This was going to be a big, big weekend.' And so it proved.

'We went down early. For some reason ITN had actually responded to the fact that it was likely to be a lively day and we were all issued with cork-lined deerstalker hats, to protect us. So I went to war that day in my old brown trousers, my ankle boots – good strong ankle boots, because it's bloody cold over there at that time of year – my old ratting coat over my sports coat, and with the potential to wear a reinforced deerstalker. And I remember we walked around quite early on, and the thing that struck me – we saw stretchers laid out, just sort of round the corner from the main streets, military stretchers for presumably their *own* casualties that they were expecting. So there was that anticipation, particularly because the Parachute Regiment were deployed, that this was a day when things were going to change, there was going to be a response from the Army. But there was also the anticipation — this is what I told London — that as soon as it got dark there would be a major gun battle. I felt very confident in my ability to report the day. I felt, This is my territory. I know the place, you know, pretty much backwards. People know *me* there. And I thought, Let it all roll out!'

And yet Seymour was to feel, at the end of a long, difficult and dangerous day, that the full story had eluded him.

'I was with Peter Wilkinson on camera and Bob Hammond doing sound at the famous barricade, where there are the pictures of the mob chucking stones and bricks at the soldiers who are responding from behind the armoured cars with baton rounds; and then quite suddenly the paratroops appeared – huge, because they were wearing those smocks over the top of their flak-vests. And they went straight past us through the line, quite quickly. About that moment we ran out of film, which happens in those awful situations, and it takes a moment to reload. Then we advanced, following them. There was the sound of shooting, and we stopped, because it's ingrained into you: if the Army are shooting, they're being shot at. So you freeze, because you think there's incoming fire, and take stock – you're continually taking stock, aren't you? And then we went forward a bit more and we saw a lot of bodies being thrown into an armoured car, and abuse between a sergeant and the priest – I remember *that*. As I came up towards the lead armoured car, one soldier was beside the open steel-plated door with his rifle up, and another one was down by the wheel in a firing position. And one of them said "Watch out – it's the f—g telly!" And his mate looked at me stuck on the ground, and I looked up and he said, "Oh, 'e's all right. It's Mr Seymour what was with us in Aden!" Then we got to the corner of Rossfield Flats, which is where there was incoming fire, which hit the masonry up above, I can remember *that*. And there was quite a lot of shooting at that stage. That sort of big "boom!". That's quite a heavy sound – that was outgoing, but there was also the "Boom! Boom! Boom! Boom!" of a Thompson sub-machine gun. Then we heard the brilliant exchange – extraordinary – between the paratroop lieutenant who was with us and his men when he shouted, "Will you please stop firing! I've told you – only fire at identified targets." And I was asked about this at the Widgery[3] tribunal, and the Lord Chief Justice looked down with a frown of utter puzzlement – a cutting look, you would have thought. He said, "Are you saying that the lieutenant addressing his men used the word 'please'?" His clerk passed up to him my statement, and his head seemed to shake – I think he'd got an MC in the Western Desert or something like that – as if to say, "Well, bloody hell, things have changed since my day!"

'It lasted a fairly short time, fifteen minutes, twelve minutes, something like that. Then we found Colonel Derek Wilford, the CO, who had no comprehension of the scale of the civilian casualties. The light was going, and I think we plonked him underneath a street-light in order to get enough light on his face – we didn't have a battery light with us. And then suddenly it's half-past four, it's dark, the street's empty, everything's gone, there's a sort of shocked quiet about the place, and there's a two and a half hour drive or whatever it is ahead of you to Belfast, to get the film in the lab.'

Seymour had been right at the front, he had seen the action, and yet he felt he could not say what had really been happening, let alone what the scale of it was. 'I remember thinking, I know what's on the film, but I don't know what's happened outside that tunnel of vision that was me looking over the cameraman's shoulder. And then we heard – on the six o'clock radio news as we drove – that there were twelve dead, thirteen injured, which was the figure at that stage. And I remember an awful sinking feeling in my gut, because that emphasised that I simply did not know what had happened and that here was obviously a colossal, major story, and I was ignorant of the basic facts, which we all needed to know. Oh, yes, you're there, a whopping great story has happened, and you almost wish it hadn't! Because of that sense of ignorance. If it had been what I'd expected, three or four dead, I could have coped with it and I would have been on top of it. And I remember *not* feeling on top of that story.

'We cut it very fast, and I read a commentary live for a ten-and-a-half minute film in a twelve-and-a-half minute bulletin, and it went flawlessly. But I remember getting a call-back, which basically told me that the second crew, our second crew, had not produced the pictures that the BBC second crew had done. So basically we'd f—d up that day and f—d up big! We hadn't got bad stuff, but we hadn't got the shot of the priest with the white handkerchief and two people behind him lugging a body. We hadn't got that. The BBC had. But that's the sort of world in which we lived, I think. The competitive edge was utterly between what we had and what the Beeb had. And that *mattered*.

The usual reaction when you're on a big story is one of arrogance, élitism, pride, smugness, whatever. "Hey, we're on the big one, and we've cracked it! We're going to lead the programme." Well, we did lead, but I remember a real sinking feeling – partly because we didn't have the best pictures but more because I didn't really know what had happened. It was a changing moment, because nothing like that had happened before. Something massive – earthquake scale – had happened in Northern Ireland, but I didn't know why it had happened, how it had happened, and why all of these civilians were dead without weapons recovered.'

In the same year that he had reported Bloody Sunday, Seymour was sent to cover an international sporting event. But 1972 was the year of the Munich Olympics, and on what should have been a feel-good story Seymour again found himself trying to make sense of the confusion of violence and death.

'In the Olympics in those days – they don't do it now – you used to have a day's break in the middle of the Games when virtually nothing happened. It was when administrators, television crews and so on could all just sag and gasp and have a bit of a rest. So we went all out for a gigantic boozing session and eventually got to bed at – I don't know – half past two, three o'clock. At around seven thirty I had my door virtually stove in by David Phillips, our field producer, to tell me there's shooting in the Olympic village. He'd just been phoned by our German student "gofer" to say there was a radio report that Palestinian guerrillas had taken some Israeli athletes hostage.

'I can remember I had this God Almighty hangover and a headache that stayed with me for the whole day. We got the crew up, dressed very fast – unshaven, of course – got the camera gear, and off we went.

'So we're then confronted by the security fence around the Olympic village. There were guards standing there looking helpless, and I just climbed over it, and the crew, being older than me, just pulled the fence up and went underneath it. And we walked into the village. When you see a policeman looking outwards, you tend to walk past him, because that's going nearer the action. And I used the trick where you turn the "squelch" up on a walkie-talkie radio and you go past guards as if you're listening to somebody in a very important way, waving your people through. And the guards were so confused, they didn't know what was going on. We took up residence on a second-floor balcony at an oblique angle from the Israeli house, the Puerto Rican team's balcony; and there we sat for the day. We had a wonderful vantage-point to see the negotiations with the kidnappers – they'd already killed two Israeli athletes. We saw the very harrowing moment when one of the hostages was brought to the window in his vest with a firearm up against his head, to be shown to the police. We had all of it, but the terrible problem was, how to get the stuff out, which is always the problem, isn't it?

'I found the manager of the UK men's hockey team, and he took film out for us.'

By the end of the day the Germans had struck a deal with the terrorists to take them by helicopter, with their hostages, to a military airbase, so that they could fly out of the country. Seymour, now with a local German cameraman, followed. 'We got in a position up by the perimeter fence, and there was a floodlit plain, aircraft in the distance. And we hadn't been there long, when "t-t-t-t-t-t", you know, the helicopters are coming in. The cameraman sat on my shoulders and he was able to photograph every-thing. And then suddenly we heard the explosions and saw the tracer, with little flashes of light. Quite stunning to me, because it was something like Bloody Sunday, which I'd just not expected on that sort of scale. And again we didn't really know what had happened. Hours later armoured cars started to come out of the main camp gate in convoy, and the guy standing in the turret of one of them had tears streaming down his face. And that was when one of the cameramen, a stills man, said, "It's a disaster," and at last I found out what had happened, that the Palestinians had killed all their hostages the minute the German security forces had opened fire.

'While this was going on, the famous news conference took place in Munich, at which they said that all the hostages were fine, "Everybody has been saved." And everybody went to bed. I got back to the television centre, where the ITN office was – course, they'd all gone back to the hotel. And I was quite miffed by this – nobody up there at all! But I remember the phone rang then, in that sort of great lonely space: "Ding ding ding!" I picked it up, and it was an Australian radio station – an affiliate of ITN or something. Anyway, they had rung our number, and the guy, the interviewer, came on, and he asked me, "What's the latest information?" And I said, "All the hostages are dead." There was this absolute stunned silence. I broke that story for that radio station in Australia – the fact that it was a terrible cock-up! He didn't believe me, of course, because he hadn't got any news-agency tape, no Reuters or UPI. And I explained what had happened. Then I went and woke David Phillips and told him. And then I went to bed to get an hour's sleep before we started again.

'What both of those stories – Munich and Bloody Sunday – taught me is that there aren't great conspiracies in this world, but there are amazing cock-ups. When you analyse them later, as people do with the benefit of hindsight, you can see the path, procedure, pattern, progress of a cock-up. But there at the time, when people are making decisions on their feet as the seconds go by, which are the ones we're part of, the ones where we're sort of standing there in the shadow trying not to be noticed and not to interfere, but trying to be a witness of people under stress, those are the best news stories, yes, but nothing is clear. You're confused, you often don't know what's really happened: just like soldiers in the fog of war.'

In the shoot-out shambles, three of the Palestinian terrorists had been captured, but in October, Black September terrorists hijacked a Lufthansa plane, blackmailed the German government (just before an election) into releasing their colleagues, and then flew them to Tripoli. At Munich airport, in true ITN style, Seymour and his producer David Phillips chartered a jet and followed with their crew. 'How much will it cost?' enquired an anxious ITN foreign desk. 'I've no idea,' replied Phillips, putting the phone down. As they flew through the night Seymour was conscious of a cash-register ringing up the ever-increasing expense of the flight.

'Young German pilot comes back and he says the Tripoli tower had just called us: "What do I tell them?" I replied, "Oh, you say it's British television and we've come to interview the freedom fighters."' The pilot asked producer Phillips to come and talk to the tower. There was an angry bark when he inadvertently referred to the Black September men as 'terrorists', but finally permission to land was given. 'The next thing is we're going down,' says Seymour. 'We land in the middle of the night, and half-past six we're in the Ministry of Information. And I've still got this cash register ringing in my head about the cost of all this! It's the Presbyterian upbringing. And I say, you know, "The world needs to hear the story from the point of view of these men, and that's what we're here for. We're asking for your help and co-operation in an exclusive interview." There's a lot of jabbering on the phone, and after we've hung around for a bit more, he says, "Right, fine, you are to return here at six o'clock this evening and it will happen." So David Phillips then decides that we have to change hotels because when the commercial flights come in during the day the rest of the world's press will be there. We can't be seen, we'd been promised this exclusive. So we go to another hotel and sit there all day looking at the Mediterranean! Meanwhile out at the airfield, of course, is still our Mystère jet: "Ch-chunk! Ch-chunk!" Fifteen hundred dollars, eighteen hundred dollars, five thousand dollars – what it was costing!

'We were taken to a villa with a high wall round it, just us and a Libyan outfit. We were there at half past six. Seven o'clock goes by, eight o'clock goes by, nine o'clock goes by. Half past nine, up the staircase, footsteps – and in walks Tom Mangold from the BBC. *Panorama*! And he must have seen my face fall about three feet! And then after a bit he sidles over to me: "I'm doing a documentary for *Panorama* about Black September. I'm going to use the Libyan television crew, but they're shooting black and white." "Really?" "Would there be any chance of a roll of colour?" And I say, "And it wouldn't go to BBC News?" "Absolutely not!" he says. So I have a conversation with David Phillips and straight away there was a roll of colour film for Mangold. So it's done! Eventually, at about eleven o'clock at night, the Palestinian guys are shown in. And one of the three spoke English. And, oh, it was fantastic. It was a world exclusive. And I was there – I'd got them. And I did one of the worst interviews I think I've ever done. I suppose I was still fresh from Munich, you know, it was a few weeks after. And I did an aggressive interview, which was stupid, because it may have reflected the views of athletes, of the general public, of white British society, but it wasn't therefore an interview from which you elicited information or, more than that, *understanding*. It was probably quite good theatre, but in terms of finding out what was inside the mind of Black September, well! And the one who spoke in English, he looked at me with utter bewilderment. Because as far as he was concerned, he was, you know, a very brave young man! And then other people started their big Black September stuff shouting and yelling at the camera. While the crew packed up I sort of gave covering fire: "Fantastic! Yes, you really put your point of view over! People are really going to understand now, the courage and bravery, etc." And then we're gone, and we're away, into the car and heading for the airport and on to the waiting jet. And Mangold is left with the crumbs to pick up. But he stayed faithful to his word and didn't give his stuff to BBC News. And what I love about that was it's the sort of deal that the two foreign editors back in London could never have made. But it's absolutely the sort of deal on the ground that two guys would make who knew each other and trusted each other 101 per cent.'

Seymour's story ran that night – though not, despite David Phillips's protestations, at the top of the ITN bulletins. None the less, sales of this exclusive interview around the world at least paid for the executive jet.

In 1975 Gerald Seymour published the first of his novels, *Harry's Game*, based on his experience of the undercover war in Northern Ireland. It was such a popular as well as critical success that ITN agreed to send him to live abroad, to help him reduce the tax he would otherwise have to pay on his book royalties. Seymour became ITN's Rome correspondent. But it was no good: he continued to write in his spare time, and his success as an author grew to the point where it made no sense for him to continue as a reporter. As editor David Nicholas told the ITN board at the end of 1977: 'Gerald Seymour will be leaving ITN at the end of his contract next summer. This is no surprise. He has three highly successful books behind him and will now take up full-time writing. He has served ITN well for fifteen years, a consistently aggressive reporter who has shone in many different skills and many different places, some of them dangerous. I do not envisage replacing him in Rome.'[4]

Tough Guy

The most durable of ITN's reporters is Michael Nicholson. True, he is now no longer, technically, an ITN man but works instead for ITV's *Tonight with*

Trevor McDonald. But when war breaks out you can bet that Nicholson will be there, and reporting for ITN's *ITV News* on some dramatic event, like the toppling of Saddam Hussein's statue in Baghdad at the end of the Iraq War.

Nicholson describes himself as an Essex boy – 'Essex boys are very aggressive' – and there is a rough, tough bovver-boy quality about him that has helped him carve out a considerable career in many dangerous situations, and then come back alive to tell the story. But Nicholson's career at ITN started slowly. He had been working in the London office of D. C. Thomson, who published the *Sunday Post* and the *Beano* in Scotland, but at his ITN interview in 1964 he gave Geoffrey Cox the impression that he was employed by Thomson Newspapers, publishers of the *Sunday Times*. That got him into ITN, but for a long time he was stuck on the newsdesk, writing and rewriting lead-ins for the newscasters, and later scripting film stories under the stern and demanding chief sub Derek Murray.

In the newsroom the atmosphere had not changed much since ITN had been formed, a decade earlier. 'The thing I remember is the noise,' says Nicholson. 'I mean, a newsroom now is like a morgue. In those days you couldn't hear yourself talk, there was so much shouting going on. Now they send e-mails to each other even if they're just a few yards apart. In those days you just screamed across the room. The air was thick with smoke, of course; I remember one of our copy tasters used to have a little bottle of gin in his left-hand drawer and there was always a box of cigars in the right-hand one.

'There was enormous sexism. Tom St John Barry, the crime reporter, used to come in after his lunch and wander round the newsroom. All the PAs – and we had some pretty PAs in those days, God knows what's happened to them – would be bending over doing something and he would pinch their bottoms. Without turning, they would just say, "Afternoon, Tom". Now you'd be sent to jail, wouldn't you? But it was that kind of atmosphere, and, of course, people like Di Edwards-Jones would be turning this smoky air blue with her asides. It was enormous fun. There is a formality now about newsrooms and about ITN which certainly wasn't around then.'

If the bulletin's 'voice', Bob Bateman, was not available to record the commentary to a film story, Nicholson might be asked to do it. 'If you had a reasonable voice you would be allowed to read your own script. And so, little by little, you kind of moved into the reporter mode; and if you had a decent face, then you got your first reporting job. But nobody got any training at it. OK, so you did the subbing, you did your scripting, you did your voicing, but nobody told you how to hold a mic, nobody told you how to do a piece to camera, nobody told you how to do a proper interview, how to dress, how to walk. You learned all this from the camera crews. The crews taught you everything.

'The very first piece to camera I did was in Lewisham. A man arrested by the police after a smash-and-grab raid was being held inside a hospital ward, because he'd been wounded. And while police backs were turned, his accomplices came in and whisked him out of the hospital. So it was quite a good story – but I hadn't the foggiest idea how to begin.

'On the way there Len Dudley, the cameraman, tuned into the BBC, and while his soundman was driving, Len wrote down all the particulars picked off the BBC news, and said "Now write your piece to camera – it's got to be forty-five seconds long." I said, "I can't do it in forty-five seconds," and he said, "If you don't do it in forty-five seconds they won't use it." So I wrote my piece sitting in the car and timed it roughly, and he said "Right, stand there, start talking, and when you see my hand go up start walking to that spot by the door." I said, "Talk and walk at the same time? I can't do that." He said, "We'll rehearse it a few times." So I did some dry runs and he said, "Now let's try a take." We did two or three takes and it went on the screen that night. It was a very important lesson for me because you don't walk unless there is a reason for it, and then it looks good. In this case Len got me to walk from where the crooks entered the hospital to the front door where they and the man they had rescued got out. Back at ITN Geoffrey Cox said to me, "That wasn't a bad start, not a bad start." I had to thank Len Dudley for that.'

Michael Nicholson shockingly reveals that his first 'foreign' story for ITN was something of a fraud. But I was not surprised to learn of the lengths to which my former colleague was prepared to go – aided and abetted by a first-class cameraman, Alan Downes.

'It was a couple of weeks before Christmas,' says Nicholson, 'and [news editor] Don Horobin had heard that there was a whisky train in Scotland that went all the way down the Spey valley, eventually to Perth, collecting these huge barrels of whisky. And apparently as it went through the last of its valleys, this train was carrying over a million pounds' worth of whisky, which in 1964 was a lot of money. So I did my first foreign trip up on the night sleeper to Scotland, with Alan Downes. Of course, the first thing I did was go to Inverness Station and I say, "Can you tell me when the whisky train comes through, please?" And they said, "Och, the whisky train, sir, at the end of every October it comes through." And I said, "No, you must have got me wrong, this is the middle of December. The whisky train, when does it come through?" "Yes, sir, the end of October," so I'd missed it by about two months.

'But this was my first big break, you know, away from the office. And I didn't dare ring Don. I thought he'd say, "You've failed, you stupid idiot, two months late!" "Well, I've only just been told about it, Don." "Come home!" That's what I expected. So dear old Alan said to me, "We've got to sort this one out. Let's ring the PR at British Railways." So I rang the PR and explained my predicament, and he said, "Well, look, I tell you what we'll do if I can get a bit of co-operation. It's a great whisky story. The whisky distillers will love it if it's on the ITN news; British Rail will love it if it's on the ITN news." So what they did, they arranged for British Rail to lay on a locomotive and wagons, and they arranged for all the distillers to have some empty barrels, and we picked up the train in the north and came slowly down, collecting all these barrels, filming all the way through. We went into the distilleries and showed the whisky, and I did my first piece to camera – well I think my second or third piece – sitting on the foremost wagon on top of a barrel, and I said, "And here I am, moving through the Spey Valley with Christmas only a fortnight away, with a million pounds' worth of the drink you want to bu.," And of course it was all empty barrels, but nobody knew. I didn't ever tell anyone. Absolute fraud!'

It was 1968 before Nicholson got abroad on his first war story. But from then on he was unstoppable, and a reporter who was more often than most in the right place at the right time.

At first it looked as if he'd got the timing wrong. Nicholson arrived in Nigeria, on the federal side in the civil war with Biafra, just as Russian tanks rolled into Czechoslovakia, putting a brutal blight on the 'Prague Spring'. That made a much bigger story, but then came a chilling incident that put Nigeria back on the news agenda. Taken to the front to show how well the federal fight was going, Nicholson and his crew, cameraman Chris Faulds and soundman Hugh Thomson, accompanied soldiers from Nigeria's 3rd Marine Commando as they laid waste the villages around Port Harcourt. It was obvious from the piles of trussed-up bodies the crew discovered that federal Nigerian killer squads were going just ahead of them, wiping out their Ibo foes wherever they found them.

The crew were with a junior commander, Lieutenant Macaulay Lamurde, when his men dragged an Ibo prisoner before them. Lamurde hit him across the mouth with the horsewhip he carried and accused him of being a Biafran soldier. The prisoner replied, in English, that he was not; that he was just looking for his family. As Nicholson later wrote: 'Lamurde smiled and prodded the man in the chest with his whip stock. "You are a Biafran soldier." He said it again in an oddly friendly way. The prisoner began to cry. We were still filming. I said to him, "You are a prisoner-of-war now and you have nothing to fear. It doesn't matter whether you are a prisoner or not – you are protected."[5]

Nicholson remembers saying something about the Geneva Convention, both to comfort the prisoner and remind Lamurde of his obligations. 'You will be taken away for interrogation but you will not be harmed. You are a prisoner-of-war.' But the Lieutenant shouted an order and the young Ibo was thrown to the ground, his hands tied behind his back and the rope looped tightly round his neck. Then, smiling still, Lamurde took a rifle from one of his men and, holding it with one hand, the butt resting on his hip, fired nine shots into his prisoner's chest three yards away. Nicholson assumed that now he and his crew would be shot, as witnesses of this war crime, but Lamurde obviously saw nothing wrong in what he had done. The ITN team was safe.

Before news of what he had filmed could leak out, Nicholson hitched a ride on a military plane to Lagos, where he could ship his film to London. He shared the flight with the casualties of war: 'As the last plastic bag was hoisted aboard I clambered aboard after it and sat for two long hours among the dead and wounded. The smell of old dressings, fuel oil and the sickly sweet smell of blood was suffocating. I tried to move but there was no room, so I vomited in the space between my legs.'[6] From Lagos airport he shipped his film to ITN, then rejoined his crew in Port Harcourt.

The story made a tremendous impact world-wide. Instead of showing how well the federal Nigerians were behaving in their campaign against

Biafra – as they and the British government had hoped – it demonstrated the savagery with which rebellion was being crushed. Furious at this propaganda disaster Benjamin Adekunle, the Marine commander, threatened the ITN crew with a public whipping and physically attacked Nicholson with his favourite weapon, a baseball bat.

The wretched Lieutenant Lamurde had now been arrested. A public example was to be made of him, and the ITN team were ordered by the Nigerians to film his execution by firing squad. They refused, but a BBC crew had also been summoned to witness the event. 'Take aim,' shouted the officer in charge of the firing detail. 'Hold on,' shouted a BBC man. Lieutenant Lamurde, now blindfolded, waited unseeing, not knowing the reason for this – no doubt agonising – delay. The BBC cameraman changed a flat battery, gave a nod, and Lamurde was shot dead.

In 1971 Nicholson was witness to another violent death: the destruction of East Pakistan and the birth of the new nation, Bangladesh. Attempts by East Pakistan to establish its independence from West Pakistan had been crushed in the most horrific way by Pakistan's military government. But this had given India the chance to intervene, and in December the Indian Army began a full-scale invasion.

At the border town of Comilla, Nicholson found himself for the first time under heavy artillery fire as the Indians began their advance into East Pakistan, where he and his cameraman were based:

> That afternoon we went forward with the tanks, walking behind one of them like infantrymen, Jacques [Chaudensen] and I enjoying every second of it. It was all we had hoped for in filming terms and we knew that when the time came all that was needed was a request on the field telephone for a helicopter to whisk us away to safety. Then came the awesome dreadful whistle, seconds later the explosion, the zing of shrapnel and searing panic as the man in khaki reeled back, red and bloody, not knowing which way to go and then falling dead, his eyes and wounds wide open. Still new to war, it never occurred to me that it was possible to be shot and not see the enemy, to see his shells exploding but not see his guns . . . We waited, hoping to hear our tanks fire back, but they did not. What we heard instead was their engines revving as they turned about. They were pulling out. We got up and ran after them in panic and when we touched the tanks we felt safer as the shelling fell away behind us.

By nightfall we were back in Dacca, feeling very brave. Safely in my room, showered and shaved, with the filthy clothes shoved into a cupboard, drinking my first beer, I could not remember being afraid at all. I had been in danger and now that I was out of it I forgot my fear, as I would forget my promises never to do it again. It had all been washed away with the adrenaline, leaving only the filtered recollection of others' fear and others' deaths.[7]

As the fighting drew closer to Dacca and the Pakistani forces pulled back, Nicholson filmed furiously while Indian planes bombed and strafed – but there was no way to get his film out. And then the Indian Army arrived and the shouts of 'Joi Bangla!' everywhere signalled the end of the fighting and the bloody birth of Bangladesh. Nicholson emerged from the Intercontinental Hotel, which had become an international safe haven, to greet my crew, Ken Taylor and Mickey Doyle, and me. We had been covering the war from the Indian side, advancing with them.

Now Nicholson demonstrated the sort of skill that made him a really useful reporter. Dacca's streets were littered with vehicles of all kinds, abandoned by their owners who had fled or been killed. In a trice he had selected something suitable as a camera car and hot-wired the starter so that the engine sprang into life. ITN was again ready to roll. And, of course, Nicholson's timing was always impeccable. While he headed home for a traditional English Christmas, I had to stay on to cover the situation in devastated Dacca.

In 1973 Nicholson was in Israel as the country reeled from the Egyptian attack across the Suez Canal into the Israeli-held Sinai desert. He and Gerald Seymour arrived together on the first plane from London. Without stopping even to check in at their hotel they went to work. Seymour headed north to the Golan Heights and the front with Syria, while Nicholson set off in the general direction of the Suez Canal and Egypt, far to the south. As the sun began to dip Nicholson at last found his target, a huge Israeli armoured column – squadrons of British-made Centurion tanks leading armoured personnel carriers, field guns and lorry-loads of infantry – on its way to counter-attack the advancing Egyptian forces. Frantically the ITN team filmed, then turned back towards Tel Aviv.

It was after five o'clock and they were nearly three hundred kilometres from the Herzliya television studios, but they made it in time for waiting

ITN film editors to cut their film – along with Seymour's – and satellite it to London for that night's *News at Ten*. ITN beat not only the papers but every other television station: a world exclusive from both fronts in the Yom Kippur war.

A few days later Nicholson and his crew were heading for the Golan Heights – he and Seymour were now alternating their areas of operation – when a jet fighter roared close overhead. At eighty miles an hour their car spun off the road, hit the edge of the Tarmac and somersaulted, landing upside down a hundred yards ahead. Nicholson was knocked unconscious and hospitalised, but gallantly got straight back to work wearing a neckbrace, in which he appeared, in the thick of the war, for his camera pieces. His devotion to duty did not impress his editor: 'Either the neckbrace comes off the screen or you do,' cabled Nigel Ryan.

With his tough, self-assured, indeed aggressive manner, Michael Nicholson has now set off on so many assignments for ITN that one would have thought he had developed some confidence in his ability to bring the story back alive. Not so, he says. 'I am aggressive – I think somebody once said I am a man driven. But reporters are all the same. We're all driven by fear of failure. I think all good reporters suffer from paranoia. I'm sure we do. There's a feeling that you are being specially persecuted while you are doing the story. And then – I don't know what the psychological description is for fear of failure – but we all fear failure, and that is our motivation. "This is the one they're going to find me out on. This is the one when they'll suddenly realise that I'm just no good at this."'

One day of great significance was 29 April 1975: the last day of the Vietnam War and the first time that the United States of America had known defeat. Despite all its military might, US forces had been unable to sustain their South Vietnamese allies in the face of North Vietnam's relentless determination to take over the whole country. At Newport bridge the day before, Nicholson and his crew, taking great risks, had covered the final battle of the war, as the last barrier to Saigon fell. It was a story that would win prizes. Now his French crew, who felt that they were more likely than American or British reporters to be acceptable to the North Vietnamese, elected to stay on in Saigon. ITN's Sandy Gall, who spoke excellent French, courageously decided that he would remain too. For Nicholson, after four exhausting months in Cambodia and Vietnam, it was time to go.

In Saigon that last day there were scenes of utter chaos. The CIA had told correspondents that when American Forces Radio played Bing Crosby's recording of 'White Christmas' they should go inconspicuously to various assembly points where they would be picked up in an orderly way for evacuation. But the record was never played. Instead buses that eventually came for the journalists had to hack their way through hysterical, panic-stricken crowds, with Vietnamese mothers clutching at the windows, begging the foreigners to take their babies to safety. Michael Nicholson vividly described the last terrifying moments of this humiliating evacuation:

> At last we were across the road from the American embassy and there was America's ignoble Dunkirk. "Don't panic", men in Texan boots and hip-holsters shouted from the other side of the high steel gates, "You have nothing to fear"... But the people clawing the gates were those who had believed in the Americans, who had worked with the Americans and fought for the Americans, and they did not hear him. They began to climb the walls to get in, and we did the same. We fought and clawed our way towards the hands of the marines who were hauling only westerners over the top. And we did fight and we did claw. I was not proud of what I did that day. No one who was there can feel anything but shame at what they did and what they allowed to happen to others around them. Marines lined the top of the wall by the back gate on Hong Thap Tu, pulling us all up and booting down the rest. They lunged with their bayonets at young girls, knocked children unconscious with their rifle-butts, stamped with their boots and broke the fingers of those who reached the top. But they pulled us up.[8]

In the embassy grounds Nicholson, cameraman Peter Wilkinson and soundman Hugh Thomson waited in line as the rescue helicopters came in, scattering scraps of paper from shredded embassy documents like ticker-tape from some victory parade. Offshore, ships from the Seventh Fleet were waiting for them. But there was one final indignity:

> As we ran out beneath the spinning blades we were directed to the rails of the ship and told to stand in line. Then a very tall and muscular black marine

sergeant ordered us to drop our trousers and bend over. One by one he went down the line and putting a condom over his middle finger, which was as large as a frankfurter, stuck it up our anuses. Someone dared ask why. 'Looking for dope, man!' 'You expect to find it up our bums?' 'Some boys will stick it anywhere.' He found me troublesome. 'Man, but you've got a tight arse.' I replied: 'Sergeant, if you'd been through what I've been through today, you'd have a tight arse too!'

Inevitably Michael Nicholson will reappear in these pages, as the reporter of other major stories ITN has covered in the course of its history. But, briefly, he tried a slightly different career. In the early eighties, not long after he had made a triumphant return from covering the Falklands War in 1982, attempts were made to turn him into a newscaster. They didn't last very long. Says Nicholson: 'There was a slot to be filled on the *News at 5.45*, and because I had a high profile after the Falklands I was made a newscaster. And there began my demise, because it was a hateful job. We all know what it's like to be a newscaster, and I loathed it.'

Under the headline 'Muddler Mike Loses the Top Spot', the *Sunday People* reported in the spring of 1986 that Nicholson's frequent slips of the tongue were about to cost him his newscasting role. 'Cross-Channel ferries', it said, had emerged from Michael's mouth as 'cross-flannel cherries', and 'a lucky young man' had become 'a yucky young lamb.'[9]

Nicholson agrees that newscasting was not his forte. 'I'd been a gypsy for near on twenty years, travelling the world, having the most exciting time. I'd been to Vietnam, Nigeria, Cyprus, Cambodia – I'd done the rounds. And then to come back and catch the eight forty train in the morning and sit all day doing bugger-all until quarter to five at night when it all started was not my cup of tea.

'I was never asked for any editorial contribution – not once. So I became an editorial eunuch, I had no balls, there was nothing I could contribute except to read this ghastly teleprompter every night, which I think dehumanises you. I always remember that when I started newscasting this director came up to me and said, "You know, Michael, the most important thing about newscasters is integrity, and once you can fake that you're made."'

With sighs of relief all round Michael Nicholson eventually went back on the road and there, to his own and most other people's satisfaction, he remains.

The Right Stuff

Tall, lean, weatherbeaten, Sandy Gall looked the way foreign correspondents are supposed to look. 'With the features of a benign pugilist, enhanced by a minicab smash, he gave the impression of a man who had become closely involved in the affray he was reporting,' says Nigel Ryan, his editor. Indeed, intrepid foreign reporting was the basis of Sandy Gall's highly successful career at ITN.

For Reuters, at the beginning of the 1960s, Gall and Ryan had both covered the Congo. Gall had spared no expense in his search for the news, and had once received a cable from Reuters that read: "Coverage superlative. Costs transcendental." Later, when both men had moved to ITN, Gall's demand for more funds provoked a further cable, this time from Ryan: "You supposed to be reporting Vietnam, not buying it."

When he joined in 1963, recalls Gall, ITN was still a small and very personal operation. It was energetic and effective but in some ways not very professional. In his view the foreign desk, under the multilingual Hans Verhoeven (who, it was said, could tell dubious jokes in six languages), did not always make the wisest of judgements about how to deploy its relatively tiny resources around the world. If he felt he was being asked to do something idiotic, Gall would often do what he wanted rather than what ITN had expected. 'We made the decisions ourselves then, in the field. You wouldn't be allowed to do that now.' Indeed not. Says Robert Hargreaves, Verhoeven's immediate predecessor as foreign editor: 'Sandy was rather difficult to deal with. He was not much interested in communication with the office – if at all. He was very independent. His stories would just turn up.'

Because he was so obviously an experienced foreign correspondent, Sandy Gall was often on excellent terms with people who turned out to be useful interviewees, both at the time and in the future. Stuck in Jordan's capital Amman after Black September in 1970, when the Palestinian uprising in Jordan had been crushed after fierce fighting, Gall was finding it impossible to get anywhere near the victorious King Hussein. In the hotel lobby he met a young Pakistani brigadier attached to his country's military mission to Jordan. Invited to supper, Gall explained his problem. The brigadier promised to help. Next morning Gall was surprised and delighted to be offered an exclusive trip with the king as he toured military bases in the countryside for the first time since the fighting had ended. Gall's cameraman Alan Downes shot prize-winning pictures as the king was carried shoulder-high in triumph by his fanatically loyal Bedouin tribesmen, and the story led *News at Ten* that night. More than that, it was the foundation of an excellent relationship, not just between Sandy Gall and King Hussein but with the helpful Pakistani brigadier. His name was Zia ul-Haq, and he would emerge just seven years later as the man who had successfully staged a coup against his country's president to become the military ruler of Pakistan.

Over years of extensive reporting Sandy Gall became both well connected and knowledgeable about what was happening on the ground around the world. Nigel Ryan, who in 1968 had become editor of ITN, says he turned down a suggestion that ITN's foreign correspondents should routinely brief intelligence people at the Foreign Office when they returned from interesting assignments. 'I told MI6,' says Ryan, 'that my reporters were free to seek information from any source, and it might be that occasionally they could offer MI6 something in return. At the same time I was not about to have people employed by me working for British Intelligence too.' But Gall was soon sought out by Foreign Office people who wanted to pick his brains or use his skills.

He recalled having a quiet lunch with the head of MI6, the Secret Intelligence Service, after one particularly interesting trip:

> It was very informal, the cook was off, so we had cold meat and salad with plenty of wine. He wanted to hear what I had to say about the war in Afghanistan. I was flattered, of course, and anxious to pass on what I could in terms of first-hand knowledge. I also decided early on in the lunch that 'M', as Ian Fleming calls him in the James Bond books, or 'C', as he really is, was unlikely to tell me anything. I therefore resolved to be completely frank and as informative as possible, and not to try to prise any information out of him in return.

That seems odd. On occasion I have been quite happy to tell Foreign Office people in general terms what I have learned on a trip to some place the FO clearly didn't know enough about. Surely we want a well-informed government rather than otherwise – the lack of accurate intelligence from Iraq is sufficient testament to that. But one can never be sure why the Foreign Office wants to know, or what it will do with the information. So, circumspection is in order. And surely, rather than just a lunch, a journalist should hope to get something by way of information back, even if it is only a better understanding of the government's position on a particular issue. But Sandy Gall's view was that if he got nothing on that occasion his lunch with 'C' might well prove helpful on a later one.

In the early 1980s Gall was asked by his intelligence contacts how the government could get better media coverage of the Afghan resistance to the Soviet invasion and occupation of the country. As a result he persuaded Central Television to commission a documentary about what was happening there, which, he says, aroused in him 'a passionate interest in the Afghan struggle for independence, first against the Russian occupation and secondly against the Communist regime which succeeded it'. Following his expedition he set up a family-run charity, that provides artificial limbs for Afghans disabled in the war and also treats children affected by the diseases bred by overcrowding in the refugee camps.

Two years later another documentary followed, this time largely funded by ITN. Gall was later told that his old friend Zia ul-Haq, now president of neighbouring Pakistan, had said to the prime minister Margaret Thatcher that 'We must encourage people like Sandy Gall to come out here and report what is happening in Afghanistan.' The idea was to go into Afghanistan with the mujahideen, the Muslim fighters, and see them mount a number of attacks on Russian and Afghan regime targets, including the ambush of a Russian convoy. This was a dangerous and arduous assignment, requiring just the qualities that made Sandy Gall such an intrepid reporter. But was the enterprise justified?

Gall had been told by British Intelligence that it was his friend Zia's idea but, from his own account, MI6 were in favour of it too. It is certainly true that, wherever the inspiration for the expedition came from, British viewers needed to know what was happening in Afghanistan. And if there was fierce fighting going on then they should see that as well. But Gall's trip came close to creating a firefight especially for television.

In Islamabad, on the way in to Afghanistan, Gall was summoned to another tête-a tête with President Zia, and asked if there was anything he wanted for his trip: "Yes," he says he replied. "Would it be possible to have some SAM 7s with us?" Zia laughed. "SAM 7s? I don't see why not. But why?" "We're likely to come under attack by Mig 24 gunships, I suppose, and it would make some spectacular pictures if one of them were to be shot down." Zia laughed again, seeing the point. "I'll see to it," he promised. "You'll get your SAMs."[10]

It's fine to want 'spectacular pictures' – what reporter wants unspec-tacular ones? It's fine to follow a war, and to get as close as you can to the action. But it's not right to film soldiers trying to kill people if the *primary* reason they are opening fire is for you to take pictures of it.

I plead guilty to this myself. I remember being with a group of Yemeni rebels dug in with a heavy mortar high on a rocky hillside above the town of Sa'ada. Every morning and every evening at around the same hour they would fire a few rounds into the town below. It had clearly become a bit of a ritual. Short of time, and anxious to move on, I asked the commander of the gun crew if on this particular day he was prepared to open fire a little earlier than usual. He was happy to oblige, but I was wrong to ask – it's not an ITN reporter's job to make war on anybody. As well as wrong, it was foolish. Gunners in the town below fired back with accuracy born of long practice. No doubt they were indignant that we had started the shooting earlier than usual.

In his expedition to Afghanistan, Sandy Gall came close to making the same mistake as I had, but he could reasonably argue that the mujahideen's war was going on with or without him. And once he and ITN had decided that the story was worth it in journalistic terms then whatever propaganda value Zia and the British government got out of it was irrelevant. Pressed on this issue Gall is quite firm: 'I was never asked to do anything which compromised my journalistic standards.'

For ITN, Gall led an eventful life. In Vietnam, in 1965, he was there to see the first American marines come ashore at Da Nang and, ten years later, to watch the North Vietnamese tanks roll into the South's presidential palace as the last Americans made that ignominious departure. Then, at considerable personal risk, he had stayed on in Saigon with his French camera crew to film the North Vietnamese consolidating their victory. When he got out three weeks later it was to learn that ITV was on strike; ITN was for some time unable to show what he had so resolutely stayed to shoot.

There were other dangerous corners in Sandy Gall's ITN career. In Uganda he nearly lost his life, and apparently it was all my fault. Idi Amin, Uganda's president, the former British protégé and now out-of-control dictator, had abruptly ordered all Ugandan Asians with British passports to leave the country. If they did not, Amin had told me menacingly, the Asians would find they were 'sitting on a fire'.

'ITN sent Richard Lindley and a crew out to cover the story,' wrote Gall later, 'but after a couple of weeks Lindley informed the foreign desk that he wanted to come home to get married.'[11] Oh dear! That does sound a bit weedy – and it's not quite right: before I left for Uganda I had told the foreign desk that I had to be back in time for this rather important engagement. Never mind: Sandy Gall, clearly made of sterner stuff, was sent to replace me. But President Amin had had enough of British journalists. A week later Gall was under arrest in the dreaded Makindye police barracks, in hut C19, which he later discovered was usually reserved for those about to die. He was lucky to be deported rather than have his head stove in with a twenty-pound hammer, the method Amin's henchmen commonly employed to dispatch their prisoners.

In somewhat similar circumstances Gall saved the life of one of ITN's best freelance cameramen, Mohinder Dhillon. In the Congo, after filming the evidence of a massacre of white hostages by Simba rebels, Dhillon had been arrested by government security men, accused of being a rebel sympathiser. Sitting in a line of prisoners, hands on head, he could hear the depressing sound of those who had been interrogated ahead of him being taken outside and shot. Soon, there were only eight left. 'I was beginning to reconcile myself to my inevitable end,' says Dhillon. 'A cold sweat and a strange numbness took over my body. It was a kind of countdown moment. And then, as I was waiting for my time to be up, my head bowed down between my knees, kind of hypnotised, getting ready for death, someone kicked me and said, "Mohinder, what the hell are you doing here?"' It was ITN cameraman Jon Lane, who had suddenly seen the forlorn figure of Dhillon in his viewfinder as he panned down the line of prisoners. Sandy Gall was with him. Soon Gall had argued successfully for Dhillon's release, flown with him to Léopoldville, and then seen him safely out of the country. Says Dhillon: 'It is a debt I owe to Sandy and Jon Lane that I will never be able to repay.'

To ITN the priceless value of Sandy Gall was his vast experience of reporting round the world. In 1970 editor Nigel Ryan decided that he should have a new role to capitalise on this. 'I remember going somewhere in a taxi with Nigel, says Gall, 'and he said, "I want you to start news-casting." Well, if I'm offered something I nearly always say "yes". So began a new phase in his career, in which a stint at the *News at Ten* desk[12] would be followed by a foreign tour. It suited him admirably. In the studio he could bring his accumulated knowledge and experience of the world to bear in presenting the news, and in the field he could demonstrate to himself and the viewers that he was not just a craggy, charismatic news-caster but still an international reporter.

In 1990 Sandy Gall retired from newscasting, but, at the age of sixty-three, he returned to reporting. And, though now only occasionally, he's still at it.

Thoughtful Daring

'By God, ITN's been good to me,' he says fervently. And Bill Neely has done pretty well for ITN too. He joined – after stints at the BBC and Sky News – in June 1989, just as the 'evil empire', the Communist bloc, was cracking and crumbling. By November he was in Germany, watching the Berlin Wall come down, the beginning, as Neely says, of two weeks that shook the world.

'I arrived in Berlin on the eleventh of November and went straight to the Wall. People were climbing on it. How could we catch up and get ahead on the story? Why can't we climb over it into East Berlin? I did a piece to camera on the Wall saying that this would have got me shot in earlier years. I interviewed the mayor of Berlin and asked him what it all meant. "It means Germany will become one country." There was a feeling that now anything in the world was possible.

'I'm a history graduate. You look back and things seem inevitable, but when you're there you don't always see it like that, but you know you're on the front line of history.

'I was in Lithuania, in Vilnius, when Gorbachev had gone there to hold back the tide of people on the streets, to try to persuade them to stay with the Soviet Union. I heard his spokesman, Gennadi Gerasimov, make some comment saying that perhaps the two countries should "divorce". I rushed up to him: "Are you serious?" "Well, yes." I could hear a bell ringing in my head – the beginning of the crack-up of the Soviet Union. I managed to get a satellite up in time, and then on *News at Ten* Alastair Burnet was reading out the news that the Soviet Union thought it might be best if it broke up.'

'There were some spectacular failures,' Neely says, 'like ITN not being in Tiananmen square when the Chinese cracked down to keep the lid on their own people, but I remember when I was at the BBC and we heard that ITN was coming it was like waiting for the cavalry coming over the hill. We still love to be fleet of foot at ITN because in military terms we're like special forces; the BBC is a tank regiment, and Sky is increasing its own firepower month by month. And, of course, the Americans turn up with absolutely everything. We have to be able to get there with daring and lateral thinking.'

Neely was offered the choice of two ITN bureaux: in the USSR or the US. With a young family to consider, he chose Washington and became ITN's youngest-ever bureau chief there. He covered the American end of the Gulf War, the presidential election of 1996, and long-running feature stories like the O. J. Simpson trial. Then, from 1997, Neely was based in Brussels, where one night he heard early reports of an extraordinary story, a car crash involving Diana, Princess of Wales. 'The definition of a great news event is whether you can remember where you were and what you were doing. I recall that I drove to Paris in two hours. There was debris – things like bloody gloves still there. I got there just after they'd pulled the car away but before the police had put up a barrier. It's true that sometimes you make your own luck.'

Now ITN's international editor for *ITV News*, Neely was one of the British correspondents 'embedded' with the coalition forces in the Iraq War: 'I am extremely sceptical about this idea of "embedding",' he says. 'I grew up in Northern Ireland with a Catholic background, and no one from there ever believes everything that the British Army says. I remember I got news from 40 Commando of a break-out from Basra. The story was that a hundred and twenty vehicles had gone south. This was considered the beginning of the end of Iraqi military resistance. They were being picked off by the Brits, was the story, but it was all wrong. I tried to get verification thirty miles away from where it was happening, but I couldn't. There was pressure from ITN to report the story. I felt I had no way to verify it, but the BBC guy was going with it and I trusted him. I was wrong.'

This, says Neely, is a good illustration of the danger he sees in the way reporting is going. With a demand for constant information to feed rolling news programmes like those of the *ITV News Channel*, reporters in the field are often tied to some satellite dish. Marooned at this fixed point, perhaps a hotel rooftop far from the action, they become mouthpieces for news fed to them from London, news that may or may not be accurate but is certainly not *their* news. They are no longer reporters but 'roof monkeys' or 'dish bitches' – ostensibly a reporter, but actually just a ventriloquist's doll. 'I don't want to be a roof monkey. I don't want that feeling of being literally chained up, unable to get out and verify anything. After all, it's your mouth the words are coming out of. Of course we need to compete, but by putting out stuff you haven't confirmed yourself you risk ridicule.'

Good news man

Later on he became one of Britain's best-paid newscasters, with his youthful looks, caring manner and friendly smile a favourite with the viewers, particularly the lunchtime audience. Derided by more cynical broadcasters, he became well-known for his advocacy of 'good news' stories – although he did not argue that all the news he presented should be good, but simply that television journalists should be as energetic in reporting the good things people were doing as the bad. But to begin with he was simply one of the best news story film-makers ITN ever employed. His name is Martyn Lewis.

Nobody else wanted the job, but in 1971, a year after he joined, Lewis saw the possibilities in becoming ITN's north of England correspondent. He negotiated a contract that gave him first call on any story ITN commissioned from the Midlands to the north of Scotland, and became a prolific and expert film reporter. 'In a sense,' he says, 'moving into the newscasting world later took me away from what had been and always will be my great passion, which is knitting together words and pictures. The secret of it is that the pictures show you "what" and the words tell you "how" and "why".

So you have this unique opportunity with television news to convey, if you do it properly, four minutes of information in a two-minute story. It's a double-barrelled assault on the senses.

It seems to me that we've really got the priorities wrong in television news, because it's considered a natural progression that you move from being a reporter to being a newscaster, because it's a higher profile, there's more money, there's more status, et cetera, et cetera, but the proper meat and drink of television news is being out in the field reporting. That means reporting as we used to do it, where you as the reporter called the shots. You didn't have producers riding shotgun, telling you what to do and what to write. One of the regrets I have about the direction of television journalism is that – apart from a few lions in the jungle – producing a report has almost become doing it by committee instead of as it used to be with us. You, as the journalist, went out, you often found the story yourself, but if you didn't, the news desk pointed you in that direction. You researched it yourself, you lined up the interviews yourself, you directed the cameraman and the crew yourself. It was your story, not something dictated from the office.'

Lewis was a shrewd operator. In order to work straight through the day and not miss any of the action he 'bought out' his camera crew's right to stop work for a proper lunch break with the promise of a decent meal on ITN expenses in the evening – a restaurant from *The Good Food Guide* guaranteed. And, although far away from ITN, he became cunning at keeping control of his story, feeding his cut film package 'down the line' to London very close to the start of the bulletin: 'I did work to deadlines a hell of a lot, and the deadlines were very tight, but being a last-minute merchant meant that, back in London, they had much less chance to fool around with the story you sent down. A technique I developed was that if you allowed the last word of a sentence to just run over the edit join, the cut to a new picture, then they couldn't easily shorten the story – take an early "out".

'The important thing, the great thing, for me about television news, and what excited me about it beyond belief, wasn't just the challenge of film-making, it was the intense nugget of satisfaction that you got at the end of each day. There are very few people who start a day not knowing what they're going to do and then have to take a project, from beginning to completion at the end of the day because today's news is useless tomorrow. It has to go out today or it's dead. I took that job in the north for two years and stayed for seven and a half, because I was on a roll, I was just enjoying it so much.'

Back in London in 1985 and already becoming known as a newscaster, as well as a reporter, Martyn Lewis was asked to make a documentary film for the then little-known hospice movement. When the Duchess of Kent came to dinner at ITN one night he discovered that she was a frequent private visitor to Helen House, the first children's hospice in Britain. Lewis persuaded her to let him film for a *News at Ten* story as she talked to the children there, none of whom had long to live: 'It was agreed that I could take a crew a day in advance, and the crew would not shoot anything on that first day, but we would simply wander around, let the children look through the lens, let them get familiar with it and say, "We're going to be here tomorrow," so all that initial stuff had been moved out of the way, which was lovely. And then, when we filmed – Bob Hammond was the cameraman – the Duchess was fantastic and we produced the most amazing footage. It was very, very powerful with those terminally ill children. In an adult hospice ninety per cent of the patients have cancer and the others have got some other life-threatening illness. It's the other way round in a children's hospice, where ninety per cent have got life-threatening illnesses of a kind that you and I have never even heard of, terribly rare debilitating diseases – like a wonderful lad we interviewed called Bruce. He was eleven but was not going to live for more than another two years because his heart and lungs were not growing as fast as the rest of his body. It was absolutely devastating, but I remember thinking that he was the kind of son that any father would have been intensely proud to have. He was a kid who'd got it right and was very sensible about it. We produced this riveting stuff.

'My problem was that the standard length of items on *News at Ten* was about three minutes. I did an edit with Mike North; we pulled it down as tight as we could, and it came out, when we'd taken all the tough decisions, at eight minutes forty-six seconds. And I thought, What do I do? I rang up [ITN editor] David Nicholas's PA and I said, because I knew the *News at Ten* output editor wouldn't even consider it, "Can you give me a quarter of an hour with David when you stop all the calls going through to him?

Don't tell him what it's about, just say I need to see him." And she said, "OK." So I walked in and I said, "David, I'm not going to say anything. I want you to watch this story. I'm not going to tell you how long it is and I want you to tell me what to cut." And David sat and watched it. He was a pretty tough journalist but, at the end of it there was a tear in his eye – the only time I've ever seen that with him – and he said, "I will mandate that to fill the second half of *News At Ten*." And it ran at the length we'd cut it.'

In 1986 Martyn Lewis left ITN for the BBC to become the first presenter there to be paid £100,000 a year. With such a high value placed on his talents, who can blame him if, from time to time, a certain self-importance surfaced. During the long ITV strike of 1979, ITN journalists were not laid off but sent to occupy themselves on useful business here and there while they were off the air. Martyn had been dispatched to New York to see the legendary newscaster Walter Cronkite, America's best-known face and most trusted broadcaster, in action. Asked if he still went out reporting, Cronkite replied that this had become difficult: there was the danger that because he was so well known his presence would overshadow the story. 'Walter, I know just how you feel,' responded the young Martyn Lewis.

CHAPTER 15

A FORCE FOR GOOD

Way back in 1956, as ITV was about to start broadcasting in the Midlands, ATV had tried to get its news material free from a local newspaper in return for an advertising 'plug', instead of taking the news from ITN. Norman Collins, as ATV's deputy chairman, wrote to the ITA proposing that: 'The reader should be announced over the air at the end of the bulletin as follows: "The newscaster was Donald Horabin [sic], news editor of the *Evening Despatch*."'[1] Keen as it was that the new companies should develop local news programmes of their own the Authority was insistent that they should take ITN's national and international service. Above all it was not going to allow the news to be sponsored. The proposal died: Don Horobin, the man from the *Evening Despatch*, did not appear on the screen at the dawn of ITV in the Midlands. However, it was not long before Geoffrey Cox heard of him, and in 1961 he hired Horobin as ITN's news editor, the replacement for Arthur Clifford who, after so much pioneering work at ITN, had been promoted to assistant editor at ITN and would shortly go off to be head of news and current affairs at Anglia Television.

Soon Don Horobin got his own tenacious grip on the news-gathering side of ITN business and, for the next twenty-three years, didn't let go. Nigel Ryan perfectly describes him:

Those who worked with him regarded him with a mixture of awe and affection. He was a professional's professional with the heart of a schoolboy. Alerted to a news story, he brought to mind a terrier advised of the presence of a rat: the gimlet eyes narrowed, the jaw clamped and the nose quivered, tuning in to strange, unseen news-gathering forces with which he appeared to be in league . . . It was Horobin's iron whisper which would come down the telephone in the middle of the night anywhere in the world into the ear of reporters or cameramen, already stretched to what they had imagined was their limit, to propose what would seem some preposterous initiative. But it would also be Horobin who organised the back-up to get his material home, and Horobin who would confront the editor to demand the funds to make it possible, and in tones which made refusal seem like treason.[2]

Together, deputy editor David Nicholas and news editor Don Horobin became known as ITN's 'dynamic duo', a Batman and Robin combination capable of making the impossible happen.

In the late sixties, after some private conversations with contacts in the security forces, Don Horobin dispatched me, together with cameraman Chris Faulds and soundman Barry Martin, to the Yemen, where it was reported that Egyptian planes were dropping gas bombs on tribesmen in the north of the country who would not toe the new left-wing, pro-Egyptian line laid down by the nationalists in the capital Sana'a.

We flew to Saudi Arabia in the company of an unexplained character who, Horobin said, had the sort of contacts in the area that we would need. As usual, he was right; the man did. Following our spooky friend's advice, we had packed large quantities of whisky in boxes marked 'Red Cross supplies' and were delighted to find on our arrival in the teetotal kingdom that cars waiting for us on the Tarmac whisked us away without contact with Customs or Immigration.

Crossing the desert border into Yemen we discovered that the rebel resistance to the left-wing nationalists was supported by the Saudis in the traditional way. Bags of gold sovereigns and the much more impressive-looking Maria Theresa silver dollars changed hands as we were passed from one group of tribesmen to another, bumping crazily in one-ton military trucks across the rocky plateau at the edge of the Empty Quarter, sleeping in a series of rather well-appointed mountain caves, and travelling by night to avoid Egyptian air raids. Progress was erratic. From time to time we would find ourselves held up, virtual prisoners, as our guides – and guards – haggled with the next lot of escorts to whom they were handing us over. And every afternoon, everything stopped for *quat*, as our hosts settled down to chew the intoxicating herb, which left them with no intention of making any further progress that day. We could do nothing but settle down ourselves and, at a tactful distance, open the 'Red Cross supplies' which contained our own western intoxicant.

Occasionally, on a mountain ridge, we would run into some SAS man dressed like Lawrence of Arabia whose job was to report by radio to Riyadh and London on who was doing what to whom in his patch of Yemen. Strangely reluctant to be filmed, these characters did their best none the less to help us find the evidence of gas attacks that we were looking for. As we drew closer to the dark tower of Sana'a we abandoned our lorries and mounted camels, but they were our undoing. After many weary days of strapping our camera gear on to these desert pack-animals in the morning and taking it off at night came disaster. A camel fell off the narrow track we were following on the side of the *djebel*, taking our sound camera with it. Over and over it went down the slope, with the silver camera box glinting in a cloud of dust and sand. From then on we were reliant on a silent camera and tape-recorder – not ideal for good television film-making.

We didn't find much evidence of gas attacks, but some people must have worried that we had. On our way back to Saudi Arabia, we were flying from the border town of Najran to Jeddah when the cabin steward urgently drew our attention to smoke emerging from one of the camera boxes that, rather than putting into the hold, we had kept with us. On looking inside we saw what appeared to be sticks of dynamite taped together with an old-fashioned slow fuse attached. The fuse was smouldering in a cartoon-like way, but by the time the plane had made a very steep descent to some desert airstrip it had burned itself out without setting off the explosive. As he rushed past us for the exit the pilot shouted that as we had brought this bomb aboard we should get it off. We did, and left it behind in the desert. So ended a typical Horobin adventure.

It was the urge to be first with the news, and finding a new way to unearth it, that excited both Nicholas and Horabin. They were the modern equivalent of the legendary Julius Reuter, who had used carrier pigeons to get news of the latest stock prices from Aachen to Brussels ahead of his rivals. Now the round-the-world solo voyage of the *Gypsy Moth* and its intrepid skipper Francis Chichester drove the dynamic duo to devise an extraordinary scheme. ITN would charter a ship, sail out into the Atlantic to meet Chichester, and transmit live pictures as he neared Land's End and the conclusion of his record-breaking voyage.

This, of course, was long before the days of portable satellite dishes, so it was planned that ITN's engineers on board the ship would send their television signal to a 'dish' mounted under a twin-engine plane circling overhead, half way between the ship and Land's End, which would then bounce it down to the GPO's receiving station at Goonhilly Down. It was a bold concept.

For the venture ITN had hired an elegant ocean-going yacht, the *Braemar*, with tastefully decorated cabins and lots of brass and mahogany in the handsome saloon. With a television camera and the transmitting equipment installed, the *Braemar* set sail from Falmouth with seven ITN engineers and me as reporter – straight into a nasty gale.

I woke in the morning, feeling queasy, to find water sloshing around the floor of my cabin as the ship rolled horribly from side to side; it seemed that the pumps were not working. Some twenty-five miles south of the Scilly Islands it became clear that this ocean-going yacht was more fitted for a gentle cruise in the Mediterranean than fighting its way through an Atlantic storm. One engine had broken down and the engine room was flooded. We were drifting, the captain informed us gloomily, towards Runnelstone Reef, but unless we ran aground he was hopeful that the *Braemar* could stay afloat for another twelve hours. There was no alternative but to send out a Mayday call. 'Rescue ships race to 20 adrift in gale – Atlantic dash to TV Yacht' was the *Evening News*[3] headline in London that afternoon.

The lifeboat from St. Mary's in the Scilly Isles was soon alongside and, as the *Braemar* threatened to sink, took us off. We were now in no real personal danger; however, given the expensive and complicated equipment that had been installed aboard the *Braemar*, which we could not afford to lose without abandoning our project, it was decided that the lifeboat would try to tow us into port. It was a cold and miserable seven-hour voyage. With the *Braemar* settling ever lower in the water we made slow progress through heavy seas, but by 3.30 a.m. we were safe inside the little harbour at Newlyn, near Penzance, where David Nicholas was waiting with hot food and sympathy.

Among those aboard the *Braemar* had been a young sound recordist from Rediffusion, Richard Spriggs. Suffering badly with sea-sickness he was taken to hospital as soon as we landed, and was expected to make a quick recovery. But very sadly his condition worsened and he died – as it transpired, from a pre-existing condition. Later a fund was established in his memory and a television studio built at Loughborough College School, where he had been a pupil.

The *Braemar* was of no more use to us, but we needed our equipment, which was still on board. The danger was that we might not be able to reclaim it before the ship was sequestrated in some argument about salvage payments. There was one indispensable piece of equipment (rented from French television) that would enable us to make the link with Goonhilly: it simply had to be retrieved. Armed with a large army clasp knife, ITN's Basil Bultitude, in overall technical charge of the project, went aboard *Braemar*, hacked through the cables and spirited this vital link ashore.

Working through the night, our engineers, among them Allen Tingay, Peter Cullen and John Gollage, reinstalled their gear in a bigger, tougher vessel, a Dutch coaster, the *Albert V*, that Nicholas had swiftly chartered. His expenses included an item that was apparently essential before we put to sea again: 300 tons of ballast at 1s. 6d. [7½ pence] a ton. Now all went well. Steaming out into the Western Approaches, we found the *Gypsy Moth*, although she was hard to spot, her pale hull barely visible, appearing and disappearing among the big white-crested waves of the Atlantic. Then, just as Nicholas and Horobin had planned it, I was reporting live, with the *Gypsy Moth* in the picture behind me, while Chichester sailed on towards a hero's welcome in Plymouth. For twenty-four hours the story was ours alone. It was great stuff – but it did not meet with the approval of all at the ITA: they saw a television stunt, a news extravaganza, taking precedence over stories of much greater significance elsewhere in the world.

Moira Kelly, one of the ITA's staff whose job was to keep an eye on ITV programmes, wrote sniffily:

> Although I was not monitoring last night I feel I really must protest at last night's 8.55 p.m. bulletin. It was several minutes before they deigned to give

us any information on the day's diplomatic activity with regard to the Middle East situation. The first few minutes consisted of a report from Richard Lindley aboard the boat due to make a rendezvous with Sir Francis and an interview with Lady Chichester. This was I felt basically not news, but promotion for the programme[4] to be shown later this weekend.[5]

Her ITA superiors agreed that, with Communist-inspired riots in Hong Kong and the Middle East moving towards the war that would break out a fortnight later, ITN had become distracted by news gimmickry, reporting events of no real significance.

But Nicholas and Horobin took a different view of coverage like this. They felt that television viewers welcomed the stirring stories they pursued about lone sailors, intrepid explorers and heroic mountaineers. In contrast to so much of the news, which was inevitably sad and depressing – concerned with war and famine, suffering and death – these stories were of hope and human achievement. And, with the greater length offered by *News at Ten*, there was often plenty of room for them.

It is true, however, that sometimes these entertaining tales strayed into areas that ITN really was hard put to justify as news. Such was the week-long search for the Loch Ness monster.

This was certainly a story that appealed to the public. A *TV Times*[6] front cover showed Reginald Bosanquet at his newscaster's desk and behind him one of those blurred photos of 'Nessie' that – like the alleged monster itself – surface from time to time. Inside, the lead article explained that ITN 'with the co-operation of the Loch Ness Phenomena Bureau' had launched 'the biggest-ever scientific expedition to Loch Ness'.

The campaign (as ever with Don Horobin, meticulously planned) began with a long 'special report' on the history of the monster, and interviews with canny Scotsmen who, for a very modest fee, told us how they had seen it themselves. Then, every night for a week, *News at Ten* carried a story about different aspects of the search. Noise-making machines were positioned in the loch to drive any monster towards sonar 'curtains' stretched across its waters; there were cameras that could 'see' in the dark, and even a miniature submarine into which cameraman Ken Taylor and I squeezed for a claustrophobic descent to the bottom, a thousand feet down. Our lights shone through the tea-coloured depths but revealed nothing much.

Finally we filmed as a bag of evil-smelling bait – anchovy paste, crushed eel, bull's blood and a hormone known to attract crocodiles – was dragged through the loch's peaty waters in the hope of attracting the monster.

The *TV Times* stayed with the story:

> Horobin's headquarters – a six-berth caravan by Temple Pier, Drumnadrochit – resembled a wartime ops room. Walkie-talkie radios linked him to ships 'sweeping' the loch with sonar. Police checked passes at the gate . . . The search revealed the floor of the loch to be rather like the Moon – rough and pitted with holes. 'Targets' were located on the bottom. But they never moved. 'It could be,' said Horobin hopefully, 'that the sonar pings are making Nessie lie low or hide in some under-water cavern.[7]

It was all, of course, to no avail. At the end of the week we wrapped up the hunt without having found the monster. With the help of a piper and Urquhart Castle behind me I ended my camera piece like this: 'If you are there, Nessie, all we can do is congratulate you on evading our attempts to find you. As our sonar screen grows dim and our noise-makers fall silent, we leave you to a sound you may perhaps prefer, the music of the pipes . . .'

Hard news it wasn't, but the viewers had found it fun. At the ITN board meeting of 15 December, Howard Thomas of ABC, referring to the Loch Ness saga, said he hoped ITN would not 'stray into current affairs', but Dr Tom Margerison of LWT said he felt the Loch Ness story 'had been entertaining and a legitimate ITN activity'.

Among the many other initiatives that Horobin launched at ITN was one that – in quite a literal sense – did not get off the ground. In 1968, as Russian tanks once again rolled in to crush dissent in a vassal state, Horobin sidled up to cameraman Jon Lane. 'Matey,' he muttered in his usual conspiratorial undertone, 'things are getting a bit difficult in Czechoslovakia. We're thinking you could parachute in dressed as a priest. What do you think?'

CHAPTER 16

FIRSTBORN GIRL CHILDREN

As a news editor Horobin was very much in the tradition of Arthur Clifford, his predecessor at ITN. But while Horobin's projects were inventive and ingenious, it was the senior partner in the dynamic duo, David Nicholas, who planned the most ambitious campaigns and carried them out with even greater panache. A believer in giving the viewers hard news with the least possible comment he was nevertheless passionate about finding the most lively and exciting way to get those viewers to watch.

'I was born in 1930 so my lifespan totally corresponds with the age of broadcasting,' he says. 'My father was a radio nut. This was a remote part of Wales, and my job was to go down every Wednesday and bring back the wet battery for the radio when it had been charged up. I remember "The King's life is moving peacefully to its close . . . ", I remember the abdication speech. And, of course, I remember the morning of the third of September 1939, and my grandmother and my mother crying. So I guess I've always been a child of broadcast. It was unbelievable what broadcasting was to one's life. But because there was no chance of working in broadcasting when I started in journalism — there wasn't much of it around – I went to Fleet Street.

'The definitive thing in my life that got me into television was when I was on the *Daily Telegraph*. And the *Telegraph* had a fantastic investigative reporter who exposed the corruption in bent elections in the Electrical

Trades Union. I used to sub his stuff and it was excellent, but it seemed to make no bloody impact whatsoever. And then sitting at home one Monday night, I saw John Freeman interviewing the ETU's Frank Chapple on BBC *Panorama*. And of course it had this huge impact, and I said, "Goddammit, I've been doing this for weeks and months on the paper and nothing." And so I said to myself, "I want to go into television."'

In 1960 Nicholas was offered a job at ITN as a sub-editor, at a salary of £1,500, and allowed to supplement his income with a weekend shift on the *Observer*. Shortly afterwards he became chief sub, and experienced the curious dichotomy that still existed then between the people writing the stories, largely from agency reports, and those dealing with the available film.

'It's difficult to believe: the output editor sat upstairs most of the time in the preview theatre seeing what pictures there were. But downstairs the chief sub was writing the running order. So what would happen was: as the chief sub, I'd be giving out scripts and stuff. "Hey, come on guys, where's your script?" Then the output editor would come down about half an hour before transmission and say, "What do you reckon?" Now, of course, he could override me. He could say, "Oh, well, that's wrong. Listen, we've got this terrific film," and I wouldn't have known what the film was. So the output editor was the boss, and the chief sub was second in command.'

Nicholas was at home, off shift, when he got a call asking him to go into the office. 'I went in in an old sports jacket, thinking, What the hell is this? I went into Geoffrey Cox's room, and I always remember being offended that Captain Brownrigg – he was chairman at the time – was sitting in Geoffrey's chair, and Geoffrey, the editor, was standing. And I thought, F—k it, no one sits in that chair, it's the editor's. And Brownrigg offered me the job of deputy editor. And he said, "By the way, you know, as deputy editor you'll be expected to dress appropriately!"'

As deputy to Geoffrey Cox and later to Nigel Ryan, Nicholas had the encouragement and support he needed to make an impact with major ITN projects.

'I used to be accused of wanting to take over ITV current affairs: I never did. In ITV there was news, and each of the major companies had its own current affairs and/or documentary department. Sidney Bernstein is quoted as saying there are two kinds of journalism: the journalism of protest and the journalism of the Establishment. And Geoffrey Cox used to say to me, "No, David. There's another form of journalism. When I was chief intelligence officer to General Freyberg, my job was to tell him all I could find out, using the best professional means, about the disposition of the enemy, and then it was for *him* to make his mind up. And that's what our job is: to put the best-quality information before the public and let *them* make their minds up." In other words, "We report: you decide." A very good maxim for broadcasting news.

'I remember saying once at some sort of news editors' conference or something – this was outrageous, now I look back on it – I said: "If we find out that they are throwing firstborn girl children into the Thames at Teddington, our job is not to say whether we approve or not but to get pictures, and the sound of the splash!"' But this attachment to hard news did not preclude special news events programmes, of which David Nicholas became the supreme exponent.

ITN's coverage of general-election-night programmes had begun modestly in 1959. Because Robin Day and Ludovic Kennedy had decided to stand as candidates – both for the Liberal Party – ITN could only offer Ian Trethowan as an on-air presenter who knew something about politics. In addition, in those early days, ITN was not equipped or experienced enough to pull the new ITV network together for such a big occasion as general election night – although it contributed what it could. The programme was therefore not an ITN production but came from Rediffusion's studio nine in the basement at Kingsway. By comparison with the BBC show, presented by Richard Dimbleby and overseen by the remarkable Grace Wyndham Goldie, it was not very good. As Geoffrey Cox reported to his board:

> The election night programme can be regarded as only partially successful. Our interpretation of the results was slower and less effective than that of the BBC . . . This was, however, the first time that independent television has mounted this particular operation as against the fourth time for the BBC. We were working with limited resources and personnel, since the two main current affairs personalities of independent television, Kennedy and Day, were out of action, and William Clarke, one of the few men in our ranks with a knowledge of the complexities of elections, was in America. As a result, we had to go into the contest largely with a team

which had already been working flat out on the arduous day by day reporting of the election.[1]

In 1964, election night was again an ITV production, but this time the programme's presenter, Alastair Burnet, was for the first time able to demonstrate his phenomenal mastery of political facts and figures, the background material that was so essential to understanding what was going on, and so valuable a resource when nothing much was happening.

But Nicholas was determined that ITN should not just contribute men and material, but take over the whole show. If ITN was good enough to cover the election campaign it should not have to bow out on election night. 'I passionately believed,' he says, 'that if we were going to play all the league matches then we'd got to play in the final as well – not hand over to other people as News did at the BBC. There, Current Affairs were the sahibs and the News people were the sepoys. I didn't want ITV to take it all away from ITN like that on the big night.'

Given the tiny majority by which Labour won in 1964 it was obvious that another general election could not be long delayed. To find out how an election-night programme might be improved, Geoffrey Cox sent Nicholas to observe the way the American networks covered their presidential election in November that year – the battle between Johnson and Goldwater. Now better prepared, ITN was, in 1966, given responsibility for the election-night programme, and Nicholas was appointed its producer. This was a role he was to keep a grip on right up to and including the 1987 general election, when he was editor of ITN, and one in which he always excelled.

Nicholas was lucky to have at his side on most of these election nights his Welsh compatriot, that most talented of studio directors, Diana Edwards-Jones. A founder member of ITN, Edwards-Jones had become a studio director in 1961. 'ITN was in the shit because everyone had gone to Israel to cover the Eichman trial,' she says. 'That's when I got my chance.' She was first asked to direct an election-night results programme in 1974. Being in charge of a programme with so many elements – scores of outside broadcasts from individual constituencies and party headquarters, studio interviews and discussions, graphics to convey the results as fast as they come in – is the most demanding of assignments. Edwards-Jones recalls a system that, by today's standards, was still technically primitive. Graphics were essentially figures and letters stuck on cardboard and put in front of a locked-off studio camera.

Whoever was giving the results read the figures off a transmission monitor. In 1974 the reader was Andrew Gardner, who had difficulty pronouncing the Welsh constituency name of Bedwellty. Simultaneously, Welsh patriots Nicholas and Edwards-Jones, listening in the studio gallery, pressed their communication keys to put him right. A foot pedal allowed Diana to speak to all directors of outside broadcasts round the country; a large red button in front of her included all the reporter/presenters in each of those far-flung locations. David Nicholas, as producer, had his own channel through which he could speak to the front-men, to alert them to a significant result elsewhere or ensure that they put a particular question to a winner or loser.

Diana Edwards-Jones's skill lay in plucking the most significant action – the exact moment of a declaration, for example – from the potentially over-whelming flood of information poised to pour in. Not every source could have its own direct line to ITN, its own television monitor in the gallery or its own videotape recording machine. As director, she had to decide second by second, on the basis of what she was hearing, rather than seeing, not only which source to put on air but which to record, and where, for playing in later. Her style was decisive, her language colourful. As her rehearsal began in typical chaos on the afternoon of election day she told the television teams up and down the land, 'Listen here, this is a rehearsal, not a f—g tea party,' and so she continued through the night. The following year the Royal Television Society quite rightly gave its award for 'outstanding creative achievement behind the camera' to Diana Edwards-Jones for her direction of the February 1974 election-night programme.

What had ended so successfully had been a fraught affair. Alastair Burnet, who had presented previous election programmes on ITV had temporarily defected to the BBC, and the brilliant but temperamental Robert Kee had been hired in his place. Since this was the first time he had ever done this particular job Kee was very nervous. At the full dress rehearsal of the programme on the Sunday before election night, some of the potted biographies of the candidates came up on his teleprompter in capital letters – notoriously harder to read than lower case. Suddenly, with television journalists and technicians around the country watching, Kee exploded. His editor Nigel Ryan, he raged, had promised him the best producers, but instead he was surrounded by incompetent hacks. So saying, he stormed out of the building.

As programme producer, David Nicholas was understandably affronted and told his editor he could no longer work with Kee. Says Ryan: 'At first David would not even speak to me, and I spent the next forty-eight hours in knife-edge shuttle diplomacy. As a last throw I told Robert that ITN would survive if he turned his back, but that he would never forgive himself. An hour or so later, I got a curt telephone call to say he had changed his mind. It is an undying tribute to the professionalism and big character of David Nicholas that he too agreed to continue, and that between them they produced such a good programme.'

The results programme for the second election in 1974, in October, suggested that ITN's election-night coverage was now on a par with the BBC's. *Broadcast* preferred it, calling it 'compact and bright' when compared with the BBC's more ponderous production. For the first time, ITN's editor told his board, ITV's figures showed that the audience was equally split. At the beginning of ITN's *The Nation Decides*, at 10 p.m., 5.8 million homes were tuned to ITV, 5.0 million to the BBC. ITN could claim to have been ahead on the declaration of 527 results, and by close-down at 4 a.m. on Friday had correctly predicted an overall majority of three seats.[2]

David Nicholas was largely responsible for ITN's growing success with these big news events. His enthusiasm was infectious and irresistible, and his relish for new ways of doing things a real challenge to production techniques that the BBC had developed. They might have Professor Bob Mackenzie and his 'Swingometer', but ITN discovered VT 30.

At the height of the first of the 1974 election-night programmes Nicholas had picked up the phone from the studio gallery and yelled down the line to the wretched academic in the studio, whose job was to explain what the onrush of election results from around the country really added up to: 'For Christ's sake, tell me who's winning!' Nicholas demanded politely. 'I can't tell you that,' replied the harassed psephologist, 'I can only tell you who isn't losing.' It was at that point, says Nicholas, that he determined that some mechanical calculating device must be an improvement on any pundit: 'I swore then,' says Nicholas, 'that we would somehow have computer graphics.'

It was Paul McKee, then working for ITN as a computer consultant, who came up with VT 30. This was a machine originally developed to allow designers of Fair Isle jumpers to see what their elaborate patterns would look like before anybody went to the trouble of knitting them. For previous general-election programmes ITN had stored masses of useful information about constituencies and their voting patterns. But on the night, it always took too long to retrieve it for it to be of any use. VT 30, on the other hand, adapted by ITN's enterprising engineers, could show graphically, with columns that rose and fell, exactly what was happening to the vote, wherever and whenever you wanted to look. Says Nicholas: 'You could see the pattern emerging – exactly like a Fair Isle jersey. VT 30 alerted us to good stories, trends that we might otherwise have missed. It was a newsmaker in itself – and it was more truly journalistic than any professor. It was so good that the American networks adopted it, and the BBC pinched Peter Snow off us just to break up our election graphics team.'

CHAPTER 17

TUSSLE AT THE TOP

When *News at Ten* went on the air in the summer of 1967 Sir Geoffrey Cox, as he now was, had been editor of ITN for eleven years. He had worked extremely hard in a senior position for relatively little financial reward. ITN was not a broadcaster, merely a supplier of news; so while many programme-company bosses had grown rich from what had at last turned out to be 'a licence to print money', he had not. With a franchise round coming up he decided that he would join one of the consortiums bidding for a regional broadcasting licence. Today he is frank about his motivation: 'It was a desire to make a decent sum of money,' he says. 'In those days a capital gain that I might make from shares in a successful bid was the only way I could hope to do that. Huw Thomas, who had for a time been a very well-known ITN newscaster, called me and said, "I'm advising a syndicate bidding for the Yorkshire contract, and I'm looking for as big a name as possible to join their consortium. Can you suggest someone?" And I said, "I'll do it." I thought it was time to try to make some money.'

The consortium Sir Geoffrey joined was successful, so even before the *News at Ten* started he had announced that he would be leaving in August the following year to become deputy chairman of Yorkshire Television. 'The new editor will be selected in the spring of 1968,' he told his staff. 'He will be chosen by the board, and under the terms of the Television Act his selection is subject to the approval of the ITA. He will be selected as someone who will maintain to the full the traditions and character of ITN as these have been developed by the efforts of all members of the staff over the past twelve years.'[1]

It seemed logical to many that David Nicholas should be appointed editor in Cox's place; he had, after all, held the post of deputy editor since September 1964. But there was, especially for Nicholas, though he did not know it at the time, a most unexpected obstacle: Cox himself. He had privately decided that although he was determined to see an ITN insider become editor his vote would go not to Nicholas but to his third in command, Nigel Ryan. 'It sounds as if I'm callous to my deputy,' says Cox, 'but Nigel was to my mind the chap to have it at that stage. David wasn't quite ready for it then. But the fact is the choice wasn't between David and Nigel, the choice was between David and Nigel, and Charles Wintour, the editor of the London *Evening Standard*.

'I was able to fight the idea of Wintour because I heard about it early. I was at a lunch at the Mansion House, and Hugh Cudlipp, who was then a director of ATV but still a big shot in newspapers, said to me, "Geoffrey, you're very lucky with your new editor, Charles Wintour." I said, "Who?" and he said, "Charles Wintour". And I said, "Oh, this is the first news I've had of this." I came back and I rang up Robert Fraser at the ITA and said, "This is what I've just heard," and Fraser said, "We've got to stop that." But Wintour had very powerful backers. ATV were entirely on his side, and so was Rediffusion. And they all felt, "This is a jolly good idea, you've got this man, a great man." I knew two things. The first was it's one thing to have newspaper flair, and second, we could not, ten years after television had come on the air, say we haven't got enough good people of our own, we've got to turn to Fleet Street.

'It was not advertised, but a committee was set up to make a selection, and we met at the ITA to interview these various people. Michael Peacock [managing director of LWT] was on this committee and when I turned up for the first meeting, he moved that I should be taken off the committee. He said, "I don't say this out of any dislike of Geoffrey, I know him well, but as a matter of principle no man giving up a job should sit on the committee appointing his successor." And I said, "Yes, as a matter of principle, but the fact is that that happens in places where a lot of people know what is required. But in this particular case, how does anybody know except me and two or three other people what you need as the editor of ITN?"

'David Nicholas was interviewed. He had all the qualities for the job but they were looking for somebody, quite rightly, with flair and Nigel had flair. David didn't display it at that time, though by God he did later. Nigel made a good impression but Wintour interviewed brilliantly. He talked a lot of stuff about bringing the arts into the news and so on which I knew to be absolute gobbledegook. He was obviously the strong candidate, but we were deadlocked. Then we adjourned, thank God. My bladder required that, and not only mine. I found myself peeing next to David Wilson [representing the smaller regional companies] and I decided the time had come to play dirty. I said to Wilson, "David, you've been a soldier and I've been a soldier. You've been at the sharp end of things, but this fellow Wintour has never been anything but a staff officer, and a staff officer in London what's more, and you can't have a man like that put over chaps who've been in the front line at ITN for ten years!" And David had been through hell as a soldier, and he said, "Geoffrey, you're right, we can't have that," and we went back into the meeting and the decision went to Nigel.'

This was a bitter moment for David Nicholas. Not only had he lost out to his junior colleague at ITN but the editor he had loyally served had not supported him. In general, ITN felt that Nicholas had been shabbily treated.

In the newsroom, as the decision about the new editor drew near, bets had been chalked on the board used to display the time at which different film consignments were expected to arrive. The odds on David Nicholas had stood at 2/1, and only at the end of a long list had Nigel Ryan's name been listed – as a real outsider. 'I came in on the morning after the announcement had been made,' says David Phillips, then a sub-editor, 'and the place was like a morgue. David Nicholas not getting the job was like Rab Butler not getting the leadership of the Tory Party after Macmillan. People were stunned, and David was sitting in his office as though he'd been sandbagged. I got a call to go and see Geoffrey Cox who told me, poker-faced, that he wanted me to produce the *News at Ten* that night – the first time I'd ever done so. I looked at him and thought, Shall I make a comment? and then, No, just shut up. But my real feeling was, Are we going to have a bulletin at all? because there was complete paralysis. I remember we took David Nicholas out to lunch to try and give him a lift.'

As Nicholas now recalls: 'I have to say it was a terrific blow for a while. But it was the right appointment. I have absolutely no doubt about that. And Nigel and I were very close chums, and we talk a lot to this day. I *did* think of quitting, I've never told this to anybody else before, I did think of quitting. And I did sound out some American networks and stuff like that. But I was not ready for the job – for sure! I think I was a good news operator as an executive, but for that sort of higher level of executive boardroom savvy, I was definitely not ready. So Geoffrey was right.'

'It was very difficult,' says Cox, 'because David was dismayed and the staff were dismayed, and Nigel was worried because he had to come in and take charge of a staff that were very, very resentful. All I could do for David was to say, 'I can't change it, and I beg you, in the interests of ITN, to stay with us.' And David was big enough to stay. And of course in the end he got his reward. He got the editorship and he got a knighthood, and he deserved it.'

Nicholas now insists: 'It was the right appointment – and it was also the making of me, frankly. When Nigel left, ten years later, I think I was ready for the job. And it strengthened me in another way too. I've had to make appointments in which people get disappointed. And I'm always able to talk to them and say, "I know what it's like." And where there's two or three people running for a job and you've made your choice, it's a heartbreak. I've had to make some painful ones like that, it goes with the territory. And I always took the view when I turned somebody down – assuming he was a serious candidate – that when he goes out of the door I've got to say something so that his head is high, something he can say to his wife. So that disappointment I had strengthened me in being able to make executive decisions of that nature in the future.'

David Nicholas had to wait almost a decade before Nigel Ryan accepted an offer from an American television network and he had another chance to become editor of ITN. By then, Cox had explained to him what had happened the first time round but, not surprisingly, Nicholas remained suspicious of what would happen this time. As Cox puts it: 'I was sitting on the ITN board as the Tyne Tees representative and David confided in somebody, "Well, Geoffrey will be against me." And I wasn't, of course. I weighed in hard. But at bottom David had a slight distrust of me, because he thought I'd let him down to a point . . . but it's all under the bridge now."

CHAPTER 18
AN EDITOR WITH STYLE

'Mr Ryan is a jolly, highly-eligible bachelor, the eldest of three brothers and the son of an Irish Brigadier,' said the Londoners' Diary of the *Evening Standard*, in covering the appointment of ITN's new editor. Ryan was tall, youthful (just thirty-eight), elegant, and wore the sort of striped suits a Guards officer in civvies might wear as he strolled down Pall Mall to visit his bootmaker in St James's. Although he had a quirky sense of humour, 'jolly' was not quite the right word for him. He was nervous, even twitchy, and his accent, after Cox's New Zealand twang, had a strangulated, distinctly upmarket tone. Different in style and mannerism though he was, he justified Cox's faith in him and proved himself a worthy successor.

After leaving Oxford, where he had been at Queen's College, Ryan spent a year 'bumbling around', as he puts it, before going to work in advertising. But, with fluent French and Spanish, it wasn't long before he had joined Reuters and been sent to Africa, right at the moment when colonial empires there began to crack and crumble. In the Congo he came across Robin Day, who was now working for *Panorama*. Day, a visiting 'fireman' paying a fleeting visit to this foreign part for the first time, needed help from the news agency man on the spot. 'Do you know this fellow Lulumba?' asked Day, (he meant Lumumba, the prime minister). Ryan was happy to be of assistance, and mightily impressed

Day with his local knowledge. The next time they met their situation was reversed.

Several months later, back in London and on the look-out for a new job, Ryan spotted Day in his bow-tie having dinner with someone he did not recognise. When he went over to them Day responded warmly: 'My dear fellow, what an amazing coincidence.' He introduced his dinner companion as Geoffrey Cox. 'I've just been talking to Geoffrey about you,' said Day. 'Would you like to work in television?' said Cox. 'Come and see me tomorrow afternoon.'

Next day Ryan reported to Lime Grove, where Robin Day worked for *Panorama*, and explained he had come by appointment to meet the editor Paul Fox. Met with blank looks he phoned Robin Day. 'Not *Fox*, you fool, it's *Cox*, the editor of ITN,' came the reply. Assuming he had now blown his chances, Ryan hastened across London to ITN's headquarters in Kingsway, where he was relieved and delighted to hear Cox offer him a job. At the editor's suggestion, Ryan rang Reginald Bosanquet at home to find out a bit more about ITN and the man he would be working for, but now there was further verbal confusion: Bosanquet was notorious for his eccentric pronunciation. When Ryan asked him about the kind of leader Geoffrey Cox was he was delighted to be told, 'He's a great warrior.' Only later did he discover Bosanquet had intended to say, 'He's a great worrier.'

Ryan joined ITN in 1961, but two years later he took a year off to work with James Mossman, one of the *Panorama* team who had decided to set up the independent company Television Reporters International. When that enterprise ran its course – the ITV network was unwilling to take TRI's programmes – Ryan returned to ITN. Moving swiftly up the chain of command, he was appointed editor in 1968.

Ryan had leapfrogged David Nicholas, who was almost exactly the same age as he was. But he discovered that there was a catch. Aidan Crawley and Geoffrey Cox had set much store by being not merely editor of ITN, but chief executive too. But now that ITN's budget and programmes had grown, it had been decided to appoint a managing director, who would be senior to the editor. Cox had originally argued against this idea to the ITN board: 'Power should be where responsibility for the product lies – with an editor-in-chief . . . To put over him, and over the general manager, a managing director would be to create a post for which no real function exists.' What of the argument that having a managing director was the best way of controlling costs on behalf of the companies? Cox pointed to the American experience, where the networks had only one man in charge, an editor manager: 'This American system is a system which has worked successfully with ITN – not least in keeping costs below those of other news organisations. To change fundamentally a system which works well seems to me to take quite an unnecessary risk with future costs and future quality.'[1]

But when it looked as though his candidate Ryan would lose out when it came to the choice of a new editor on the grounds of inexperience, Cox had hastily changed his tune. Before Nigel Ryan was appointed editor of ITN it was announced that Donald Edwards, a former editor of News and Current Affairs at the BBC, had been given the top job. 'Yes, I did support the idea of having a managing director at that point,' says Cox. 'I backed the idea of Nigel and Donald Edwards as a way of beating Wintour. But I think Edwards regarded us as a bunch of suckers. Really, he was being paid to do nothing.'

Says Ryan: 'I had understood that they were going to put in a managing director on a temporary basis. I was told that, if I got the editor's job it would be up to me to show that I didn't need a chief executive above me.' And indeed, after three years, when Edwards's contract was up in 1971, Ryan was confirmed as both editor and chief executive of ITN.

Sensibly, given the early hostility within ITN to his appointment as editor, Ryan decided to let his defeated deputy, Nicholas, play a major role in running the ITN news operation while he concentrated on strategy. 'My greatest achievement was getting David to stay on at ITN. To make *News at Ten* fly properly it needed someone who really knew the nuts and bolts of the operation very well. So I took every morning meeting, and the "look ahead" and evening conference while David ran the machine. I thought *my* job was to organise the shape of programmes, and get the style right.'

Geoffrey Cox had been concerned lest the man he had argued for might not be able to overcome internal opposition to his appointment. 'I was worried about Nigel. I thought that he mightn't carry the staff with him. But in fact what he did was very skilful. He struck up a rapport with David and he gave David a hand, and Nigel represented ITN to the ITA and the public outside, and of course he did this very well. David came to me, after about a year, and said, "You know, this chap's bloody good, this chap Nigel Ryan."'

Ryan's particular skill was indeed in establishing good relationships with important people in the companies and at the ITA. 'I realised that what Nigel did was to get the money,' says Cox. 'I think that Robert Fraser[2] [ITA director general] was very taken with him. He regarded him as the son he'd never had, and he was prepared to back him. So Nigel could get money out of the companies through him.

'When Aidan Crawley went he left me a very handsome letter in which he told me never to trust the Authority. "Never go to the Authority for anything," he said, and I never did – until I wanted to get *News at Ten*. I always felt that if I'd done that the companies would have felt that I was going behind their backs, and they wouldn't have trusted me. But they didn't feel that with Nigel. They felt that Nigel was a lad who needed a bit of ITA protection. By this time the companies were very well established, they had lots of money, and the outcome of this, of course, was that because Fraser backed Nigel, they did give ITN lots of money. Nigel got much bigger budgets through the ITN board than I could have done. And as a result David Nicholas once said to me, "Well, Nigel gets us some money." He didn't say, "He needs me to spend it properly," but he did.'

'It was the duty of ITN's editor to decide each month by how much he should exceed the budget.' Nigel Ryan sums up with conscious irony what many of the ITN board were convinced was secretly his own conviction. It was certainly his excellent relationship with the Authority that helped him persuade the companies to swallow their medicine.

As David Nicholas puts it: 'I once said to Nigel, "When I was a kid my mother said if you had to take cough mixture or whatever, there's a glass there and you have to put hot water in. But if you put a spoon in first, the hot water won't crack the glass." And I said, "The IBA's[3] the spoon – it stops the glass cracking!"'

Ryan needed all the help he could get to push through the increases in the ITN budget that he was sure were needed. 'Being first is an expensive and often wasteful business,' he told his board, 'but it is the lifeblood for a good news organisation. We need to be able to take more long shots.' He pointed out that ITN had not sent a crew to Hong Kong to wait there for permission to enter China. The BBC had done that and had eventually got

in. ITN had not sent anyone to Chile when Allende came to power as the
leader of the first democratically elected Marxist government, and had not
had the resources to investigate allegations of Communist conspiracy at
Ford's Dagenham works. 'The result of our economic approach is that
instead of going out and gathering this sort of news, ITN is often forced to
react to news developments collected by other media. We need to have on
our staff one or two people of calibre to keep track of what is really going
on behind the scenes. . . This would reinforce the authority of the
programme which, at times, is in danger of becoming good television but
divorced from the reality it is there to report.'[4]

Ryan's demands meant an increase in the budget for 1971–72 to
£3,298,000 – a hefty rise of 13.7 per cent on the estimated costs for the
previous year. When the board next met,[5] the IBA representative Brian
Young urged the directors to 'respond positively' to Ryan's proposals, but
they decided to set up a sub-committee to scrutinise the figures. The
following month[6] Aidan Crawley, returning briefly to ITN as a director of
LWT, pointed out that ITN's proposed budget was now ten times larger
than it had been when he was editor. In his view it was not ITN's main job
to be first with the news, and he thought that some of the stories ITN had
missed did not matter. Norman Collins said he hoped it would not be
assumed that ITN's expenditure would always go up. But Sir Robert Fraser
told the board firmly that he endorsed the budget. 'Finally it was unanimously agreed that the budget should be accepted.' Such, then, was the
power, or at least the influence, of the television regulator.

And that was usually the way it was for many years to come. The editor
asked for more, the companies grumbled but, urged on by the Authority,
eventually paid up.

In a chapter drafted by Nigel Ryan, the official history of Independent
Television sums up the improvement in ITN's fortunes that had occurred
under his aegis: 'In 1968 staff numbered 278 and there was an operating
budget of £2 million; ten years later staff numbers had risen to 511 and the
budget to £10 million. Costs had increased threefold through inflation,
ITV's advertising revenue fourfold, and ITN's budget fivefold.'[7]

News at Ten had begun with ideas of offering background features and
live interviews as well as news stories. The mix had not worked well, and
within days the programme had become pretty much a longer, though

much more effective, version of the bulletins of earlier years. All the talk of including more background and analytical pieces had not come to much; indeed, Nigel Ryan felt that, if anything, things were moving in the other direction. The pressure to include more and more 'hard news', he told the ITN board, was growing:

> This is due mainly to the advances made in communications since 1967. Newly launched satellites now link Europe to all the other continents except Africa; Eurovision has spread its tentacles into North Africa, Portugal and Greece; links with the Communist bloc through Eurovision have strengthened; airlines have speeded up: telex and telephones and radio circuits have been modernised. The total effect has been a vast increase in the total bulk of daily news available to report. *News at Ten* is increasingly a vehicle for this extra quantity of material . . .
>
> For this reason it would be hard to increase significantly the 'in depth' element in *News at Ten* at the expense of the 'hard news' element; put another way, to lessen the number of items carried when the pressure is to increase it.[8]

Ryan was concerned, now that *Dateline* and *Roving Report* had gone, that there was nowhere else in ITN's output where the news could be presented in a more than superficial way. Initially he proposed a new weekly Sunday-evening programme, or even an extension of *News at Ten*, but soon he was agitating for a serious lunchtime news.

His case was strengthened in November 1971 when Christopher Chataway, ITN's first newscaster and now Conservative minister for posts and telecommunications, halved the levies that the ITV companies were paying to the Government, reducing them from £20million to £10million a year. These reductions, he said, '. . . are designed to enable the companies to improve the quality of their programmes and those of Independent Television News.'[9] When in January the following year Chataway removed controls on broadcasting hours Ryan redoubled his efforts to get more airtime for ITN. In April 1972 he told the network: 'Our first preference remains for a half-hour programme each day at 1 o'clock. This would have the advantage of providing a good and easily remembered title (*News at One*), a traditionally important start time for news, a reasonable amount of time for preparation, and a chance to take on the radio programme – *The World At One*.'[10]

The ITV companies wanted a twelve noon start to get the news out of the way and allow them to ring up the curtain early on their afternoon entertainment programmes. Ryan felt that this would not attract the politicians and other 'opinion-formers', who at present listened to *The World At One* – it was too early in the day.

'I remember a stand-up fight,' Ryan says, 'with Donald Baverstock of Yorkshire Television, who was in charge of ITV's daytime scheduling. Donald was a cold-war warrior from the BBC in the days when News and Current Affairs there were in deadly competition with each other; once in ITV his hostility to ITN seemed to be visceral. It was important to ITN that its new programme should not be buried alive, particularly as it was launching a new way of presenting news, and we did not want to lose both the audience and the experiment. I remember appealing to the ITA and declaring it a resignation matter.'

Giving its support to ITN, the ITA said it would not approve any of the ITV autumn schedule unless it included a lunchtime news starting after twelve thirty p.m. and running for at least twenty minutes. Grudgingly, the companies acquiesced, and agreed to a twelve forty start. A twenty-minute weekday lunchtime news from ITN would begin in early October 1972. The ITN board approved an annual budget of £330,000. But who was to be in charge of the new programme?

Barrie Sales had been a serious player at the BBC. In the running for the editor's chair at *Panorama* in 1968 he had lost out to ITN's Brian Wenham. As Wenham headed west for Lime Grove and the BBC, Nigel Ryan picked up the phone to Sales and asked him to make the reverse journey to become producer of ITN's *News at Ten*. It was a straight swap with Wenham that did them both good.

When in 1972 *First Report* was given the go-ahead, Sales applied to run it: 'It was all about serious programming in the new daytime hours, but – very like *News at Ten* – the programme companies didn't believe in it. I thought about it and went to Nigel and volunteered to do it. I took everyone by surprise. They couldn't understand why I would give up *News at Ten*. But I saw the potential. I immediately thought of competing with *The World at One* and William Hardcastle on BBC Radio.

The BBC scarcely had a lunchtime *television* news at all – it was a desert – and I thought this new ITN programme was a chance to set the agenda for the day. I saw it as a branch of the ITN tree. I didn't want it to be divisive, setting one ITN programme against another in the way that often happened between BBC programmes at Lime Grove. *First Report* had a corner in a sort of alcove in the main newsroom and I wanted us to remain part of a family, but I did want it to be distinctive. I deliberately called the subs "item editors", because they were going to be stirring things up more than just writing. The fact was that you couldn't have produced a traditional news bulletin at that time of day because there were no pictures in yet: it was just too early, so it had to be "live". The regions could initially make very few contributions – they simply weren't up and running at that time of the day.

'Editing *News at Ten* is a subbing job – you're cutting stuff out or down – but most mornings on *First Report* you had nothing to sub. But I was used to bashing phones to get stories. Nigel had never really thought about the content. In his mind it was just going to be news headlines plus the big interview. I thought that would be boring, but I did it like *News at Ten* with several stories, not many pictures, because there weren't many available, but several live interviews.'

The newscaster for this programme would have to be exceptionally talented. He would not only be reading the news headlines but interviewing national figures live on a wide range of topics. Nigel Ryan persuaded Robert Kee to take on this demanding role.

'I was at the Fountainebleu Hotel in Miami,' says Barrie Sales, 'when I was offered the *First Report* job. When I got back, Nigel told me that Kee was available. I didn't think about anybody else.'

Robert Kee was a distinguished journalist. Like ITN's first editor Aidan Crawley, he had been a Second World War pilot and prisoner of war. He was a man of great intelligence and wide interests who had worked equally successfully as a reporter for the great popular weekly *Picture Post* and as literary editor for the *New Statesman*. Moving into television he had been for many years one of the celebrated team of reporters on BBCs *Panorama*, doggedly dragging the truth into the light however deep he had to dig for it. He was quite a catch. 'You're risking your reputation for not much money,' Nigel Ryan told him.

Says Sales: 'The risks for Robert Kee on *First Report* were even greater than they were for me. We'd be juggling the running order all the time; it was much hairier than *News at Ten*. But Robert was nerveless.' Says Kee: 'It was because it was hairy that it was fun. Almost every day we'd discover that there was no news at all. We had to go and find it. Barrie Sales used to keep a car ready at Westminster until about eleven thirty a.m., and if there was really no news he'd grab an MP and drag him into the studio for me to interview.'

The first programme did not go well. The minutes record Nigel Ryan as telling the board that there had been an outside broadcast failure. Nevertheless, 'From the trial programmes it was obvious that the key to its success was the use of live material, including the OB unit, and of live injects from the regional companies; he was also placing emphasis on girl reporters.'

First Report did give a chance to 'girl reporters'. First came Carol Barnes and Joan Thirkettle, and later Sue Lloyd-Roberts and Sarah Cullen. These last two were both 'item editors' trying to get out of the office and start reporting. As Lloyd-Roberts recalls, *First Report* would give one of them a ring at home when they were off duty: 'Sue? Are you free? If not, don't worry, we'll call Sarah'; and, of course, they would try it the other way round. As a result, the two women ended up working enthusiastically as reporters on their days off, and appearing on air at least as often as 'proper' reporters.

First Report aimed to seize the news initiative. Says Sales: 'I knew that our audience was women and the unemployed, but the opinion-formers had a TV set in their offices. We soon had no difficulty in getting people in – or on the screen via our mobile OB unit. We did well with material in Northern Ireland and abroad. Robert Kee was invaluable to us because he was very knowledgeable indeed about Northern Ireland. It was a political decade – the Heath government, industrial strikes, prices and incomes stories, inflation. We could set the agenda and the *Evening Standard* would pick it up.'

The format seemed to work. By January 1973 ITN's chairman, Sir Robert Fraser, could tell the annual general meeting that in the first three months *First Report*'s audience had grown from 1 million to 1.5 million homes. 'By using *First Report*'s Outside Broadcast camera unit,' said Fraser, 'the news presenter is also able to interview the public on the spot, and the public is increasingly able to express its own attitudes in return. And housewives have become accustomed to watching *First Report* for the weekly survey of food prices . . . It would not be immoderate,' he concluded, 'to say that the programme has been a true success.'[11]

As ITN's editor, Nigel Ryan, reported to his board in the same happy vein: 'Ratings apart, the programme is acquiring a prestige and an impact of its own. With the full blessing of the Downing Street press office, the word has gone out in Whitehall and through the House of Commons that it is a programme to appear on if possible. Recently Mr [Robert] Carr came out of a Cabinet meeting to make a statement on inflation in *First Report*. Both Ray Buckton and Clive Jenkins have said they consider *First Report* has superseded *The World at One*.'

Some viewers complained about Robert Kee's obviously spontaneous and unscripted interjections. Nigel Ryan recalls him commenting on a story involving President Nixon, 'Tricky Dicky strikes again!' Today Robert Kee says: 'I remember being ticked off by Nigel Ryan for my ad-libs: I think I was probably a looser cannon than I realised at the time.'

'I do wish Robert Kee would keep his remarks to himself,' wrote one correspondent. 'Surely he is there to report on the news and not to furnish us with his own news.'[12] From the Authority, now the IBA, David Glencross wrote to Nigel Ryan asking for his comments on what Kee was up to. Ryan sent a rather smug, lordly reply. While of course ITN's policy was not to permit its programmes to be used for the expression of newscasters' personal opinions,

> At the same time, the special business of setting the news in its context and pointing up its relevance has sometimes given rise to controversy, especially amongst viewers who place a different interpretation on the significant of events to our own. This is very much the area in which *First Report* specialises. It is an experimental programme, and occasionally may, therefore, make a false step. However, it is my judgement that in the main it is a highly successful experiment, and Robert Kee's own contribution to it is immeasurable. The programme's aim is to elucidate and to humanise, not to editorialise – to analyse rather than to comment. Clearly the line between these two is sometimes a narrow one but we feel that in the main we keep to the right side of it.[13]

Having made their point, the IBA decided to back off rather than up the ante.

'All of us here,' wrote David Glencross, 'would agree that *First Report* has extended the range of television news presentation and makes an important contribution to ITN's news service as a whole. We also recognise that Robert Kee is an important element in this new development. On those occasions when we have had reservations about some of the off-the-cuff comments I feel sure that you and your colleagues have on the whole shared our views.'[14]

First Report's initial success continued, and in October 1974 the programme moved to one p.m., the start time Ryan had originally asked for. He told the board that this should '. . . further promote the by now thoroughly tried formula for producing news with an element of evaluation and examination, but without injecting opinion or abandoning impartiality.'[15]

In 1976 Ryan finally got his preferred title – *News at One*. In that year, duty more than adequately done, Robert Kee left the programme and Leonard Parkin, another former *Panorama* person, took over. ITN reporter Peter Sissons followed as presenter in 1978.

By 1979 *News at One*'s audience was 3.4 million. It had been a remarkable success. 'Without doubt,' says Ryan today, 'the reason for moving *First Report* to one o'clock was its success, both in ratings and in esteem. It had, consistently, a gratifyingly good press as ITN's answer to the BBC's *World at One*. I'm more proud of *First Report* than of almost anything else I did as editor. *Newsnight, Channel 4 News* – both look back to *First Report* as the moment when newscasters took the story further.'

With *News at One* Nigel Ryan got the news extended into new areas, with extra time to go into the detail of what it was reporting, but he had always hankered after a weekly programme, perhaps on Sunday, which would take the big news story of the week and analyse it thoroughly. In a memorandum to the Authority and programme companies, he wrote:

> Today there is an important and unfilled gap in ITV's weekly programming. There is no single programme devoted to the considered evaluation of the main issue of the week, undertaken with clarity and impartiality in such a way as to inform the viewer of the ingredients in the case, but leaving him free to make up his own mind about it. This is the gap which ITN would like to fill, and feels uniquely qualified to fill.

In America Ryan had seen that the people who did the news – CBS, ABC, NBC – did the current affairs too. It seemed to him to make sense that ITN, the company with the technical resources and the journalists familiar with doing things quickly, should make more use of its resources than news bulletins alone – even ones like *First Report* – could do. This was how he set out his stall:

> ITN's business is news, and the programme envisaged would not only handle news, but would make it as well. By live discussion and reaction, by special film contributions, by bringing the story right up to date it would itself become part of the news . . . Whether it is a question of handling an actively moving event requiring instant evaluation – such as the near disaster of Apollo XIII – or of quickly pulling together a mixture of recent newsfilm and studio material, recorded or live – as in the case of the assassination of Robert Kennedy or the sudden resignation of President Johnson – no company can match ITN's technical experience and equipment; and no company can deliver the goods more cheaply. The material is flowing constantly into the building, and the basic staff is there: it is a question, in part, of simply putting them to this further use.[16]

Today Ryan is adamant that all he wanted to do was break down what he saw as a meaningless barrier between news and current affairs, and he certainly never wanted to stray, for example, into the troublemaking territory of Granada's *World in Action*. His point was that the companies' current-affairs programmes could not be relied on to deal with the week's top news story. They might just as likely choose any one of a number of interesting issues and make a film about it. But although Ryan might insist that all he wanted to do was tackle the top news story in depth, in a straightforward way, and that he would stick strictly to the news agenda, his colleagues in the network didn't believe him. They saw his proposal as an assault on their territory.

At London Weekend Television Cyril Bennett, who had previously run Rediffusion's current affairs, including *This Week*, wrote in answer to Ryan, pointing out that there would be weeks in which there simply was no news story that would justify a half-hour programme. 'All current affairs programmes have had to face this problem. They provide for it by producing programmes on issues which have nothing to do with that week's news. If that is the area you want to get into, let us be clear what you are asking for – it is for ITN to take over the responsibility for all ITV's current affairs output.'[17]

Nigel Ryan tried again: 'ITN does not want limitless extra time. Nor is this a bid to take over current affairs in ITV. Let a thousand flowers bloom. We are asking for one extra programme: we need to have it.'[18]

It was not to be. While Ryan, with the help of the ITA heavy mob, got his *First Report* at lunchtime, his weekly round-up programme on ITV never materialised.

In the country at large the seventies were a difficult and unsettling time: inflation was taking off and, in its wake, as the government sought to impose wage restraint, industrial unrest. In 1974, with annual inflation running at around 17 per cent, ITN's eighty journalists decided to join their colleagues in the ITV regions and, for the first time, and in defiance of the dispute procedures, go on strike. Their stated aim was that their pay should match what their opposite numbers at the BBC were now getting – though catching up with their cameramen's earnings was their real objective. Clutching banners that read "Parity with BBC, not Charity with ITN", well-known newscasters and reporters stood on the picket line in solidarity with the newsroom subs, demanding a 30 per cent rise. 'No news was good news yesterday . . . for the profits down at the Green Man pub at least,' reported the *Daily Mail*. 'Those waiting their turn to carry the banners were providing landlady Mrs Judy Embleton with her best trade for months. The strike is about pay, "But they are all very good spenders," said Mrs Embleton, surveying her bar as the pints went down the ITN throats. "And they're such a nice, polite, charming lot."'[19]

With a general election looming, the strike instantly attracted the politicians' interest, and the prime minister, Harold Wilson, referred the dispute to the new Conciliation and Arbitration Service, ACAS. The strike was settled before election day,[20] but it had crippled news coverage on five of the thirteen campaign days. While the ITN board congratulated Nigel Ryan on the election results programme, 'The Editor expressed his disappointment that the ITN journalists had withdrawn their labour during an election campaign when ITN's role of impartially reporting events was of such importance.'[21]

The strike had been only partly about pay. Staff numbers had risen, the coverage budget had increased, but despite that, disaffection spread. A series of specials about the American presidential elections was cancelled after threats had been made by ITN's journalists to 'black' them. *Broadcast* reported: 'NUJ [National Union of Journalists] members claim they have been pressing the management for two or three years to introduce more "consultation" regarding ITN specials. They say they have been met with sweet noises but little action.'[22] Michael Green, ITN's industrial correspondent at the time, remembers a growing sense of malaise at ITN, a feeling that the place wasn't being well managed, that internal communications had suffered a breakdown. This feeling grew so strong that some of the senior reporters decided to act. According to Robert Hargreaves, 'During my time there was a little mutiny at ITN; I think there was a slight feeling that ITN was rather rudderless; that the captain had left the bridge.' Julian Havilland, ITN's political editor, was deputed to speak to the chairman, John Freeman, who gave him a rather dusty answer. However in the autumn of 1976 Nigel Ryan commissioned an investigation by John Pearson of the Industrial Society 'to look into working relationships at ITN.'

Pearson's 'strictly confidential' report, in April the following year, was distributed to managers and union representatives and uncovered considerable unrest within ITN:

> Twenty-four per cent of the comments and criticisms made to me were the absence of any form of constructive communication . . . In no way can an organisation in the front line of the communications business justify the extent of frustration that exists at all levels, with the most moderate people, because of a lack of involvement . . . My findings clearly indicate employee-management relationships at all levels are in need of overhaul. Had it not been for the fact that employees like working for ITN, and there is little where else to go, the situation would have deteriorated even further.

By way of remedy Pearson suggested setting up various committees designed to promote the exchange of information and ideas, better training and appraisal systems, and a clarification in the different chains of command. Introducing the report, which cannot have made pleasant

reading for him, Ryan undertook to consult managers and union representatives, and declared that: '. . . following these discussions the Management
will introduce any changes which it considers will improve the structure
and working relationships within ITN.'[23]

Later in 1977, the year in which Pearson reported, Nigel Ryan decided to
leave ITN and work in American television. He told Jean Rook of the *Daily
Express*:

> When I joined ITN, ten years ago, I was fired with enthusiasm, and
> brimming with new ideas. Recently, when I was working on the up-coming
> political conferences, and I thought about Blackpool and that frightful
> journey, and the awful hotels when you get there, I realised I just wasn't
> excited any more. And ITN's editor must be excited, and bursting with bright
> ideas and fresh thinking. When you start smoking, for the first time in all
> these years, like I've just done, you know you're stale, and it's time to quit.[24]

The *Daily Mail* saw more in Ryan's abrupt departure – he resigned while he
was away in America – than simple boredom:

> Behind his departure are the frustrations of a long-running squabble going
> back many years over ITN's place in the ITV family. Quite simply it has been
> a row between what Ryan has wanted ITN to do and what the ITV
> companies – who control the ITN budget and air time – would permit him
> to do . . . The jealously guarded preserves of each individual ITV docu-
> mentary and current affairs department have proved paramount . . . Ryan
> told me: 'We have earned the right to a weekly current affairs programme on
> the network. But the companies will not allow it. In America, current affairs
> and news are regarded as the same thing. I am going to America because I
> can do there what I always wanted ITN to do here.[25]

But as a vice president of NBC News in New York Ryan found that
American television had its own constraints. Within three years he was
back in Britain, as director of programmes at Thames Television.

John Freeman, the chairman of London Weekend Television, had also
chaired the ITN board for some of the time that Ryan was editor. He had a
high regard for him, though not for his expansionist plans. 'It's terribly

important not to underestimate what Nigel Ryan achieved; he made it professional and respected in a number of ways,' he says. 'ITN was one of the most valuable subsidiary interests which my company [LWT] owned, something we would have struggled to have gone without. The prestige of the system could be thought of like goodwill – and ITN was the lynchpin of that.'

But Freeman, like his colleagues in the rest of the network, thought that the proper study of Independent Television News was the news – no more: 'I held the view that the only way that ITN could survive was if it remained a nuts and bolts operation, without fancy points. I would never have supported an expansion of ITN's coverage into anything like current affairs. So there, I think, Nigel's ambition – though honourable – was mistaken.'

Nigel Ryan was unsuccessful in getting ITN to break down what he saw as an unnecessary barrier between news and current affairs, then advance across the border to seize new territory. But he added lustre to ITN's reputation and lucre to its budget; and, above all, he kept the programme that had become the main source of news for the people of Britain on the road. As he puts it: 'We believed that with *News at Ten* we had a magical opportunity. It was a Rolls-Royce. I didn't build it, but I didn't drive it into the ditch either.'

CHAPTER 19
OUT OF THIS WORLD

In 1961 Peter Fairley, a London *Evening Standard* reporter, had predicted the precise launch date of the rocket carrying the first man – Yuri Gagarin – into space. Fairley was interviewed on ITN's *Dateline* programme, soon became a fixture in ITN's studios, and was eventually appointed its science correspondent. It had been the toss of a coin that decided him on science rather than transport as the subject in which he was going to specialise, but it was the right choice. From the moment in 1957 that the Russians launched Sputnik 1, Fairley made himself a master of space science and technology.

Through the sixties, as the Americans invested heavily in catching up with the Russians, space became an increasingly important story, mixing superpower rivalry and the fear of war among the stars with the exciting and romantic prospect of exploring the new world of space. As the US Apollo missions got ever closer to the goal of putting a man on the moon Fairley left the *Evening Standard* to work exclusively for ITN and the *TV Times*. He had been described by the magazine *World Medicine* as 'portly-built', and editor Nigel Ryan apparently threatened to put a clause in his contract requiring him to 'stay in reasonable shape'. Since Fairley was constantly having to squeeze into some mock-up of a space suit for his studio appearances this seemed only sensible. But his most engaging characteristic was his enthusiasm, which all the best science experts on television, like the astronomer Patrick Moore and ITN's current science editor Lawrence McGinty, seem to share.

Infected by Fairley, ITN was also enthusiastic for space, but the unimaginative ITV network had to be persuaded that putting a man on the moon was worth anything more than an extended news bulletin. While Apollo 11's touch-down was scheduled for 19.22 on Sunday, 20 July 1969, the actual moon walk would probably happen in the dead of night, at 05.12. Editor Nigel Ryan sent a proposal to the companies' programme controllers that ITV should cancel all its usual programmes and stay on air through the night as long as necessary to broadcast the moon landing live. He suggested that they might plug the gap in the early hours with a film and that 'ITV could mount a Moon Hogmanay party (say) with Eamonn Andrews and/or an open air party with Eidophors [large television screens] carrying the moon story in Hyde Park.'[1] The programme controllers' group was unconvinced and, along with his deputy David Nicholas, Ryan was summoned to a special meeting of ITV chiefs in Sir Lew Grade's office at Marble Arch. Warned by a secretary that they had just seven minutes to put their case, Ryan did his best but found the network men 'wonderfully unenthusiastic'; for most of the time that he was making his pitch, showman Grade was on the phone to Hollywood. While Granada seemed ready to go for an all-night programme, the rest of the network thought this extraordinary event could be perfectly well covered with occasional newsflashes.

The two ITN men were abruptly thrown out of Grade's office to make way for a sub-committee come to talk about religious broadcasting. As they waited despondently outside, Nicholas said to Ryan, 'If we go back to ITN and tell Don Horobin that all we've got is newsflashes just imagine what he will say.' It was enough. The thought of Horobin's remorseless, accusing glare should they have to admit failure was more than they could contemplate. When they went in again Ryan made what he describes as 'a Henry V type speech', which had the desired effect. Purple in the face, thumping the table with his fist, Lew Grade half rose to his feet and bellowed his unequivocal support for ITN's proposal: 'Why,' he shouted, 'this is the biggest story since the birth of Jesus Christ!'

Planning for the programme was carried out over lunch at the Boot and Flogger pub in Southwark, in a glassed-off inner nook conveniently close to the bar. Secrecy was important: ITN did not want the BBC to hear of its plans for what would be a highly visible head-to-head contest. The team was led by David Nicholas, with Jon Lander as his associate editor, Frank Miles as chief writer and Peter Fairley, of course, as the studio expert. On the night they would be joined by Alastair Burnet as the main presenter of the programme and a former 'Voice of Apollo' commentator from the space agency NASA, Paul Haney. Over the years Fairley had struck up an extremely good relationship with the space centre at Houston and had now acquired the two-inch thick flight plan for the Apollo 11 mission, which became the basis for the ITN team's planning. Miles got to know the plan so well that he was able to alert NASA to an inconsistency in it about the exact time that the Stars and Stripes was to be raised on the lunar surface.

On one point everyone was agreed. During the previous Apollo flight experts in the studio had talked all over the conversation between the astronauts and Mission Control in Houston. This had jarred with many viewers. 'We must never trample over astronaut sound again,' pronounced Nicholas. The problem was that the exchanges to and from space were so cryptic that they meant nothing to the ordinary viewer. '1202, do you copy?' for example, meant 'Shall we abort the mission?' But how would anyone ever know that without some intrusive commentary?

Fortunately, ITN's chief engineer Cyril Teed, visiting an exhibition of television technical equipment in America, had noticed an interesting gadget made by a small but innovative company called Visual Electronics. Their machine was called Titlefile, and it could memorise up to a thousand separate captions – subtitles – and display them on command. In the days before computer technology had arrived this was the first character generator with a memory. Once acquired, Titlefile was hidden away in a locked room and only a very few people at ITN even knew of its existence. In secret, Frank Miles, following the NASA flight guide sequence of events, painstakingly programmed the device with simple explanations of those otherwise meaningless codes the astronauts would be using – and others that would signal some emergency or change of plan. Paul Haney's contribution would be to talk about the astronauts as people he knew well, and explain the dangers they faced – sitting, as he put it pithily, on top of two million parts, every one of which had been manufactured by the lowest bidder. 'Impact engineering,' he explained drily, was the astronauts' euphemism for kicking machinery that wouldn't work.

Having decided after all to make the moon landing a big television event ,the ITV network went to work on the entertainment that would fill the long hours when nothing much – barring an accident – would be happening in space. Out went Eamonn Andrews and in came David Frost, with an incongruous collection of guests signed up to join him in his London Weekend Television studio at Wembley. The stars included singers Cilla Black and Engelbert Humperdinck, with the politician Lord Hailsham and actress Dame Sybil Thorndike answering phoned-in questions from viewers. To make sure the 'moon-related' entertainment side of the programme would not overwhelm the news story of the moon landing, David Nicholas and Alastair Burnet flew to New York where David Frost was working. Frost readily agreed that he would hand over to ITN from the LWT studio immediately there was any news from space to report. Hospitably, he invited Nicholas and Burnet to stay overnight with him on Long Island, where he had rented a house, but due to some miscalculation, they ended up having to share a bed. It is, Nicholas insists, the only occasion on which an ITN newscaster has slept with the editor.

The night of the moon landing was stiflingly hot, in fact the hottest night of the year. In the cramped Television House studio – which ITN would soon leave for larger premises – the temperature rose to 92 degrees Fahrenheit, but the programme went exactly as planned:

> As the lunar module *Eagle* went behind the moon for the last time before starting its descent, the first caption appeared. Only the voices of the astronauts and Mission Control were heard as each caption built up the suspense during the countdown. A simulated film sequence prepared from the NASA flight plans and synchronised to the second was run. From that moment the captions exactly matched the exchanges between *Eagle* and Mission Control in Houston, Texas. For the first time viewers could simultaneously see, hear and understand.[2]

Then, half-way through the final descent, the Titlefile machine began fainting away, overcome by the heat in the studio. On the preview screen the carefully prepared captions turned to gobbledegook, and a desperate

Frank Miles was unable to give the programme director the signal to transmit them. It seemed as if their programme's secret weapon would fail them. Just in time, engineer Mike Neusten, with the help of a Morphy-Richards hair-dryer and a film can full of dry ice, directed a blast of cold air at the machine. Titlefile revived sufficiently for it to subtitle the last few moments of the descent and the landing itself.

'TOUCHDOWN' read the triumphant caption on the screen. But Miles wanted more drama: 'Make it flash,' he urged Hilary Deed, the production assistant at the Titlefile keyboard. Swiftly she moved the cursor to the beginning of the word – but not quite far enough. 'OUCHDOWN' flashed the caption – rather appropriately. Then, before any word came from NASA in confirmation, but confident he'd got it right, Miles cued the historic words, 'The Eagle has landed.' A moment later, almost as if he was reading from the ITN screen, the voice of astronaut Neil Armstrong was heard saying, 'Houston – this is Tranquillity Base. The Eagle has landed.'

The programme proved an astonishing success for ITN, and for the network as a whole – '. . . the ITV men were definitely separated from the BBC boys,' said Stanley Reynolds in the *Guardian*. 'At times the BBC coverage was so inept by comparison that I thought someone at the BBC must have decided the moon project was not worthwhile and should be rushed off.'[3]

When ITV at last closed down at 06.22 on the Monday morning it had completed its longest ever continuous broadcast, and the ITA was quick to congratulate ITN on making such a success of its ambitious plans. 'Dear Nigel,' wrote Bernard Sendall the same day. 'May I write to record my deep satisfaction, which is shared by my colleagues, with ITV's moon landing presentation? It is now self-evident that the whole conception was absolutely right, and if the audience figures do not bear this out I, for one, will never believe them again!'[4]

'TV's most exciting show of all time' was the *Daily Telegraph* television critic's verdict. 'Independent Television scored heavily over the BBC by combining extreme suspense with maximum information . . . Unlike the BBC, ITV had captions on the screen explaining the lunar module's position minute by minute and naming the speaker.'[5] 'Peter Fairley's rotund, whimsical but professionally informed presentation added more lustre,' said the *UK Press Gazette*. 'After months of pantomime perform-

ances in space suits and gravity-free simulators, Fairley was able to show his true mettle on the night. One got the impression that he had rehearsed the operation as often as the lunarnauts themselves – he never missed a detail, but he never stepped beyond his scientific beat.'[6]

In the *Listener*, the much respected broadcast journalist William Hardcastle said that given that the BBC and ITV had exactly the same basic material to work with, something of significance had happened: 'In the past the BBC has generally tended to excel in the handling of such material, partly through experience and partly through the national cohesion of its network. It was therefore quite striking to see on Sunday night how ITV rather than the BBC rose to the event.'[7]

Later came confirmation that at peak moments during the night, ITN had overcome the viewers' traditional allegiance on big occasions to the BBC. At 4 a.m. 3.5 million were watching ITN's coverage of the moon walk, and only 2.5 million the BBC's.

This was a high point in ITN's fortunes. In the most convincing way it showed what the news company could do to beat the opposition both in quality and in audience share on a big international, indeed universal story. No wonder that at ITN they filled their mock-up space helmet with champagne to celebrate both the success of the Apollo 11 mission and their coverage of it.

It was a triumph for editor Nigel Ryan, who had sold the idea to the network; for David Nicholas, who today is still widely rated the best live-event producer ever, and his deputy on the programme Jon Lander; for Alastair Burnet, Peter Fairley and Paul Haney in the studio – with their director Gordon Hesketh; and for Frank Miles, who had made himself such a master of every detail of the Apollo programme. When Miles retired from ITN in 1988, nearly twenty years and countless space flights later, David Nicholas could rightly say, 'Twelve men have walked on the moon's surface. In spirit there was a thirteenth present – Frank Miles.'

CHAPTER 20

A DOUGHTY WARRIOR

From 1977 to 1989 David Nicholas was ITN's editor. During those years it was the energy and tenacity that he demonstrated in getting the best possible show for the efforts of his ITN team that made him so popular and so well respected. The Falklands campaign for example in 1982 saw hard fighting by British forces at the other end of the world. But at the civilian level no one could have fought more fiercely than David Nicholas in London to see that news of the conflict, of the hardships endured, the casualties taken, was brought before the public. It was Nicholas who led the never-ending battle against that most obdurate enemy the Ministry of Defence to tell the truth about what was happening in the campaign to recapture British territory from the Argentine invaders.

'We were caught short,' says Nicholas. 'Foreign editor Mike Morris had been trying to persuade me to let him send a crew to the Falklands. But I held off: I didn't think it was the moment, and in fact the night before the Argentine invasion we led *News at Ten* on rumours about [Soviet president] Brezhnev's health. The next day I was being driven back to ITN from the BBC at White City – I'd been on a *Did You See . . . ?* programme – when I heard the news on the car radio. The rumour was the BBC *did* have a crew on the island, so Mike Morris was crowing over my mistake. It was a Friday and we were told the Task Force would sail on Monday – I couldn't conceive that there would ever be a chance to join the fleet later, as there later turned out to be. But the Ministry of Defence were utterly opposed to taking reporters. I was on the car phone reminding them as forcibly as I could that even in the Second World War, on D-Day, there were corre-spondents and cameras there, side by side with the soldiers. I got no joy at all so I phoned [press secretary] Bernard Ingham at Number Ten. I got a call-back in the car saying, "Yes, you can go on Monday." Then we had to find Michael Nicholson, who was staying in the Lake District on holiday with his family, and out for a stroll. Thank God, he came walking back past the hotel earlier than expected and someone ran out to give him my message. We chartered a plane and got him down to Portsmouth in time to join the fleet. The war was a constant struggle for all the media. Editors like me would have these meetings at the MoD in which people like Frank Cooper, the permanent secretary, would solemnly ask us not to mention the weather in the South Atlantic – when I could pick up any newspaper and read it there.'

Throughout the conflict it was a frustrating business trying to get news of what was happening. In evidence he later gave to the Commons Defence Committee, Nicholas set out the extraordinary delay between film being shot and finally reaching the television screen via a satellite feed from Ascension Island. For example, the repossession of South Georgia by British forces – twenty-three days; Goose Green and casualties – sixteen days. 'In fact,' says Nicholas, 'the only combat footage we were able to show while hostilities were still under way was the burned-out hulk of the *Sheffield*.'

ITN made great efforts to get its pictures satellited from *Hermes*, the Task Force flagship. It might have been possible but, equally, the time taken to make the transmissions might have imposed unacceptable delays on military communications. But that was never put to the test. In his submission to the Commons Defence Committee inquiry after the war was over, David Nicholas argued, 'ITN was convinced that satellite pictures could have been transmitted from *Hermes*. But there was an absence of will by high authority to try it.' He concluded: 'Insufficient attention had been paid by the Ministry of Defence to the importance the public would attach to seeing pictures of British forces in action.' Now he says, 'We were getting letters from viewers saying, "You're not telling us anything because it's all gone wrong." We had got the network to give us a part three for the *News at Ten* to cover the news of the Falklands and we were begging the MoD for news, any news, of the war effort.

Sometimes we would get a voice-piece from Nicholson, but we never knew when it might come in. I remember one Friday night we were running a long interview with Labour's leader, Michael Foot, when suddenly the sound department shouted, "Nicholson's on the line." We banged him on air and I said, 'Run every word we get.' I got on to the network at LWT and told them we needed an overrun, but they told me John Birt [director of programmes] had given them an instruction that that was not to happen – we'd been doing it too often. I demanded Birt's home number – couldn't get it. So I told the network controller, "We're going on running this voice-piece till it ends. If you take us off-air that's down to you." He didn't, and I'm glad to say that next week when I went to a network controllers' meeting I got the backing I wanted. I told them we ought to have a red alert system like the Americans. ITN ought to be able to pre-empt the schedule while we are at war.'

It was in the year of the Falklands that John Toker arrived at ITN, hired by David Nicholas as his deputy news editor. After three years on the *Liverpool Echo* Toker had gone to work for Granada, covering the Toxteth riots in Liverpool, the worst civil disturbances in Britain for a century. It was his work there, on a big and dangerous story, that had got him noticed. 'What I loved about ITN,' says Toker, 'was that people like David Nicholas and Don Horobin were hacks, just like me. They believed in the four Es: exclusivity, enthusiasm, excitement and enterprise. At the sight of a story you could see David's eyes just light up. He absolutely loved the news business.'

Toker was soon entrusted with making the ambitious television news coverage that David Nicholas planned actually happen. In 1986 he went to China with ITN engineer Peter Heaps. Equipped only with a compass and a pocket calculator, they worked out how, with a portable satellite flown to the site by Chinese military helicopter, ITN could broadcast live pictures of the Queen's historic visit to China's Great Wall. Says Toker: 'With David Nicholas ITN did deliver, and as a result the reputation of *News at Ten* was fantastic. ITN always looked as if it knew what was going to happen. The Romanian revolution, for example, in December 1989. It was a brilliant call to send reporter Paul Davies on the story when they did.'

Flying in to Bucharest in a small charter plane, Davies and his crew were refused permission to land. A battle for control of the airport was going on below. Only when their pilot told the airport tower that they were about to run out of fuel were they finally allowed in. Through some ferocious fighting Davies contrived to get his team into the television station at the heart of the battle for the capital. 'We were surrounded by the Securitate,' says Davies, 'and the people in the station had virtually no arms at all. They expected that the building would be stormed that night and that we would most likely all be killed, but though there was quite a lot of firing it didn't happen. Little by little over the days that followed, junior army officers who could see which way things were going came to join us, so we began to feel a bit safer.'

Davies and his team stayed in the television station for the best part of two weeks of revolutionary struggle, with the station staff only too anxious to help him satellite his reports to London more or less whenever he needed to. Short of food – Christmas lunch was bread and cheese that had been smuggled in – they were never short of news. The Royal Television Society later voted Davies Journalist of the Year.

But this was only one element in ITN's coverage of the Romanian story. 'I remember Nigel Hancock, the head of news input, saying: "This is huge. We must record it for history,"' says Toker. Hancock told Penny Marshall, who had been covering the 'Velvet Revolution' in Czechoslovakia, to try to get into Timisoara, where protests against the Ceausescu regime had set off the much more violent Romanian revolution. 'This was my first foreign trip,' says Marshall. 'Every day we'd drive to the border and say we wanted to cross over to go skiing. They knew perfectly well that we were journalists, and they kept saying, "No." But one day, as the revolution looked like succeeding, a border guard said, "You want to go skiing? Then go!" and we did.'

Marshall made an arrangement with John Toker that if she didn't soon return to their Budapest hotel in neighbouring Hungary it would mean she had got across into Romania. He would then drive to the border with editing gear, ready to handle her material when she returned. And that was what happened. She reached Timisoara, filmed the aftermath of fighting – the bodies in the mortuary – and when her tape material had been edited at the border it was sent to London from a feed point on the Hungarian side.

But Toker had reinforcements, a second wave, to cope with: reporter Colin Baker and his team, along with their satellite equipment, and nearly a hundred other assorted journalists, all flying in on a much bigger charter. Unable to land in Romania because of continued fighting they were diverted to Budapest. It was Christmas Eve, and none of them had visas for Hungary. Says Toker: 'I went out into the street and hired this gang of ruffian lorry drivers. The only way to keep them with me was to put them in the restaurant and ply them with food. Then we drove to the airport, which of course had closed for the night. With my translator I dug out an immigration officer who said, "No visas." I said, "Is this a Marlboro problem or a dollar problem?" It turned out to be a dollar problem: a hundred dollars each for a hundred people: he knew it was the biggest opportunity of his life.' Soon Colin Baker and his team were on their way to Timisoara, running the gauntlet of gunfire on their way.

Toker goes on: 'We knew this story – the overthrow of Communism in Europe – had to be reported from beginning to end. And the point is that with ITN there was a degree of humanity. They understood that it was a human story too that had to be told. It was not just a matter of geopolitics. I was in Bavaria, in Germany, just before the Berlin Wall came down when I got a call from London. On the Czech border Geoffrey Archer had interviewed a young East German refugee couple. Their passion was ballroom dancing, and they had told him their great dream was one day to dance in the Blackpool Tower ballroom. It was only ever going to be an "And finally . . . ' item, but ITN had fastened on to the idea of two young people from the Communist bloc discovering the possibilities that life in the West might offer. We were going to make that couple's dream come true. We had no names, we didn't know exactly where or when they had crossed the border or where they were in Germany now. All we knew was that they were in a little Trabbi car and that they were going to stay with some Germans who were also keen dancers. I went into a refugee camp, hired six students and told them to ring every dance club in Germany and find this couple. Eventually some guy near Munster said, "Yes, they're my friends, they're coming to stay with me." I hired a Lear jet in Munich that could get us to Blackpool and flew down to meet this couple – I actually got there before they arrived. I rang Young's dress hire in Blackpool and organised evening dress outfits, and then I called the Blackpool PRO to tell him what we wanted. And so at the end of *News at Ten* we just said, "Do you remember this couple, and what they told us their dream was as they crossed into the West?" and then we cut to these pictures of them dancing happily under a "welcome" sign at the tea-dance in the Blackpool Tower ballroom. I thought it just summed up the human story of that extraordinary year. I think the point is that ITN then expected you to put just as much of those four Es – exclusivity, energy, excitement and enterprise – into a tailpiece, an "And finally . . . " story, as you did into the rest of the programme.'

Editor David Nicholas brilliantly combined dramatic coverage of great events with human stories that made them comprehensible. But even he suffered an occasional setback. One evening, as editor and chief executive, with his chairman Lord Buxton, he was preparing to host a rather grand dinner party at ITN House. They were both ready and waiting on the steps as the car bearing their star guest George Howard, the chairman of the BBC, drew up. As they stepped forward to greet him there was a ghastly accident. Nicholas denies that it was he who slammed the car door shut prematurely but, however it happened, the rotund and flamboyant Howard got his fingers agonisingly caught. Leaving Buxton to look after their other guests Nicholas got Howard back into the car, and drove with him to the casualty department at the Middlesex Hospital, just round the corner. There they gave their names and sat down to wait for attention, surrounded by derelicts, drunks and drug addicts. Howard was in considerable pain and Nicholas was conscious of his other guests waiting at ITN. Politely he approached the nursing sister in charge of Reception to ask for immediate treatment, only to be told to take his turn in the queue like everybody else. 'I don't think you understand,' said Nicholas. 'Shortly this place will be full of journalists and people taking pictures of us. You do realise, don't you, that I am the editor of ITN and this is the chairman of the BBC?' Came the tart response, 'Yes, and I'm the Queen of Sheba.'

CHAPTER 21

ITN AT WAR

First Casualty

'The holes in my legs stay with me. I can feel the throbbing in my feet now, because the nerves to my feet go past where the damage is in my legs. Never an hour goes by without my feeling it.'

Peter Sissons was the first ITN reporter to be badly injured in a war zone in the line of duty. It was in Nigeria, as the federal government slowly shot their way to victory over secessionist Biafra.

'With hindsight, when you think how thoroughly people prepare before they go off to cover a war now, it was totally irresponsible of ITN to send me,' says Sissons. 'Remember, I was just twenty-six. I had done time in the Middle East, but that was after the Six Day War was over. There was still sporadic firing down at the Suez Canal, but no more than that. We found an ammunition train in the middle of the Sinai desert still with corpses lying next to it. Spread all around for half a mile was ammunition of all kinds. We walked through it – we must have been out of our minds. I think the lucky thing for me was that both in Sinai and in Nigeria I was with marvellous crews.

'In Nigeria it was being said that the war would be over in three weeks, so I was sent out with Cyril Page, ITN's most experienced cameraman, and soundman Archie Howell. He'd seen it all too. For ages we kicked our heels in the Federal Palace Hotel in Lagos trying to get to the front. Eventually, at the airport, we just jumped on a DC-4 full of empty coffins packed with mortar-bombs. I remember that oil was pouring out of one of the engines and streaming down the wing. We learned later that the plane that had taken off just in front of us had crashed. In fact, we flew over the wreckage – there had been forty soldiers on board.

'At Port Harcourt, near the front, we found our way to Brigadier Adekunle's HQ and managed to get hold of a long-wheelbase Land Rover. We teamed up with Morley Safer from CBS and Time-Life photographer Priya Ramrahka. Looking for a slice of the action, we got as far as Owerri, but couldn't find anyone to say which side was actually holding the town. We came to a trench dug across the road so we got out of the Land Rover and went forward on foot, with some of Adenkunle's Black Scorpion soldiers around us. I remember their brigade badges – a blue octopus on a red ground.

The sound camera had gone down, so Cyril was carrying a silent Arri [Arriflex] and Archie Howell had a tape-recorder. I recorded a wild-track commentary describing the scene as we walked along. Suddenly there was a bit of sporadic incoming fire from up ahead of us. No one at first thought it was anything to worry about. Our guys knelt down and just hosed the area with automatic fire, and then we went on advancing down the road. Suddenly, as we rounded a bend, there was more firing – now the bullets were pinging on the road all around us. I'd never been that close to incoming fire before. It became very, very heavy and everyone scattered. Cyril got behind a tree and stopped filming; Archie kept recording. I dived into the bush about ten feet off the road, but there I was lost.'

Now firing started up from another direction. Lying low in the mud Cyril Page shouted, 'Leave the gear, let's crawl.' But the photographer, Priya Ramrahka, still had his cameras and lenses strung around him and could not crouch low enough. He was hit, and mortally wounded. Between them Page and Morley Safer dragged him, dying, out of the danger zone and got him into their Land Rover. Archie Howell too managed to crawl to safety. But as they began to pull out they realised Peter Sissons was missing.

As Sissons lay in the bush the firing died away. He shouted, 'I am a British journalist,' and then, to his horror, heard someone close-by bang in a new magazine.

'He must have been firing blind, but he loosed the whole lot off at me,' says Sissons. 'As I flung myself into a sort of foxhole I got one round through both legs. I looked down and saw that my trousers were red from the waist down. I felt no pain. I shouted again, "I'm a British journalist. I've been hit." Maybe I passed out. Then through the bush came a Nigerian army major and a signaller: they pulled me out on to the road. Suddenly Cyril Page and Archie appeared, pushing a child's pram, a Silver Cross.' Page had remembered seeing it, symbol of a safer and more civilised world, abandoned in a roadside rubbish dump as they passed. Using the soldiers' webbing as tourniquets for Sissons's wounded legs, Page and Howell got him on to a plank, which they put on top of the pram, then pushed him to safety. By now, although he has no memory of it, Sissons was screaming in pain. Not far away they found a little local hospital, but there was no doctor, just a rusty Red Cross box with iodine and bandages.

Priya Ramrahka was now lying dead in a room next door, and Sissons was badly wounded, with the nearest proper hospital seventy miles away. There was an ambulance outside but the driver wouldn't budge. 'I didn't have a gun or I would have shot the bastard,' says Page. 'Instead I bribed him to let me take the ambulance. It was the longest journey of my life.'

All the way, as the ambulance bounced through the night along deeply rutted roads, Page was standing up in the back with the dead Ramrahka on the floor between his feet, trying to stop Sissons being tossed out of his ambulance bunk. 'I must have come round because I remember it beginning to hurt badly,' says Sissons. 'I was bumped out on to the floor and fell on Ramrahka's body.'

At Port Harcourt there was little that could be done for Sissons: he needed major surgery. For two agonising days he lay on the Tarmac at the airport in the shade of an aircraft wing, while Page and Howell covered him with a white hospital sheet to keep the flies off his wounds, and fanned him with a piece of cardboard to keep him as cool as possible. At last a plane with a load of coffins – full of bodies this time – took them back to Lagos. There Page and Howell got Sissons into hospital, and put a call through to London. ITN flew out a British orthopaedic surgeon, Ken Hesketh.

'In Lagos,' says Sissons, 'I remember lying in bed watching huge lizards walk across the ceiling. My only emotion was of anger at the world in general – not ITN, not [deputy editor] David Nicholas: "Why am I sitting in this ghastly hole in this bloody country bleeding to death?" There was lots of muscle and nerve damage; to this day one leg is much thicker than the other. The left leg, the second one to be hit, got the worst damage. Naturally enough the wounds had become infected – I'd got a shovelful of Nigerian earth in each leg.'

The bullet had missed the femoral artery by less than half a centimetre, but because of the spreading infection, the Nigerian doctors were preparing to amputate Sissons's legs as the only way to save his life. Hesketh arrived just in time to operate, and save the patient's legs.

Back in Britain his recovery was slow. In hospital, round the corner from ITN, a bored Sissons was frequently visited by colleagues trying to cheer him up. Once, Ivor Mills and Steve Wright smuggled him out of his room and, between them, 'walked' him to a nearby pub. Afterwards, says Sissons, 'Even if I'd had the use of my legs I wouldn't have been able to use them.'

At last he was getting better, and beginning to walk again. But what was he to do now? 'I was twenty-six, crippled, and I began to wonder if I had a future in journalism. I was told by general manager Bill Hodgson that there was always a job of some kind for me at ITN, but that if I pressed a compensation claim they would pay up, but then let me go. The NUJ said they couldn't help – what had happened was simply an occupational hazard.' So Sissons left the union and got his own solicitor to deal with ITN on his behalf. 'The fact was,' he says, 'that at that time, so far as I know, ITN had no insurance for this kind of thing. I was the first reporter to have stopped so much as a piece of shrapnel.'

There followed some rather protracted negotiations. It was not until 1971 that the board minutes recorded a settlement.

> The board had considered this matter in March of this year and had agreed that an ex-gratia payment of £3,000 should be made to Mr Sissons in compensation for some permanent partial disablement resulting from the wound. The Management had carefully reconsidered the matter and having taken account of all the circumstances recommended that this sum should be increased to some £5 – 6,000. After some discussion the board agreed to such an increase and left it to the Chairman and Management to determine the most appropriate way of paying the compensation.[1]

Peter Sissons had gone back into hospital for a tendon transplant to stop his foot dragging. But after that he was still left unable to run or take evasive action in another dangerous situation. Clearly, if he was to stay with ITN he would have to change his job. 'My silver lining was that I had this enforced change of direction just at a time when the trade unions were becoming hot news – and would remain so for another decade. So in 1972 I became an industrial reporter, and I made my name far more quickly than I would otherwise have done.'

In 1972 Peter Sissons became industrial editor, and then in 1978 began a new career as a newscaster, when he took over as presenter of ITN's *News at One*.

Heavier Fire

The wars ITN's reporters went to in the sixties were, by and large, mere skirmishes by comparison with today's conflicts. In Egypt, in Hungary, in the Yemen and in Nigeria, there was always the chance of stopping a bullet, as Peter Sissons discovered, but that was different from the experience of reporters who came later: they might easily find themselves under heavier, and more deadly fire – in Vietnam, the Balkans or the Middle East.

Actual fighting in the two wars between Israel and the Arabs, in 1967 and 1973, had been covered largely from the Israeli side, not from any bias but because it was so difficult to persuade the Arab countries involved to let Western journalists anywhere near the action. But in Lebanon, in the summer of 1982, ITN's journalists and camera crews were on the Arab side, and on the receiving end of a powerful and sustained air and artillery assault by Israel.

For many years Sam Hall had been a 'fixer' for ITN – or, as he and others like him preferred to be called, 'field producer'. 'As a fixer,' says Hall, 'you were a dogsbody – keeping your reporter supplied with coffee and sandwiches. You set up satellite feeds and sometimes might have to write the reporter's scripts. You had to maintain contacts wherever you were operating – you were constantly on the phone, and you were always backtiming: your whole life was going backwards from *News at Ten*, working out when you had to finish filming, when you had to stop editing, when you had to start getting the cut story to the feed point and so on. Everything conspired against you. I remember once in Leeds running down a maze of corridors that led off the cutting rooms. We'd promised we could be ready and the *News at Ten* newscaster was already beginning to read the intro to our film – I could hear him! I got to telecine, the operator stuck the film in the gate and just let it spool on to the floor as it ran.'

As a fixer Sam Hall had learned how to make it happen: how to get the story on film or tape, and how to get it back to ITN in time for the bulletin. But in 1979 he had become a reporter in his own right, and in July 1982 he was sent to cover the situation in the Middle East. The previous month Israel had launched 'Operation Peace for Galilee', designed to drive the Palestine Liberation Organisation out of neighbouring Lebanon. Now Israeli tanks and artillery were on the outskirts of the capital Beirut and had sealed off the western section of the city. Inside it were some six thousand heavily armed PLO fighters along with the civilian Lebanese inhabitants. Hall's brief from the ITN foreign desk was to tell the story of what life was like inside the besieged part of the city.

Hall flew to Larnaca in Cyprus with cameraman Mike Inglis, soundman John Soldini and picture editor Peter Blanchard, then got his team aboard a dilapidated cargo vessel for an uncomfortable fourteen-hour voyage to the Lebanese port of Jounieh. In the relatively safe east Beirut, the Alexandre had become the press hotel; in the evening journalists went up to the roof with a few cans of beer to look on as the Israelis shelled west Beirut from the surrounding heights. After a series of false starts Hall found a driver prepared to make the dangerous journey through half a dozen roadblocks into west Beirut, the Israelis' target area, and early on the morning of 8 July the ITN team arrived at the Commodore Hotel, which now became their head-quarters, where they were welcomed by their fixer, Michael Crick, who was already there. Through the days that followed, Hall kept a diary.

> Thursday, 8 July. In the afternoon we began editing my first story, and during it all there was a big gun battle right outside the hotel . . . I taped the battle and have to admit I was quite frightened, particularly when a gun crew with a recoilless rifle (a big gun anyway) mounted on the back of a jeep, aimed it inside the hotel lobby. Everyone hit the deck and then scrambled for the stairs to get away. Later, it turned out the battle was between two factions of the PLO.

> Friday, 9 July. The [Israeli] bombardment began this afternoon with sporadic shelling but it gradually intensified as the evening wore on and it is now clear

that this is one of the heaviest bombardments since the war started, and the heaviest since the siege began . . . You can hear the shells whistling overhead and the crump of one explosion after another.

Saturday, 10 July. Up at 6.30 a.m. with shelling continuing sporadically . . . 50 people were killed and 200 injured in last night's bombardment. We were out early, filming the wreckage, which was quite incredible . . . fires every-where . . . vast areas of the city are now just devastated. We worked out that the area in which every single building had been hit was about four square miles, about the size of London's West End.

Monday, 12 July. Feel awful and can't sleep because of shelling. At 9 p.m. ceasefire. Heaven. The traffic outside my window seems quiet by comparison.

That night Hall's script read: 'The bombardment lasted seventeen hours. All told, nearly eight thousand rockets and shells fell on the Lebanese capital – nearly a quarter of them in one, unforgettable, hour alone.' In a telex message from London, ITN was doing some morale building:

Tuesday, 13 July. Tks for everything you have done. We feel that things are going extremely well and everybody rooting for you. Good luck and keep your heads down.

Monday, 19 July. Israeli jets flying overhead with ack-ack fire from around the corner. Noisy. Scary. There are now strong rumours that Israelis WILL attack West Beirut – possibly on Wednesday morning.

In the Commodore, Coco the parrot had grown skilled at imitating the sound of incoming shells: reporters new to the hotel ducked or took cover. A previous ITN crew had been kidnapped and held hostage after they had been blamed for the death of their Lebanese driver. It had cost ITN forty thousand dollars to get them released and out of west Beirut, so Hall and his team were keeping a low profile, conscious that ITN was not popular with the locals. Their fixer Michael Crick had been replaced by Mike Nolan. Every day, between shelling and during brief ceasefires the crew went out to report death and devastation, homelessness and hunger, anger and misery.

As his diary shows, the daily Israeli bombardment was getting on Hall's nerves.

> Friday, 23 July. More heavy shelling and bombs at 2 p.m. Getting very tired of it.

> Saturday, 24 July. Renewed PLO passes. Feeling very tense and basically want out. Missed lunch to try to get some sleep. Not feeling very well – I think probably it is shock from shelling on Thursday and yesterday. 'Tis taking its toll. Heavy shelling again afternoon . . . incredibly close bombs and outgoing ack-ack. Did story. Bed early after discussing latest rumour that final push by Israelis is due any moment. UPI and Newsweek have been told to evacuate the city.

> Monday, 26 July. Extremely heavy shelling and bombing. Got terrific pix from Bahsali flat of ammo dump going up just 150 yards away. Noise unbe-lievable. Could actually see a red-hot shock-wave travelling down the street. Tried desperately to get the story on *News at Ten* but the tape went missing! . . . feel depressed and very, very tired.

> Tuesday, 27 July. Rang London who now say they having difficulty finding replacement for me and can I stay on another week. Feel EXTREMELY UPSET and VERY ANGRY! Bastards. In the end they rang back to say that David Smith is coming out to relieve me. So I should leave Sunday . . . Dear sweet God make that happen. Shelling today is heaviest yet. Dreadful noise. Can't sleep at all. Very frightened.

> Wednesday, 28 July. Up at 6 a.m. editing yesterday's story, which [has] unbe-lievable pictures. 106 dead. 200 injured – all civilians, Lebanese police say. Strain here now is almost intolerable. I'm shaking like a leaf half the time. Very high state of tension – but all pictures and voice pieces now in London so we are on all three bulletins and should have a fantastic showing including ammo dump. Went to bed at 1.50 p.m. to try to relax. Have packed a survival bag and carry pen torch all the time now in case we are trapped in a cellar. Dave Smith leaves [London] tomorrow. Please, please God let me get out safely now.

Hall added a hand-written paragraph to his script: 'Every hour here is a day long. It is virtually impossible to eat, rest or sleep in peace because every time you try to relax the planes come back, dive-bombing the city, sonic booms crashing overhead, in a deliberate attempt to keep the population on a knife edge.'

> Thursday, 29 July. Late at night ITN telexes: 'Your piece tonight has led *News at Ten* again, as you expect. But we felt it was one of the best pieces you have sent. It put the story on another plane and left everyone here delighted. BBC pictures were no match at all.

> Friday, 30 July. Did my last story today, about the people of west Beirut flocking to the Red Cross for help now that there is a ceasefire . . . and how the Israelis for the fifth day running have cut off the water and electricity . . .

On Saturday, 31 July, David Smith, Hall's relief, arrived at the Green Line separating east and west Beirut, and managed to cross safely. That night at the Commodore there was a party to welcome him and say goodbye to Hall – with twenty bottles of champagne and chip butties. The ITN foreign desk cabled Hall:

> Sam, before you go, and in case you are in any doubt, this is to let you know that your reports have been the real guts in many of the bulletins for the last few weeks, and will probably be remembered long after many of the so-called lead stories have disappeared into obscurity. It's not easy for people here to appreciate the hardships and risks that you, Mike [Inglis], Mike [Nolan], John [Soldini] and Peter [Blanchard] have gone through to send those words and pictures. But you may like to know that the editor has mentioned you all, individually or collectively, many times and in glowing terms.

The party over, Hall went to bed at 1am; but not for long.

> Sunday, 1 August. Two hours later we were all on the roof again, filming the most ferocious land, sea and air bombardment of the war so far . . . Even the Commodore was hit! My heart sank. I could not envisage getting out of west Beirut now . . .

But at ten thirty the next morning one of Hall's colleagues burst in to say that there was a way out. A driver for ABC Television was taking a tape shipment as far as the Green Line, where another car would be waiting on the other side to take it on to Damascus in Syria, or even down to Israel. In what must have been a truly terrifying journey, Hall finally left west Beirut:

> We drove at a furious pace with shells exploding all around us. The driver bumped his way down rubble-strewn streets, stopping at every crossroads to make sure it was passable. At one point there was a terrific explosion just behind us and the whole car leaped forward – lifted clean off the ground. Miraculously we were not blown sideways and simply landed five–ten feet further along the road. The driver skidded about a bit but quickly regained control. By this time I was almost on the floor of the front passenger seat, quaking.

Once across the Green Line, Hall was soon swallowing several large whiskies in the Alexandre Hotel, before laboriously retracing his steps, via the port of Jounieh and Cyprus, to London. He arrived home safely in the evening of Wednesday, 4 August. In west Beirut, ITN's coverage of the destruction of Lebanon's capital continued. The massacres of Palestinians in the refugee camps of Sabra and Chatila would soon follow.

A Woman at War

Of course, there are excellent newscasters who have never done much reporting at all, people who cope calmly while a studio director screams instructions into their ear-piece, and pronounce perfectly the names of faraway places they know nothing about. But, by and large, it helps to have been there yourself. Typically it is the male newscasters who have come inside after some years on the road, while women get the studio job with little or no experience of anything more than the local news. As a result the women tend to carry less authority. Who really wants to be told about a war by a newscaster who has obviously never been near one?

Andrea Catherwood is a relatively rare example of a woman newscaster who has been there and done that. She started young, and that perhaps is part of her success. At sixteen, working for BBC Radio in Northern Ireland, she had won a Presenter of the Year award and then, after travelling and working for Ulster Television, had spent five years reporting for America's NBC in South East Asia. Based in Hong Kong, she shared an office with the ITN bureau where Mark Austin was the reporter in residence, and it was he who suggested she apply to ITN for a job. She sent them a letter and a tape, and was invited to fly to London for an interview. ITN's Nigel Dacre telephoned the day afterwards to offer her a contract. 'I think that by the time they'd paid my business-class fare,' says Andrea drily, 'they were of a mind to hire me.'

For Catherwood it was not a matter of getting her feet under the ITN newscaster's desk and relaxing – 'the fighting o'er, the battle done'. Unlike many other women presenters she still wanted to report. For the first six months she spent one week getting up early to read the read the 5.30 a.m. news and the next making special reports for *News at Ten*. Soon she graduated to weekend newscasting. But while she liked the mixture of reporting and presenting, she didn't find it sufficiently exciting: she wanted to report from abroad.

'It's been very difficult over the years for women to break into foreign reporting,' she says, 'but I've done it. By the time I came to ITN I was twenty-nine, and they knew I'd got the experience. I was keen to get abroad again. I was used to it and I wanted to travel. I didn't worry about missing dinner parties, the social life, because I came from Northern Ireland and then Hong Kong. London was for me another foreign posting. I didn't live here. I wasn't from here. I was extremely determined to travel – I was single and I was single-minded about it.

'I remember fighting tooth and nail to get sent to Kosovo in 1998. ITN had the A team in place – all of them men – and I remember walking in one day and saying, "Do you realise that the BBC has three women there and we have none?" There was no woman travelling for ITN at that point. A war was about to happen and there was no woman covering it. I pestered Nigel Dacre, the editor of ITN's News on ITV. On Good Friday I was reading the news, watching Tom Bradby report from Kosovo, and thinking, Why aren't I there? When I did finally get sent I think some of the camera crews felt I was just a girl who reads the news, and it took them a while to realise that I could get them to the front-line stories. Sometimes it's the older cameramen who are more prepared to see your good points. I had to prove my credentials, but being from Northern Ireland helped a lot when it came to trusting me not to get them shot: I was quite street-wise. I think if I'd come from the Home Counties that would have been an added difficulty. It is the experience that counts.'

Later, Andrea Catherwood reported from Afghanistan – with its anti-female prejudice no easy assignment for a woman reporter, and thoroughly dangerous in every way. Hitching a lift on a barge bringing relief supplies into Northern Alliance territory, Catherwood and her cameraman Phil Bye were taken to local warlord General Dostom, who had just captured the town of Maza-I-Sharif. His Taliban prisoners, herded into the fort there, had not been properly searched. As Catherwood and her crew filmed the scene, there was an explosion.

'One of the prisoners being frisked detonated a grenade, which killed the local police chief. I knew I was injured in my leg. There's a hot burning sensation as shrapnel goes in: it actually cauterises the wound. We ran and I didn't look down. While Phil turned for a moment to film what was happening I tried to pull up my trouserleg to see how bad it was. The interpreter screamed, "Don't! It will upset the Taliban," so I did a piece to camera without looking. Then, when there was more shooting, "We have to go!" It was getting dark when I finally had a proper look at my leg. There was not too much blood.'

Did Catherwood ever feel, as a woman reporting fighting, that she was being exploited? Was she sent because viewers found it exciting to see a woman at war? 'I've never felt I was being used by ITN, because I was always so desperately keen to go. I think we are much more concerned about quality – doing a good story – than getting someone under fire because it's sexy. I remember being told that if I did one more camera piece without my flak jacket then I would not be used.'

In 2003 Andrea Catherwood was in Baghdad as America and Britain invaded and then occupied Iraq. 'Iraq this time was more frightening. I was in ITN's armoured Land Rover in Baghdad when one guy emptied an AK47 into us. The bullets were bouncing off the windshield inches from my head – I could see him shooting at me. It's more frightening than a one-off grenade because you don't know when the shooting's going to stop. In that sort of situation you just focus very sharply. I had the map, but of course I couldn't read the road signs so you're looking for railway lines to help you find your way. The adventure of it is incredible: your brain is so active. I remember we were travelling very slowly with two tyres shot out. It hasn't put me off war reporting, but I don't seek to be in these situations. You need to see what's going on without becoming the target.

'I think my foreign reporting gives my presenting credibility; and in the same way, a face that's familiar from newscasting is good for my reporting. I guess women reporters have a shorter shelf-life than men because we're starting families. As a reporter the foreign stints are often months long, but I hope, now I'm a mother,[2] I can do shorter targeted stints. But they are so keen now to "brand" the news that they want the same people presenting all the time, not dashing off reporting. Nigel Dacre said to me, "It won't be for ever you can combine the two: you'll have to choose."'

The Pity of War

'My subject is war, and the pity of war', wrote that great poet of the First World War, Wilfred Owen. His words are inscribed on the memorial in St Bride's, the journalists' church near Fleet Street, in memory of those who lost their lives while covering the most recent war in Iraq.

On 22 March 2003 Terry Lloyd became the first ITN staffer to be killed in a war zone. In the same incident his cameraman, Fred Nerac, and their translator, Hussein Osman, went missing and are now presumed dead. Even that was not the end of it. 'ITN had never lost a journalist in action before the Iraq War,' said Mark Wood, ITN's chairman, 'yet in the space of a week we had the death of Terry, the disappearance of Fred and Hussein, and the death of Gaby Rado, of *Channel 4 News*, who died in Kurdish northern Iraq.'[3]

Truly, the price of reporting war had risen high.

Terry Lloyd had been with ITN for twenty years, and at the time of his death he was its longest-serving reporter. Modest, unpretentious, effective, he had travelled a good deal over the years: to Vukovar in former Yugoslavia, to report on the discovery of mass graves thought to contain the remains of hundreds of Croat refugees; to Kosovo, as the first correspondent to get inside the region, while the rest of the press waited for the Serbs to let them in. He had watched Sir Richard Branson attempt his round-the-world balloon flight, and seen Andy Green take the world's land-speed record in the Nevada desert. And in Iraq, in 1988, he had been first into the Kurdish town of Halabja, to find the population – men, women and children – lying dead in the streets, victims of gas bombing, the horrific demonstration of Saddam Hussein's readiness to use chemical weapons.

In March 2003, when the Iraq War began, Lloyd went in as a 'unilateral', one of those journalists who operated independently, not attached to (and under the control of) some military unit but making his own way as best he could. With his team, Nerac, Hussein and another cameraman, Daniel Demoustier, he had left behind the border with Kuwait and was driving up the road to Basra, following the speedy advance of coalition forces.

Like every other journalist in the area Lloyd wanted to be first into Basra. With Demoustier driving, and followed by Nerac and Osman in a second car, he pressed on up Highway 80, past checkpoints and coalition positions. Soon they were in that dangerous territory, no man's land, on a battlefield that was shifting fast. Daniel Demoustier later described[4] how they passed a group of American tanks just off the road and then, at a bridge just ahead, saw armed Iraqi soldiers. Demoustier decided that this was too dangerous – he did a U-turn and headed back down the road. In his mirror he could see their second car, with an Iraqi vehicle next to it. As the two ITN cars started moving again an Iraqi truck pulled level with Lloyd and Demoustier, its occupants making what seemed friendly gestures, as if, perhaps, they wanted to surrender. Then, Demoustier says, 'Hell broke out.' Heavy machine-gun fire shot out the windscreen. Instinctively he ducked beneath the wheel but somehow kept driving. Glancing to his right he saw that the door was hanging open and Terry Lloyd was no longer in the vehicle. The car ran off the road and stopped, its dashboard shot to pieces and the roof ablaze. Still under fire, Demoustier flung himself out. As he tried to dig himself into the sand at the side of the road, the car exploded.

Demoustier told of how he later broke cover later and tried to join an Iraqi family walking down the road with a white flag, but he again drew machine-gun fire and had to run back to the relative safety of the ditch. Later still, a car carrying British journalists arrived on the scene and Demoustier made a successful dash to it. Back in Kuwait he was safe, with only minor injuries, but Lloyd, Nerac and Osman were missing.

ITN began at once to try to find out what had happened, and whether the missing men were alive or dead. Among video material pouring in by satellite came footage from the Arab television news channel al-Jazeera. It provided ITN with the melancholy evidence that Terry Lloyd was dead. From the tape, his ITN editor and great friend David Mannion was able to identify his body. It was later confirmed, by an autopsy carried out when the body had been brought back to Britain, that he had been killed by two bullets, one American and one Iraqi.

Terry Lloyd and David Mannion had first met when they started out in journalism together in Derby, working for a local news agency. In his obituary Mannion wrote:

> If Terry, my closest, dearest friend for thirty years, were guiding my hand now, what would he wish me to say of him? Probably not much at all. He died doing the job he loved at a time in his life when he was personally and professionally happier than I had ever seen him . . . Some have described Terry as 'fearless'. He wasn't. He feared many things. He was afraid of letting his mates down (which he never did) and he was afraid of failing to be the perfect father to his children. But he was never afraid of 'the story'.[5]

For many weeks the Ministry of Defence refused to help ITN find out how Terry Lloyd had met his death and what had happened to his two missing colleagues. ITN's chief executive Stewart Purvis declared himself 'amazed' by defence secretary Geoff Hoon's decision that he would not investigate the case unless ITN could provide evidence that a war crime had been committed. But in May 2003, following further pressure from ITN, the MoD changed its mind, and the Royal Military Police began to conduct a full inquiry. So far it seems most likely that all three men in the ITN team died because they were caught in crossfire between American and Iraqi forces. Traces of DNA have now been matched to other members of Hussein Osman's family, but of Fred Nerac there has so far been no trace. Both men must now be presumed dead, two more to add to the roll of eighteen journalists, cameramen and assistants who were killed during the Iraq War.

As the fighting ended, news organisations round the world tried to learn the lessons of this war, in which proportionately more media people had died than in any previous conflict. The BBC commissioned research from the Cardiff University School of Journalism, Media and Cultural Studies. Their report[6] found that the American military felt no obligation to Western journalists operating as unilaterals. If they were working on their own, or in Iraqi-held territory, then too bad if they got hit. Only journalists 'embedded' with military units of the coalition could count on not becoming targets: 'The death of unilaterals – many of whom were killed by US forces, none by British forces – was regarded by the Pentagon as the inevitability of a certain kind of warfare. In short, fair warning had been issued, and that was the end of the matter.' The British Ministry of Defence, though it did explicitly state that unilaterals were to be afforded the same protection as any other civilian, said that they would not be given the same level of protection as embedded journalists.

Despite Terry Lloyd's death, ITN did not withdraw its other unilateral journalists from Iraq. But the concern now is that in future conflicts news organisations will regard it as too dangerous to send correspondents and camera crews to cover wars independently, and that this is what both the military and the politicians want. Yet, as the Cardiff research shows:

> One of the areas in which both broadcasters and the public are in emphatic agreement is that a *multiplicity of sources and perspectives* is essential for objective and balanced war coverage. In short, we need to know not only how it looks from beside the missile launcher, but what happens when the missile lands. Embedded reporting may be a useful addition to the mix, but there is broad agreement (outside the Pentagon) that it should remain part of a picture that includes independent reporting.

Will that be possible in the future? ITN's Mark Austin was a unilateral reporter, as well as news programme presenter, in Iraq: 'One danger I think is that the MoD and the British forces will start to use safety as a reason to stop journalists going into an area and I think this is likely to happen. It's almost that safety and fear become a form of censorship . . . where you sit in the Hilton Hotel in Kuwait, you wait for daily press trips to safe, well-prepared areas, which everybody will go on, real media-circus operations, and you just sit there and wait till your number comes up and off you go. Which in my view is no way for a journalist to cover the war.'[7]

Ever since the Vietnam War, when television told viewers what was really going on so vividly and accurately that public opinion turned against American involvement, governments have been keen to keep journalists under their control. Censoring their copy or their pictures doesn't look good: making it too dangerous for journalists to operate independently seems to offer a better option. ITN lost three people in the fighting during the Iraq War: even if brave newsmen are still prepared to go, will ITN be prepared to risk sending them next time?

42 Commando
of the Royal Marines

The G CO
Buck Howes

They could not guarntee
the safety of any journalist
who was not embedded
The truth is they want
out of their way to
make life difficult for TV

teams & other journalists
who were intent on
entering the battlefield
in Southern Iraq
on their own

CHAPTER 22
REGGIE

Riding High

News at Ten had been launched in the summer of 1967 with Alastair Burnet as its main presenter, but he had always made it plain that he could not, as editor of the weekly *Economist* magazine, go on indefinitely doing two jobs at once. Indeed, from the beginning, Burnet only presented *News at Ten* on three days of the week, and he did not shoulder the burden of a half-hour programme alone. Just as ITN had copied the American networks with an in-vision, personable presenter so now *News at Ten* adopted the networks' notion of having not one newscaster but two. To some extent at least, the success of a news bulletin now depended on the 'chemistry' between them.

Originally the idea had been that Andrew Gardner would be Alastair Burnet's regular partner, with Reginald Bosanquet and George Ffitch conducting interviews in the second half of the programme, 'after the break'. But the interview idea was quickly forgotten when Burnet left *News at Ten*, taking George Ffitch with him, to return to *The Economist*. Bosanquet and Gardner soon became not the only team presenting the *News at Ten* but the pairing that worked best.

'I like doing it with anybody,' Bosanquet told the *Observer*, 'but most of all I like doing it with Andrew. The only person I didn't like doing it with was Alastair Burnet, who wasn't, actually, very good at it. We had nothing going between us you see.'[1] Bosanquet and Gardner used to compare themselves to that other double act Morecambe and Wise, with Gardner as straight man to Bosanquet's Eric Morecambe. It was indeed a perfect partnership.

Andrew Gardner had come to ITN from Rhodesia, where he had been working for the Federal Broadcasting Corporation, via a short stint at the BBC. There, chairing *Table Talk*, a daytime conversation programme, he had caught the eye of ITN's deputy editor Denis Thomas, who had got him in for interview. Despite being, at six foot five, one of those tall men that Geoffrey Cox liked to have about him, he had not at first impressed ITN's editor. But when Cox himself saw Gardner in action on television he called him in again. 'I was watching [*Table Talk*] one day and I saw Andrew Gardner,' says Cox, 'and I thought, My God, that's the man! Andrew came to see me and when he came into the room he said, "You know, you interviewed me last week," and I said, "Surely I didn't?" He said, "Oh, yes, you did," and I suddenly remembered I'd thought this chap was too pallid to be a newscaster. But there was an extraordinary difference between what people are in the flesh – well, "pallid" is not the right word, but "quiet" *is* the right word for Andrew, and of course the moment he came on the screen for ITN he was a great success.'

From the beginning of their television partnership Bosanquet greatly valued Gardner's steadiness, his reliability: 'What Andrew did for me,' he said, after a decade of newscasting together, 'was to make things relaxed, which is a vital element in live television. He was safe and super-reassuring. I've done *News at Ten* with quite a few people who are very nervous and don't communicate or have any rapport with you. This makes you nervous. Andrew and I were always aware of each other's problems. We took to each other instantly. We share the same sense of humour, which is a bit sophisticated. What I do for Andrew is make him laugh.' Gardner agreed: 'We've always confided in each other, though we're complete opposites. Reggie is very volatile, warm, big-hearted, a larger-than-life character. I think I'm more serious, without wishing to sound pompous, but I do have a sense of humour, and we've always shared the funny side of things, too.'

The problem about newscasting is that it fosters a sense of insecurity and encourages a lack of self-discipline. What is this job, where you work fewer hours and are paid more than others? Where you no longer toil in the fields to produce anything, and where other people do most of the spinning for you?

Where after reading a few scripts from a teleprompter you become someone nationally known and admired, and where no one is likely to tell you off? It takes a strong sense of self-worth and a determination not to let yourself get sloppy if you are to be a long-term success as a newscaster, because it *is* a stressful job. All the effort that has been put into gathering the news, crafting film or tape reports and producing the graphics now depends on you to make good use of it. You are now the one who will make or mar this particular bulletin. And, of course, with millions watching, it only takes one stupid mistake to blight your career. Some, like Andrew Gardner, conscious of the important job they did but not carried away with a sense of celebrity, were capable of doing it well whenever they appeared. Reginald Bosanquet was not.

The whole point about Reggie was his unpredictability: it made him exciting to be with and, as a viewer, exciting to see, but as the years went by his bosses increasingly watched him through their fingers, hearts in their mouths. 'Vroom, vroom,' he would shout, stamping on an imaginary accelerator beneath the newscasters' desk as the *News at Ten* title music swelled. It was like watching a highly charged racing car about to leap from the grid. Everyone was waiting to see if the car made it round the circuit or came spinning off the track to crash spectacularly at some particularly tricky bend.

As Bosanquet's second wife Felicity recalls, Reggie had only been doing the *News at Ten* for a few months when editor Geoffrey Cox left ITN: 'He told his successor Nigel Ryan he didn't think Reggie should continue to read the news because he was too nervous. Nigel didn't agree. He thought that Reggie had that rare extra quality, which, in the cinema, is called box-office appeal, that people would not only want to watch the news, but Reggie as well, which is what happened in the end.'[2]

He had star-quality all right. The writer Jilly Cooper first caught sight of him at Oxford, sitting on the riverbank with a friend, laughing as she floated by in a punt. Nearly thirty years later she wrote: 'It was Reggie I remembered, aware even in those few seconds of a superb arrogance, animal health, raging high spirits – coupled with a slight detachment which made him still more irresistible. He looked like the young Cary Grant with a touch of Belmondo's earthiness and sensuality. I fell in love instantly, but knew it was the desire of the moth for the star.'[3]

Some time after they had parted (with considerable acrimony) Felicity summed up her former husband like this: 'He can be kind, warm-hearted, generous, enthusiastic. He is clever, knowledgeable and extremely good at his job. He has a magnetic personality which he manages to put across on television – authority mixed with charming vulnerability. Who else could become a show-business celebrity merely from reading the news? At the same time he is prone to bouts of utter gloom. He is extravagant, frequently lazy, and an incurable romantic. Some of my happiest times were when he would read poetry to me. Reggie loves poetry and he reads it beautifully, better than any actor I've ever heard.

'He also loves to drink, and he does that well too. He can get through enormous amounts without showing the signs of being the worse for wear. He is not one of those people who have to drink for some neurotic reason. He simply likes it. He will have a glass of beer where someone else might have a cup of tea.'

In the end drink became the big problem, but to begin with it was Reggie's determination to live beyond his means that caused most difficulty for Felicity. Reggie's ITN colleagues were the happy recipients of her husband's wonderful hospitality – which she found herself obliged to go along with.

In 1964 Reggie's second marriage had got off to a slightly unorthodox start when he invited Karin, the first Mrs Bosanquet, to be his witness at his marriage to Felicity: both women's names therefore appeared on the marriage certificate. Shortly afterwards Felicity discovered she was being taken on honeymoon to the same house – near Deià in Majorca – to which he had often taken Karin on holiday. But it was the house that he decided they should buy that proved most troublesome.

Though he was well paid at ITN Reggie was by no means a rich man, yet now he determined to live like one. Brushing aside Felicity's doubts, he bought a country house that even its previous owner, the film star Rex Harrison, had found too expensive to run. Tidebrook, on the Kent-Sussex border, was big, with nine bedrooms, forty acres of grounds and two large ponds almost the size of lakes. It cost the Bosanquets £19,000, a considerable sum in the mid-1960s. As Felicity says, 'Reggie's dream was to live the life of a country squire, sitting on the terrace at Tidebrook, glass in hand, directing a brace of gardeners. He was the cosiest person in the world, but he needed luxury in order to enjoy life.'

Reggie adored Tidebrook, and was soon inviting hordes of friends down for the weekend. As these lucky people, many from ITN, drank and laughed the weekend away Felicity too often found herself far from the fun, trying to cook meals in a distant corner of the house. Though Tidebrook boasted four kitchens, the only working stove was a Baby Belling, with two rings and a tiny oven. But food was not the priority.

During a weekend at Tidebrook guests would be woken in the morning by the unmistakable sound of a champagne cork leaving the bottle – the jaunty announcement that Reggie Bosanquet's day had begun. Through a glass, darkly, I recall a late breakfast of bacon and eggs accompanied by a couple of glasses of Tolly ale and, out on the delightful terrace before lunch, a bottle or three of white wine, glinting encouragingly in the sun. When the bottles were empty Reggie would send them spinning high in the sky to splash in the pond below. Then it was into the kitchen to 'help' Felicity serve lunch.

Funds had never run to furnishing Tidebrook in a more than vestigial – though most charming – way, but there had been enough money to purchase a serious piece of equipment normally seen only in pubs and clubs: a handsome brass cylindrical machine, screwed to the kitchen dresser, that pulled corks splendidly: one stroke of the lever pushed in the corkscrew, another pulled the cork out. It was almost too easy to operate, and made drinking on and on, through lunch, and through a long lazy afternoon of billiards afterwards, really no trouble at all.

Reggie's drinking was on a gargantuan scale. Felicity recalls their first weekend at Tidebrook – at Easter. They had decided they were overweight and were taking slimming pills. On top of that Reggie swallowed a bottle of champagne, another of white wine, one of red, and finished off with half a bottle of port. During the night Felicity and their guests woke to the noise of carpentry. Reggie was discovered on the eighteenth-century staircase, sawing through the banisters, to which he had taken a sudden and inexplicable dislike.

In winter, the central-heating system was incapable of keeping Tidebrook warm. Reggie seemed not to mind, but others did. Felicity recalls taking tea to a couple who had been staying overnight only to find a note pinned to the pillow that read: '2am. Sorry, we were too cold to stay so we've gone home.'

Frequent guests at Tidebrook were Nigel Ryan and Antony Rouse, another ITN producer and typically eccentric Old Etonian. As they huddled round a roaring fire one Christmas, very drunk indeed, the chimney caught alight, and the fire brigade was summoned. Staggering outside with the others, Rouse carried a milk jug full of water as his contribution to dealing with the blaze, but was overcome by the beauty of the leaping flames: 'It looks so pretty,' he said wistfully. 'Can't we just let it burn?' When the fire brigade arrived Reggie, playing the local squire, dispensed more wine to his guests and beer to the fire-fighters. The fire finally out, their chief proceeded to the paperwork. 'What name shall I put down?' he asked. Somewhat taken aback Reggie replied, rather huffily, 'Reggie Bosanquet'.

'Roger Basingstoke,' the fire-chief wrote down carefully.

Eventually Reggie was forced to admit that he could not afford Tidebrook. Although he was the highest paid person at ITN (including the editor) he never earned more than £22,000 a year, and that was not nearly enough to sustain Tidebrook's running costs. But selling the house was one of the greatest disappointments in his life, and it provoked a normally sunny and generous-spirited Bosanquet into a burst of snobbery: 'I had to put it on the market. A man in a big vulgar car and his wife with blue-rinsed hair came to look at it and offered me a good price. I could not bear the thought of them living in it. I sold it at a lower price to a very nice family named Wellesley.'[4]

At work, on the *News at Ten* treadmill, Reggie was now becoming both lazy and bored. When he was asked to come in to ITN during the morning and record an interview with somebody he might say, 'Must I? I'm playing tennis.' 'The great pity,' says Anthony Rouse, 'is that ITN didn't make Reggie stick to interviewing. He was brilliant, the quickest man on his feet I've ever met, bowling his father's googlies, metaphorically, at unsuspecting victims. He was incredibly perceptive, and frightened of no one.' After lunch, at an editorial conference, Reggie might doze off and awake with some inappropriate comment. At one such meeting David Nicholas had been talking about getting to the 'coal face' of a story; Reggie came to and joined the conversation under the impression that they were discussing the miners. And working on the bulletin scripts in the newsroom he seemed to be more interested in the 'And finally . . .' tailpieces than anything else. That is not to deny that he was good both at writing those stories and delivering them.

One of his favourites, which divided the viewers into those who thought it appalling and those who found it very funny, was about a cat. Let Reggie tell it:

This was during the firemen's strike, when the Green Goddesses were brought into action, and the story concerned a dear old lady who had phoned the fire brigade in distress about her beloved cat, which had climbed high up into a tree and couldn't get down. It was the classic firemen-come-to-the-aid-of-cat-up-a-tree situation and these temporary firemen did not let the old lady down. They arrived in their Green Goddess, sent the big ladder up and rescued Tibby or Samantha or whatever the cat's name was. The old lady was so grateful she insisted that they let her give them a nice cup of tea. Then after a pleasant interlude of tea and home-made cakes they took their departure. They got into the Green Goddess, reversed, and ran over the cat.

The newspapers maintain that I collapsed in laughter on the screen. It is not true. I did not move a muscle. In fact I was proud that I was able to keep my cool as a newscaster in very testing circumstances.[5]

When it came to his marriage Reggie was not so well-behaved. Living in a flat in London instead of spacious Tidebrook he and Felicity had not been getting on well. Reggie didn't start work until the afternoon; she had to get up early to pursue her high-powered public relations career. But in the small hours the click of billiard balls and noisy laughter of Reggie and various disreputable ITN hacks playing billiards in the room next door made it impossible for her to sleep. Married life became unendurable. In May 1976 ITN bosses opened the *Daily Mail* to find a five-column picture of Reggie sitting disconsolately on the bare boards of a room in his London flat. In the accompanying article he complained: 'I've lost a lifetime of trivia, much of it of great sentimental value . . . My God, even the lavatory seat has disappeared.' Granted a divorce on the grounds of Reggie's 'unreasonable behaviour', Felicity had been to collect the furniture that belonged to her. 'I decided it was time to move,' she was quoted as saying, 'and I am sure that everything Reggie owned is still there.'[6] As for the lavatory seat, Reggie must have forgotten that it had been smashed and thrown away after he had, for some unknown reason, stood on it.

Admonished by his editor – and close friend – Nigel Ryan that he was in danger of becoming the story rather then the storyteller, Reggie was suspended and sent off on an extended holiday – exiled to a Greek island. The papers loved it. 'Is this Reggie's Elba?' asked the *Daily Mail*. 'Shall we live to see Napoleon Bosanquet's Hundred Days with our hero bursting from a sealed boat-train at Waterloo and being carried shoulder-high by a mob of Southern Region commuters to storm Sir Lew Grade's penthouse?

Or is this Reginald Bosanquet, *News at Ten*, St Helena?'[7]

The *Sunday People*, under the headline 'You Want Reggie!', reported:

> Reginald Bosanquet is the greatest! That's the overwhelming verdict of *Sunday People* readers who responded to our 'Hands Off Reggie' article last week . . . This typical reaction comes from Mrs. V. T. Stevens, of Wem, Shropshire. 'Reggie is the favourite newsreader of myself and my husband. The expression on his face, whether the news is good or bad, always reflects the right mood. And we miss that "good night" with a smile.'[8]

Reggie returned to continue newscasting on *News at Ten*, but while his personal life had been in the public eye a backstage battle had been going on about the shape of ITN's bulletins and who would present them. After a brief defection to the BBC and a rather unsuccessful few months as editor of the *Daily Express*, Alastair Burnet was returning to ITN on a full-time basis. There had been speculation that Nigel Ryan wanted him to present *News at Ten* on his own, rather like Walter Cronkite on CBS News in America. There had even been a suggestion that the programme would move to nine o'clock, in direct competition with the BBC. In the event, Burnet began by taking over the early-evening news, now slightly extended to fifteen minutes at five forty-five, while *News at Ten* continued with Andrew Gardner and Bosanquet as its most familiar pair of presenters.

But Gardner was restless: he felt that, on just £15,000 a year, he was undervalued. When Thames Television asked him if he would like to present their early-evening news programme *Thames at Six* he was ready to listen. Although he would be seen only in the London television area he would earn a good deal more money and be driven home in time for dinner with his family. He decided to accept the offer, and in July 1977 it was announced that he would be leaving ITN.

This was a considerable blow to Reggie Bosanquet. His whole life, says his devoted daughter Abigail, was one of loss, starting with the death of both his parents by the time he was seven years old. 'ITN was the first family Reggie had ever really had,' she says. '*News at Ten* was a sort of marriage with Andrew. There was a strong emotional love there, between two people who had a deep affection for each other. When Andrew left the programme Reggie was exposed. His really was a history of loss. He lost Tidebrook, a huge and devastating loss. He lost a first and second wife through divorce. He was even losing me because I was getting married. And he lost Andrew. In the end he had no one to look up to, no one to aspire to.'

'After we had to leave Tidebrook,' says Felicity, 'and after our divorce, I think Reggie really lost interest in life. He became a completely different person. He was bored, but he didn't have the self-discipline to do anything else except be a newscaster. But *News at Ten* became just a meal-ticket to him. He only went on with it to keep the money coming in – and, of course, to keep himself in the public eye, which he adored. He had a desperate need for admiration.' One year Reggie's Christmas card was a cartoon of a TV breakdown announcement, with the words: 'We have temporarily lost the will to continue – please stand by.'

'Why do you drink so much, Reggie?' asked producer Sue Tinson.

'To ease the pain of living,' he replied.

Reggie Bosanquet's drinking started to interfere more often in his work. Viewers began to watch just to see what state he was in. Sometimes it was not too good. At a board meeting in early 1977, 'Several members of the board expressed concern at the standard of newscasting on *News at Ten* the previous Friday, 14 January, which had resulted in their receiving a number of letters of complaint from viewers.' Nigel Ryan had decided that he could no longer avoid discussion by the board of his notorious newscaster's behaviour. He had, he said, told Bosanquet 'that his work, on this occasion, had been well below the level expected of ITN'[9] he had warned Reggie that if it happened again he would be taken off the air. When Bill Brown, managing director of Scottish Television, began to speak, Ryan was full of anxiety, fearful of some Presbyterian diatribe against ITN's toleration of drunkenness. But, to his relief, Brown took quite a different tack. 'You mean,' he asked, apparently aghast, 'that we are in danger of losing ITN's greatest asset?' It seemed to Ryan that with this director at least profit took precedence over propriety.

Soon after his return to ITN Alastair Burnet had moved from *News at 5.45* to lead the *News at Ten* team. Like Bosanquet, Burnet liked a drink but, unlike him, he didn't seem to suffer any consequences, and he is critical of the way Reggie allowed his drinking to affect his performance: 'He was a bloody nuisance, pissed as a newt. Andrew Gardner was a saint to look after Reggie, in every way, and there was no doubt in my mind that the important thing to do was to have Reggie fired.'

Burnet did not enjoy Reggie's idea of a joke: 'The doorbell went at three o'clock in the morning, and I went to the door – I was living in this block of flats and I had to go down the bloody stairs and all the rest of it to open the door. And there was this poor little girl who said, "Mr Reginald Bosanquet said I should call round here and you would pay my fare back to Wolverhampton." So I did. He was a bloody nuisance!'

Martyn Lewis was still an ITN reporter, not yet a regular newscaster, but he had been tried out once or twice on *News at Ten*. 'On two occasions [deputy editor] Don Horobin called me into his office when I was the late duty reporter, and he said, "I don't want you to tell anyone about this in the newsroom, but here is a set of scripts for *News at Ten* and I'm going to decide just before the bulletin starts whether Reggie is going to go on air tonight or whether you are going to stand in for him." And so I sat there at that lonely desk, where you're the only reporter, waiting for the big late-night story, and went though the scripts, half of me hoping that I was going to get the opportunity to do the programme and the other half of me hoping that I was not because it would be awful if Reggie had to be told he couldn't do it. It didn't happen.'

And then, for Reggie Bosanquet, came a temporary reprieve in the shape of Anna Ford. A former academic and Granada reporter who had joined the BBC to help present *Man Alive*, Anna had – in 1977 – been unsuccess-fully wooed by Nigel Ryan. Rejecting his advances, his invitation to join ITN as a newscaster, she had told him crushingly that she had no interest in either fame or money – which seemed to leave little to talk about. But a year later Ryan's successor David Nicholas craftily agreed that Ford could combine newscasting with the role of medical correspondent, which she was interested in, and this persuaded her to join ITN. She was to be the first woman newscaster on *News at Ten*, ITN's answer to the BBC's Angela Rippon, and she became an excellent screen partner to Reggie Bosanquet.

Reggie had publicly declared his antipathy to women newscasters in general, but to Ford he could not have been kinder or more supportive. 'When I arrived at ITN,' she recalls, 'one of the first things Reggie said was "Do you play darts?" I said, "I do." He closed the door of the office and on the back of it was a well-used dartboard full of holes and he handed me a set of darts for a game. He said to me, "You may have read that I don't believe in women reading the news, but I think I will make an exception for you."'

Ford had not been long in London and did not know many people. Reggie urged her to 'get a life'. After the programme he took her to parties and introduced her to people – they included her future husband, the cartoonist Mark Boxer. There was no romantic attachment between Reggie and her – at the time she was more interested in another ITN man, Jon Snow – but the satirical magazine *Private Eye* seized on the idea of the old *roué* Reggie exploiting an innocent Ford's blind and passionate devotion. 'After the Break' by Sylvie Krin chronicled the relationship between Ford and 'bluff, convivial, hard-living Ronnie Beaujolais' (like Reggie, he wore a toupée to hide a bald forehead):

> The story so far: After downing a Mexican Bollock Shaker, Anna Ford, the beautiful doe-eyed newscasterette has fallen head over heels on to the floor of the ITN hospitality room. NOW READ ON:
>
> . . . Now it was all coming back to her. She must have passed out in the hospitality room and Ronnie Beaujolais was taking her home. What a kind, thoughtful man he was to be sure. Just being near him made her feel safe . . . Anna surrendered to his touch. 'Yes, yes,' she said quietly, 'I am yours', and as she spoke her hand reached up to caress his brow. The cab lurched to a halt at some traffic lights and they were thrown forward together. There was a ripping sound and to her horror Anna found herself clutching something damp and furry. Horrified, she opened the window and threw 'the thing' out. 'You silly bitch,' yelled Ronnie. 'That wig cost me fifteen quid!' She looked up, and in the car's mirror she could see the driver's face smirking evilly at her. Would Ronnie ever forgive her?

Anna Ford and Reggie were both intelligent and well-read. They enjoyed swapping bad verse with each other in the studio, as they waited for their next cue:

> Anna thinks that Obolensky
> Murdered Lenin and Kerensky.
> Little does she know the bugger
> Ran a hundred yards at rugger.

Ford's reply is unfinished, interrupted by the next story she had to read to the studio camera:

> No, I don't. It was Rasputin.
> All the rest is high falutin'.
> Never—

Some of Reggie's lines were innocuous enough:

> When I hear the name of Ford
> I always think of Anna.
> But Henry, of the company name,
> Thinks about a spanner.

Some were more risqué:

> There was a young lady called Anna
> Who pleasured herself with a spanner.
> She gave it a twist
> With a flick of the wrist
> In a most extraordinary manner.

And some were unprintable.

Anna Ford was not fazed by anything that any of the ITN men could throw at her. She'd reported some tough stories herself – in the often violent area of Liverpool 8, for instance – and, as a young academic, she'd lectured Provisional IRA men in Long Kesh, the Northern Ireland internment prison. At ITN she found it stimulating to sit next to highly experienced journalists, like Sandy Gall and Alastair Burnet, exchanging ideas as they worked on the *News at Ten* together. As for Reggie Bosanquet, she says, 'His eccentricity was balanced by his real journalistic talent. But the trouble was, he had no faith in himself, so from time to time he did get cantankerous. I know that ITN did try to help with his drinking. It paid for him to go and dry out.'

Nemesis

'Nigel Ryan said to me as he went out of the door, "Be brave and sack Reggie,"' says Sir David Nicholas. When he took over as editor in September 1977 Nicholas had been given the same advice by Nigel Ryan as Ryan had received from his predecessor Sir Geoffrey Cox nearly ten years before. Now things were coming to a head, but deciding when to get rid of Reggie was a difficult call. While Nicholas worried about his unpredictability, and whether, some night soon, he'd fail to make it to the end of the bulletin, he was aware of his popularity with the viewers. In the end the need to maintain professional newscasting standards won. 'Reggie was becoming a laughing-stock,' says Nicholas. 'The problem was that as he read the News at Ten he would get slower and slower – particularly in the second half. The output editor had to keep dropping stories from the running order. No bollocking had any effect on Reggie. You could plug him into the mains and it would make no difference. You could take a blowtorch to his hide and you would be lucky to get his name, rank and serial number. The only thing that worked was to appeal to him on a personal level, ask him to behave well for your sake, to do it for you. And that brought out Reggie's generosity, and for a few hours it would work and he would do his best to behave, before the effect wore off.'

The end came soon after an ITV strike in the late summer of 1979 that had taken ITN off the air for eleven weeks. While reporters were given stories to work on and research to undertake, Reggie had moped about, increasingly fed up, with nothing to do. Back on air he seemed demoralised, his newscasting even more erratic. His daughter Abigail says, 'He was bored. That's what it came down to, and they could have done so much more for him. Reggie absolutely loved ITN and everything News at Ten offered him. He knew that was the job for him.'

It was the habit of Alastair Burnet, News at Ten editor Barrie Sales and studio director Diana Edwards-Jones to adjourn after the programme to the Cavendish Hotel in Jermyn Street where, in the days of strict licensing regulations, they could get a drink after hours with something to eat. There one night, after a particularly difficult broadcast, they decided Reggie had to go, that they would tell David Nicholas the time had finally come to deal with the Bosanquet problem. Nicholas regretfully agreed. Not long after, at an emotional meeting, when tears were shed, it was decided that Reggie would leave ITN.

Reggie Bosanquet read the *News at Ten* for the last time on Thursday, 8 November 1979. Due to newscast again the following night, he had hoped to be allowed to say goodbye to the viewers but, fearing that Reggie might find himself unmanned by emotion, Nicholas decided that he should not. He told his board: 'Reginald Bosanquet has left the Company after nearly twenty-five years' service, most of that time as a newscaster. No doubt members of the board will be aware, from the hectares of press coverage, of the circumstances involving his departure.'[10]

'Only when he left ITN did he realise how much he was loved,' says Abigail. 'Never have I seen so much publicity.' Reggie Bosanquet was indeed loved by a great many people. Somehow a man who had nothing much in common with the common man, an old-fashioned, upper-middle-class maverick, who could have stepped from the pages of an Evelyn Waugh novel, had struck a chord that for a long time reverberated in the nation's heart.

Reggie's first wife, Karin, recalls how, long after their divorce, an Irishman she happened to meet reacted on hearing her surname, Bosanquet: 'Is it himself?' the man asked, almost reverently. 'Reggie,' says Karin, 'was recognised for what he could give, and he gave it. He was the most lovable of people: he had the gift of being loved.'

Reggie had never worked for anyone except ITN. When he left he was without serious occupation. Serialisation of his memoirs brought him quite a lot of money; he appeared in some silly commercials; he was in demand to open fêtes and train company directors in television techniques; he played tennis; he wrote a book for children, and he was a loving father; but he never again found a proper full-time job. Asked what he was going to be doing in three years' time he replied, 'I don't know', and added, after a pause, 'Nothing is deader than an ex-broadcaster.'

Good company though he usually was, Reggie Bosanquet was funda-mentally melancholy. He didn't think enough of himself to make more of his life. It seems that life, past and future, was for him something best forgotten, and in his cups he was prone to pronounce, 'Life's not worth living.' Reggie had found a favourite verse in *The Rubáiyát* of Omar Khayyám:

> Ah my beloved,
> Fill the cup that clears
> Today of past regrets and future fears.
> For tomorrow I may be myself
> With yesterday's forgotten years.

In 1984, five years after leaving ITN, Reggie Bosanquet died of pancreatic cancer. At his memorial service his old newscasting partner Andrew Gardner recalled the many sides of a man for whom so many had so much affection: 'We can all rejoice in our own special memory of that extraordinary man because he left us so many Reggies to cherish. The *Wind in the Willows* Toad of Toad Hall Reggie; the eighteenth-century-squire Reggie; the wine, women and song-but-I-am-tone-deaf Reggie; the humorous Reggie; the unpredictable Reggie; the intellectual Reggie; the witty Reggie; the mine-host Reggie; the infuriating Reggie; the generous Reggie; the mischievous Reggie; the daddy and the father Reggie; the husband Reggie; the intuitive Reggie; the happy Reggie; the squeezable Reggie; the lover Reggie; the impossible Reggie; the canny, questioning and challenging Reggie; the independent Reggie; the ITN Reggie; the to-hell-with-the-lot-of-you Reggie; the reckless Reggie; the naughty Reggie; the very naughty Reggie; the cheering-up Reggie; the gourmet Reggie; the good-to-be-with Reggie; the caring Reggie; the lovable Reggie; always Reggie. The list is endless, and its ingredients have added richness to the lives of all of us who were lucky enough to be numbered amongst his friends.'

Without doubt it is Reggie Bosanquet who remains the best – and perhaps the most fondly – remembered of all those who have worked for ITN.

CHAPTER 23

TURNING OVER

As ITN grew up, its early cameramen grew older. Gradually these tough ex-newsreel characters, who had done so much to get ITN on the air, were replaced by a new breed of younger men. Nigel Ryan believes that it was because they were younger, because they had therefore had the benefit of the better state education that post-war Britain offered, that they were more flexible, readier to fit in with the demands of television news than the men who had grown up in the more predictable cinema newsreel.

One reporter of that time says bluntly: 'There was a problem. You set out with a terrific zest but you ended up running a three-legged race with the cameraman.' It was rare, almost unprecedented, for reporters to enter the camera room, where camera crews relaxed and did their expenses between assignments. But as new cameramen and sound recordists were appointed – men who were just as interested in what was going on in the world as any reporter – so the relationship between them all improved, and in trying situations they worked better together.

'When Jon Lane arrived,' says Nigel Ryan, 'there was a sense of relief. ' Lane was indeed remarkable, and not just for being one of the first of a new breed.

He was a failed public-schoolboy from Dulwich College. He'd joined the classics stream, he says, because his friends had done so, but that hadn't helped him much. In the library he would sit for hours reading travel books and he ended his school career at the age of seventeen with one O level. 'Actually one and a half,' he says, 'geography and French oral. I always felt I'd be all right if I knew where to go and what to do when I got there.' But for Lane there followed a busy higher education in the university of life. He toiled in Bristol docks, shifting bulk cargoes of carbon black and fertiliser, and worked his way on an oil tanker to New Orleans, where there was jazz and his was the only white face in the crowd. Applying for early call-up, he did his National Service in the Commando Brigade, 45 Commando, and in 1956 found himself landing at the foot of De Lesseps's statue at the entrance to the Suez Canal on day one of the ill-fated British invasion.

On coming out of the army Lane didn't know what to do – only that he wanted to travel. He decided he would hitchhike to South Africa, but for that he needed money so he took a temporary job sorting the mail in the ITN postroom. And then he was asked if he wanted to be an assistant to an assistant film editor. Cleaning the film joiner, topping up the acetone bottle, he listened while Brian Lewis and his assistant John Boorman cut *Roving Report*s and talked about television news. By the time his three months' attachment was up he was hooked – and as soon as he got the chance became a trainee cameraman. Almost at once he was sent on assignment to the Congo. 'When am I supposed to be going?' he asked film manager John Cotter. 'You'll be flying from Brussels tomorrow, so you'll need to get a plane there tonight,' was the answer.

Lane parlayed that first foreign trip – all the horrors of the Congo, as commercial interests, imperial powers, black African tribalism, nationalism and the United Nations all collided – into a three-month tour, shooting silent film on his Bell and Howell clockwork camera. Listening to Brian Lewis had paid off. 'Try not to look at things from eye-level,' Lewis had told him. 'Try to go higher or lower.' 'I tried to get different angles,' says Lane, 'and I used a tripod less than the standard five foot five inches high. And, of course, I took the camera off the tripod a lot. I'd been a marksman in the army and I treated the camera like a rifle: take a breath, let two thirds of the breath out and you'll be able to hold it steady – even with a long telephoto lens. That can be useful. I remember Cyril Page once had a man being killed close-up on a wide-angle lens. It was just too brutal to be used. Martin Gray in Hungary got a shot of a secret policeman being killed by the crowd at the end of a long lens. Somehow it was more effective.'

When Jon Lane returned from that first trip he knew he had found his vocation. 'I was absolutely over the moon,' he says. 'I was travelling, doing all the things I wanted to do, and now I could see that the camera could help me do it. I bought an E-type Jaguar on the proceeds of that trip.'

With his equally talented young colleague Alan Downes, Lane soon became one of ITN's most sought-after cameramen because he was always thinking of interesting new ways to tell a story in picture and sound. He was also good company, but as ITN's first hippie – very modern and laid-back – irritatingly superior. He rarely allowed himself to look foolish, but there was a nice moment as he set off, with the equally stylish Hugh Thomson as soundman and me as reporter, on a trip to Biafra.

The journey really began in Lisbon, the centre of the sanctions-busting operation flying supplies of every kind into the beleaguered Biafran enclave. It was always a terrifying journey. After a brief refuelling stopover on the island of São Tomé the plane would take off in darkness and fly towards the Biafran coast, searching for the landing strip that daylight would reveal as no more than a relatively straight section of unfinished motorway. Overhead droned a Nigerian bomber trying to destroy the 'runway' and anything landing on it. In the relief plane, typically filled with crates of hand grenades masquerading as humanitarian supplies for starving Biafrans, some television crew would sit petrified with fear as the ageing aircraft lurched and bumped its way through a tropical storm towards a hair-raising touchdown. At the last moment paraffin flares would be lit along the roadside airstrip. Suddenly there would be a crashing thump and trees would be rushing past the windows, just a few feet from the wing tips, as the pilot fought to hold the plane steady – and pull it up before it piled into all the others that had finished up in a nasty mess at the end of the road.

On this occasion, in Lisbon, as the ITN team climbed nervously aboard their clapped-out Constellation, they met the classic Hollywood-disaster-movie air crew: the red-eyed, whisky-swilling American pilot, the black-leather-jacketed one-armed German engineer, and the clearly barmy British navigator. Lane and Thomson took one look and promptly swallowed the handfuls of pills they had – with typical forethought – brought with them for just such an eventuality, and which quickly rendered them unconscious. Not for nothing were they jocularly known at ITN as 'the drugs squad'. But for once Lane's cool sophistication had let him down. Despite all the efforts of the pilot and his crew the plane's engines failed to fire. Tediously, the ITN team had to disembark and wait until repairs had been made. Far too worried to have taken any sleeping pills myself, I was delighted to see the oh-so-cool Lane, together with sidekick Thompson, staggering across the tarmac in a narcoleptic stupor, heading dozily back towards their Lisbon hotel.

Jon Lane shot great pictures. On that same Biafra trip one of his images in particular remains in the memory: a starving Biafran boy helping his younger brother climb a little flight of stairs, the two of them so weak and slow-moving, like old, old men. Where other cameramen might have changed the shot, moved in for a close-up or a different angle, Lane held his camera steady to allow the full pity of the image to sink in: small children on the edge of death.

'I wanted to take pictures that people would remember', he says. 'But I came to the conclusion that nothing I was shooting made the slightest difference to anybody. I was poking my camera into people's faces and saying, "Sorry, I know this is a terrible time, but my pictures will change the situation." But they didn't. What was I doing as a news cameraman if I wasn't changing anything?' So in 1974 Jon Lane decided to leave ITN and go freelance, in order to make longer films, documentaries, in which he would have time to tell a story properly in a way he felt might have more than a fleeting impact.

Nonetheless, Lane's years at ITN were happy ones: 'We had the best times,' he says, 'without a doubt.'

Switching Off

It's usually easy to decide when to film and when not. In principle the job is to 'turn over', for the cameraman to switch on and record whenever he can see interesting action in his viewfinder. It's his job to get it 'in the can': time enough, when the material is viewed during editing, in the field or back at ITN, for decisions to be made about whether it's too dull – or too horrific – to show the viewers. But there are occasions when cameraman – and reporter – have to make their decision on the spot.

When Michael Nicholson's team in Nigeria filmed the shooting of an Ibo prisoner there was nothing premeditated about it. They had no fore-knowledge of what was going to happen, no time to discuss whether they were going to film or not. The camera was running, sound was being recorded, and what happened before their eyes ended up on film. Even so, cameraman Chris Faulds afterwards regretted what he had done: 'I'm sorry I filmed it. My immediate reaction should have been to switch off the camera, but you can't suddenly sever your news instincts – it was happening and it had to be filmed, otherwise nobody would have believed it. The moment haunted me for years afterwards, and I know now what I should have done.'[1]

It's not surprising that Faulds was haunted by the memory of the cold-blooded killing he had filmed, but he surely had no reason to feel he had done anything wrong. As he said afterwards, 'It had to be filmed, otherwise nobody would have believed it.' The same had not applied to the execution by firing squad of Lieutenant Lamurde, the Nigerian officer who had killed his prisoner so brutally. On that occasion ITN had refused to film what was essentially a piece of theatre laid on for the cameras, an execution carried out for their benefit. But when exactly should a television team walk away?

At the end of the fighting between India and Pakistan, which saw an independent Bangladesh rise from the ruins of East Pakistan, there were scores to be settled. Local Bengali resistance leaders emerged from the backwoods to claim their share of the spoils of war and take revenge on the Biharis, the Urdu-speaking collaborators who had sided with the now defeated Pakistan armed forces. Two days after the victorious Indians arrived in the capital Dacca, a large crowd gathered in the stadium to be addressed by one of the most charismatic of the guerrilla leaders, Abdul Khader Sidiqui. Prostrate before him, bound hand and foot, were a few of his captives.

ITN was the only television crew there, with Mohinder Dhillon as cameraman, Satwant Singh as sound recordist and me as reporter. If it turned out to be interesting our coverage would be exclusive – always a nice position for a television crew to be in. As Sidiqui ranted on, his armed supporters began to torment the prisoners, burning them with cigarettes and prodding them with bayonets. We remonstrated with Sidiqui's guards. When that had no effect, we ostentatiously put down our equipment to show that we were not going to film any more of what was plain torture. But still it went on: indeed, it threatened to get worse.

Mohinder Dhillon, who was having to look through his lens at the unpleasant detail of what was happening, was not unnaturally the one most affected by it. Some years before, filming in Aden at the beginning of a long career working as a freelance with ITN, he had taken his camera off his shoulder and walked away when it became obvious to him that two Arabs suspected of treachery were about to be lynched by the mob – as indeed they were. Now in Dacca he faced what he felt was a similar situation. Even though he was no longer filming he was worried that our presence might be making things worse.

Reluctantly I decided that Dhillon was right: there was now a real danger that the prisoners were being tortured for the benefit of the television camera. And so, along with stills photographer Penny Tweedie, we left. Two other photographers, Horst Faas and Michel Laurent from Associated Press, left too, but then returned to the stadium. There, they took some dramatic pictures as the captives were finally beaten and bayoneted to death. In 1972 those photographs, 'Death in Dacca', won Faas and Laurent a Pulitzer prize, America's most prestigious award for journalism. But ITN had no coverage of the horrific climax to this incident. The foreign desk was understanding, but no 'herograms' winged their way to Dacca.

Had our presence had any effect on whether the captives lived or died? Probably not, but who can say? Rather than walk away, should we have stayed? In some quarters we were regarded as idiots for leaving, in others as high-minded heroes – indeed, we rated a mention in John Pilger's book of that title.[2] It would be nice to think that on this occasion we did the right thing, as Mohinder Dhillon still believes. But to this day I have my doubts.

CHAPTER 24

LOSING CONTACT

Far away from home, based in some foreign country or stuck out in the
wilds on some outlandish journalistic venture, reporter and crew feel
vulnerable. What's happening back in the office? Who's in, who's out of
favour? Who's going to decide whether to use the story? How much do they
really want it? Where are other teams deployed, and how are they getting
on? In short, please tell us how we're doing, whether we're ahead or behind
the rest of the pack, and please, please, tell us that you love us still and value
what we're trying to do in difficult circumstances.

Improvements in communications mean that news bulletin editors can
now speak directly to reporters and producers in the field much more often
than they used to, but the foreign editor remains the link between ITN and
its reporting teams spread across the world. It is the foreign editor who
must point the reporter and his colleagues in the right direction, and
smooth their path with hotel bookings, phone calls to stringers, local
contacts and foreign governments. It is the foreign editor who must argue
inside ITN on behalf of those in the field and 'sell' their stories to the
output side. It is the foreign editor who must keep the crews informed of
what has happened to the material they sent back and explain why it was
cut short or didn't run at all. It is the foreign editor who must pass on
praise or blame from the editor. It is the foreign editor who must constantly

motivate people far away so that they redouble their efforts despite difficulty or disappointment. It is the foreign editor who must reassure teams that all is well at home, and reassure those at home that their loved ones, whom ITN has perhaps put in harm's way, are – so far at least – unharmed.

It is not enough for ITN's foreign editor to know what stories around the world should be covered and – within the budget – do his best to see that they are. He must also be the dependable friend, the reassuring counsellor, the voice on the phone that calms and cajoles, that cheers and cares. Some are better at it than others, and best of all was John Mahoney. I still recall being woken by my bedside phone ringing in the middle of the night in August 1968. In his quiet, calm yet urgent voice, Mahoney explained that the Russians had invaded Czechoslovakia, that tanks were in the streets of Prague and that airport and borders had been closed. I was to get down to Heathrow immediately, rendezvous with the crew, catch a 7 a.m. plane to Vienna, then try to get into Czechoslovakia and report what was happening. Mahoney made me feel I had been waiting all my life for just this wonderful opportunity: he was a great motivator.

John Mahoney had come to ITN from the newsfilm agency Visnews. There, he had only had to deal with camera crews, but at ITN he was required to cope with reporters, all replete with pride and paranoia. They were not all convinced that ITN cared much about them when they were away on a story. Out of sight, out of mind, they felt was the norm. But even the most cynical reporter made an exception for Mahoney.

'I think the only person who really ever worried about us was John Mahoney,' says Michael Nicholson. 'He was the finest foreign editor you could ever have. The way he looked after us was to look after the people at home. I mean, I don't want people ringing me up when I'm away saying, "How are you? Are you doing well?" I want them to be ringing up my wife saying, "How are you? Is there anything we can do for you?" And John used to do that every night. Those were the days when you didn't have mobile phones – and often international phone calls were impossible too. He had to sit on the telex every night and type it out to us, or telephone the wife or girlfriend of the crews who were away. He used to ring up my wife Diana and say, "All right? Nick had a piece on tonight, did you see it? No? Don't blame you! Anything you want? No? Ring you tomorrow." Boom. And of course she adores the guy. I mean, any wife who's ever had anything to do with John Mahoney will raise a hat to him. He was absolutely marvellous. But otherwise I wasn't ever aware that ITN was really concerned about me. I knew that if I was in trouble, they would pull out all the stops to get me home, I never had any doubt about that, but all of us who've been through some sticky times felt "Christ, I wish I'd had a few more herograms or a little more communication from them." But Mahoney was marvellous.'

In the mid-seventies, when ITN opened a bureau in South Africa Michael Nicholson was the first correspondent to be based there, with his wife and young family. One night when he was away reporting the final days of white rule in Rhodesia, Diana woke to hear someone trying to break into the house. Calling London in considerable fear, she got Mahoney, who kept the line open for half an hour, talking to her reassuringly, until the would-be intruder had given up and left.

By 1978 Angola, the former Portuguese West Africa, was in turmoil. As colonial rule collapsed, civil war had broken out between different nationalist factions, with the Communist government of the MPLA trying to crush the widespread insurrection led by Jonas Savimbi and his UNITA party in the south of this vast country.

In London John Mahoney had left ITN and been succeeded as foreign editor by Mike Morris. At considerable expense, and after great argument with the apartheid South African government, ITN's bureau was now firmly established in Johannesburg. Nicholson was there with his family; cameraman Tom Phillips and sound recordist Mickey Doyle had joined him on six-month unaccompanied postings. Phillips had been the soundman on that extraordinary day in Vietnam[1] when Alan Downes had filmed the unforgettable shot of nine-year-old Kim Phuc running towards him, her naked body ablaze with napalm after a South Vietnamese airstrike. Now he had picked up a camera himself.

Once the crew was in place in South Africa and costing money it was important to everybody concerned to justify the expense. The team had been busy filming in Mozambique, another former Portuguese colony, on the other side of Africa, when they got a message to return immediately to Johannesburg. A 'facility' trip – an offer from UNITA to get them into Angola for an exclusive interview with rebel leader Jonas Savimbi – had come up, and, in London, foreign editor Mike Morris had approved the venture.

'There was probably no risk assessment at the beginning of all this,' says Morris. 'I think I might have done a bit more work on it myself. I might have asked, "Is the story worth the risk?" but there was not much going on out there. The feeling was, "We're paying for the crew in South Africa anyway, so why not go?" It never occurred to me that there was a risk.'

In Johannesburg there was a brief shopping expedition for the crew to equip themselves for what they guessed might be a bit of a hike through the bush to reach Savimbi's headquarters. Because they would most likely have to carry the camera gear themselves they cut it down to the minimum. All the shiny aluminium equipment cases that usually accompanied them were left behind. The camera went in a canvas hold-all.

On Sunday, 6 August, the team flew from Johannesburg to Kinshasa, in Zaïre. There, they were met by security police and, without passing through Customs or Immigration, were taken directly from the plane to a small hotel in the hills overlooking the city. They were not asked to sign in. Zaïre was currently well disposed towards Savimbi and UNITA, but had no wish to be seen helping Western journalists gain access to him. If anything went wrong, no one would have heard of Nicholson and his crew; they would simply have disappeared somewhere in Africa. There would be no record that they had ever been in Zaïre – formerly the Congo, Joseph Conrad's 'heart of darkness'.

'We'll be gone for a week or two,' Mike Morris remembers Nicholson telling him, but in the hotel bar in Kinshasa the ITN team met a French journalist who was less sanguine. Says Tom Phillips: 'He shook his head and just said, "Long time, lots of walking."'

In the early hours of the following morning they were taken back to the airport, put aboard a small twin-engined Fokker Friendship plane and flown across the border into southern Angola, landing on a grass airstrip deep in UNITA-held territory. They were expected, and soon were on their way to meet Savimbi, wedged into a lorry already packed with UNITA soldiers, travelling at night to avoid the government helicopters out looking for any rebel movement. So far south it should otherwise have been relatively safe, but within forty-eight hours the lorry was ambushed by MPLA ground forces and their Cuban 'advisers', armed with machine-guns and grenades.

As Nicholson recalls it: 'The noise and commotion were frightening, the men's rifles were on the floor, hidden in the tight mass of bodies. Tom and

Mickey were trapped in the front cab with the driver, watching everybody jump from the lorry; some were killed as they ran. I saw nothing for the first few minutes, hiding between piles of backpacks, lying as flat as I could, pressing my nose against the filthy floor as bullets hit the side. There was a loud explosion and shrapnel skidded off the cab roof – a mortar or more probably a rocket. The crates of ammunition were a yard away.'[2]

Remarkably, the MPLA soldiers who had lain in ambush now disappeared, the ITN team were unharmed and the UNITA men straggled back to them. Before the men who had set the ambush could decide to return to the attack, Nicholson, Phillips and Doyle, with a ten-strong escort, abandoned their transport and set off on foot. It was to be a long walk. Savimbi, alarmed by news of the ambush, hurriedly left the camp at which he had planned to meet them: he suspected that the MPLA had cracked the code his forces were using in their radio messages and were now determined to prevent him giving an interview to ITN that might help swing Western support behind him, and against the MPLA government. It was to be a matter not of days but weeks before the interview took place.

Now Nicholson, Phillips and Doyle began a weary march through the bush, a journey which, it seemed at times, not all of them would survive. In the exhausting heat of central Africa thirst came to dominate the day. As the team sweated along, loaded with their personal gear and camera equipment, they gulped from their water bottles until they were empty. But to the fury of Nicholson and Phillips, Mickey Doyle showed enormous self-discipline: desperate as all three men were for a sip of water, Doyle refused to drain his water-bottle dry but instead kept just an ounce or two sloshing around at the bottom. The sound drove his companions almost mad. 'I don't know if you've ever been without water,' says Nicholson, 'but you become almost hysterical. I imagine it's like being taken off drugs – cold turkey style. It was dreadful, dreadful, dreadful. And the more I think about it now, the more dreadful it seems to be. But Mickey always kept that little drop of water in the bottom so he could hear it and we could hear it, and Tom will tell you there were times when we could have strangled him.'

At fifty, Mickey Doyle was a good deal older than his two companions. It was his self-discipline, his assertion of mind over matter, that kept him marching on. But the boots he was marching in were nearly the end of him. Bought in Johannesburg on that brief shopping trip before they left, they were a size too big. Worse, in crossing one of the rivers they occasionally encountered, he insisted on keeping them on – understandably he was worried about bilharzia, the parasite carried by snails that thrives in slow-moving tropical waters and can prove fatal to humans who catch it. But keeping his boots on turned out to be a mistake. Within two days Doyle's feet had blistered so badly that he could no longer walk. His ankles were swelling and he was developing a fever. Nicholson lanced the blisters but Doyle's ulcerated feet continued to fester. Yet the long march had to continue lest the MPLA establish the ITN team's location and attack.

There was no question of leaving Doyle behind to recover in some village in the bush while the others pressed on: without his armed escort his life would be short. So, dragged along for some days in a hollowed-out tree trunk behind two oxen, carried on the backs of their UNITA escort, sometimes managing to walk for a while in a pair of Nicholson's shoes, Doyle staggered on. But one afternoon he could go no further and collapsed unconscious. His toenails were now black and horribly infected: his feet were rotting. It was only a matter of time before infection spread to the rest of his body. Without anything stronger than a miniature bottle of whisky to use as disinfectant there was nothing more that Nicholson and Phillips could do to help.

It was extraordinarily lucky that at this moment they fell in with another group of UNITA fighters – and the medicine man travelling with them. He used no modern drugs, but at once mixed a draught the colour of tea for Doyle to drink.

> Mickey's pupils grew blacker and larger [wrote Nicholson], his head sank back and he stared, unseeing, at the sun. The medicine man, his bifocals perched at the end of a long thin nose that dripped, spread out a dirty towel, monogrammed with the name of a hotel in Luanda, and with the unster-ilised blade of a knife carefully cut the black nails from the ten diseased toes. It took half an hour or more but Mickey never murmured and when it was done another, different-coloured potion was poured into his mouth and the magic was done.[3]

Thanks to the skill of UNITA's medicine man, Mickey Doyle made a remarkably speedy recovery, and the pain he had suffered seemed only to have strengthened his self-discipline. At the beginning of their trek Doyle, the oldest and least fit member of the team, had trailed the others; now he led.

On 14 September, five weeks after they had started their journey, Nicholson and his crew made their rendezvous with Jonas Savimbi. As they entered his camp the ranks of ululating UNITA women fighters parted before them and the ITN team, followed by their escorts, were guided towards the imposing figure that awaited them. 'Welcome!' said the highly educated Dr Savimbi. 'I believe you are a little late.' With some feeling, Nicholson agreed that they were.

After a week spent filming their interview with Savimbi and other sequences that would help explain the nature and extent of UNITA's military campaign, the ITN team were ready to go, and desperate for home. The plan was to head south, then cross the border into South West Africa – now independent Namibia but then under South African military control. Another long walk lay before them.

Four hundred miles and three weeks later they arrived at the border, the Okovango River, and waited while their UNITA guides made contact with the South African forces on the other side. There was a delay, but four days later a message was relayed back to them. It was the worst news they could have received: 'Under no circumstances will Nicholson and team cross into South African territory. They will re-route and exit elsewhere.'

The ITN crew had now been gone nine weeks: what was happening in the office in London?

Adventurous, yes, dangerous, possibly, but to the foreign desk it had seemed a fairly routine assignment. Having dispatched Nicholson and his crew on their way to Angola Mike Morris had taken some holiday owing to him and gone to Ireland. On his return he was told that nothing had been heard from the ITN team. At first he was not worried. But Morris's partner at the time was another ITN employee, the intrepid foreign reporter Sue Lloyd-Roberts, who clearly felt kinship with other reporters far from home and out of touch with the office. 'One evening,' says Morris, 'Sue said to me "Why aren't you worried?" and I suddenly got a terrible feeling in my stomach that something was wrong. It never left me until the whole thing was over.'

The families of Nicholson, Phillips and Doyle were certainly concerned that they'd heard nothing from the men. Nicholson's wife Diana was accustomed to his unpredictable comings and goings, his unforeseen and sometimes lengthy absences, but this was out of the ordinary. 'Diana has never ever harangued ITN when I've been away about what's happening,' says Nicholson, 'but I had told her we were going to Angola for ten days to a fortnight, and seven weeks later, *seven weeks later,* she hadn't heard from me, *nor* had she heard from ITN. It was Keith Hatfield, sent out to Rhodesia to report because I wasn't available, who kind of broke the story. He was passing through Jo'burg, took Diana out for dinner, of course, and after too many wines probably, she started to cry and said, "Do you know what's happened to Michael?" And she told him the story. Keith Hatfield blew his top, because he was that kind of guy, and he rang the editor David Nicholas, got him out of bed and, Diana said, just blasted him on the telephone. And it was only then that they started to do things. They flew Diana's parents out to Johannesburg. From then on they couldn't do enough.'

Sir David Nicholas does not remember that call, but there is no doubt that once he had understood the seriousness of the situation ITN's editor did not let up in his determination to rescue the team: 'We must get them out' became his constant theme. Tom Phillips says, 'All the time we were out there in Angola I felt confident. I thought that we were working for the best news organisation in the world, and that David Nicholas would not rest until we were home again.'

Foreign editor Mike Morris now focused on UNITA as the only possible means of contact with the ITN crew. Alone or with ITN deputy editor Don Horobin he made more than one trip to Paris, where UNITA's representative in Europe had his headquarters. Despite all manner of reassurance it became plain to him that no one there knew any more about the ITN team's situation than he did himself.

With nothing useful to be learned in Europe, Nicholas sent Morris to Kinshasa – where Nicholson and his crew had boarded the Fokker Friendship to fly into Angola – to talk to the UNITA people there. They agreed to help, but before they made their plane available for a rescue they demanded that ITN supply radar equipment and other spares. In Kinshasa, Morris handed over the equipment, only to have UNITA's men tell him it didn't work.

In Angola the ITN team – exhausted, desperate – pondered what to do. They guessed why the South Africans had refused to allow them to cross the border to safety. Three years before, on an earlier visit, Nicholson and his cameraman Alan Downes had spotted and filmed South African military forces deep inside Angola, giving secret military support to their protégé Savimbi in his struggle for power against the Communist MPLA government. The story had a tremendous impact: the revelation of Savimbi's collaboration with white apartheid South Africa had done him little good in the rest of black Africa; and South Africa's neo-colonial military adventure in Angola had been exposed, and had to be abandoned. Now someone on the South African side was taking their revenge for Nicholson's earlier journalistic coup. Says Nicholson: 'A few days after I finally got back to Johannesburg BOSS[4] came to interview me. And they said, "You've only got yourself to blame."'

Since it seemed that the objection was to him, not his crew, Nicholson tried to persuade Phillips and Doyle to cross the border without him, but they refused. 'We got the message that they would let the crew across but they wouldn't let me, and I said, "Right, fellows, off you go." And they said, "You've got to be kidding. We've been together this long, we'll stay together." They could have crossed, the South Africans would have let the crew go across, and they said, "No". So they stayed with me for, what, another month, five weeks. There was no hesitation.'

'It was the only way to survive,' says Phillips, 'sticking together. When you are part of a TV crew you probably see more of each other than you see of your wife.' That, of course, had its drawbacks. As they reluctantly turned back from the southern border and trudged off once more into the Angolan bush, it became increasingly difficult to live in such close proximity to each other day after day. 'In those situations,' says Nicholson, 'you become excessively polite. You have to guard each other's space carefully. You know that if you start to go wrong, it could go terribly wrong; and so we were immensely polite to each other – astonishingly polite, looking back on it.'

'Someone might just say, "I'm having a bad day,"' says Phillips, 'and then we would just leave him alone until he said he was better.' Back and forth and round and round they trekked through the bush, shaking poisonous snakes and scorpions from their sleeping-bags at night, and by day covering up to protect themselves as best they could against the flies that swarmed around them. Unable to disinfect his contact lenses Phillips never took them out. 'In the heat of the day', he says, 'you would just sit with your back against a tree with your shirt over your head in an effort to keep the flies off your face, then just stare at the little patch of ground between your feet – study it in minute detail hour after hour.' They rationed their toothpaste, choosing whether to brush their teeth in the morning or at night, and to save the batteries they would only switch on their radio once a week or so – wildly conducting to 'Lillibullero', the music which heralds the BBC's *World News*. As Nicholson recalls, 'We listened as the season of cricket passed into the season of football, two popes died, Liberal MP Jeremy Thorpe was tried for murder, Kenya's Jomo Kenyatta died, Egypt's Sadat met Israel's Begin in the spirit of Camp David, P. W. Botha became South Africa's president, the Shah declared martial law in Iran, a poisoned brolly killed a Bulgarian defector in London and Mao's *Little Red Book* was denounced in Beijing. But we did not hear of a British crew who had disappeared without trace . . .'[5]

The team heard nothing about themselves on the news for a very good reason. ITN was trying hard to keep their disappearance quiet. David Nicholas had come to the conclusion that if the missing crew were still alive then to publicise their plight would only encourage the MPLA to find and kill them – to prevent their interview with Savimbi surfacing. 'In confidence we told the rest of the ITN camera crews exactly what the situation was,' says Nicholas, 'but a shop steward who obviously didn't think we were doing enough tipped off Fleet Street. I remember phoning round newspaper editors explaining why we thought it would be so dangerous to the crew to print the story. It didn't appear.'

But Michael Nicholson thinks Nicholas was wrong. As the ITN team tramped agonisingly on in Angola, trying to reach a suitable jungle airstrip without first being intercepted by the MPLA, the attitude of their escort had begun to change. The ITN men had become a burden, a distraction from the war Savimbi's forces were fighting. How much easier it would be to kill the crew and be rid of them. Nicholson believes that publicity about their plight would have made it harder for Savimbi's men to dispose of them. 'I didn't know until much later,' he says, 'but a very good friend of mine who used to work for the SIS,[6] was in Jo'burg – a good friend, and his wife was a great help to Diana – and of course he was making enquiries through the network, and he heard from our ambassador in Luanda, the Angolan capital, that UNITA had actually chopped us, and that Savimbi's people were saying, "Look, these guys are just a burden. We can't have thirty, forty guys looking after them, you've got to just get rid of them." Savimbi said, "No," but I think if it had been publicly known that we were still there, the pressure would have been on Savimbi to get us out alive. And it might have actually persuaded the South Africans to let us across the river when we got south, and they didn't, you see.'

Part of the problem was that while the crew had gone missing in Angola the politics of the region had been changing. Angola's neighbour Zaïre was now much less supportive of Savimbi than it had been, much less willing to be the base for a rescue attempt. And since Britain recognised the MPLA government in Angola, the Foreign Office was not helpful. Mike Morris recalls a conversation in Kinshasa in which the British ambassador Sir Alan Donald made it plain that he was not supposed to help find the missing ITN crew. Morris got a different response when he turned to the Americans: they helped to persuade the Zaïre government to co-operate unofficially in the coming rescue attempt.

Most of August, all of September and most of October had passed without any contact between the ITN crew and the outside world. On 31 October, to establish whether or not they were still alive, Mike Morris persuaded his UNITA contacts in Kinshasa to have a message for Nicholson relayed through UNITA's network of radio stations to the crew's escort in the Angolan bush: 'What is the name of your new dog?' At last Nicholson and his colleagues knew that they were not forgotten, presumed dead, but that a rescue attempt was under way. 'Badger,' Nicholson replied, but to his fury some UNITA radio operator refused to pass on the message, perhaps assuming it was a code word that might have unknown consequences. Furiously, desperately, Nicholson offered an alternative phrase that he thought might identify him and his team to ITN in London.

Relayed from operator to operator, from Angola to Zaïre, from Africa to Britain, the message received at ITN was at first indecipherable. '*LINEU STOP HEBEERS STOP*, it said. The best journalistic brains in the ITN newsroom studied the garbled sentence – to no avail. Then, after scarcely a glance, deputy foreign editor Barbara Gray cracked the code. 'It says, "Line up the beers," she said, 'It must be them.'

The rescue attempt was set for 22 November, but as UNITA's Fokker Friendship taxied out of its hangar in Kinshasa a propeller sheared from its engine. The rescue was off. But speed was now essential: UNITA said that the crew could not stay at the airstrip where they were for more than a day or two longer without risking an MPLA attack.

Now ITN showed how well it could perform when it put its mind to a story. Reporter Anthony Carthew had flown to Zambia to see if he could charter a suitable plane there, and in London Peter Snow identified two pilots with a plane in South Africa who might be persuaded to make the trip. Reporter John Suchet was sent to make contact with them. It was later said that at this stage David Nicholas commanded the third largest airforce in Africa.

In South Africa the two pilots considered the proposition Suchet put to them. There was considerable risk – not least that they might be shot down by Cuban pilots flying Russian Mig fighter planes for the MPLA. But Roy Mathews, formerly of the RAF, and his co-pilot Johnny Adams, formerly of the Fleet Air Arm, decided to take on what they later described as 'the most lunatic mission of our lives'.

In their Hawker-Siddeley jet, the two pilots flew first to Kinshasa to be briefed on exactly where they were to land inside Angola. Then came a refuelling stop further south in Lumumbashi, closer to their target area. Here there was unexpected trouble: their credit card was not acceptable. The pilots had to pool their cash reserves before they could pay for their fuel and take off. Then, instead of returning to South Africa as their flight plan said, they flew across the border into Angola.

At Coutado do Macusso, where the crew had now been waiting with increasing impatience for five days, their escort had tried to improve the state of the mud and grass airstrip, clearing it of the metal spikes driven into the ground to prevent just such a landing as this. It was still not suitable for a jet but, after a pass to check it out, the HS25 landed, scooped up the ITN crew and was quickly airborne once more. Refuelling again in Lumumbashi there was a final heart-stopping moment. The crew had stayed on board their plane, out of sight, once again not officially in Zaïre, while reporter Anthony Carthew (who had arrived from Zambia to help) plied them with cold beers purchased from the airport bar. But as they prepared to take off for the last leg of their journey the plane was surrounded by police vehicles with flashing blue lights. All aboard thought their number was up, until the police made their demand: could they have the empty beer bottles back, please? Apparently there was a shortage in Zaïre.

At Johannesburg airport Sandy Gall, yet another of the ITN army recruited to get their colleagues released, greeted Nicholson, Phillips and Doyle with superior champagne. But Carthew, who had flown in with them, found himself detained in custody overnight before he was deported. Like so many journalists before him he had at some time in the past been banned by the government for his reporting from South Africa.

But from Lumumbashi Carthew had already sent a cable to ITN: 'I have the chickens safely back in the nest.' All day long the two duty foreign editors, Tony Millett and Maggie Eales, had taken turns on the desk, desperate for news of the rescue attempt. 'We heard nothing for ages,' says Millett, 'and finally I went home and took my wife out for an early curry. We got back at about seven thirty to find a note from the babysitter, which said simply: "Maggie rang: they're out." I drove in to ITN and had the best drink in the ITN bar I ever had.' At Wells Street relief and euphoria fuelled an impromptu but classic celebration. ITN had been behind on this story but had caught up with spectacular success. Yet in the excitement no one remembered to tell Diana Nicholson that her husband's plane had landed safely. 'The first she knew,' says Nicholson, 'was a knock on the front door. And there, in the dim porchlight, she saw an almost naked scrawny brown man with a mass of wild hair, a wide ginger beard and a walking stick.'[7]

The others were also changed men – in some ways, at least. 'I'd gone into it at fourteen stone,' says Phillips, 'I came out at nine. But when we all went for a check-up in Johannesburg the doctor told us he had rarely seen men so fit. Mickey always liked a glass or two of whisky. When we started out his eyeballs looked like a map of the London Underground; afterwards they were as white as marble. And he found he didn't need his reading glasses any more.'

On 18 December 1978 a greatly relieved David Nicholas reported to the ITN board: 'An elaborate operation culminated in the rescue from the Angolan bush of Michael Nicholson, Tom Phillips and Mick Doyle after 110 days and 1,500 miles on foot with the forces of Savimbi, the rebel leader.'

Needless to say, the cost of the operation was a matter of concern to the directors. Nicholas assured them that it had been £25,000, not £100,000, as had been reported.

CHAPTER 25
THE AGENCY GAME

From the beginning it was clear that ITN, like any other news organisation, would need access to news that it could not cover itself. And as *television* news it was obvious that it would need more than the words that came clattering out of a news-agency teleprinter. ITN had been set up to offer not just local London stories or even national ones, but international news too. However, it had few cameras of its own and little money to deploy them at any great distance from its Kingsway headquarters, so one of the first things Aidan Crawley did when he was appointed editor of ITN was to try to arrange a supply of foreign news. On a flying visit to the United States he struck a deal with an American broadcaster in which he would pay partly for their news stories with material ITN generated itself. So began not only an arrangement for ITN to buy in newsfilm material from other sources, but also the idea of ITN paying its way, even making money, by selling what it produced itself to other broadcasters around the world.

In May 1955 the *Manchester Guardian* reported: 'ITN has made an agreement with the Columbia Broadcasting System of New York for an exchange of news on film. CBS will supply ITN with film taken on the American continent and in the Far East, and ITN will supply film that it takes in the United Kingdom and abroad. For film from Europe and the Middle East ITN is making its own arrangements.'[1]

Crawley asked the BBC if it wanted to co-operate in setting up a British news agency to supply them both. As both ITN and the BBC had now each made their own arrangements with American broadcasters, 'The most likely form of co-operation between the BBC and ITN, therefore, would seem to be in the forming of some agency to handle film coverage outside the United Kingdom and the United States.'[2] The BBC said they were interested, but next month, following a lunch with the director general Sir Ian Jacob, his adviser Harman Grisewood and editor of news Tahu Hole, Crawley told his board that he would be surprised if anything came of the negotiations.[3] He was right, and it had surely been a mistake even to try. What was the point of a new television channel if it was to show exactly the same foreign film material as did the BBC?

ITN now began to set up its own network of stringers – freelance cameramen – around the world, whom it would call on for whatever foreign coverage it could afford. Its own material was sent to CBS as part of the deal that had been struck, and syndicated to anyone else outside America and other CBS 'territory' who would buy it. Frank Miles was recruited to make the syndication system work: 'It meant coming in at night,' says Miles, 'getting longer cuts made of film stories, writing scripts to them, and seeing them shipped out. I was already in a job, in public relations, and this was to be part-time. I went in at seven o'clock in the evening and stayed till three in the morning, and I was back to my other job by ten in the morning till about five. So I did this for about six months and then I went to Geoffrey Cox and I said, "This is too much. I can't go on with it, it's affecting my health," so he got Chris Barlow to come in and we did alternate nights until eventually, in August 1958, Geoffrey offered me a permanent job.'

In 1959 syndication became a six-days-a-week operation, which it was estimated would cost ITN £28,000. The company was trying hard to expand its sales abroad, but it could not compete with Visnews, a much more comprehensive service involving the BBC, the Canadian and Australian Broadcasting Commissions, the Rank Organisation and Reuters. The board was warned that 'ITN's syndication is losing money and may well lose money for some years to come.'[4]

So it did. The CBS deal had not worked well, with CBS selling ITN material in areas of the world where ITN could have sold it itself. But, the board was told, 'There can be no future for ITN syndication unless an effective ally can be found.' So in 1966, when United Press International, in America, suddenly found itself in need of a partner for its film agency business, ITN was ready. Together they set up UPITN. The ostensible benefit was that together ITN and UPI would deliver a much better and more competitive news service. Privately ITN management also hoped that UPI camera crews around the world would reduce the need to dispatch ITN's own crews to foreign parts. Their first-class travel and overtime agreement made it too expensive to send them abroad very often.

The deal was not popular at ITN, not least because it would make nearly all the syndication team redundant. 'It was decided,' Frank Miles says, 'almost behind our backs, that there would be a merger with United Press. There were by this time seven of us employed, but we found that in merging only I would be offered a job. Everybody else was being made redundant. We were just a small unit working during the night, and we didn't really know the rest of ITN, but now for the first time I felt the power of a union, and the marvellous backing we didn't even know we had from people in the newsroom. Jon Lander, chief sub and father of the NUJ chapel, called a meeting to which we were invited, and we found that not only were they prepared to strike on our behalf, but also that they had fed the story to the national papers. It had made the front pages of all the nationals – that there was going to be a strike to protect the jobs of the seven journalists. And we were amazed.

'This resulted in a meeting in Geoffrey's office. I had had a call at home from Hugh Whitcomb, the editor of our newsfilm service, who said, "I want you to understand that we are prepared to offer you a job." So we filed into this meeting and Geoffrey Cox said, "Would you like to come and sit with me?" and I said, "No, I'll sit with my colleagues, if you don't mind." The upshot was that we were all offered the alternative of a new job at ITN or redundancy pay. Chris Barlow, Derek Dowsett and I all chose to stay on at ITN and the rest, I think, took their redundancy money.'

It wasn't just those directly affected by the merger who objected to the deal with UPI. As Nigel Ryan later wrote: 'In the ITN newsroom the venture was eyed with the deepest suspicion. The foreign desk was reluctant to loosen its absolute control of coverage and feared a blurring of objectives. It wanted any growth to be in material tailor-made for its own needs rather than aimed at a mass market. The counter-argument was also a strong one: the agency could generate more funds, and without funds there would be no growth.'[5]

Foreign editor Robert Hargreaves was dead against the merger. In his view the money that would have to be invested if UPITN were to succeed would be far better spent setting up more ITN bureaux abroad – in 1967 there was only one, in Washington. Reporters were not enthusiastic about the new arrangement either. It was all too common to arrive in some foreign country and be met by a UPI crew that was either ill-equipped or simply incompetent, able to shoot a few feet of news-agency footage, but not to the sort of standard that ITN expected and got from its own camera crews. And, of course, those ITN camera crews were not happy to see inferior material on the screen while they were travelling less.

UPITN got off to a bad start. The very day the merger went into effect, in June 1967, the Six Day War between Israel and the surrounding Arab states broke out. The new agency was caught somewhat unprepared and as a result ITN did not do as well as it might have against the BBC. More importantly, hopes that the merger would be justified by increased profits proved illusory. UPITN expanded, but did not make money. As Sir Geoffrey Cox recalls, feelingly, 'We went on and on but we never could get this bloody thing UPITN to break even. I needed the time for editing ITN, but here I was travelling round Europe taking editors of television stations out to sleazy nightclubs persuading them to buy the service.'

Two years later ITN reviewed the situation.

Following a first-year loss of $241,000 it was predicted that in its second year UPITN would still lose between $50,000 and $100,000. More expensive colour film was coming in and there was a danger that some substantial European contracts would be lost. For the next four years the agency continued to expand, but disappointed its owners with what Nigel Ryan, ITN's new editor, described as 'undramatic but persistent losses'.

In 1973 UPITN's competition in America upped the ante with a decision to supply its customers there with news stories delivered electronically by landline. ITN had to increase its stake or get out of the game. But all seemed set fair when Paramount Pictures, flush with the profits from its latest picture *The Godfather*, decided to take a 50 per cent share of UPITN. Nigel Ryan had to negotiate the terms of the deal with some pretty tough characters who, he joked, could have stepped straight out of the film: 'There were bizarre moments. When the ITN and UPITN executives entered the Paramount boardroom in the Gulf and Western building in New York, they found themselves confronted by two Paramount executives with only pocket calculators on the table in front of them; on the wall was Marlon Brando in his Godfather posture, making the offer that his business partners "could not refuse".'

Pushed along by Paramount, UPITN found itself going for broke, and that was pretty much what happened. Unlike its competitors in the United States UPITN had no link with any major American television company and had to generate all its own US material. This was very expensive. By May 1975, after racking up losses of $3.5 million, UPITN abandoned its electronic delivery service.

Paramount now wanted out, but neither UPI nor ITN was keen to spend its money buying up Paramount's shares. Back in Britain some of the ITV companies were adamantly opposed to becoming further embroiled in the tangled affairs of UPITN. Peter Cadbury, the chairman of Westward Television, wrote to Nigel Ryan:

> I have always expressed the opinion that the initial venture into UPITN was an error, that it was an extravagance that ITN cannot afford and that there are inherent dangers that could be very serious financially. I have never varied from this opinion and I have always urged the board to close down the whole operation if it were practical . . . Dealing with multi-million dollar American corporations is not a game to be taken on lightly from this distance and I am very nervous of the outcome if and when the gloves are off.[6]

ITN had been talking to America's ABC network but, because of legal hitches, nothing had been agreed; without a deal with a major American network it looked as if UPITN might have to be wound up, at a cost to ITN of £624,000. And then, suddenly, a saviour arrived.

John McGoff, a Michigan-based publisher, owned a string of papers in the American Mid-west. He was known to hold strong right-wing views and was an open supporter of South Africa and its apartheid policy. In other words, he was not the partner an impartial television news organisation like ITN was looking for. Nevertheless, there was no legal reason to say no to his money; no one else wanted to help, and beggars can't be choosers. For 50 per cent of UPITN the flamboyant Mr McGoff paid $1,350,000.

UPITN staggered on, though by 1978 it was again in financial trouble, with a projected loss for the year of $800,000. But in March the following year a far more worrying development was reported to the ITN board. A rumour was spreading that McGoff had bought his share of UPITN with South African government money.[7] This was serious. ITN had just run an extract from a UPITN interview with the South African President John Vorster, which had been conducted by the man McGoff had installed as UPITN chairman, Clarence Rhodes.

UPITN's executive vice president Ken Coyte assured the Guardian[8] there was 'no possibility whatsoever' that South African money was involved, but the news got worse. At UPITN McGoff himself twice denied that he had been bankrolled by the South Africans, but on 21 May 1979 ITN decided it wanted that assurance in writing: 'It was agreed that unless there was a satisfactory reply, the reputation and the future of UPITN would be at critical risk. Whatever statements were made, the dilemma could only be resolved by the removal of Mr McGoff as a shareholder.'[9]

No reply was forthcoming, so now ITN's chairman John Freeman wrote a stiff letter making it plain that, if necessary, ITN would pull out of UPITN: 'My board . . . do not find it acceptable to be associated in any way with a company which is not in a position immediately and unanswerably to refute the allegation that it may have been covertly penetrated by foreign government funds.'[10]

On 4 June, in South Africa, the Erasmus Commission, which had been looking into the allegations of an undercover and illegal propaganda campaign, published its report. All was revealed. The South African government had indeed secretly financed the purchase of McGoff's UPITN shares from a $70 million 'slush fund' set up by the information ministry for just that kind of thing. Eschel Rhoodie, the minister's right-hand man, later boasted of how the investment in UPITN '. . . gave South Africa virtually unlimited access to all of the international outlets of this television news distribution agency.' Of the UPITN interview with the South African president, Rhoodie wrote: 'That interview was eventually screened in ninety countries, some of it during prime television time. In terms of buying time on television that one Vorster programme more than repaid the investment of $1,350,000.'[11]

'It was undoubtedly one of the department's biggest coups,' said the *New Statesman*. 'What effect the Department of Information's takeover has had on dissemination of news across the world is still a matter of speculation, but it is disturbing that the fact has slipped by so largely unremarked.'[12]

It was all a huge embarrassment, and to demonstrate that its hands were now clean ITN had to buy McGoff's shares for what he had paid for them – less the losses UPITN had incurred since he had taken over. As for the now notorious interview with Vorster, supplied to ITN and UPITN's other clients round the world, ITN editor David Nicholas robustly defended his decision to run an extract from it: 'The two minute interview was the first time anyone had got him [Vorster] to say anything about Angola on camera. He admitted that South African troops were in Angola, that the MPLA was making advances, and he criticised the free world for not backing UNITA. These were all strong news points. I would run two minutes with Gaddafi or Lucifer on similar terms if I could get them.'[13]

Yes, but the viewer might have looked at the interview differently had he known it was being carried out by a company part-owned by the interviewee.

Once again UPITN was groggy, on the canvas, but to ITN's relief the legal problems that had prevented an earlier rescue were resolved, and ABC Television climbed into the ring to haul UPITN to its feet. With an American broadcaster involved, UPITN stood a much better chance of success. The company fought on.

But in 1984 the ITN board noted 'with misgivings' the reported financial problems of UPITN's other co-owner, UPI. The following year UPI filed for bankruptcy and in April 1985 UPITN was renamed WTN, Worldwide Television News, with ITN and ABC as its owners. But, as a McKinsey study showed, neither party was getting a good deal – they could perfectly well have set up a 'swap' arrangement without the need for WTN at all. And WTN was making it difficult for ITN to become the world player some wanted it to be. The then chief executive of ITN, David Gordon, argued in 1993 that 'The prime objective of establishing a worldwide sustained news market was hindered by the WTN agreement.'

So in 1994 ITN finally ended its involvement with WTN and replaced it with a cash contract to take news footage from Reuters. This would inevitably be costly, the ITN board was told, but management would redouble their efforts to sell ITN's own material to pay for it: 'We are reasonably optimistic about increasing overseas sales to show a surplus over these costs.'

The fact was that, nearly forty years after it had first set up its own syndication business, ITN was pretty much back where it had started, always hoping but never quite succeeding in selling its material for more than it was paying for other people's.

To keep its programmes fully fed, ITN now takes news-agency film from Reuters Television (the successor to Visnews) and from APTV, a newer agency. The relationship with ABC in America has ended and ITN is most closely associated with NBC. An agreement is in place for ITN's terrestrial programmes to have access to the American broadcaster CNN for breaking news in return for ITN reporter packages.

CHAPTER 26
SCOOP!

Welcome to Cyprus

'If I had any particular ability, it was to grab at luck and even on occasion turn bad fortune to advantage.'[1] This was how Michael Nicholson began his account of what was perhaps his greatest scoop, a huge success for him and for ITN, born out of what looked like a succession of failures.

It was July 1974 and he had been reporting from Cyprus, assigned by foreign editor Tony Millett, who had a hunch that something dramatic was about to happen. Tension on the island, with its mixed Greek and Turkish populations, had been increasing. The fear was that mainland Greece might make some military move to bring about Enosis, the union of Cyprus with Greece, and that Turkey would intervene with military force to prevent it. Now the Cyprus National Guard, with mainland Greek rather than Greek Cypriot commanders, seemed to be throwing its weight about on the island. 'Something is up,' Nicholson reported, but it was not clear what it was. Tension remained, but there is a limit on how long any television newsdesk can keep a crew hanging about 'just in case'. With no specific developments to report, Nicholson prepared to return to London. He ended his short tour by interviewing the Cypriot president, Archbishop Makarios.

While they were doing their 'two-shots' at the end of the interview, with the sound still being recorded, Makarios insisted that nothing exciting was going to happen and that Nicholson could let ITN recall him: 'I am perfectly safe,' Makarios said. Nicholson flew back to London, and his interview ran in Friday night's *News at Ten*. It didn't seem very exciting, and, indeed, the foreign desk had to get David Nicholas to intervene to ensure that the interview was in the bulletin at all. But on Monday morning Nicholson got a call from senior foreign editor John Mahoney: 'Are you sitting down, Nick?' Mahoney asked. 'If not, I suggest you do.' A military coup had been staged by the National Guard and Makarios had been assassinated. Nicholson had missed it.

With considerable difficulty Nicholson managed to get back into Cyprus to report on the aftermath of the coup. 'Some houses had been demolished, others were barely standing,' he wrote. 'The walls of some government buildings had been neatly patterned by the snipers' succession of single bullets and from a distance looked like clever graffiti. Army jeeps and lorries were wrecked and still smouldering, tanks had torn up the gardens of the Archbishop's palace where I had sat with him only a few days before.'

Better than nothing, but there was no disguising that ITN had not been there for the coup. And now Nicholson managed somehow to miss the press conference given by Nicos Sampson, the puppet the Greek government had installed as president of Cyprus. Arriving just as it ended, he nonethless persuaded Sampson to talk to him, and a couple of other television crews, and seized his opportunity. As cameraman Alan Downes said later: 'Nicholson was at his best and really screwed Sampson into the ground. He took over the whole thing and, at the end, Sampson was virtually steaming with anger.' This was better, but that seemed to be it: the excitement was all over.

Nicholson had planned to hand-carry his Sampson interview to Tel Aviv in Israel, where an ITN film editor was waiting to cut and satellite the story to London, but the flight was delayed, and he decided to let an American colleague take the film for him while he stayed in Cyprus overnight. That evening there was a bit of a party at the Ledra Palace Hotel and Nicholson, thinking his trip was over, crawled into bed at about three in the morning rather the worse for wear. He was woken by a phone call from London and a whispered message from diplomatic correspondent Peter Snow: 'Sources here tell me that *they* – you understand me, I can't be too explicit on the phone – *they* are coming in tomorrow, landing in the north at Salamis Bay.'[2]

Badly hung-over, Nicholson got out his map of Cyprus and struggled to make sense of the message. Was this the Turkish invasion? He thought Snow had spoken of Soldana Bay. Could it be Salamis Bay? But that was in the east of the island not the north. Which way should he go? Deciding that the northern coast, closest to Turkey, was the most likely landing place he tiptoed down the hotel corridor to wake up cameraman Alan Downes and sound recordist Bob Hammond. They pushed their rented car silently out of the hotel car park to avoid alerting their BBC rivals and set off towards Kyrenia, in the north.

Then it seemed that Nicholson had made another blunder or, just as fatal for a reporter, was again suffering from bad luck. He had been responsible for renting the car, but a few miles outside Nicosia it stopped – out of petrol. Worse, moments later two BBC crews swept by, laughing and jeering at ITN's predicament. Nicholson had lost the initiative and, it seemed, the story.

Then, close overhead, they heard the heavy drone of C-130 aircraft. Soon the sky was full of parachutes: the Turks were coming by air as well as sea, landing in the centre of the island as well as on the northern coast. ITN's car breakdown, Nicholson's failure, had brought about success. A Cypriot student just back from Britain recognised the ITN logo, enthusiastically bundled them into his car and drove them towards the drop zone. They were briefly detained by a truckload of Turkish troops and forced to follow them in the student's car, but as they twisted and turned through the narrow streets of a village, the vehicles were separated, and the crew jumped out. 'We ran through the village,' Nicholson recalled, 'down alleys and backyards and suddenly we were out into the fields, under the men falling. What I did next must have seemed a little surprising, given the circumstances. I stood and applauded them down and as the nearest of them landed and gathered in his parachute I ran to him and shook him by the hand and said above the din, "I'm Michael Nicholson of ITN. Welcome to Cyprus."'

Soldiers descending by parachute feel exceedingly vulnerable to fire from the ground. Seeing cameraman Alan Downes with a large black object on his shoulder and soundman Bob Hammond with his 'rifle' mic, both pointing in their direction, would certainly have had the Turkish soldiers' fingers itching on the trigger. Nicholson's friendly overtures must have prevented them being shot up. 'They were completely bemused by this incredible figure who kept rushing up to them,' Downes says, 'shaking them by the hand and saying, "Welcome to Cyprus." It was a very clever move, because, although the Turks were understandably a bit on edge, it caused no alarm and gave me more time to film them.'

Then came the helicopters, line after line, one after another disgorging Turkish troops. As Greek artillery shells and mortar fire began to find the range it all made a perfect backdrop to a dramatic piece to camera by Nicholson. Dodging more Greek bombardments the crew made their way back to Nicosia. There they found that another ITN crew – reporter Christopher Wain, cameraman John Collins and soundman Tony Piddington – had spent a busy day filming their own dramatic material of British holidaymakers diving for cover in the hotel lounge as bullets smashed through the windows. Greeks and Turks had apparently been firing at each other from opposite ends of the hotel swimming-pool.

ITN now had a great story. But sitting in Cyprus, where there was no film processing and even if there had been, no satellite, it was as good as useless. With the civilian airport closed, the only possible way to get it out seemed to be courtesy of the RAF. Next morning, during a UN-organised one-hour ceasefire, Wain set off for the British military base at Akrotiri with his crew, carrying his and Nicholson's material. With luck and tenacity they made it through police and military checkpoints, travelling across a Cyprus now at war, and arrived at Akrotiri minutes before an RAF VC-10 was taking off for Britain.

At seven thirty that evening a helicopter chartered by ITN met the VC-10 at RAF Brize Norton, scooped up the film and flew it to the Battersea heliport in London. Dispatch riders got it to ITN by nine o'clock, and an hour later the story was on *News at Ten*. Next day the London *Evening News* said: 'The ITV switchboard was jammed with complimentary calls after last night's *News at Ten* programme. Some callers said it was the best television news coverage they had ever seen.' The London *Evening Standard* agreed. Of the 'Superbly Informative ITN' it said: 'The past few days have confirmed what many of us suspected after ITN's coverage of the last Middle East war – that BBC News will have to get a lot sharper, a lot fresher, a lot more flexible, if it is to match *News at Ten* when the big stories break.'[3]

ITN had had a world exclusive with material no other network could match, even when their own crews' footage reached the screen days later. No one except Nicholson and his team had been in the right place to greet the invading Turkish forces. Overcoming failure and back luck, he had turned disaster into triumph. The *Daily Mail* concluded, 'If ITN does not collar all the Newsreel of the Year awards for its footage from Cyprus this week, then the prizes will not be worth their silver plating.'

Desert Story

At 1.45 p.m. on Sunday, 6 September 1970, El Al flight LY219 was climbing out of Amsterdam's airport on its way to New York. Shortly it would cross the English coast above Clacton-on-Sea in Essex, at twenty thousand feet.

Suddenly two passengers, a man and a woman sitting together in economy class, jumped from their seats and rushed headlong through the dividing curtain into the first-class cabin, making for the flight deck. They were screaming – it might have been 'Yallah!', 'Let's go' in Arabic. But the door to the cockpit was locked and the pilot would not open it. A furious fight developed. The man pulled a gun and seriously wounded a cabin steward before he was shot down by El Al's armed on-board air marshal. Meanwhile the woman was brandishing two hand grenades and threatening to blow up the aircraft. When the pilot put the plane into a steep and sudden dive she lost her balance, was thrown to the floor and quickly overpowered by cabin crew and passengers. Fortunately she had not pulled the pins from her two grenades.

The woman was Leila Khaled, an Arab born in Haifa in what had once been called Palestine but was now part of Israel. It was on behalf of the Popular Front for the Liberation of Palestine that she had tried to hijack this flight from Israel's national airline. The plane made an emergency landing at Heathrow airport and Khaled was detained. But the story of her hijack war was only just beginning. It would end with a tremendous exclusive for ITN.

Forty-five miles north of Amman, the Jordanian capital, lay a desert runway last used by the RAF in 1947, as the British abandoned the UN Mandate in Palestine and left the Jews and Arabs to fight it out. Then the British had called it Dawson's Field. Now known to Arabs as Ga'Khanna, it was about to be renamed Revolution Airstrip. In an audacious plan the

PFLP had decided to hijack three commercial airliners, compel their pilots at gunpoint to fly them to this desert runway, then hold the passengers to ransom. The price: the release of other PFLP hijackers held in Europe. In addition they wanted to exchange Israeli passengers for Palestinians imprisoned in Israel.

On the Sunday evening, as it grew dangerously dark, two of the three hijacked planes, a TWA B-707 and a Swissair DC-8, landed safely at Revolution Airstrip, just as the PFLP had planned. But the El Al plane – the only one to have an armed guard aboard – had escaped, and Leila Khaled was now in British custody. So that they could bargain for her release the PFLP now seized a British plane, a BOAC VC-10. Hijacked after leaving Bahrain on a flight to London, it joined the others at Revolution Airstrip. On board were fifty-two Britons, including twenty-one children returning to boarding-school at the end of their summer holidays. In all, more than three hundred hostages were now being held in the desert.

The PFLP set a deadline for the following Sunday. If their demands were not met then the planes would be blown up with the passengers strapped into their seats. Days of dramatic activity followed in Europe and Jordan as the nations whose citizens were being held captive negotiated with the PFLP for their release, and go-betweens flew back and forth. At Revolution Airstrip, conditions aboard the planes, sweltering without air-conditioning in the desert heat, quickly became unpleasant. To reinforce their demands the PFLP ostentatiously strapped explosives to the aircraft. Journalists were taken out to see some of the passengers and allowed to question them.

Then, at last, on the Saturday, as it was confirmed that the Western governments involved had agreed to release the PFLP prisoners, the hostages were allowed to leave the planes and were brought to the Intercontinental Hotel in Amman, first the women and children, and later the men. But more than fifty, including all the Israelis, were spirited away by the PFLP, to ensure that the deal went through.

In Amman, following every twist and development in 'Leila's hijack war', were two ITN crews, led by reporters Gerald Seymour and Michael Nicholson. In London, ITN's deputy editor David Nicholas decided that their material, when he got his hands on it, might make more than just a *News at Ten* story: it might justify a special news programme for the ITV network. To help co-ordinate the filming in Amman, and pull together an instant documentary, he dispatched a field producer.

David Phillips, ten years at ITN, was a very safe pair of hands indeed in which to place such a difficult project. He was a typical ITN entrepreneur, dashing, decisive, determined. During the current crisis not much was flying in or out of Amman, but early on Saturday morning Phillips had caught an Arab Airlines flight out of Beirut that would get him to the heart of the story. As he flew in to Amman he could see, way down on the desert floor, the three hijacked planes – they looked like dots on a domino tile. On the ground Phillips talked his way through what seemed an endless succession of PFLP roadblocks to reach Amman's Intercontinental Hotel. Soon after he got there ITN filmed extraordinary scenes as the women and children among the hostages arrived at the hotel, led by triumphant Palestinian guerrillas singing the PFLP revolutionary anthem and firing their rifles into the air. It made an excellent sequence: Phillips could now be sure he had all that was needed to make a special programme for ITV. But the story wasn't over.

As Michael Nicholson, in his hotel room, typed away at his script for what he had been filming, he was interrupted by ITN's local freelance cameraman Ghassan Dalal. Nicholson must come with him at once, back to the hijacked planes out in the desert, he urged. 'We got to the strip just as the last of the men hostages were leaving,' wrote Nicholson, 'but they were not Ghassan's concern.' As they watched they saw Palestinians jump from the planes and sprint away.

> As Ghassan braced himself, with his camera wedged hard against his neck, I realised what they were about to do. I heard the camera running and I counted. At five the VC-10 exploded – first the nose, then the tail. The TWA Boeing went up in a flash of flame seconds later. Then a pause, and the Swissair DC-8, twelve million pounds' worth of aircraft, suddenly disintegrated in front of us, a mass of black and grey and orange. I sat down in the sand and watched.[4]

Back in Amman, forty-five miles away, David Phillips saw a great cloud of smoke climb into the sky and realised that the planes had been blown up. Dalal, a PFLP man himself, had been given exclusive access to film this extraordinary event, carried out by local militants at Revolution Airstrip against the wishes of the PFLP leadership. But the film was not yet in ITN's possession. The militants now began to discuss with Dalal how to get the most propaganda value out of this exclusive. One suggestion was that it be auctioned among the many television networks vying with each other in Amman.

In the early-evening twilight Phillips was driven to a rendezvous with the PFLP militants, where it turned out that the decision as to what should happen to the film had been left to Dalal. He told Phillips that ITN could have its film, but only if the local CBS cameraman (a relative, of course) could have a copy. 'At this point,' says Phillips, 'I became aware of CBS producer John Lane lurking behind me. Some rather intense argument ensued. My point to Ghassan was that the film belonged to his employers, ITN and UPITN. It was not for him to say who should have it. But it was half an hour before the film – this scoop of scoops – was actually in my hands. What made Ghassan hand it over? My guess is that materialism conquered his idealism. He saw that he could lose his job. This way, he would be able to go on filming his Palestinian revolutionary comrades. Anyway, we now had everything, and all I had to do was get it out. We were already in the satellite age, but the television station in Amman was shut, for fear of a PFLP takeover. Hand-carrying the film to London was our only hope.'

But as Phillips set out for the airport, only hours after he had arrived there that morning, CBS producer John Lane stuck close to him, refusing to give up hope of getting his own hands on the film. 'Thank God he did!' Phillips now says.

At the airport the apron was virtually bare. Given the dangerous situation, all commercial flights had been cancelled. Was there a small plane to be hired, asked Phillips urgently, a Cessna or anything that might get him somewhere where he could pick up a flight to London? No, there was not. But on the tarmac stood a large eighty-nine-seat Caravelle. It was supposed to fly – empty – next day to Cyprus, for servicing. For a price, it was suggested, it could take off that night. 'How much?' asked Phillips. 'Six thousand dollars,' came the reply. Phillips had a decent advance to help him pay ITN's way, but nothing like as much as that. 'I think I can help,' said Lane. 'If I can, I want equal access to the film.'

Phillips struck a deal: if Lane could get the money *now*, CBS could have a copy of it in London, the moment ITN aired the material in the UK. With America five hours behind Britain, that would give CBS plenty of time to satellite the story to New York for their main evening-news programme. ITN would have its exclusive in London, CBS in America. Lane got on the phone to the Intercontinental; it was not long before his colleague Bert Quint, the celebrated CBS bag-carrier, arrived. 'I remember Quint had this Gladstone bag,' says Phillips, 'which he held high upside-down in the air while all these dollar bills poured out, six thousand dollars of it in little bundles.'

At Nicosia, the Caravelle, the first plane out of Amman since the hostages had been released, was met by hordes of expectant journalists, but to their disappointment just two people, Phillips and his CBS shadow Lane, came down the steps. A BEA flight was leaving for London at 3 a.m., but it was full. Thinking of the VC-10 exploding in the desert, Phillips asked to speak to the local BEA manager. Waving his bag of unprocessed film in front of him Phillips explained his difficulty: 'I think your bosses in London will want to see this,' he said. Soon he was sitting in a jump seat aboard the plane on his way home to the UK.

By 9 a.m. Phillips was at ITN and David Nicholas was negotiating with the ITV companies for a special programme that evening. There was so much material that, for editing, the footage was divided in two. The brothers David and John Harwood worked on the first part, Leo Rosenberg on the second. After a day's desperate editing in which the two cutting rooms had been ceaselessly at work, *Deadline at Dawson's Field* finally ran, twenty-five minutes in length, at 5.30 p.m. A shorter version ran in the late news that night.

Afterwards, as they were pouring their several celebratory drinks there was a congratulatory phone call for Phillips. It was from former ITN producer Brian Wenham, now editor of *Panorama* and a rising star at the BBC. Would Phillips like to join his flagship programme, he asked. Phillips declined. ITN was just too much fun.

CHAPTER 27

COMING INDOORS

By 1976 ITN producer David Phillips had come indoors and been domesticated. While he still relished the role of field producer for the really big story, his experience was now being put to good use in his role as one of the output editors of *News at Ten*.

News at Ten, which had begun almost a decade earlier in 1967, had now become pre-eminent in British news broadcasting. Three times in five weeks, boasted an ITN press release, *News at Ten* had headed the list of the twenty most popular television programmes. At lunchtime *First Report*, which had begun in 1972, had established itself as much more than the housewife's choice, a serious programme in which live interviews with newsmakers of all kinds drew a large, attentive audience. Only the early-evening programme remained unsatisfactory. 'I felt that the six o'clock news was a disgrace,' says Phillips. 'It was a rag-bag filled with scraps from here and there – it just picked up what was available; bits hacked out of reports done for *News at Ten*, items from Eurovision [the daily news exchange between television companies in Europe], and hand-drawn captions. When, for scheduling reasons of their own, the ITV companies asked us to change the time of the programme, I suggested to Nigel Ryan that we really could make it ITN's third proper show.'

Ryan liked the idea. The new early news would be fifteen minutes long and start at 5.45. He seized the opportunity to 'brand' all his programmes in the same way. ITN announced, 'All the ITN weekday programmes will have the same name style from August 30. *First Report*, which was launched in 1972, will be retitled *News at One* in line with *News at 5.45* and *News at Ten* . . . we are titling our programmes as "news at. . ." so that people will naturally switch to ITV when they want the news.'

By happy chance this was the moment at which Alastair Burnet had decided to return to broadcasting, and to ITN. It was envisaged that he would ultimately find his place again as a *News at Ten* newscaster, but to reintroduce him to the ITN audience it was decided that he was the ideal man to launch the new programme *News at 5.45*, as he had *News at Ten*. Intellectual though he was, Burnet also had a popular side. He was, for example, a keen sports fan – of football, racing and cricket.

Together Phillips and Burnet went to New York to see in particular how the great CBS front-man Walter Cronkite managed to present his programme with the wonderful blend of cosiness and authority that had made him the nation's favourite newscaster.

When they returned from their tour of American television studios and control rooms they presented Nigel Ryan with their detailed proposals. 'I put it to Nigel,' says Phillips, 'that at fifteen minutes the *News at 5.45* could be like a London evening newspaper at its best. It would be up-to-the-minute in news but also highly visual.' Phillips had adopted a technical system the Americans were using in which sharp, clear images could be presented over the newscaster's shoulder to illustrate the story and give a sleek, individual look to the programme.

Perhaps most importantly he was determined that ITN's reporters should work as much for 5.45 as for the *News at Ten*. In August, shortly before the new programme began, he told them: 'What I am proposing is that reporters write and record two scripts – their *NaT* script and a shorter one for the 5.45, with of course a "News at Five-Four-Five sign-off". This means the film editor can put aside the *NaT* wildtrack [recorded commentary] and select the sequences to cover the 5.45 script, which will be the guts of the story. I assure you that sequences will not be butchered to suit our length and so spoilt for your *NaT* package.'[1]

Generally, reporters welcomed Phillips's proposal. Their only concern was that *News at Ten* would take the lazy way of simply rerunning the shorter packages that had been cut for the *News at 5.45* rather than restore the material to the length they had intended for *News at Ten*.

News at 5.45 went on the air at the end of August 1977 and at once did well: the audience was 11 per cent up on the six o'clock programme of the previous week, and one third as large again as the BBC's early news – a television rating of 28 as opposed to the BBC's 21. 'The figures do tend to indicate,' wrote ITN's Paul McKee cautiously, 'that the 5.45 News may have succeeded in pushing up the network audience share by 1 per cent or 2 per cent at this critical early evening period.'[2]

Now at last, with three well thought-out, complementary bulletins, ITN was a coherent whole, a vital and valuable part of ITV, at the height of its success. Once again, the network had cause to be grateful to its news provider. With chief scriptwriters like Frank Miles and programme editors Derek Dowsett and Phil Moger, *News at 5.45* would endure to the end of the century.

But after the successful launch of *News at 5.45*, David Phillips grew restless. In America he had seen how quickly the networks had adopted ENG, the new electronic news gathering system based on videotape. At a stroke they had done away with the time-wasting business of processing film. ITN was taking the first steps towards acquiring the new technology but Phillips was worried – rightly, as it turned out – that in Britain the unions would take their time in agreeing to operate it. Rather than wait he decided to move on, and in 1979 he joined the American NBC network to work in its London bureau, once more travelling the world.

CHAPTER 28

A DIFFERENT NEWS

'Any train that leaves the station,' said ITN editor David Nicholas, 'I want to be on it.' First had come expansion in what ITN provided for its owners, the ITV companies – *News at Ten, News at One, News at 5.45.* Now, in the early eighties, ITN was for the first time looking to supply news programmes to a different broadcaster altogether.

In early 1981 Nicholas told the ITN board: 'ITN is at a crossroads. In the months ahead, a series of interlocking judgements need to be made which will determine how the company is to develop over the next decade. It is, perhaps, as important a time as any in the company's twenty-five years of existence, to be compared only with the major policy decision in 1967 which traded off *Dateline* and *Roving Report* in exchange for a twelve-week experiment with a nightly half-hour news.'[1]

Television in Britain had been slow to expand. First there had been the long monopoly held by the BBC; in 1955 ITV had been established; then, in 1964, came BBC2. Nearly two more decades had passed before expansion picked up speed. It was 1982 before Independent Television got its own second channel, Channel 4.

Naturally Channel 4 would have news programmes; naturally, thought David Nicholas, they should be provided by ITN, and his lobbying seemed to produce results. In 1979 William Whitelaw, the Conservative home secretary, was already saying that the *Channel 4 News* 'was clearly a job for ITN, with the resources to do it, and its admirable record'.

The IBA, the Independent Broadcasting Authority, agreed. It strongly supported the idea that ITN should do the *Channel 4 News*. But Jeremy Isaacs, the first chief executive of Channel 4, was not at all sure that ITN was capable of giving him something sufficiently different from the kind of news it already provided for ITV. As Isaacs put it:

> Liz Forgan, senior commissioning editor for news and current affairs, had decided to offer, against two rival submissions, the channel's major news commission to Independent Television News, ITN. We knew there might be a real difficulty for ITN in making what we wanted, which was a different sort of news programme, with a different news agenda from what they already successfully purveyed on ITV. It might require, someone observed, an effort amounting almost to collective schizophrenia on their part to get both right. We also knew that to give this one major contract to ITN was to risk running counter to the whole pluralistic purpose of the channel. We ought, surely, to be diversifying the sources of news, rather than perpetuating and extending the BBC/ITN duopoly. But ITN, we were agreed, was our best practical hope of a considered, serious news magazine programme.[2]

And so, rather grudgingly, Channel 4 gave ITN its news contract.

But what exactly would Channel 4 want? 'The general theme of two informal discussions with Jeremy Isaacs,' Nicholas reported, 'has been that the news programmes, like all other programmes on the Channel, should be as different as possible from those on ITV. This was further defined as "news by exclusion", that is no news about, for example, the royal family, film stars, sport, crime or major disasters.'

As Isaacs recalled:

> In public utterance, and in meetings with ITN, I stressed that we wanted a news that not only did not rely on but actively eschewed violent incident for its own sake. If such incident were portrayed it must be justified, whether in Ireland or in Israel, by the political context. We did not want stories of individual crime, or of minor natural disaster. We did not want coverage of the daily diaries of the Royal Family. *Channel 4 News* would deal with politics

and with the economy. It would bring coverage of the City, and of industry. It was to report on developments in science and technology, and in the arts. It was to cover the politics of other countries and to supplement that reporting with the output and insights of foreign television news programmes.

Who was to present the new programme? Thinking that Isaacs would be overwhelmed by the generosity of his offer, David Nichols prepared to pluck the finest flower in ITN's garden, none other than Alastair Burnet, star of *News at Ten*. Says Isaacs: 'David Nicholas told me quietly one day that, if I was interested, it was just possible that Alastair Burnet, who had after all edited *The Economist*, might be prepared to give up presenting *News at Ten* to front the new programme. I dismissed the idea. Though no one doubted his abilities, it seemed to me wrong that we should rest our appeal on Burnet's familiar image.'

Isaacs wanted someone new, but before he was turned down for a job he obviously did not want, Burnet took part in an early pilot for the new programme. 'Have you ever seen the pilot?' Stewart Purvis, who later became editor of *Channel 4 News*, says gleefully. 'It's wonderful. Alastair sits there sulking throughout the entire thing . . . The pilot is really quite interesting. But Burnet clearly hated it – hated every minute of it.'

In January 1984 an *Observer* profile accused Sir Alastair – he had been knighted in the New Year Honours – of behaving unprofessionally, and suggested that 'Burnet's undisguised dislike of *Channel 4 News* springs from his recognition that its thoughtful liberal tone constitutes an implied critique of *News at Ten*'s fast-moving tabloid style.'[3] The following Sunday Burnet responded with an angry letter insisting that while he had not liked the pilot, and had said so, 'I have consistently supported ITN's *Channel 4 News* contract with the IBA, Jeremy Isaacs of Channel 4, the ITN board and my colleagues.'[4]

But it seems that Burnet remained underwhelmed by *Channel 4 News*. In the book he published after he had left Channel 4, Isaacs concluded: 'In all the years *Channel 4 News* has been on the air bringing credit and distinction to ITN, of which he is a director as well as an employee, Sir Alastair Burnet has never uttered a syllable of commendation of it to Liz Forgan or to myself.'[5]

David Nicholas insisted that the choice of editor for the new programme should be his, although Channel 4 had to be consulted. The eventual appointment was a curious one. Derrik Mercer had shown himself an able managing editor (news) at the *Sunday Times*, then in its heyday, but he knew little about television. Yet now he was to be responsible for a daily one-hour news programme made by ITN for a very demanding new broadcaster.

The first demand that Channel 4 made was that ITN should cut the price of the product. ITN's original bid of £6,722,000 had already been reduced to £6,166,000; but Channel 4 was insisting that it be cut to £5,427,000. At an ITN board meeting on 20 October 1981 Brian Tesler and David McCall, who were directors of both ITN and Channel 4, pointed out that Channel 4 was not all that keen on taking its news from ITN. With the IBA's director general Sir Brian Young, they persuaded ITN to accept this rock-bottom, if not loss-making, price.

Soon after *Channel 4 News* was launched on 2 November 1981, it became clear to everyone involved in making the programmes that Derrik Mercer was not cut out to be a television editor. Peter Sissons, who had finally been chosen as the programme's main presenter, remembers it as a miserable time: 'I hated going in to *Channel 4 News* while Mercer was there, trying to do a valuable job for the company, working for someone who was so obviously out of his depth – and he hated it too. It was the only period in my life when I hated going to work at ITN. We used to sit there cringing at the morning meetings. The programme was so awful, with a ghastly set. When you work in television it does help if the person you're working for commands your respect. I loathed the way things were going, so much so that I was ready to risk anything to try and turn things round.'

At the first meeting of the joint ITN/Channel 4 editorial Review Committee Mercer reported that the programme had broken new ground in all the areas it had set out to target. It had been the first to reveal the government's worries about the exchange rate, Labour's plan to deal with Militant and, in the arts, the Whitbread literary awards. 'There is no doubt,' said the embattled Mercer, 'that the programme is achieving its brief of widening the agenda of television.'

But nobody was watching. Audiences for the News fell below 250,000, when Channel 4 had – though quite unrealistically – been hoping for 1.5 million. ITN's chairman, Lord (Aubrey) Buxton, was worried; he wrote to

ITN board members about his 'concern that the *ITN News* on Channel 4 may become the scapegoat for some of Channel 4's failures' because the flagship news programme was the obvious target. 'It is becoming intellectually trendy to be complimentary about some Channel 4 programmes, but the fact remains that the service is diabolical as far as normal viewers are concerned.' Buxton wanted the ITN board to discuss this so that ITN would not 'unwittingly get boxed into an unwarranted defensive position, simply because the specification was impractical and unrealistic.'[6]

By June 1983 Isaacs was in a rage at the way *Channel 4 News* was failing, and he felt that David Nicholas and his senior ITN colleagues were not paying it sufficient attention. At a meeting on 28 June Nicholas and Lord Buxton met Isaacs and Edmund Dell, Channel 4's chairman:

> Edmund Dell spoke of Channel 4's dissatisfaction with the quality of service being provided in the *Channel 4 News*. The original requirement was for news headlines and a number of stories in depth. Instead of headlines, they were now getting a series of news stories that were getting longer, with no sense of treatment in depth. The quality of distinctiveness, which they had hoped for, was not being provided.[7]

It is clear that ITN accepted the force of these criticisms. The next day Buxton wrote to Dell saying that Derrik Mercer would 'stand down' immediately as editor and that, pending a permanent replacement being found, ITN's Paul McKee would hold the fort – which he did, very creditably.

Meanwhile the search began for a new editor. At ITN, Stewart Purvis began to look like a possibility.

Purvis had been a television presenter at Harlech Television while still a student but had then joined the BBC radio news trainee course because, in 1969, the BBC still offered no training in television news. Bored by the BBC's bureaucratic systems, and told he could only go to the television newsroom if he dropped a pay grade, he soon departed for ITN. There, just as others were beginning to feel that they'd had more than enough of Northern Ireland, Purvis was ready, willing and able to take their place. 'It was "Step forward, Purvis,"' he says.

In the Middle East, as a fixer during the Yom Kippur war of 1973, Purvis had learned to finesse the competing egos of rival reporters – in this case

Michael Nicholson, Gerald Seymour and Christopher Wain – as each argued fiercely for the single press pass that would get an ITN crew across the Suez Canal with the Israeli Defence Forces. Later, on a bank holiday evening in 1980, he bravely browbeat the ITV network controller into taking *Coronation Street*'s end titles off the air in favour of ITN's live pictures of what turned out to be the SAS as they burst into the Iranian embassy to save the hostages there.

After that Purvis moved quickly through the ITN ranks, particularly well-regarded for his special news events programmes, like the Pope's visit, and 1981's royal wedding between the Prince of Wales and Lady Diana Spencer. Stewart was the friendly producer to whom the Prince confided, 'I talk to the plants.'

But in 1983, and now one of the two duty editors of *News at Ten*, Stewart Purvis had just hit a pothole in the pathway that seemed to lead to the top of the company. What looked to him like a clever career move backfired: 'I remember lobbying – I'd never lobbied for anything in my life at ITN curiously, but that's the one thing I lobbied for – that there should be one editor overall for *News at Ten* and, of course, that it should be me. And by that point I'd won a few Royal Television Society awards, and was looking in reasonable shape, so I lobbied David Nicholas, and David called me one day and said, "I think this is a really good idea, we *should* have an editor for *News at Ten*, and it's going to be Alastair Burnet." Ah! Not quite what I had in mind, but as a result, "This is awful and I'm now worse off. At least there were two of us before. Now there's one and it's Alastair!"

'The Alastair issue became quite big because of the influence he had at ITN in more ways than one. Editing a programme as I was, and trying to choose a lead story when the presenter, Alastair, was described as the editor – well, we got into some difficult bits. At that point, I did consider leaving ITN. And also at this point *Channel 4 News* was getting into desperate trouble and Burnet, with whom – it's no secret – my relationship was never warm, called me and said that Jeremy Isaacs had rung him up and said what should he do about *Channel 4 News*, and that he had told him that I should be the editor. Now, maybe he saw this as a way of getting me off *News at Ten*. Anyway, faced with what appeared to be going nowhere on *News at Ten* because of the new system, I agreed to do *Channel 4 News*.'

Before being offered the job, Purvis was given the once-over by Channel 4 board members. As Jeremy Isaacs recalls it: 'Edmund Dell and I, joined by [deputy chairman] Dickie Attenborough, had lunch with Stewart Purvis. Over the pâté, the fish salad, the duck, Edmund quizzed Purvis on his views on the IMF, third world debt, the EMS and other such topics. Purvis manfully responded. At the end of it, Dickie Attenborough leaned forward and put a hand on his arm. "Darling," he said, "we are all, you know, in show business. Never forget that, will you?" Out on the pavement Purvis was understandably bemused.'[8] He must have asked himself if Channel 4 had the slightest idea of what it really wanted.

Unknown to Purvis, Isaacs had laid down a rather brutal condition before Channel 4 would agree to the new editor's appointment. If, after another year, the News was not being watched by an average 750,000 a night then Channel 4 would have the right to 'determine' the contract – to go elsewhere for its news.[9] It was only after he took up the job on 17 October 1983, and went through the files, that Purvis discovered that he was standing in unfriendly territory on the edge of a precipice: 'There was a basic hostility, but absolutely all credit to Jeremy. After a week he came in and he stood on the Channel 4 newsroom desk, and it had a very low ceiling, and Jeremy, he almost bumped his head, even being quite short, and he just said, "This is going really well. This is what we want. Stewart has our complete support," that sort of thing. So quite quickly we were perceived to be turning it round.'

Channel 4 News had hired distinguished specialist journalists to present their stories in the studio, but some couldn't hack it. Sarah Hogg, in particular, was just not comfortable on television. Says Peter Sissons, the first main presenter of *Channel 4 News*: 'The only thing Sarah has ever failed at is being a television presenter.'

Purvis tried to use her journalistic talent in a different way: 'I persuaded Sarah that she should stop being a presenter and try and get on screen this unbelievable journalism that she had. Sarah is the only person I knew who had really – and it's maybe because her husband was a leading politician – really penetrated how Westminster works. So we'd come in, and the big story of the day is so-and-so, and she would say, "No, it isn't. The real story is that this cabinet committee is meeting, and they're making this decision about a Bill which is going to come out in three months, time." And I would think, "F—k, I don't know how to handle that because that's not on anyone else's running order."'

Sarah Hogg tried making films for the programme but she was never easy in the television reporter role either. Rather reluctantly Purvis said goodbye to her, and at the end of October she left to become economics editor of *The Times*. Says Purvis, 'I do think it's a bit of an indictment of the industry we all know and love that somebody who did come to it with an absolutely different take on life found the medium so frustrating.'

Arriving at *Channel 4 News* Purvis found a team mesmerised by the first computerised newsroom anywhere in the country. 'The amount of intellectual and emotional energy which that took up was spectacular. People would say, "I've worked out a new way of splitting the screen," and by that they meant on the computer, not on the air, and therefore they had this massive technology distraction when it was really a simple case of just writing a script.'

Channel 4 News had only four 'dedicated' camera crews but, despite the inevitable shortage of their own material, there had been a strange and disdainful reluctance to use the 'video river' that flowed into ITN from thirty-five camera crews working for the ITV bulletins – even though it was available to Channel 4. Purvis changed that, and also saw to it that stories were commissioned much earlier in the day so that people had time to work on them properly.

But he felt he was operating in enemy territory: 'I did try a number of different things with different people, all of which created extraordinary hostility within the Channel 4 newsroom. They were very conservative. The people I inherited from Derrik Mercer were deeply conservative about the way they'd done it. But I just don't think that you throw away the kit of tools of commercial television, and public service television, in order to create something which says, "I am not television." Yet that was absolutely the attitude I found. So, for example, on one occasion there was a big national health scare about something and it had arisen from food in a hospital, and I said, "I want to see a graphic of what the patients had for lunch." Now that actually was a piece of analysis, and I was using the metaphor of the lunch graphic as a way of trying to make a scientific story, about what germs were where, understandable. But that was seen as downmarket journalism. I deeply resented that.'

Today Peter Sissons recalls enthusing about the choice of his new editor: 'They came up with Purvis: it was a master-stroke. He was the best, pushiest and most adventurous *News at Ten* producer ITN had. Stewart knows everything about television. He knows exactly what it can do in the sense that every device can be stretched to the limit to do something different for your programme. He knows how to extend the range of everything.'

That was not how it felt at the time, says Purvis – even though he wanted to focus attention on Sissons as his main presenter: 'I completely redesigned the programme around him, created this second-presenter slot, which still exists to this day. And I think that was one of the best decisions I ever made. And it worked fine. But Peter was probably suspicious, as most people were, about me, about where I was taking the programme, because I'd made my name doing "Royals". I mean we're talking about the royal wedding, I'd done the Pope's visits, and therefore I was regarded as a kind of populist broadcaster.'

Channel 4 was hostile, his own staff was suspicious, and ITN was irritated by a programme that seemed to call into question the value of the news it had for so long produced for ITV.

'Well, it was exciting but it was pretty stressful, and at one point I nearly lost it, to be absolutely honest. The pressure was just so unbelievable, because there's no news programme I've ever known since where somebody said, "If the ratings don't go up, we're going to shut you down." In *Broadcast* there's a picture of me, and my office in Wells Street had one of those mini-balconies, and they said could they take the picture by the mini-balcony because of the light. Everyone said it looked like I was about to jump. Everyone presumed that *Channel 4 News* would fail, and lots of people in ITN wanted it to fail, because it was seen as a critique of *News at Ten*. So even the company was mixed up about it. And I got pretty mixed up about it as well.'

Did Purvis actually have a breakdown?

'Nearly. Let's leave it at that. But then, of course, the miners' strike came along and that was what the show needed, a big story. As the Falklands had made BBC *Newsnight*, the miners' strike made *Channel 4 News*.'

It was indeed the miners' strike in 1984 that gave the programme its first taste of real and continuing success. As Jeremy Isaacs says: '*Channel 4 News*, with space to play in, rose to the challenge. Only the ablest journalists working together . . . could hope to do justice to the seriousness of the issues, the strength of emotion, the particularity of local incident, the complexities of statistics bandied about by both sides, the tactics, argument, recrimination of both protagonists, the rights and wrongs of police behaviour. *Channel 4 News* made a better fist of reporting the course of events and examining both cases than did others. Stewart Purvis brightly invited Arthur Scargill and Ian MacGregor each to make a separate report putting the argument. These were broadcast on successive days. A debate between them, on Wednesday, the twenty-second of August 1984, was a major off-again on-again coup. It brought *Channel 4 News* its highest audience to that point.'

In September the ITN board was told that the Scargill/MacGregor debate had attracted two million viewers: 'The Channel 4 company had noted their pleasure at the progress of the programme, and our relations with them are in excellent order.'[10] The following month, with continuing coverage of the miners' strike, *Channel 4 News* had reporter Jane Corbin living for ten days in the mining village of Shirebrook: 'Her account of how the wives and children of strikers and non-strikers heckled and swore at each other ran for twenty-four minutes on *Channel 4 News* and six minutes on *News at Ten*. It made a deep impression on viewers; the prime minister remarked in a newspaper interview how much it had moved her.'[11]

In December, with the *Channel 4 News* audience running at a steady 750,000, television critic Peter Fiddick named it Programme of the Year. In March the following year the Broadcasting Press Guild made *Channel 4 News* the best news and current affairs programme and also gave an award to Peter Sissons. The Royal Television Society gave Jane Corbin's Shirebrook report a prize as Best Topical Feature.

In July 1984, *Television Weekly* reported that *Channel 4 News* had been given a budget increase well above inflation and sufficient to fund six new reporters and another camera crew: 'One and a half years after the avowedly new-look news programme was launched to considerable criticism and near-zero ratings, the increase in resources is being seen as a vote of confidence by C4 in the vastly improved programme.'[12]

Stewart Purvis had turned the programme round, there was no doubt about that, but there was a nasty moment to come when Peter Sissons and the *Channel 4 News* team felt that he had let them down on a matter of principle. At the height of the Westland helicopter affair, defence secretary Michael Heseltine had agreed to debate the issue live in the Channel 4 studio with Admiral Sir John Treacher, the Westland chairman. Sitting in the studio, listening to Sissons's introduction, Heseltine was infuriated to hear for the first time that Clive Ponting, a former Ministry of Defence civil servant who had revealed details of the sinking of the Argentine cruiser *Belgrano* during the Falklands War, would also be in the programme. Heseltine abandoned the up-coming debate, flounced out of the studio, and retired sulking to the Green Room. It was a rehearsal for his dramatic walk-out from the Cabinet Room over the Westland affair a few weeks later.

Instead of telling Heseltine to get lost, Purvis said that if he would only return to the studio and carry on debating he would drop Ponting's interview from that night's programme. It was an understandable concession, but one he still regrets: 'I should have said "If you don't like it . . .", but I didn't know exactly what had happened and I was making it up as I went along, and therefore I made the concession. This went down like a bloody lead balloon. Peter Sissons was furious. I remember going upstairs to the newsroom and virtually nobody would speak to me, and this went on for a few weeks. And undoubtedly Peter was the organiser of that sort of thing. So that was quite a bridge to rebuild, and I'm delighted that we did rebuild it pretty quickly. I think Peter and I were deeply stressed at one point, and we are now reconciled.'

A sin of commission, perhaps: editors must not hand over decision-making to their studio interviewees – however important. But it was a sin of omission, if you can all it that, that Purvis is most sorry about: 'The one thing I nearly did, and I deeply regret to this day that I didn't, was that John Ware came to see me from *World In Action*, with some colleagues, including Paul Greengrass. They wanted to sell themselves to me as a package. They would all come to *Channel 4 News* and form a kind of body, and that was a great idea. It was a kind of independent production implant sort of thing, an investigative unit, but it was miles ahead of its time, and it would have caused terrible trouble with the rest of the team. Of course, Greengrass went on to make *Bloody Sunday* and *The Bourne Supremacy*, and Ware did *Who Bombed Omagh?* for *Panorama*.'

Through tenacity and his ability to get the utmost from every resource available to him – from both people and machines – Stewart Purvis had overcome hostility from the programme team and brought them all success. And now that he had got the audience up to what Channel 4 had demanded, his bosses were happy too. 'We had a lovely little event recently on the anniversary of Channel 4', says Purvis, 'when I got a poster made of *Channel 4 News* and it said, "Three people's vision", and that was Jeremy Isaacs, Liz Forgan and David Nicholas. Then I said at this party, "The pity was that they were never the same vision," and they all laughed, so that was rather nice.'

His time at *Channel 4 News*, difficult though it was, was certainly the moment in his career when Stewart Purvis showed that he was capable of going to the top of ITN. He left the job in 1987, to be replaced by a recruit from the BBC, Richard Tait.

There is a postscript to this chapter of the *Channel 4 News* story. In 1989, Peter Sissons, who had, as its much-prized presenter, fought so determinedly to preserve the high seriousness of *Channel 4 News*, was lured away to the BBC. ITN was in uproar at this defection, and David Nicholas in particular was beside himself with rage – so much so that he insisted on suing. In June 1989 writs were served on both Sissons and the BBC, seeking an injunction to stop him working for the Corporation, and damages, and damages against the BBC for inducing him to break his three-year contract with ITN. It was, Nicholas told the board, important to make a stand as a point of principle. A hearing in the Queen's Bench Division was set down for 12 July.

'The BBC had always nibbled away at me,' says Sissons. 'By 1989 I had done *Channel 4 News* for seven years and was ready to go. ITN said they would match any offer, but what they couldn't match was the chance to chair *Question Time*, which the BBC was offering me. David saw it all as a BBC attack on ITN, and decided he wouldn't let them steal me. He came round to see me and we went for "a walk in the woods". But I'd been at ITN for twenty-five years, all my working life. I had to go to the BBC, just to see what it was like. When I dug in my heels the atmosphere changed: David got pretty nasty.'

Eventually a deal was done: the BBC compensated ITN for some Channel 4 debates Sissons had been contracted to chair and he was free to go. 'I doubled my money,' he says. 'It was half a million pounds over three years. The row kept me off the screen far longer than I would have liked, but I'm glad to say that within six months David Nicholas and I were happily sharing a bottle or two together.'

While Sissons settled in at the BBC, ITN searched anxiously for a replacement. Jon Snow was reporting in Berlin when he was summoned back by Stewart Purvis to fill in for three days presenting *Channel 4 News*. Stop-gap duty done and heading back to Germany, Snow was asked if he could stay on for a bit while ITN went on looking for the right presenter. Fifteen years later, Snow is still there, except that he manages to return from time to time to what he says is his first love, getting the news himself. 'I still have to fight to keep that mix of presenting and reporting,' he says, 'but it's on the road that you really show you can cut the mustard.'

As ITN's *ITV News* struggles to keep its quality despite increasing commercial pressure, *Channel 4 News*, made for a company which is not yet required to produce profits for its shareholders, looks better by comparison. Under Jim Gray, whom Snow describes as the best programme editor he has ever worked for, the programme has kept both its liveliness and its relatively serious agenda. And while the *ITV News* has careered around the clock *Channel 4 News* has hung on to its 7 p.m. slot. It seems to have benefited: the programme has put on viewers – in 2004 its audience was up 16 per cent on the previous year – and now a million people watch it regularly. Following the Iraq War, in which all its reporters, but in particular Lindsey Hilsum, did so well, *Channel 4 News* carried off three strongly contested prizes: an international Emmy in New York, and Best News awards from the RTS and BAFTA. And in 2004 the programme won yet another Emmy for its coverage of the Madrid terrorist bombings.

Best of all, given the suspicion with which it was regarded by Jeremy Isaacs and the early Channel 4, *Channel 4 News* is now recognised as being at the heart of the channel's remit – the programme that gives it its identity. It is true that *Channel 4 News*, which began with a commitment to have nothing to do with royal stories at all, recently led with a story about a royal butler. But that, says Jon Snow firmly, was a mistake that will not recur.

CHAPTER 29
TELLING THE TRUTH

Due Impartiality

It sounds so simple, doesn't it, the idea that television news should tell the truth fairly and impartially? But somebody's truth is another's conscious distortion or unconscious bias. Today, as news channels proliferate, it is fashionable to ask whether the concept of impartial news is any longer worth upholding. Why not abandon the first and greatest commandment of television news in Britain? Why not accept that there are different ways of looking at the same thing, and licence television news channels that make a distinctive perspective – or bias – a basic part of the service they provide? That, indeed, was one of the conclusions reached by a report for the Independent Television Commission in its dying days before it was subsumed in the new regulator Ofcom, in December 2003. Among other things, the ITC report *New News, Old News* suggested that:

> In the interests of achieving greater diversity of television news, to serve a wider range of audience interests, Ofcom could use its freedom to interpret the principle of 'due impartiality' and might be given the power to recommend to the Secretary of State the terms on which particular television and radio services might be authorised to depart from standard rules and codes on issues such as impartiality.[1]

Perhaps that will come, but will it really prove an adequate replacement for news services like ITN's, which have always sought to show 'due impartiality', as the law has required? After all, the evidence over many years past is that the public values television news more highly than it does the newspapers. The reason? Because television news is more likely to tell the truth, more likely to report what has happened without bias.

As Anthony Smith, the inspiration for the creation of Channel 4, wrote: 'Broadcasting absorbed the highest version of journalism's most sacred code – that of precision and factuality. In the West at least broadcasting built its news ethics around an extremely highly developed sense of pure truthfulness.'[2] Surely it was that which led to its growth in credibility over other media. People saw that broadcasting in Britain, unlike the newspapers, was trying to tell the truth and be impartial.

A recent 'YouGov' poll for the *Daily Telegraph* bears this out. People were asked: 'How much do you trust the following to tell the truth?' Eighty-one per cent trusted journalists on ITN's news on ITV and on Channel 4, and on BBC news programmes, to tell 'a great deal/ fair amount of the truth.' They were at the top of the trustworthiness chart. Judges came in at 68 per cent, broadsheet journalists at 65 per cent, and the wretched hacks on the 'red tops' at just 14 per cent.

Even though they were ready to countenance the idea of television news stations that were consciously not impartial but had a built-in bias, the authors of *New News, Old News* found that viewers were still very keen on the idea of impartiality: 'Almost all (97 per cent) say that impartiality is fairly or very important,' they said. 'MORI and ITN data show clearly that journalists as a group are not highly trusted as truthful sources of information, but that television newscasters are.' Trust in the impartiality of television news varies, depending on the particular channel, age, race and social class of those asked for their opinion, but the research revealed a real desire to see the principle of impartiality sustained: 'The focus-groups confirmed strong resistance to any relaxation of the laws on impartiality: they wanted the standard maintained, even if it was difficult or impossible to achieve.'

As channels proliferate they naturally want to differentiate themselves from each other. Increasingly they want their news programmes to take on the character of the rest of their output. So it is likely that news on different channels in the future will look different. Ian Hargreaves, one of the authors of the ITC report, is now a member of the Ofcom board. Ofcom is already thinking about whether it should still insist on 'due impartiality' for channels that want to present the news from their own point of view.

So how long before television news, in its agenda and treatment, is allowed to be whatever its channel and its owners want it to be – just like the newspapers?

As Adrian Monck, until recently the deputy editor of ITN's Channel 5 *Five News*, recently wrote: 'At a time when political journalism in print has become a kind of organised lobbying, and where television retains its credibility precisely because it is regulated, we're seeing not an extension of the rules that preserve that credibility to newspapers but instead a weakening of the pillars that support the nation's most trusted media.'[3]

At Ofcom, as the all-digital army advances (rather like some terrifying scene from the film *Lord of the Rings*), there is the sound of paper-shredding. The Authority seems to be preparing a fall-back position, a retreat to safer ground. If, in a multi-channel world, it is increasingly difficult to enforce due impartiality then why not abandon the obligation on broadcasters to observe it? That seems to be the way that the regulator is tending.

Following the tradition established by the BBC, ITN has always been determined to report the news with accuracy and due impartiality. It has prided itself on its success, so any suggestion that it has failed in this endeavour has always provoked an angry response.

In 1976 a number of academics – the Glasgow University Media Group – published a study entitled *Bad News*.[4] In it they examined twenty-two weeks of television news broadcast in 1975. The period included the mounting economic crisis, the resignation of Edward Heath as Conservative leader, the Common Market referendum campaign, IRA bombings, and the Communist victory in Vietnam. It was a wide canvas, but the authors' primary concern was the biased way in which they thought industrial disputes were being reported. In their study they accused television news of the 'laying of blame for society's economic problems at the door of the workforce', and came to the conclusion that for the news organisations simply to *claim* objectivity was inadequate; all sorts of 'filters' were operating to preclude even-handedness, filters that the journalists simply refused to acknowledge.

'One gets the impression,' wrote Richard Hoggart, in his introduction to *Bad News*, 'of a trade which has hardly ever thought out its own basic premises but continues, come hell or high water, to rest its case on a few unexamined assertions.' That comment had some force. ITN journalists wouldn't let an interviewee get away with saying he was right just because he said he was. It was reasonable to ask the journalists to explain why they were so sure they were impartial in the way they delivered the news.

To find out why the biases they thought they had found existed, the *Bad News* team wanted to study what happened as a news programme was being put together. The BBC was hostile, but allowed an observer into its newsroom. 'Our relationship with ITN has been very much more straight-forward,' the group reported. 'There has been no hostility and equally almost no co-operation.' A researcher had managed 'to snatch five days under-cover observation at ITN' by visiting friends there. Though she said she had been told that at no time had people received a directive from the editors about inclusions or exclusions from the bulletin, she felt sufficiently confident of her own research to conclude that 'Obviously, both BBC and ITN rely on selected recruitment and conditioning of personnel to produce a continuing auto-censorship.'

When it was first published *Bad News* made the serious allegation that ITN's news bulletins were at risk of being affected by commercial pressures. The *Daily Telegraph* reported:

> Critics' review copies of a book about the British press and television suggested that Mr Frank Duesbury, ITN's public relations officer, had sought to influence news presentation to meet the wishes or convenience of adver-tisers, a High Court judge was told yesterday. If the allegations in the book *Bad News* had been true Mr Duesbury would have lost his reputation and been guilty of breaking independent broadcasting's legal obligation to present news impartially.[5]

Frank Duesbury received damages and his costs and, as part of his vindi-cation before the book's general release, *Bad News* was altered to withdraw the imputations that had been made against him and ITN.

Bad News was not a very good book. Other academics found it difficult to replicate the Glasgow University Media Group's research to see how well it stood up, but some came to the conclusion that the book had been motivated not so much by a desire to help make the news more impartial but to make it more left-wing. None the less, *Bad News* was a useful reminder to television journalists that they should ask themselves about the attitudes, prejudices and conventions they were bringing to their work – if only because others would be doing so: 'Broadcasters have to come to terms with the fact that media studies are here to stay,' wrote Martin Harrison, of Keele University, 'and that most of its practitioners are thoroughly scholarly and professional, although what they say may at times be remote from the realities of the newsroom or over-fond of jargon. A handful of academics still need to realise that media studies is not a continuation of revolution by other means, and that what counts is their scholarship rather than their ideological stance.'[6]

The attack on ITN's impartiality was renewed – or, at least, that was how ITN's editor at the time, David Nicholas, saw it – when Channel 4 set up in business. ITN was delighted to be supplying Channel 4's news – stressful though making the programme was – but it did not like what Jeremy Isaacs and his commissioning editor Liz Forgan planned to do. Their idea was that while the news programme would run daily, for nearly an hour, from Monday to Thursday, it would be shorter on Friday to make room for something else. *The Friday Alternative*, made by the independent Diverse Productions, would present the stories of the week from a different perspective, and comment on the way they had previously been told by the media – including ITN. To add injury to insult it would require the use of ITN film to question whether ITN had got it right. The inclusion of Greg Philo, one of the Glasgow University Media Group, in *The Friday Alternative*'s production team did not exactly reassure ITN.

Sure enough, early in 1983 there was a major row. A furious Nicholas complained to his board: 'The 7 January edition on the coverage of the Falklands had been a farrago of distortion and misinterpretation with the motives of the television news programme makers being impugned. To some extent the assertion in the 14 January edition that ITN had taken the Government line in reporting the Andropov peace proposals was even more offensive.'[7]

Isaacs later admitted that ITN did have a point:

This element of *The Friday Alternative* appeared consistently if not exclusively to present only one alternative viewpoint, that of the left. In the end there was no defending this. The channel had a clear obligation to political impartiality overall, and must fulfil it . . . The staff of *The Friday Alternative* equally could take the line that all news had a bias; theirs had a different bias. Surely, at half an hour a week only, that need present no problem. But ITN refused to admit a bias. The IBA would not have it said that ITN showed bias. Anyone might get an emphasis wrong on occasion; nobody is perfect. But ITN and ITN's *Channel 4 News*, like other elements in our output, aspired to objectivity. No other week-in-week-out contributor, whether of the left or of the right, could be licensed to put across only one view of the world. It was an abuse of the Act, and an infringement of the channel's hospitality.

ITN could not afford to agree that their point of view was simply one among many others. A letter to Jeremy Isaacs complaining that *The Friday Alternative* was using ITN's material to make political points evoked an uncharacteristically soothing reply: Isaacs knew he'd be stuck if ITN refused to allow *The Friday Alternative* to use its material. 'I am satisfied,' he wrote, 'they are not of malicious intent but are honestly trying to do something new and different, which I want to encourage. I hope therefore that your board will give them the benefit of further doubt. If you still have reason to complain of political bias, then I shall understand if you seek, within the terms of our contract, to withdraw your material.'[8]

Nicholas, momentarily mollified, replied saying that while for the present things could continue as they were, 'I cannot over-emphasise the unanimous strength of feeling expressed by the ITN board about the loaded way in which *The Friday Alternative* has been using our material.'[9]

ITN continued to be unhappy about the use of its news material in what it regarded as a biased and unprofessional programme, and came to the conclusion that *The Friday Alternative* was damaging ITN's reputation as a source of impartial news. That was a serious matter, and the IBA now brought its guns to bear on Channel 4. Jeremy Isaacs, with his own chairman against him, was forced to surrender:

Against ceaseless pressure from the IBA, who were sometimes particularly responsive to hurt yelps and cries of foul play from ITN, Liz Forgan and I strove to ensure that Diverse Production's contract to continue *The Friday Alternative* should be renewed, even if the programme format was modified. Edmund Dell [Channel 4 chairman], on this issue in agreement with George Thomson [IBA chairman], was adamantly against. The Board of Channel 4 determined that *The Friday Alternative* should vanish from the air. At a meeting on 21 July the decision to kill it was taken.

Jealous of its reputation for impartiality, ITN had been understandably unhappy at the idea of its *Channel 4 News* being attacked by a programme that immediately followed it. For the same reason it was consistently unwilling to surrender editorial control over its material to others.

When the IBA advertised the new 'breakfast' franchise in 1980 its hope was that the winner would use ITN to provide news programming, and when TV-AM won the contract[10] its chairman Peter Jay had 'long and basically friendly, though by no means easy'[11] discussions with ITN's David Nicholas as to how this was to be achieved. Jay wanted all the material that flowed into ITN to be available to TV-AM to edit and use as it saw fit. But ITN was unhappy with that: it wanted to make the programmes itself and then deliver them to TV-AM. As Nicholas explained the problem to his board, TV-AM wanted to interweave news and news background: ITN was nervous about that because it wanted to keep editorial control of its news. 'Were ITN now to become a supplier of raw material to another UK broadcaster, then the whole basis on which ITN is established would be called into question.' How could political balance be maintained if TV-AM was free to use political interviews as they wished? ITN's reputation might be ruined if its material was 'to turn up haphazardly on a regular basis in someone else's programmes.'[12]

For rather different reasons ITN's owners, the ITV companies, were just as unhappy as ITN management. At a meeting with the IBA's chairman Lord Thomson the companies said that from their side 'TV-AM would be regarded as a competitor to the existing service and that, in seeking access to ITN's material in the way it had suggested, it would be like handing TV-AM a pistol and asking ITN to supply the bullets. Lord Thomson acknowledged the force of that point.'[13]

Despite the wishes of the IBA, TV-AM and ITN could not find a satisfactory basis on which to work together. As a result their deal did not go ahead: TV-AM set up its own news service; ITN hung on to its editorial control, and its reputation.

Lies, the Law and Videotape

None of the threats to ITN's impartiality, or the suggestions that the impartiality it claimed did not exist, was anything like as serious as the allegation made against it by *LM*, a small political magazine that had originally been published by the Revolutionary Communist Party under the title *Living Marxism*. In its first edition, in February 1997, *LM* carried an article that, in effect, accused ITN reporters Penny Marshall and Ian Williams of lying.

'It was the most traumatic thing, other than my father's death, that has ever happened to me,' says Marshall. 'The columnists laughed at that – "She must have led a sheltered life," they said – but fundamental to a journalist's life is telling the truth, and to be accused of lying is to say that twenty years of trying to tell the truth has been worthless.'

In August 1992 Marshall and Williams were in Bosnia. Stories of atrocities being committed on all sides were rife but needed documenting. Says Marshall: 'This was before the UN arrived and it was pretty wild, with armed men high on drugs manning endless roadblocks. We travelled in the mornings early, before they all got drunk on slivovitz. There were endless columns of displaced people, refugees. It was almost like Africa. Humans were the currency in this war. There was always the sense that the Muslims were the underdogs in this struggle, though there were plenty of horrors on their side too. Most of the news stories were coming out of Sarajevo, that was the daily life-threatening thing, but ITN told me to stay out of daily coverage and try to pin down the atrocity story that was being talked about: there had to be a kernel of truth in what the refugees were saying. Sue English from *Channel 4 News* had good contacts with the Serbs and got permission for ITN to visit two of their camps with a Serb escort, so we joined in.'

Obviously the Serbs wanted to show that all was well at the camps, that no one was being ill-treated. 'The first one we came to,' says Marshall, 'was an extremely evil place, very horrible, and I tried to convey that. There was silence: your hair stood up. But we had to admit, "We can't tell what is happening here."'

Then, at the second camp they were taken to, Marshall's team filmed the sequence that would make her decide, eight years later, she had to go to court, backed by ITN, to defend her reputation as an honest and impartial reporter.

As the *Guardian* later put it:

> The single image that touched the consciences of millions of viewers around the world was that of Fikret Alic, an emaciated Bosnian Muslim man standing shirtless behind a barbed wire fence in a Serb-run camp at Trnopolje, in northern Bosnia. Although just a brief moment in ITN's lengthy reports [on ITV and Channel 4] broadcast on 6 August 1992, the emotive image of Alic was taken as the evidence of Serb atrocities that the western powers had been waiting for. The picture quickly zoomed around the world, prompting numerous headlines comparing the camps in Bosnia with those of the Holocaust, though that was not a comparison made by the ITN reporters.[14]

'When I got back to my base in Belgrade to edit,' says Marshall, 'my producer in London suggested we start the report with that image, but I wanted to "join up the dots", to tell the story in a linear way. I thought you should put it in context. This was the most horrific discovery in Europe in 1992. It had to be shown, but because it was so powerful it had to be shown with the utmost care because there were people around who did just want a "horrible Serbs" story. Nevertheless the image was in the *News at Ten* headlines – one of the "bongs".'

Awards for the story followed, and Marshall's and Williams's reports were credited with speeding up Western military intervention; but five years later came the *LM* article under the title 'The Picture that Fooled the World'. It was written by Thomas Deichmann, a German journalist and expert witness on German media at the war crimes trial of Bosnian Serb Dusko Tadic.

Deichmann had seen all the footage shot by Penny Marshall and her colleague Ian Williams because ITN had sent it to the tribunal, and he now argued that the transmitted story did not represent the truth of the situation at Trnopolje. It was Marshall and her camera crew, he said, who had been behind the wire fence as they filmed, rather than Fikret Alic. Far from being some kind of concentration camp, Trnopolje was a just collection centre for refugees, who were always free to leave.

In February 2000 the High Court heard that *LM* had alleged that the ITN team 'fabricated and broadcast grossly distorted television footage which sensationalised the treatment suffered by Muslims detained at the camp.'[15]

As soon as ITN saw a press release for the *LM* article it demanded that the magazine pulp all the copies it had printed. When it did not, ITN issued a writ for libel. But this did not receive universal support. Was it really the business of journalists to sue each other, it was asked. Why was the ITN elephant going to court to squash this gnat of a magazine? Why not argue out the issue in public debate to see where the truth lay?

But as Penny Marshall explains, that was unacceptable to her: 'I had already been involved in huge debates about this vivid image, and how it had been used, but no debate at all was possible about whether or not I was telling the truth – whether I was a liar. That's not something you can discuss.' And so it was that the case went to court.

'ITN faced a dilemma,' wrote Richard Tait, editor-in-chief of ITN. 'We were initially reluctant to sue *LM*. But the reaction of some reporters was "If you don't sue there must be something in the story." The moment we did sue, the press line became: "Why are you bullying a harmless little magazine?"'[16] ITN realised that was a problem. Penny Marshall says: 'I was a bit surprised when Richard Tait asked me and Ian Williams to sign the papers. I hadn't realised I was suing in my personal capacity – I assumed ITN was doing it – but ITN thought a poor helpless individual like me would be more effective.' But there was no lack of support for Marshall and Williams from ITN and their colleagues, or from Ed Vulliamy, the *Guardian* correspondent who had been with them that day in Bosnia.

LM had its own supporters, like the distinguished journalist Harold Evans, and the BBC's John Simpson was ready to give evidence on its behalf. 'I was quite devastated to see John Simpson in the legal documents,' says Marshall. But although Simpson gave the *LM* team's lawyers his advice his evidence was ruled out as hearsay: he had not been at the camps. The most effective witness turned out to be a Bosnian Muslim doctor who had been interned at the camp. He had appeared in Marshall's original report in an interview in which he was plainly terrified, and he now convinced the court that Trnopolje was indeed a place where many Muslims had been beaten, tortured and killed by their Serb guards.

As the *Daily Telegraph* reported, the jury brought in a unanimous verdict: 'Two television journalists accused of sensationalising the image of an emaciated Muslim behind barbed wire at a Serb-run detention camp in Bosnia, won libel damages of £150,000 each at the High Court yesterday ... after a jury unanimously found that it amounted to a highly damaging attack on their reputations and professional integrity.'[17]

ITN was awarded £75,000, which it announced it would donate to the International Red Cross. Its reputation for telling the truth to the best of its ability in an impartial way had been vindicated.[18]

CHAPTER 30
EXPAND OR DIE

As we have seen, when Alastair Burnet returned to ITN in 1976 it was the third time he had brought his great talents to ITV's news operation. To begin with he had been ITN's political editor, then the first presenter of the *News at Ten*, and now he was back to read the news again, initially for the *News at 5.45*. Some people were rather sniffy about that. Was it really all he could do? Surely a man who had edited *The Economist* with great success – even if he'd failed to turn the *Daily Express* round – could find a better use for his time than reading a teleprompter! But Burnet was interested in doing more than that.

First, of course, came increasing recognition that he was, as a newscaster, without peer. In March 1978 Burnet moved from *News at 5.45* to *News at Ten*, where he grew in authority and stature. On just one extraordinary day in 1982, when the Pope's visit coincided with the Falklands War, Burnet interviewed the Prime Minister and the Archbishop of Canterbury, presented a special programme on the Pope's visit and anchored *News at Ten*.

After the end of the Falklands conflict and a great victory parade programme, the *Sunday People* headline was: 'Alastair Burnet doesn't just read the news, he talks to the nation.' Burnet (pronounced *Bur*net, not Bur*net*) told the paper: 'I have no regrets. Had I been given the perfect choice, I would have much preferred to have been a millionaire. I could have written a couple of bad books and got away with it, for instance. When you are rich you can afford to make mistakes. I could never have been a politician, I'm not clever. I'm really flattered that people find me interesting. I didn't set out to make television my way of life, but I am glad I did. I enjoy it.'[1]

Burnet certainly enjoyed the confidence of his editor, David Nicholas, who made him an associate editor, in overall charge of *News at Ten*, ITN's flagship. The idea was that he would bring consistency to a programme edited by different shift editors, acting as 'continuity-girl', as he self-deprecatingly put it. In fact, as Stewart Purvis had been irked to discover, Burnet's was a powerful voice in editorial decision-making.

When Burnet was knighted in 1984 there were those who didn't like the idea of such an important influence on the news receiving an honour from the Thatcher government. 'His values and political perspectives,' said an *Observer* profile, 'are those expressed by *News at Ten*. To the viewing public, he is simply one of two presenters on any night, assumed to be answerable to the programme editors. In practice his authority is decisive.'[2]

The following week Burnet's colleagues, past and present, as well as Burnet himself, hurried to correct what they saw as an unfair and damaging article: 'Sir Alastair undoubtedly does have a strong voice in the *News at Ten* programmes and often writes many of the stories which he reads,' wrote Robert Hunter, a former ITN producer, but 'during the years I edited *News at Ten* I never witnessed him failing to be convinced by rational argument or, if unconvinced, refusing to read a story . . . It is true that he is a power behind the throne at ITN, but that throne is firmly and effectively occupied by David Nicholas, who is the dominant influence on all ITN programmes. Sir Alastair is not the only senior counsellor to whom he turns for advice.'[3]

Fair enough, and few argue that Burnet, as a broadcaster, ever forgot his obligation to impartiality, whatever his political sympathies. But he was influential at ITN far beyond his editorial role on *News at Ten*. In 1982 he became a director of the company and was in a position to affect not just ITN's programmes but its future. In that role, his standing with the prime minister, Margaret Thatcher, would be crucial.

As the eighties wore on, and trade-union reform was pushed through Parliament, Mrs Thatcher made it plain that she thought television was 'the last bastion of restrictive practices'. Her opinion was confirmed by the Peacock Committee when it reported in 1986. 'We received evidence from a number of contributors,' said Peacock, 'that the broadcasting industry was wasteful of resources through over-manning and self-indulgent working practices.'[4] The Prime Minister wanted reform of the ITV system primarily because she felt that money that was subsidising high wages, high manning levels and excess profits should more properly go to the Treasury and back to the taxpayer. Commercial television seemed to be escaping the discipline of the market. In principle, she felt that was wrong.

There may have been another motive. An ITV programme, *Death on the Rock*,[5] which revealed the truth about how the SAS had killed IRA terrorists in Gibraltar, had profoundly irritated her, even more so when a rigorous investigation by a former Tory minister, Lord Windlesham, gave the programme a clean bill of health. Taking money out of commercial television and giving market forces free rein would inevitably mean that relatively expensive, relatively small-audience current affairs programmes would be replaced by cheaper and more popular ones less willing or able to tackle difficult but important subjects.

In time, the Thatcher government's reforms certainly had this effect: long-running current affairs series on ITV like *This Week* and *World in Action*, which had once been given the resources to investigate and challenge authority and the peak-time slots to present the results, would soon be dead, ousted in favour of more popular series that were not so interested in questioning the government of the day.

The government's reaction to the Peacock Report made it apparent that in future commercial television companies would have to compete for their licences to broadcast, with the licence for each region going to the highest bidder. Television would become just another commodity in the market-place. Price would be everything: never mind the quality, count the cash.

The IBA, the broadcasting regulator, made it clear that ITN also would be expected to run on much more commercial lines than hitherto. Instead of being a cost to the ITV companies, a cost which up till now they had agreed grumpily to bear more or less in relation to the money they earned from television advertising, ITN was to become a profit-making organisation. In future it would sell its services, its news programmes, to the ITV network and anyone else – like Channel 4, or foreign broadcasters – who might buy them, with the idea of making a profit for the owners of ITN.

But who would those owners be? From the beginning, ITN had been owned by the companies that took its news service – there had been no outsiders. The owners had also been the customers. But now the government and the IBA had decided that this was inappropriate in the new commercial environment – much too cosy. In future, it said, the broadcasters would only be able to own a minority share in ITN, less than 50 per cent. Outsiders would have ownership of the company.

This threw the directors of ITN into confusion. For decades, they argued, they had stood behind ITN, building it up without any financial reward, only to find that now, when at long last they might have expected to see a return on their investment, they were to be forced to give up or reduce their shareholding and lose control of their company. They might even have to pay more for the news service they got – because it now had to make a profit for ITN – while looking on impotently as more than half of those ITN profits went to new investors.

With David Nicholas now chairman, and Stewart Purvis on the board, the ITN board minutes of 20 February 1989 record a hot discussion on how ITN should respond to the government's proposals. Directors from some of the companies emphatically stated their view that ITN should continue to be their creature, their news supplier, and no more. Leslie Hill of Central Television

> suggested that ITN was in effect an in-house service for ITV, a point rein-
> forced by Mr [James] Gatward who said that his own company saw ITN as
> TVS's international news room. Mr. Gatward said there was a strong
> argument for ITN retaining its present relationship with the ITV system
> rather than seeking a radically different financial relationship ... Without the
> firm base of an ITV contract, ITN could find itself fighting for survival.

As the directors, in angry, worried mood, considered their options, a division opened within their ranks. While the non-executives, the directors who represented the ITV companies, were all for pressing the government to back off and allow them to continue their exclusive ownership of the news company, some of ITN's managers, the executive directors, took a different view.

David Nicholas and Sir Alastair Burnet believed in the expansion of ITN, and they thought the time had now come for it to escape the clutches of the ITV companies to make that expansion happen. They had become convinced that people who were concerned primarily with a low-cost news supply for themselves would never have sufficient incentive to invest in ambitious new projects. Indeed, as the attempt to do a news supply deal with TV-AM had shown, many of the ITV directors were unwilling that ITN should try to sell its product to other broadcasters who might be in competition with it. Nicholas and Burnet felt that ITN was tethered to the ground when the time had come for it to fly. In their opinion the only way it could take wing would be if money was forthcoming from new investors who wanted to make ITN a worldwide news provider, not just a wholly-owned subsidiary of the ITV companies.

'I wanted ITN to be more independent, and get away from being just a loss-making subsidiary,' says Burnet. 'The companies regarded ITN as a burden – they were against news and they always had been. They were entertainment people. Yes, I was very keen to extend the shareholdings, but the companies did not want to relax their grip on ITN – after all, there was a 15 per cent premium on the advertising space around the *News at Ten*.'

There was also a political argument for widening the ownership. Burnet felt that opening up ITN to new investors would not only bring in new money for expansion but would also help see off the more extreme of the market-forces advocates among Conservative ministers and advisers, the people who were a real threat to the future of ITN. 'It was important to say to the Tory maniacs that we would widen the ownership. Because that would, in a way, absolve them from insisting on market values and so on. And I think people should understand that. The idea of widening the ownership was to allow Tory stalwarts a foothold in their struggle against yet more market madness.'

On the issue of ownership Nicholas saw eye to eye with Burnet, but Stewart Purvis was not convinced: 'I think that the ITV companies *could* have been interested in the growth of ITN – I can't see why not,' he says. 'But David and Alastair were convinced that ITV would always be anti-ITN, and so they thought the way forward was to grow, but to block ITV

Via satellite. In Bangkok, producer David Phillips and film editor Leo Rosenberg cut a story for satellite transmission to ITN in London, 1971. (Courtesy of Leo Rosenberg.)

UPITN/ITN scoop. The Popular Front for the Liberation of Palestine hijackers blow up airliners at Dawson's Field, Jordan, 1970. (Courtesy of ITN.)

Cameraman Tom Phillips leads sound recordist Mickey Doyle and reporter Michael Nicholson on their long march through Angola, 1978. (Courtesy of Tom Phillips.)

President Idi Amin of Uganda gives an informal interview to reporter Richard Lindley and freelance cameraman Peter Frense in Kampala, 1972. (Courtesy of Africapix.)

'Bloody Sunday', Northern Ireland. Cameraman Peter Wilkinson, reporter Gerald Seymour (standing) and (behind soldier on right) producer David Phillips, 1972. (Courtesy of David Phillips.)

The picture that changed everything. An emaciated Fikret Alic in the Serb-run Trnopolje camp, in Bosnia, 1992. (Courtesy of ITN.)

First Report. News editor Peter Cole, programme editor Barrie Sales, and presenter Robert Kee confer, 1972. (Courtesy of ITN.)

Programme producer and ITN deputy editor David Nicholas briefs presenter Robert Kee for a General Election results programme, 1974. (Courtesy of ITN.)

Newscaster Andrew Gardner leaves ITN for Thames Television. With director Diana Edwards-Jones, newscaster Reggie Bosanquet, editor Nigel Ryan, and newscaster Leonard Parkin, 1977.

(Courtesy of ITN.)

ITN's first two newscasters, Robin Day and Chris Chataway, are reunited with former production assistant Diana Edwards-Jones, 1985. (Courtesy of ITN.)

Dame Sue Tinson, producer in charge of Gulf War coverage, in Saudi Arabia, 1990.

(Courtesy of ITN.)

For the first time ITN's journalists go on strike. Picketing ITN House in Wells Street are (front row left to right): Gerald Seymour, Anthony Carthew, Norman Rees, Keith Hatfield, Gordon Honeycombe; (behind them left to right): Michael Nicholson, Peter Sissons, David Rose; (top right): Ivor Mills, 1974.

(Courtesy of the *Daily Mail*.)

Tape editor Mike North works on an 'And Finally…' compilation with reporter and newscaster Martyn Lewis, 1984.

(Courtesy of ITN.)

A fine ITN romance. Reporter Jon Snow and newscaster Anna Ford are briefly engaged, 1979.

(Courtesy of ITN.)

Channel Four News: an uncomfortable start. (left to right) presenter Peter Sissons, foreign editor John Mahoney, studio director Malcolm Johnson, editor Derrik Mercer, 1982. (Courtesy of ITN.)

Prime Minister Mrs Margaret Thatcher in the Portakabin 'studio' as John Suchet presents the ITN World News, 1987. (Courtesy of John Suchet.)

Michael Green, the 'ruthless charmer', and chairman of ITN, 1993. (Courtesy of ITN.)

The end of an era. Nigel Dacre, editor of the ITN News on ITV, addresses his troops on the last night of News at Ten, 1999. (Courtesy of ITN.)

Keeping the show on the road: ITN chief executive Stewart Purvis, 2001.
(Courtesy of ITN.)

Woman at war. Reporter Andrea Catherwood with friends in Afghanistan, 2001.
(Courtesy of Andrea Catherwood.)

The most trusted newscaster in British television. Sir Trevor McDonald stars in ITN's
'theatre of news', 2004. (Courtesy of ITN.)

from controlling it. And I remember the first time David ever told me that he was going to do that with Alastair. I didn't quite take it all in really. I didn't quite understand the rationale for "growth equals blocking ITV". Alastair and David were totally committed to it. I went along with it, there's no doubt about that, but I didn't get involved. And I do remember a most curious encounter with Greg Dyke, when he invited me over to London Weekend to ask, "Which side are you on in this?" and it was an uncomfortable meeting. I fudged it, but I don't think he fell for the fudge. I clearly recall him concluding that I was more on the side of David and Alastair than on the side of the ITV companies. And I think that partly explains Greg's hostility to ITN when it tried to get into other new ventures in competition with the ITV companies – as happened with breakfast television, for example.'

The coming Broadcasting Bill threatened ITN's owners with losing control, but before this issue could come to a head ITN discovered that its very existence was in peril. One morning in 1988 Sue Tinson, by now a senior programme editor on *News at Ten*,[6] took a call from Bernard Ingham, the prime minister's press secretary. He had been reading the first draft of the Broadcasting White Paper, drawn up by the team at the Department of Trade and Industry under Lord (David) Young, a free-market favourite of Margaret Thatcher. 'Bernard said to me,' says Tinson, '"Do you realise that this Bill does not have any 'must carry' obligation as far as news is concerned? None at all." I said, "Heavens, gosh, bloody hell! I'll get hold of David and Alastair and get back to you." So I did, and they both went round to No.10 and had a session with Maggie.'

'Lord Young had come up with this extraordinary idea,' says Stewart Purvis, 'quite early on in his time at the Department of Trade and Industry, that the new licences, when they came round, would have nothing about news in them. I remember him coming to dinner at ITN and Alastair and David Nicholas arguing for the fact that there must be clauses about news and he was saying, "Well, I'm sure they want news from you, old boy, we surely don't have to put that in the Bill or anything."'

Lord Young's vision of the future of commercial television in Britain had been shared by the head of Mrs Thatcher's Policy Unit, Brian Griffiths. But Lord Griffiths (as he is now) says he was differently motivated. In his view, reform of the system was needed simply because there would shortly be a sharp increase in the number of television channels available: 'The tech-nology was exploding. The question was, how to stay level with it. We all wanted quality news,' he insists. 'We all spoke from the same page. This new world could not be a totally free market – there had to be safeguards – but there was talk of becoming global, of becoming a real international news business.'

It is hard to see how ITN could have had a global business if it could not even be confident of keeping its place on ITV, Britain's key commercial broadcaster.

At a board meeting in September 1988 the chairman of ITN, George Russell, referred to press speculation on the forthcoming Broadcasting Bill, saying that ITN 'appeared to have been more or less forgotten by those drafting the White Paper'. He wanted ITN to try to insist on being given long-term contracts with ITV and Channel 4, with its income from those contracts guaranteed. He suggested the contract price should be linked to inflation, or to advertising revenue, and he went further: 'An alternative radical solution would be for a new franchise to be created on a national basis for the hours 10 p.m. to midnight.' ITN would be guaranteed this contract for seven years before the IBA decided whether it should be put out to tender. Nice work if you can get it, but such suggestions never stood a chance.

There followed a discussion about how best to get 'mandatory news' into the Bill, but it was thought that even if that were achieved, it was unlikely that ITN would be named either in the Bill or the Act that would result. The chairman said, 'ITN would be delighted if it was the designated company to meet the requirement, but the company was confident it could obtain a contract in its own right.'

It was agreed that ITN's views would be made known 'in a discreet manner' to Downing Street before the Cabinet approved the white paper. Richard Dunn, from Thames Television, said it was important that ITN should not look 'insecure' about its position.[7]

Without an obligation to carry the news, who could say that the ITV companies would in future do so? In the tough commercial climate that was so obviously coming, wouldn't they be likely to ditch proper news programmes altogether in favour, perhaps, of a 'rip and read' service of headlines or a downmarket pop product? Never mind who the new owners of ITN were going to be: it looked as if ITN's services might not be required at all – at least not by ITV, far and away its most important customer.

But this was not necessarily something that would worry Margaret Thatcher. Tough, she might say. If that's what people want, so be it. That's the market! But in their meeting with the prime minister and her press secretary Bernard Ingham, Burnet and Nicholas deployed another, very telling, political argument. How would the prime minister feel, they asked, if there was only one proper news programme for people to watch – the news from the BBC? 'The case we made was this,' says Nicholas. '"We know Thatcherism is all about choice, but this is depriving people of choice – you are actually taking television back to pre-1955, in which there was just the one broadcaster, the BBC. Are you happy with having the news only from the BBC?"'

Now, if occasional ITV programmes like *Death on the Rock* made Margaret Thatcher cross, that was as nothing compared to her loathing for BBC News and Current Affairs, which she had often made plain. She felt that the BBC was essentially a left-wing, anti-Conservative broadcaster – and she had only recently put in a new chairman, Marmaduke Hussey, who had immediately sacked the BBC's director general, Alasdair Milne.

When Burnet and Nicholas suggested that the proposed Broadcasting Bill, as it stood, might mean the end of any real alternative to the BBC's version of the news, and in particular of election and political coverage, she took the point rather quickly. 'Bernard was outraged, really, I think,' says Nicholas, 'and he put a paper in for the prime minister – we were told it went into her box when she did a September visit to Balmoral, and she allegedly read it there; and that, of course, changed the whole thing.'

Naturally, Burnet and Nicholas wanted it both ways. They longed for the freedom to develop into what they hoped would be a big international business, but at the same time they wanted to be protected against the possibility that their main customer, ITV, would no longer buy their product. This was inconsistent. We all want to do as we like and still have a guaranteed income, but it's not really a reasonable expectation. None the less, knowing they had the prime minister's support for ITN to go on into the new television economy, Burnet, with his ITN colleagues Nicholas and Tinson, went to work to get the Broadcasting Bill changed. Their argument was that as long as the BBC held on to its role as a news provider, so should independent television: 'As long as the BBC was entrenched,' says Burnet, 'there should be something else to fight it.' 'When British Airways was privatised,' David Nicholas told an interviewer, 'it did not have its routes taken away.'[8]

'We had got the message about what was planned,' says Burnet, 'and George Russell, who was chairman, said, "Good heavens! This is the end of ITN," so we went to work. And it was reasonably sensible once we had Maggie – once she got the line that reducing ITN meant that the BBC was cock of the walk. That meant that the BBC ran election coverage – and she wasn't a fool. But these little somnambulist people [in the Conservative Party] who wanted to impress the free-marketeers – they never understood this. And they were reasonably well-informed people, including the then chancellor of the exchequer, Nigel Lawson, and [former chancellor] Geoffrey Howe – a couple of unintellectual people.

'I talked to Maggie, I talked to Bernard Ingham, I talked to the Home Office minister David Mellor – Sue Tinson and I had lunch with a fair number of people. But Maggie got it from the beginning. And this was what Lord Whatsit of Wales [Brian Griffiths] never understood. I remember him coming with a face as long as all-get-out and saying, "Maggie wants ITN to go on."'

David Nicholas, too, recalls his fellow-Welshman and good friend Griffiths calling in for a drink following a meeting with Mrs Thatcher to discuss the Bill. The prime minister had demanded to know why news was not a requirement. 'Brian paced up and down,' says Nicholas, 'and he said to me, "You know, I guess I was so committed I didn't quite see the politics of this thing."'

It was in 1990 that the Broadcasting Act became law. The new system would come in at the beginning of 1993. ITN's lobbying had had its effect. The Act now made plain that 'news programmes of high quality' would be required from a 'nominated news provider' and would have to be carried by all the ITV (Channel 3, as it was now called) licensees at the same time, including peak viewing times. What was not clear was whether that 'nominated news provider' would be ITN only, or whether another company might also get the stamp of approval and be free to pitch for the news contract with Channel 3. This was not altogether re-assuring for the ITN directors, but IBA chief executive David Glencross, with a wink and a nod, told them that 'it would be surprising if the IBA were to choose any organisation other than ITN'[9] as its nominated news provider.

The IBA had always felt they had to protect ITN against the programme companies. Peter Rogers, its finance director, had been sympathetic to Alastair Burnet's view that they would never help ITN expand. 'I didn't think the companies had it in them to make a success of ITN in a wholly competitive world,' he says. 'In practical terms, because of their own protected existence within a monopoly, they didn't have the capacity to go out and develop ITN. The fact is that when it came to successful diversification, the ITV companies had a very poor record. If they were going to make a success of ITN it would really need to be picked up by someone from outside who had already succeeded.'

But Rogers had doubts about Burnet's campaign for new ownership: 'I think it was quite OK for the IBA to argue about the future and advocate change, but for an employee of ITN like Alastair to argue against the policy of his company was intolerable. I really thought Alastair was disloyal, and I found it difficult to see why the board didn't dismiss him. But the problem was that he had the ear of Mrs Thatcher, who was no friend to the companies. If the companies had dismissed Alastair she would have seen that as a snub to her.'

In effect Alastair Burnet had struck a deal with government. In return for letting ITN continue as commercial television's national news provider there would be wider ownership of the news company. 'I believe,' Burnet would tell the ITN board, 'that this is the least bad way of tackling the highly desirable but anomalous continuation of ITN's near monopoly of the supply of national and international news on Channel 3.'

It was quite a coup, as Peter Monteith of *Television Week* spotted:

> The Broadcasting Bill is likely to guarantee ITN a monopoly supply and, as part of the protection needed to guarantee news independence, be immune from any take-over. So we have the remarkable situation of a Bill which introduces competitive tendering for ITV and a greater pressure on programme standards, costs and good management, creating a monopoly situation in which a company has a guaranteed supply contract with no pressure on staffing, costs or good management.[10]

But the majority of the board could not see that they'd got a good deal. Whatever work he had done to get the news requirement written into the Act, Burnet had been active in encouraging the government to take control of ITN away from the programme companies. From the beginning of 1993, when the Act came into effect, no single broadcaster would be allowed to own more than 20 per cent of ITN, and all the broadcasters taken together would not be allowed a majority shareholding – they would lose control.

On 19 February 1990 a dramatic scene took place in the boardroom of ITN House in Wells Street. The directors representing the ITV companies were furious with Burnet. His, they felt, was an act of betrayal for, as a member of the board, he had urged the passage of a law that would damage their interests. A paper was put forward urging the government to think again, and let broadcasters retain at least a two-thirds majority share in ITN. David Nicholas and Stewart Purvis decided they must go along with the non-executive directors. All present supported the paper: all, except Alastair Burnet.

Well aware of the hostility the board felt towards him and his policy on the ownership issue, Burnet had come to the meeting fully prepared with a neatly typed statement of resignation, which he now produced and read to his fellow directors:

> If there is little or no change in a commercial, near monopolistic system after thirty-five years, the likelihood is that the components of the near monopoly will persist in adhering to defensive, suspicious policies . . . In a television news company, facing new competitors and opportunities – and their attendant risks – I think that the lesser risk lies in going with new ideas, new finance and new shareholdings. I doubt frankly if many of the managers and shareholders of regional television companies are likely (or should be expected) to put capital and enthusiasm for an international news service as a high priority. In essence, to most businessmen (and certainly to their share-holders) 49 per cent of a successful company is better than 51 per cent of a defensive and threatened one.

It would be hard, Burnet insisted, to get new investment if ITN remained 'wholly subservient' to Channel 3 licensees. Change was necessary. He concluded:

I do not wish the perception of ITN, especially in predators' eyes, to be the creature of an evident cartel, the sole relict of the pre-1993 system, and the target of any political or commercial campaign against what will be called a stitch-up. It is with regret that I am unable to add my voice to others round the table, and I shall give my resignation from the board to the chairman immediately.[11]

So saying, Burnet rose from his chair, slipped quietly through the door directly behind him, and vanished from the boardroom to go back to his work as a newscaster. It was a stunning performance, which left the board collectively open-mouthed.

That Monday night *News at Ten* carried a short announcement of Burnet's resignation, read by Trevor McDonald, his newscaster partner for the evening. A few days later the press had some unkind gibes to throw at him when he was found by the police to be rather the worse for wear after apparently colliding with a lamp-post near his home in Kensington; he had to be taken to hospital. To help the battered Burnet avoid the press while his bruises and abrasions healed, ITN smuggled him into a room at Berners Hotel. There, he complained to Sue Tinson, he was troubled by a series of phone calls from 'some woman' wanting to speak to him. Eventually he was persuaded to take the call. Tinson recalls the wounded knight springing to attention. 'Alastair, what have you been up to? Are you all right?' enquired the mystery woman. It was, of course, his great admirer, Margaret Thatcher, the prime minister.

It had not been a good week for Burnet, but although he had lost his place on the ITN board, the television news deal, which he had struck, stuck. He had – for the moment, at least – reinforced ITN's monopoly of ITV's news, and, to the indignation of his fellow board members, helped ensure that they would soon have to sell some of their ITN shares to non-broadcasters. In November 1990 it was announced that ITN would indeed remain the sole 'nominated news provider' for ITV, and that that decision would not be reviewed until 1995. At the same time the IBA said that it would postpone until the end of 1994 the date by which the ITV companies must have sold off their majority shareholding in ITN.[12]

CHAPTER 31
TOMORROW THE WORLD

How big, and in what way, should ITN try to grow? That had been the argument over the years. While there had been one channel and not much money about, it was clear that ITN should concentrate on providing a national and – so far as could be afforded – an international news service for ITV. Under editor Geoffrey Cox, ITN had added other programmes for ITV – *Dateline* and *Roving Report*. Then it had made the jump to *News at Ten*, a nightly half-hour news for ITV. Next, with the addition of new channels and the breakfast franchise, came attempts (some successful, others not) to supply news tailored to what these new customers said they wanted. There were other ventures: selling ITN's studio-based services to commercial companies; trying to make a go of syndication and of UPITN, later WTN; and later still supplying a satellite service, Superchannel. But through the 1980s ITN had chafed at the reluctance of its owners, the ITV companies, to give wholehearted support to its desire to grow.

In fact, the clearest criticism of this reluctance came from the representative on the ITN board of one of those same reluctant companies, Lord (Aubrey) Buxton, a founding member of Anglia Television. During his time as chairman of ITN (from 1980 to 1986), he had on several occasions urged his colleagues to be more energetic in thinking about ITN's future development, and in 1987 he circulated another paper, 'Thoughts on Future Strategy':

> I sometimes wonder whether the board is fulfilling its proper role as a policy maker, aiming to build up and develop ITN as a major programme component of ITV, as the top national news service and as one of the main world news operations of renown and rising reputation. For example, there is little doubt that if one of the contractors owned and operated the daily ITN programme service, it would be supported by massive promotion and PR, and would be proclaimed, day in and day out, as a television spectacular.

This was a point constantly made by ITN management. He continued:

> As things are, the board seems to operate primarily as a watchdog to ensure that nothing gets out of hand, and is not much more than a management committee, concerned primarily with finance and administration . . . It has to be said that if there are any prospects in the new era for ITN making money and increasing revenue nationally and internationally, it is not going to do it by being contained in a strait-jacket . . . A watchdog is inadequate and will simply miss the opportunities that are looming.[1]

Others shared Buxton's view that ITN's owners were letting things slide, and that a decision should be taken as to what kind of company ITN was going to be.

The IBA regarded ITN as its pride and joy – it had, after all, been created by its predecessor the ITA at the very beginning of the world of commercial television. It looked on its creation, and saw that it was good. But the IBA's director of finance, Peter Rogers, felt it was high time ITN made up its mind about what it was trying to do.

In 1987, when the IBA's director general asked for his comments, Rogers responded with a memo that was sharp and to the point:

> The ITN business is now developing rapidly, so that there is no longer an identity between investors and customers . . . The present structure of ITN is wholly unsuited to the scale and diversity of the development referred to . . . because this structure:

- provides an inadequate capital base
- increases the exposure of ITV contractors to a range of business risks which do not arise out of the provision of the ITV/Channel 4 news services
- generates inadequate commercial incentive and motivation within ITN
- has produced a business management which, on the business side, is not in my view fully up to the much larger, more difficult and diverse tasks envisaged
- has produced an ITN board of directors in which the main interest and expertise of the very powerful non-executive directors (each one of them representing an investment stake) is focused on just one part of the ITN business. Moreover this is the part in which substantial growth is not anticipated.[2]

In other words ITN didn't have enough money or incentive to expand, didn't have owners who could be expected to take an interest in new ventures, and didn't have managers who were capable of handling them.

Later that year Rogers put forward what he saw were the two options facing ITN:

i   that ITN should be required to limit its horizons to the provision of news services to ITV, Channel 4, BSB and possibly Independent Radio. In this case there need be no major structural reform, although some limited but worthwhile changes might be made in the composition of the ITN board and the approach to business planning generally;

ii   accept the desirability of a growth and diversification strategy. If, however, this wider remit is to be successful, then there will have to be changes in the ownership, corporate structure, funding and management of ITN.[3]

Rogers and the rest of the IBA staff recommended the second strategy, and this course was accepted by the members of the Authority. So now those at ITN who wanted to expand, to shout 'Tomorrow, the world!' had the approval of the regulator. Of course, that did not mean they would necessarily succeed, or that they would have the full-hearted support of the ITN board in making the attempt. As Peter Rogers says today: 'Everybody could see the excitement of a world-class free-standing news service, but no one had done it successfully. There was no one in the world making money out of news. People were putting mega-bucks in, but not getting profits out. On the other hand it was a bit dreary just going on being a service provider to ITV. The idea was to find something in the middle.'

Under David Nicholas ITN wanted to grow, and in one sense at least it had to do so. It was symptomatic that the news company was now physically bursting out of its headquarters in Wells Street, not far from Oxford Circus, which it had occupied since 1969. Although it was a decided improvement on its former cramped premises in Kingsway, ITN House had always been a rather tacky building. On the day ITN moved in, the tall and energetic Peter Snow had punched a hole in a lavatory cubicle wall to demonstrate his contempt for the poor quality of the hardboard partitions. Over the years, as the number of people on ITN's staff increased to deal with its new programme responsibilities, so the accommodation became more crowded, until officers and other ranks alike were close to mutiny.

A search began for new premises. At a board meeting in early 1987 Nicholas insisted that ITN had to stay in central London. It wasn't like a newspaper where the journalists could be miles from the printing presses. As he later said: 'I thought we had a great asset in being in central London, in touch with the people who made news – in flesh touch . . . Lots of MPs and big people were in and out of the ITN building all the time. They'd have a drink with young journalists in the Green Room or go across to the wine bar. And I always felt that was a terribly important way, especially for young journalists, to keep contact. Whereas the BBC moving out to White City was remote . . . '⁴ Alastair Burnet supported Nicholas, saying that ITN had to be close to Westminster and its politicians. As to the overcrowding, 'As an occupant of the present accommodation he could testify to the fact that the problem was now extreme.'⁵

ITN rather fancied the elegant Bedford College in Regent's Park as its new address, but the Crown Commissioners wisely decided that the kind of changes ITN would have to make to the building would ruin it. Other sites considered included a new building in Euston Road, rejected as too expensive, and an old London Rubber Company condom factory south of the river. Nicholas pointed out that, had this been the option eventually chosen, his office would have been in the former latex rubber retort room.

He might then have been called the best-protected editor in British tele-vision. Finally, ITN's attention was drawn to a building owned by the media tycoon Rupert Murdoch. It had been built for the *Sunday Times*, but Murdoch was now intent on producing his papers with new technology in Docklands, and 200 Gray's Inn Road was for sale. It was a massive building, far too large for ITN alone, but Nicholas was thinking big. ITN would make the new building into a giant media centre by letting space to other companies in the same line of business: 'Spare space,' deputy chief executive Paul Mathews told the board, 'could command premium rents from others in the television industry.'[6]

At the same time that ITN was planning to exchange its cramped condi-tions at Wells Street for something bigger, it was trying to expand into new programme areas. Protracted negotiations to supply news had been held with British Satellite Broadcasting, BSB, which was planning to bring programmes to British viewers via a satellite and a 'squarial' dish. The deal had foundered when the two sides could not agree on the circumstances in which ITN would deny BSB access to a hot news story until it had first run on ITV's bulletins. But there was another interesting venture, which ITN hoped would get it into satellite broadcasting abroad.

Superchannel had promised the 'Best of British' programming, but a series of miscalculations meant ITN's news programme was really the only good thing about it. ITN signed a three-year contract to supply a half-hour news bulletin at 10 p.m. every evening, a deal worth £2 million in the first year, £2.57 million in the second and £3.26 million in the third.

'I was a reporter and part-time newscaster,' says John Suchet, 'when David Nicholas said to me, "We are going to begin the most exciting new project. This is a chance to take the lead in television news, to put out the first British news to a foreign audience." He told me, "I have selected you to present it because you have a clear voice without a regional accent."'

There was a basic problem: there was no room to make the new programme in ITN's Wells Street headquarters. The solution was to hire a Portakabin and park it on a flat portion of the roof. ITN had no planning permission for this: they just got on with it. 'On a Sunday morning,' says David Nicholas, 'they closed Ridinghouse Street, and a bloody great crane came and lifted a Portakabin on to the roof – long before any of our neigh-bours could say it interfered with their light or any of that crap! And there was a gantry outside in the open air going across to the main building – like a wobbly sort of gangplank.'

Superchannel opened for business on Friday, 30 January 1987, and ITN's first newscast for the new channel was on the following Monday. Says Suchet: 'My opening words were "Welcome to the *ITN World News* – the first television news bulletin to be broadcast by satellite across Europe from London." To make sure I was understood in these European countries I spoke more slowly than usual – two words to the second instead of three. Letters poured in from all over Europe. I remember being stopped by people in Oslo when I was there. We heard that people in Eastern Europe were using dustbin lids as satellite aerials. We had an international agenda on the *World News* – we could lead on the resignation of the Portuguese prime minister. People in Europe told us, "We trust the news from Britain." I cut my teeth as a newscaster going out to a foreign audience. I'd given up my reporting career for the *World News*, but I really believed in what we were doing.'

Because the prime minister hated what she saw as the monopolistic fat-cat tendencies of Britain's broadcasters, she loved the leanness of ITN's Superchannel operation. As it happened, the BBC had been pitching to the government for funds to start its own television version of BBC Radio's *World Service*, but now that ITN was doing it (or something like it) without subsidy, as a commercial enterprise, Nicholas rang the Foreign Office to protest at what he saw as unfair competition in the offing: 'I was bloody outraged! "First of all," I told them, "we don't think that public money should be going into this. We think it's doing the market down; we are already doing a foreign news service on Superchannel. But *if* public money is going into it, then we should have the right to tender." I heard the intake of breath down the telephone, and then I was taken to lunch by the permanent secretary of the Foreign Office. He said, "Well, if I have to tell you the truth, we didn't know there was another game in town, something that already existed." They didn't have a clue. So, of course, Mrs Thatcher, when she got to hear about it, was extremely keen on what we were doing. And we invited her round one night, and took her up to see John Suchet doing the Superchannel news. And there was a bloody gale blowing; and she had to walk across this gantry holding her skirt tight. John was doing the programme, and there was virtually no room there between them. She stood in there while the Portakabin swayed in the gale. She loved it.

'A few weeks later there was a reception at Number Ten – I think it was for some foreign visitor – and my wife and I were invited. So Mrs Thatcher is going down the line with him and she says, "Ah, this is David Nicholas — he runs the best news service in the world." And then she said to me, "Have you heard the news? The BBC are not going to get the money."'

All seemed set fair for ITN, but Superchannel was watched by only a hundred thousand people across the whole of Europe. Very soon it ran into financial difficulties, and by November 1988 it owed ITN nearly £450,000. When the channel refused to pay up, ITN cut off the news service it provided, and its satellite adventure was reduced to virtually nothing. It was not until 1992, when the American broadcaster NBC bought Superchannel to carry its own material in Europe, that ITN's *World News* revived and began to bring modest returns, shown on Public Service Broadcasting stations in America, and channels in Australia, Japan and New Zealand. But it was always a shoestring operation.

In the early nineties *World News* acquired its own studio, but it was even smaller than the original Portakabin, scarcely bigger than a broom cupboard. At times, to save money, bulletins were not broadcast live, but transmitted from tape: links recorded by the newscaster would be edited together with the reporter packages drawn from ITN's other programmes, then fed to the satellite when editing was complete. It did not add to the immediacy of *ITN World News*.

In the end, despite ITN's bold initiative, it was the publicly funded BBC that became the dominant British broadcaster abroad, able to offer other programmes as well as news bulletins to its clients. *ITN World News* finally closed down after its principal customer in New York lost its transmitter on top of one of the towers of the World Trade Center, on that dreadful September day in 2001.

CHAPTER 32
OUT OF CONTROL

ITN's attempts to expand and sell its news programmes to other new satellite broadcasters did not prove particularly successful. Sky's Rupert Murdoch had suggested that he might be interested in taking his news service from ITN – so intoxicating a prospect that David Nicholas allowed himself to be flown to Hollywood in Murdoch's private jet to discuss the deal. But it seems more likely now that Murdoch just wanted to see ITN's figures to help him set up his own operation, as indeed he did.

Despite this disappointment Nicholas was still bent on expanding ITN's accommodation. While Murdoch had declined to buy ITN's news service he had agreed to sell to ITN the former *Sunday Times* building at 200 Gray's Inn Road for £7 million. But there was a hold-up. Labour councillors in Camden, furious that Murdoch was taking the printers' jobs away from their borough to Docklands, tried make ITN pay a 'voluntary donation' towards helping unemployed printers and their families before they would give planning consent to the development of the building. The ITN board was split on the issue, with Nicholas all in favour of paying up in order to get on with a move he felt was now absolutely imperative. But the non-executive directors, the ones with the votes, thought otherwise. It was decided to call Camden's bluff and buy the building without planning permission. If that was refused, ITN would go to court. In the event it proved the right move. Though still obstructive, Camden eventually gave way and granted the necessary permission. It was time for the big decision.

In March 1988 Nicholas told his fellow ITN directors that this was one of the most important meetings ever held by the board: the long-term future of ITN would be decided by its outcome. ITN had been searching for new premises for six long years, and the company was now on a knife-edge, with staff overcrowding that bordered on illegality. The Gray's Inn Road building was clearly a good investment in a developing area and ITN's advisers believed that there would be no difficulty in attracting tenants at premium rates. Paul Mathews said reassuringly that the increase in rent and rates that ITN would now have to pay if it moved to Gray's Inn Road would, to a substantial extent, be met by operational savings. It was agreed that negotiations with Stanhope Properties to develop the site should go ahead.

The following month the decision was taken to proceed to contract. In retrospect this was when ITN set out on the path that would bring it to the edge of the abyss, the brink of ruin. There had as yet been no real expansion to bring increased revenue, and just as ITN committed itself to develop new and costly premises, its coverage costs, the money it spent on gathering the news, were starting to run out of control. At this same board meeting Nicholas explained that 'unbudgeted accommodation costs for the crew in Moscow, the Middle East bureau and events in Gibraltar and Ulster had led to a budget overspend. Stringent measures had been put in hand, and every effort would be made to contain the situation . . . ' Plans to present *News at Ten* from Moscow during the Reagan/Gorbachev summit, he said, would have to be scrapped, and the availability of camera crews had been reduced to twelve a day.

At first it looked as if ITN was getting a grip on the cost of coverage. The operating budget presented in June the following year by the new director of finance Penny Bickerstaff was well received: 'Mr Brian Tesler said that the budget was quite the best budget the Committee had seen from ITN; that it demonstrated impressive imagination in addressing the control of costs.' But in that same meeting Nicholas, now Sir David and chairman as well as chief executive of ITN, 'gave a presentation on recommendations to purchase a helicopter'.

Penny Bickerstaff had come to ITN on secondment and joined the staff in June 1988. She found an organisation where coming in on budget was regarded by ITN's journalists, understandably, as of secondary importance to getting the news. 'David Nicholas would blow up,' she says, 'at the idea of missing a story, not of overspending.' At the weekly Friday meeting to discuss coverage costs she found a reluctance to get to grips with making any economies. 'I said to them, "If we are going to spend on covering everything you don't need me – it's about making judgements about what *not* to cover." When, on one particular project, they explained to me how difficult it would be to decide what to cut out, and how long it would take, I said to them, "Well, I don't know anything about news, but give it to me and I'll do it in five minutes: all I'll do is take out everything beginning with B. Then they said they would do it themselves after all.'

When it came to the purchase of the helicopter that Nicholas had set his heart on, Penny Bickerstaff offered him a deal: if she could take £300,000 out of reporters' expenses, particularly taxi fares, he could have his helicopter. She compiled a list of dodgy-looking taxi-company bills – three-hour waiting times at nearby restaurants, that kind of thing – and got Nicholas to write in cloudy but menacing tones to a variety of ITN people about reducing their expenses claims. The management's eye, they were meant to feel, was upon them.

Bickerstaff says she felt then that ITN was putting out all the wrong signals – being a big spender at a time when commercial television was about to be reorganised in a way that would force it to be much more cost-conscious. As far as the new headquarters in Gray's Inn Road was concerned: 'I thought the building was too costly and too risky. It was wrong in look and in feel: it sent the wrong message, and I was dead against it. I even wrote formally to [deputy chief executive] Paul Mathews to say so.'

Costs were mounting. Good coverage made everyone at ITN happy, but it was increasingly expensive. In January 1990 the new editor, Stewart Purvis, told the board that 'because of the success of the Romanian coverage, staff morale was very high. Paul Mathews said that this coverage would cost an extra £300,000 to £400,000 in excess of the budget.'[1] A month later Purvis reported that the costs of the Romanian coverage were now standing at £500,000. 'History would record,' he stated boldly, 'that money had never been better spent.'[2]

It got worse. By March the estimate was of a £1.5 million loss. 'Mr [Richard] Dunn [Thames Television] said that, as a shareholder of ITN, he would be happy to support the Romanian coverage and the *World News*. However, he wondered whether such a view would be taken by a future shareholder whose business was unrelated to news . . . there was a real fear among the shareholders of another Romania . . . The chairman pointed out that no one would have believed, when producing a budget in June last year, that Eastern Europe would collapse in twelve weeks. ITN was currently taking austere measures to ensure that the forecast could be delivered.'[3]   *— 1990*

Come May, and Paul Mathews's financial report revealed a forecast net deficit of £1,986,000 for the year to July 1989 – which did not even include the overspend on the Romanian coverage. And the new building at Gray's Inn Road was now beginning to look more of a burden than an opportunity. ITN had sold it to the developer and was now leasing it back at a rent of £5,750,000 a year, with the idea of sub-letting it to other media organisations, which, it had been assumed, would be queuing up to rent space. But now Mathews 'asked the board to note the depressed state of the property market.'[4] In the event that all the five available floors could not be sub-let, ITN would have to meet costs of some £4 million a year.

Over a series of board meetings Greg Dyke, the ITN director representing London Weekend Television, attacked ITN's handling of its finances again and again. Costs were not under control, he said in September 1990; how had ITN turned the £24 million price on the sale of its Wells Street headquarters into a £1 million overdraft, he asked in October. ITN had been mismanaged, he asserted in November: savings must be made, and could not wait.

It was in October that the *Guardian*'s media editor, Georgina Henry, reported on a leaked letter from Sir David Nicholas to the home secretary, which confirmed that ITN was on the brink of serious instability and had run out of cash. Given that ITN's future was uncertain, the banks were unwilling to lend the money needed to get the company into the new Gray's Inn Road building.[5] 'ITN fears it could be "broke within weeks",' was the *Sunday Times* headline a few days later. 'Independent Television News, facing a financial crisis, will tomorrow ask the ITV companies that own it for an immediate injection of £6.5 million to see it through the next six weeks. If it fails to get the money ITN could be broke within weeks . . . '[6]

In the event, reminded by the IBA that they had an obligation to see that the ITN was 'effectively equipped and adequately funded', the ITV companies paid up, and ITN staggered into its grand new quarters in Gray's Inn Road, a building empty of other tenants.

In March 1990 Penny Bickerstaff left ITN to help Thames Television prepare its bid to remain London's weekday ITV contractor. She had detected nothing fundamentally amiss at ITN, and the computer system for the accounts department, which had a habit of crashing every Friday, was well on the way to being replaced. But, disastrously for ITN, her successor was not found for some time. It was only when Clive Timms was appointed finance director many months later, in September, that anyone began to plumb the depths of the black hole ITN was in. It was much more than just a short-term cash-flow problem.

Weighed down with the problems involved in controlling coverage costs, burdened with the continuing expense of an empty new building, Sir David Nicholas was not in a good position to pursue ITN's expansion. He realised he could not continue as both chairman and chief executive. So at the ITN board meeting on 21 January 1991 there was a new face at the table, a new chief executive designate. Nicholas had approached Bob Phillis who, in the eighties, had been on the ITN board representing Central Television, and was a warm supporter of ITN. Recruited from Carlton Communications – which, later that year, would win the London weekday franchise from Thames – Phillis thought he was coming to lead ITN into the new, competitive, cost-conscious world. Instead he found himself dealing with potential catastrophe. 'I didn't know anything about this until three weeks before I took up my appointment,' says Phillis. 'Clive Timms came to see me, David Nicholas called in Paul Mathews and we found a black hole in our accounts. Over the past couple of years ITN had failed to pick up significant expenditure – it was really the cost of covering Afghanistan and Eastern Europe. Unless the shareholders had agreed to continue their support ITN was effectively bankrupt. ITN couldn't explain it, and our auditors hadn't picked it up. It was a bloody disaster. "Jesus Christ! We have some explaining to do here!" I was amazed: I was surprised. It changed the focus of my job from growth and expansion to a rescue.'

Phillis wasted no time in trying to find out what had gone wrong. Essentially it was a matter of coverage commissioned but not properly costed or tracked so that, much later on, huge bills – for endless satellite transmissions from the Gulf, for example – would turn up unexpectedly for payment.

At his first board meeting as chief executive, in February, Phillis presented a paper on the accounts for the year 1989/90. Because of the incompetence of certain key staff in the finance area which the report revealed, he said, they would be asked to leave once the investigation was complete. The auditors, from Coopers and Lybrand Deloitte, were quizzed as to why 'lack of procedures had gone on so long'. They replied that it was because 'no one within the organisation appeared to be taking the action that was necessary to put things right.'

Greg Dyke asked whether they felt responsible. Not in the least, they said. It was 'a matter for management, and the auditors had regularly drawn management's attention to the problem.'[7]

It was pretty clear that the lack of financial control had continued into 1991, for in May that year editor Stewart Purvis reported that 'the estimating processes adopted in January and February to assess the future costs of Gulf War coverage have proved inadequate in a number of key respects.' As a result, a bureau manager and a foreign manager had been replaced.

Greg Dyke had only recently returned from taking an MBA at Harvard Business School, where he had been taught how to read a balance sheet. As a result he had begun to look very shrewdly at the ITN accounts and would claim to be the first person to spot the 'black hole' that a close study of those accounts had revealed. At another board meeting 'Greg Dyke expressed the view that ITN still did not seem to know what it was spending, and that in a normal commercial situation the shareholders would seriously question whether to provide continuing support to what, to him, appeared a bankrupt organisation.'[8]

By now the papers were on to the story. In the *Independent*, under the headline 'What's the bottom line? It's news to ITN', Maggie Brown wondered, 'Who would buy shares in a company that has been incapable of balancing its books?'[9] It was confirmed that, in all, a whopping £9.8 million was unaccounted for. Bob Phillis told *Broadcast* frankly: 'Although it should be said that this money wasn't lost, it wasn't embezzled, it wasn't fraudulently misused, it was spent, and it was spent by ITN. Of course it was the accountants' failure to add it up, but they didn't spend the money. It was the other 850 people who spent the money.' But surely, he was asked, heads would have rolled at any other company. 'I don't disagree with that comment,' Phillis replied. 'There's no glory and no credit to ITN in what has happened . . . David [ITN chairman Sir David Nicholas] was mortified and distraught when he heard of this problem. Of course he feels responsible for the problems that have arisen. We have to focus our attention on the future and not be vindictive about the past.'[10]

'In my book,' says Phillis today, 'David Nicholas was a superb editor, a great journalist, an inspirational leader, a tremendous manager of colleagues and staff. What David was not, and never was, was a chief executive in the terms we now understand in broadcasting. ITN was not a company concerned with the bottom line: it was a cost centre within ITV. The board itself must bear some responsibility for not having recognised the situation. I have absolutely no doubt that the auditors were considerably at fault, but they had not brought their worries about suspension accounts to the board's attention. David unwittingly took on too much, even though he would say he successfully delegated. David picked good people, the heart and soul of what ITN used to be, but were those people accountable? ITN was journalistically led, and journalists are not always good at financial control. When I got there, the accountants would be hidden away somewhere. They would scarcely see the editorial teams on ITV or Channel 4. No one was picking up the cost when people and projects were being commissioned.'

These criticisms led Sir David Nicholas to consider his position. He had not been due to retire until the following year, in January 1992, but when the ITN board met in June 1991 he announced that he intended to go earlier than planned. 'ITN,' he said, 'had established and demonstrated that public service quality can be encompassed within the environment of commercial television.' But now Bob Phillis and the papers he was presenting to the board signalled 'the start of a new era', and so he proposed to retire in October, five months before he was due to do so. Nicholas added that his old friend and former ally on the board Alastair Burnet would stop presenting *News at Ten* in August.[11]

The resignation of its two television knights was a significant moment for ITN. As the official ITV history recognises, it

> marked a watershed in the evolution of ITN from personal to professional management . . . Nicholas, like his predecessors, had sought to command all the news ground on behalf of ITN. He would often personally direct his troops to what needed to be covered. It was, he sometimes appeared to feel, his duty to rise above the mundane commercial concerns of his share-holders to achieve the greater journalistic good. He was a brilliant instinctive editor, to whom the audience owed much . . . His was an achievement in accord with the educational traditions of his Welsh blood and upbringing. That was not diminished, only tarnished, by the events of his three years as chairman – which many of his colleagues feel, with the benefit of hindsight, was a role too far.'

At the ITC David Glencross, soon to retire himself, had worked closely with Nicholas and come to admire him greatly: 'He had a tremendous flair', says Glencross, 'for recognising a news story and knowing how to pursue it. He had a rare talent for picking talent – in front of and behind the screen. He had nerves of steel in dealing with politicians. His election night programmes when he was executive producer were wonderful. He had skills and enthusiasm which he never lost. But his weaknesses were that he was first and foremost a journalist, and the administrative and financial cares of ITN were to him of lesser concern. He hoped – he *thought* – that those details would look after themselves.'

CHAPTER 33
THE DOOMED BID

It says a good deal for ITN and its new chief executive Bob Phillis that even as the news company was paddling furiously to stay afloat it was still trying to flap its wings and fly. It still wanted to develop and expand. Up for grabs was the breakfast television licence and ITN became the lead partner in a consortium bidding to take over from the current holder TV-AM. As well as ITN, with 20 per cent, Daybreak's shareholders included the *Daily Telegraph*, MAI, NBC Europe and Carlton Communications.

Daybreak set out to offer 'something more substantial for breakfast', as its publicity put it, something for all those potential viewers who were turned off both by TV-AM's rather juvenile approach and the much more upmarket BBC breakfast programme. Non-executive directors included the television star Sir Robin Day, passionate about getting viewers interested in current affairs, and Carole Stone, a former BBC Radio 4 *Any Questions?* producer, who was expert at bringing people together in lively discussion of topical issues. Chairman of the bid was Sir Paul Fox.

But Daybreak wasn't the only contender with TV-AM for the breakfast franchise. London Weekend Television and the news agency Visnews had put together another bid, called Sunrise.

In many ways the Daybreak bid looked superior: its production base would be in ITN's new Gray's Inn Road building, while Sunrise would have its 'intake' at Visnews in West London, and its 'output' miles away at LWT's studios on the South Bank of the Thames, surely a recipe for trouble. And while Daybreak had the vastly experienced ITN to supply it with news, Sunrise was relying on a news agency, Visnews, that had never made news programmes before.

But though this last point looked like an advantage to Daybreak and ITN it was also a difficulty. Unlike ITV, which for the next five years was required to take *ITN News*, the successful breakfast contractor could get its news from any supplier it chose. For the ITC to give the licence to Daybreak would mean that ITN was the sole supplier of news to all of Britain's commercial television broadcasters – great for ITN, but against the spirit of the times. ITN argued to the ITC that 'There would be a substantial advantage to Channel 3 [ITV] as a network if Daybreak were to be awarded the licence. It would allow ITN to provide round-the-clock news coverage, generating economies of scale and helping to make the Channel 3 news provider more competitive.'

Exactly how strengthening ITN's monopoly on the supply of news would make it more competitive was not immediately clear.

Provided they passed a basic 'quality' threshold, the ITC's decision on the breakfast licence applicants – just like those it had made on ITV bidders – had to be on financial grounds. How much were they prepared to pay for their licence to make money? But Sir Paul Fox, leading the Daybreak bid, tried a little special pleading with the ITC. In August 1991 he wrote to its chairman Sir George Russell, who was performing his now practised role of trying to get people who wanted to make money to take at least some interest in making good programmes:

> At the risk of this letter being out of time and quite possibly out of order, I feel compelled to write to you about ITN. You and I have been Chairmen of ITN and do have a special regard for it.
>
> As a part-time observer through my link with Daybreak, I have seen ITN at work in recent weeks and I have watched quite a few programmes. Not surprisingly, there is a loss of confidence within the place and too much hostility within the industry. There is a scepticism about ITN among opinion formers. Bob [Phillis] and Stewart [Purvis] and their colleagues will have to work hard to restore ITN to its rightful place: a centre of distinction and achievement.

What ITN needs is a shot in the arm; something to boost its confidence and underline its unique role within Independent Television. I remain convinced that only ITN can provide the 24-hour news service that ITV (Channel 3) needs. Any other system – especially a new and untried one – is likely to be damaging and wasteful.[1]

Russell's reply was carefully worded: 'There are no indiscreet letters to the ITC, only the possibility of indiscreet replies back. So, in the circumstances, I am sure you would not expect me to comment on the points you have made.'[2]

When, on 16 October, the ITC announced the result of the breakfast licence auction, Daybreak discovered it had lost. The existing contractor, TV-AM, had bid £14,125,000, less than half what Daybreak had offered – £33,260,000 – but, lo and behold, Sunrise had bid almost exactly the same as Daybreak, £34,610,000 – just £1,350,000 more.

At an ITN board meeting on 21 October, chief executive Bob Phillis reported that if the Daybreak board had accepted the recommendation from the executive team led by ITN, its bid would have been the highest: it would have won. Through gritted teeth he congratulated Greg Dyke from LWT on the success of his Sunrise consortium, but ITN's disappointment turned to fury when it transpired that Carlton (a major shareholder in the Daybreak bid) was now joining the successful rival Sunrise, conveniently filling a gap that had been left open in its funding. The suspicion grew that somehow Sunrise had become aware of how much Daybreak was bidding and had therefore been able to bid just that little bit more to gain the prize.

Says Bob Phillis: 'I have very strong reason to believe that the Sunrise bidders knew what we at ITN were doing with our Daybreak bid. The outcome was an absolute tragedy for ITN: it was a travesty.' Today Greg Dyke cheerfully admits that, as leader of the Sunrise consortium, he did indeed discover what Daybreak was going to bid; but he denies that the information was leaked by Carlton.

CHAPTER 34

LEANER, FITTER – OR WASTING AWAY

As ITN's *Channel 4 News* service had prepared to start up in 1982, the ACTT, the Association of Cinema and Television Technicians, had demanded more money for its ITN members before they would work on it. It was a familiar tactic of the time, in which a company that tried to develop new products or markets would have to pay its workforce more, up-front, to obtain their co-operation. For the manager charged with getting *Channel 4 News* on the air on time, as ITN was contracted to do, without conceding the 10 per cent wage demand, it was a stressful time, and he had a nervous breakdown. Mike Morris, former foreign editor, and now on the first step of the managerial ladder, looking after ITN's journalists as editorial manager, found himself drafted in to deal with the ACTT. 'I was absolutely terrified,' he says. 'I hadn't smoked for years but I remember I went out, bought a packet of cigarettes, and smoked ten of them straight off. You have to remember that this was before the Thatcher legislation took effect. People could and did walk out at the drop of a hat, and the ACTT could stop *Channel 4 News* getting on the air.'

Morris had no extra money to offer so there was nothing to negotiate about. Certain that on this occasion the union had no real case he went to arbitration – 'flip-flop' arbitration, in which one side or the other wins outright. He won, and found himself launched on a new ITN career. Morris was appointed director of personnel and industrial relations and promptly sent off on management courses at Ashridge and Henley. 'They opened my eyes to professional management,' he says. 'It started me thinking. About this time ITN was having discussions with the new American television company CNN in Atlanta. "We cannot believe your numbers," they said to me, "what it's costing you to produce your news stories."'

Compared with CNN's new electronically based operation, ITN – like the rest of the British television industry – did indeed still look like the last bastion of restrictive practices that Margaret Thatcher so resented. For example, it had taken nearly three years after the board had approved the purchase of new electronic cameras for the technical unions to agree even to a six-month trial of them. Now, in the late eighties, as ITN tried to introduce mobile edit vans, the unions were demanding that four people should ride in them: a driver from NATKE (the National Association of Theatrical and Kine Employees), a tape editor and a sound engineer from the ACTT, and an electrician from the ETU. It was an exhausting dispute, and Morris remembers writing a memo that in effect said, 'We've run out of road with the ACTT – there must be another way.' In April 1988 he presented to the board his working practices action plan 'Into the Nineties', designed to make ITN fit for life in the more competitive world that lay ahead.

'Change is necessary to ensure that ITN has a competitive cost structure and can provide its existing and potential customers with ever greater value for money,' said the plan. 'The forces for change, both within the independent television industry and from the government are growing stronger.' At the time at least it seemed pretty radical stuff. Labour costs were to be reduced by £4.6 million, and staff numbers from 1,067 to 931. ITN was looking for retraining, multi-skilling and greater rostering flexibility. And for people who didn't fancy the future there would be generous pay-offs – four weeks' money for every year of service, with a maximum of £71,238. Morris was able to tell the board that the ACTT was accepting the proposals in principle, provided that the redundancies were voluntary; it was the journalists in the NUJ who were most hostile, concerned at being required to work longer hours than at present. However, 'Our assessment is that the NUJ will make a lot of noise, but will agree to work the new rosters.'[1]

In the end they did. Meetings went on through the summer. Details of the deal were argued out at a union conference centre in two sessions, each lasting several days. It was clear that the unions could see the future of television as well as anyone else and knew that ITN had to slim down to prepare for it. Says Morris: 'They bought into annual salaries with no overtime – the whole culture of the organisation was changed by this. The fact was that we'd had Wapping, when Murdoch destroyed the print unions, and TV-AM, where they'd locked out their unions and never let them in again. Every time I drove past TV-AM I used to think, As long as management don't give in here, ITN will win this one. We made it plain that we were absolutely determined to go on, and once you've taken that step then your body language shows people you mean business.'

By the time he left ITN to try to sort out even more complicated workforce problems at the Royal Opera House, Mike Morris could boast that in three years he had reduced ITN's wage bill from £42 million to £26 million – without a strike.

The restructuring of ITN's working practices, the saving of money, became urgent when in 1990, ITN belatedly discovered that it was standing on the edge of the 'black hole' of missing millions. Suddenly 'Into the Nineties' looked far from radical, not nearly tough enough. In January 1991, when Bob Phillis arrived to take over some of David Nicholas's burden as chief executive, it was obvious that changes had to be made quickly. Hopes that it could all be done over a period of time, and by agreement, were abandoned.

In June ITN announced that there would be 137 compulsory redundancies, twenty-one journalists among them, and a year's pay freeze. ITN's bureaux in Paris and Berlin would be closed, staff in Johannesburg and Moscow reduced. The famous ITN helicopter would be mothballed. 'It's all bad news for ITN' was the *Observer*'s headline, and in the *Daily Mirror* newscaster Julia Somerville was quoted as saying that 'Only a fool would say morale is high at ITN.'

After some decided to go without being pushed and others were redeployed within ITN, only seventy-nine people were in the end made redundant against their wishes. They included reporters Sarah Cullen and

Giles Smith. Two other well-known reporters, Keith Hatfield and Desmond Hamill, decided to go voluntarily. Only three years before, Hamill had won the Royal Television Society's TV Journalist of the Year award; now he felt the golden age was over, and in the *Guardian* he blamed a lack of good management for the crisis:

> It's not just extravagance which has brought ITN low. Any high-spending organisation operating in such an uncertain world as news coverage will spend too much from time to time. The problem lies deeper and stems from the belief that only journalists can manage journalists . . . On the whole, jour- nalists do not make good managers. We are conditioned to break – or at least bend – rules and regulations. However, it helps if someone is around to establish guidelines and it makes sense to run an organisation which is finan- cially sound enough for people to get on and do their jobs.

Now, said Hamill, ITN would no longer have the resources to let him do that:

> My job of covering hard news stories and special reports had gone. No longer would I be able to examine the plight of the rainforests of the Amazon and Nepal, follow the illegal ivory trade route from Africa through the Gulf and on to Hong Kong, investigate Aids in Africa or travel with the Mojahedin deep into Afghanistan. It was made clear that I could stay on but would undoubtedly become very frustrated. That is why I decided to take the voluntary redundancy offer. I was very sad but there now seems little room for real, original story- telling. I hope in the drive to cut costs that skill is not killed off altogether.[2]

The *Daily Telegraph* reported, 'Staff at the Gray's Inn Road Headquarters say that few foreign correspondents nowadays are likely to get further afield than a videotape editing suite. "Where have you been lately?" runs the current in-house joke. "I've been in Baghdad VT2."' 'It's not really a joke,' Hamill told his interviewer Sue Summers. 'That kind of report should be the exception rather than the rule, but if you haven't got the money to send people out, you will get a lot more of it, and quality will fall.'[3]

ITN's editor-in-chief Stewart Purvis wrote indignantly to point out how many ITN reporters were still out and about in the world, but Hamill had a case. The trend towards a reporter 'packaging' other people's material from the many sources flowing into ITN, rather than travelling to a faraway location to shoot his own story, had intensified. For example, in July 1992 ITN director Clive Leach (from Yorkshire Television) asked whether the cost of ITN's service to ITV 'could not be significantly reduced by the substitution of much of the original foreign news-gathering activity by agency pictures and reports'. This stung David Glencross, the IBA's representative at the meeting, into saying that the regulator 'would not consider the quality of international news to be adequate if it relied exclusively or significantly on news agency pictures, reports and voice-overs'. In their applications for the new ITV licences due to start in January 1993, the successful bidders had included an average figure of £60.3 million at 1991 prices for what they said they would spend on the news – equivalent to nearly £64 million in 1993 values – but now they were trying to cut back.

It was hard for an ITN management required to accept less money to do their job to say that the quality of the news they produced would be unaffected, but they had to try. Stewart Purvis, as editor-in-chief, told the board that 'There were many areas where he believed, with further investigation, significant savings could be achieved within the next few years.' Asked whether he could maintain quality with an ITV contract worth only £53.64 million, he replied that 'there was a period in the past when ITN could have been accused of "hyperactivity", so far as news coverage was concerned, producing more news stories than were needed or could be used. The philosophy now was to cover both national and international news in a cost-effective, controlled and measured way. A major news story breaking meant that other coverage could be forgone.'[4]

Presumably news editors had now grown so skilled that no reporter would ever be dispatched on a story that turned out to be a dud; no venture would ever have to be written off; every assignment would produce a high-quality news report well worthy of transmission.

Now began a gruelling time in which ITN found itself no longer on a get-fit regime but a diet of the most drastic kind, that was to continue on and on. In September 1992 ITN cut another 112 jobs, which reduced the workforce to 638.

Morale was not helped when Andrew Quinn, the chief executive of the ITV Association, representing the ITV companies, declared that ITN's shares were of 'nil value'. 'No major news service in the world makes money as a stand-alone commercial organisation,' he said. 'Of course morale is low,' said Bob Phillis. As Melinda Wittstock wrote in *The Times*, 'Mr Phillis has been put in the unenviable position of justifying drastic cost-cutting to his staff as a guarantee of ITN's long-term future, only for them to hear from Mr Quinn two days later that ITN will always be unprofitable, regardless of staffing levels.'[5]

But Quinn's estimate of ITN's potential was not shared by everyone. In a coup that caught everyone, including Bob Phillis, by surprise, ITN was taken over by a consortium led by the new star performer of commercial television, the 'ruthless charmer', as *The Times* called him,[6] Michael Green.

Green had become a media tycoon in short order. Already boss of Central Television, he had just outbid Thames Television to take over the coveted London weekday licence with his Carlton Television. Now that ITN, too, was to be run on commercial lines like any other television company, he saw an opportunity. Green's offer to buy it was accepted and at a board meeting held by telephone on 31 March 1993 it was resolved that Michael Green (Carlton), Sir Christopher Bland (London Weekend Television), Gerry Robinson (Granada), Leslie Hill (Central) and Mark Wood (Reuters) be appointed ITN's new directors. On 29 April, when the new board met for the first time, Michael Green was appointed chairman.

Says Green: 'I think first and foremost it was a business opportunity; it was one of the better transactions I can remember. I did it with Christopher Bland. Christopher came to me and asked what I thought of the idea. I said, "Marvellous, you must do it." He said, "No, no, *you* must do it", and we had an argument about who was to be chairman and how he was going to do this. And, yes, I fronted it, but there's no question about it. Christopher was behind me the entire time.'

ITN was struggling: the black hole of unaccounted-for spending, the declining value of the *ITV News* contract, low staff morale and a huge rental bill to pay on the new Gray's Inn Road building all added up to a heavy burden that was driving it to its knees. No wonder some ITV executives regarded the company as worthless. But Green and Bland were smart enough to see that ITN's difficulties offered just the right moment to step in with a generous helping hand to put it on its feet again.

'Well, I remember talking about the company being bust,' says Green. 'The directors were worried about signing the accounts, saying, "The company's insolvent!" And there was some truth in that because if you looked at the rent liabilities and the folly of Gray's Inn Road! A beautiful building, a magnificent Norman Foster building. I knew the landlord Stuart Lipton well, I went back many years with him. That's why Christopher [Bland] thought I was capable of solving ITN's problems, because it actually was a property play. If you didn't sort out the ownership of the property and the rental, I think I could put forward an argument to you that ITN *was* insolvent. We valued ITN at just £1 million then and, just to give you an idea, in year two it made £17 million profit. It was one of the most exciting transactions that Christopher and I, over many a glass of Armagnac, reminisce about – why didn't we buy it ourselves? Why did we buy it for our companies? It's absolutely true!'

Green says he told the landlord, Stuart Lipton's company Stanhope, that there was a danger ITN would not be able to find the rent money: 'I said, "I tell you what, we cannot pay this rent, we'll have to buy the building." I bought it off Stanhope – I think about £72-, £74 million. We bought the freehold . . . and that is how we got ITN out of its serious financial difficulties and that rope from round its neck . . . It allowed ITN to survive and prosper.'

Michael Green, going about his business, had come upon a badly injured ITN lying by the roadside, had picked it up, bound up its wounds and, in general, looked after it. However, unlike the Good Samaritan, he was not doing this out of goodwill. ITN was not an object of charity. As a businessman, he had made an investment and, perfectly naturally, he wanted the best possible return.

After their successful takeover of ITN, the new owners, led by Carlton's Michael Green and Granada's Gerry Robinson, stepped up the pressure to make ITN ever leaner. In January 1994 David Gordon, whom Green had brought in as chief executive to replace Bob Phillis, reported to the board that since April the previous year another fifty-three staff had been made redundant at a one-off cost of £1.3 million, with payroll savings of £2.4 million. Manpower was now down another 8 per cent from 683 to 630. There had been salary reductions for twenty-seven people, and 59 per cent of staff had received no pay increase on 1 January 1994. 'Now that the cuts have been made, and some management changes within departments have been implemented,' said Gordon breezily, 'the morale of the company is being restored.'

'Yes, ITN had been over-manned,' says Michael Green. 'There were some Spanish practices operating there. I came from the printing industry many, many years ago and it reminded me of SOGAT, NATSOPA and NGA, and it needed dealing with. I don't think ITN's staff respected ITN's management. If staff are allowed to get away with certain practices that they know are cheeky, they actually lose respect for the company.'

It went far beyond cutting existing staff and holding down salaries. The way to get costs down from now on, Gordon argued later in the year, was 'the introduction of new employees at much lower pay levels. This is well in hand with the News Assistants Scheme, under which ITN recruits and trains young people from college.' The news assistants – university graduates – were being paid just £12,500 a year.

In the past ITN had been a public service to be carried by more commercial parts of the schedule. In this new, more commercial world, ITN was no longer simply providing a service to its customers at a price but was required to make a profit for its owners. When the board considered the 1995 budget, Robinson, supported by Green, said it was disappointing that profits were only moving up by about 10 per cent; 15 per cent would be a more reasonable target. In his opinion ITN was not being aggressive enough in reducing staff in the short term. There was now constant pressure on ITN to make savings to enable the company to live with a lower income from ITV *and* turn a profit.

Barely out of intensive care, still convalescing, ITN now faced a pretty gruelling regime that grew tougher as the decade went on. Not only was it expected to supply news more cheaply than before and make a profit, it had to maintain its high standards – or at least convince its customers and the ITC that it was doing so. It became the task of Stewart Purvis, the editor-in-chief who in 1995 became ITN's chief executive, to reconcile these conflicting imperatives: to sell news cheaply to ITN's television-company customers, to make money for Michael Green and his fellow shareholders, and to produce news programmes that he and the people who worked for ITN could still feel proud of.

'Stewart was asked to do more than any one man could have done,' says newscaster Jon Snow. Purvis was certainly the right man for this near-impossible job. He was steeped in ITN tradition, yet not uncritical of it. Intelligent and shrewd, he knew what good journalism was while at the same time recognising that it was ITN's job to make the good popular – as well as making the popular good. He was well aware of the suspicion that the pressure to be popular would drive out good reporting and lead to a general 'dumbing down' in the news agenda. When Green asked him at a board meeting if the ITV service supplied by ITN had gone 'down-market' Purvis replied carefully, 'A more populist approach had been adopted but that this did not mean that the product had been taken "downmarket". The approach now adopted was to cover stories from the viewers' point of view – that is, to cover important stories that interest viewers.'[7]

Logically, therefore, there was always a danger that important stories that did not interest viewers would not be covered.

Purvis had had a major success with *Channel 4 News*, taking over when the new channel was threatening to cancel its contract with ITN and turning a failure into a modern, stylish programme that was inventive and original. He was also well known at ITN for his love affair with royalty, and in 1985 had struck a deal with the Prince's Trust, for two special programmes. In the first, Sir Alastair Burnet would interview the Prince and Princess of Wales in the first such interview since their marriage; in the second, ITN's cameras would follow the royal couple over a year for some exclusive fly-on-the-wall filming. ITN would pay the Prince's Trust £400,000, plus a share of the profits. Purvis also agreed – contrary to ITC rules – that ITN would give editorial control of what was in and what was out to the Prince. As a result a charming sequence of Charles and Diana swimming with their children in the open-air pool at Highgrove was removed by royal command, and now exists only in bootleg form.

Purvis makes no apology for putting the royals high up his running order: many viewers are fascinated by them and, after all, the BBC's *Panorama* certainly doesn't apologise for its famous Diana interview.

Perhaps what put Purvis ahead of the pack in ITN was his interest in finding new ways to do things. He recalls an incident in the seventies, early on in his ITN career, when videotape recording was still in its infancy. 'Somebody in VTR – remember, we had the big two-inch videotape spools, the first kind of videotape – showed me how he'd worked out that if you pulled the plug out at a certain moment you could freeze the video. There was a Cabinet reshuffle one day, under Harold Wilson, and I suddenly had this idea that you would walk the people down Downing Street as they went in, and then you would freeze them and put their names up. At ten to ten I was still standing with this videotape machine, pulling plugs out and putting supercaptions on, and people were absolutely knocked out by the result and said, "Jesus, how did you do that?" And I suppose that was why it kind of worked in the office – that I had ideas. And I think the editor, David Nicholas, probably spotted me around that point when he asked, "Who did that? How did that happen?" I did have ideas and I was encouraged to demonstrate them.'

In some ways Purvis was unlike many ITN staffers. 'I was more obviously enthusiastic than some people, if you like, and of course you have to remember there was this curious culture that somehow looked down on enthusiasm. It's an odd fit, isn't it? It seems to run completely against the ITN culture but there was a group of people to whom being seen to be too keen was not a very good idea. And this showed itself particularly at weekends. A certain output editor used to invite all the young producers, script writers, to go round to this Greek restaurant at lunchtime and then there would be kind of "last back is a sissy" game, which I found a little bit odd, because the news on a Saturday used to be on at five past five, or something like that, so the lunch would go on till about four, and then it would be who could be last back in time to produce a bulletin by five? So I suppose the culture was that when you're in the field it was work hard, play hard, but I was surprised in the office. It was play hard, play hard!

'I tried to be a drinker, but I wasn't very good at it. I had been a bit of a classic sort of student drinker and a bit of a drinker at the BBC, but funnily enough it was the ITN drinking thing that got me, partly because it was much more open. There were people drunk in the office, let's be honest about it. I never saw anyone drunk in the office at the BBC.'

When Purvis reached the top of the management tree to emerge, in 1989, as editor, and in 1991 editor-in-chief, ITN became a more sober and disciplined place. In February 1994 ITN's policy on alcohol was discussed by the board. 'It was agreed that a reference to maintaining the company's reputation should be included, and that the third paragraph [of the policy] should be altered to read ". . . potentially leading to summary dismissal".

The new policy was to be included in the company handbook and displayed on noticeboards.

One day, the ITN bar on the first floor of the new Gray's Inn Road building disappeared. Earnest sobriety was now the way ITN worked.

It was not only alcohol that was frowned on. That had been just an obvious aspect of an expansive, rip-roaring style that was incompatible with a much more carefully costed and controlled system of management. Those used to making the grand expensive gestures to celebrate a win over the BBC or to reward a crew for a tour of duty well performed suddenly found their style was out of fashion. Very senior figures who had flourished in the old free-spending days of the seventies and eighties went. Nigel Hancock for instance, the head of news input, was asked to resign following 'systematic irregularities in his expenses claims.'[8]

'Tears at Ten as Executive Quits in ITN wrangle' was the *Daily Mail*'s headline. Hancock admits that he spent freely on entertaining on behalf of ITN and, when he came to do his expenses, couldn't really say where the money had gone – other than insist that it hadn't ended up in his pocket. He points out that he was told to leave at the very moment when coverage of the first Gulf War, which he had had a big hand in organising, was being recognised by awards at home and abroad. Said the *Mail*: 'Mr Hancock was given much of the credit by colleagues for ITN sweeping the board at the Royal Television Society journalism awards two weeks ago.'[9]

'When friends ask me what it was like working at ITN at that time I reply that it certainly beat work,' says Hancock. 'Yet all the people there worked incredibly hard and long, mostly without complaint. There was such a spirit of adventure and excitement in the newsroom then that journalists reached heights they could not possibly have done if they had been working at another less-motivated place. But after the Gulf War in 1991 the whole atmosphere began to change. ITN was beset by falling news budgets causing many redundancies, a diminution in the quality of its programming, and above all by the lowering of its journalists' morale. In short ITN became merely a place to work – not a place where inspired dreams could become reality in a story that told the British public exactly what was going on.'

Says Hancock's former ITN colleague Nick Pollard, now the head of ITN's rival Sky News, 'Nigel was demanding, aggressive, flamboyant and talented. He was also volatile, infuriating, illogical and unreasonable. He was an excellent journalist, a great motivator and a heroic drinker. A conversation with Nigel was just as likely to make you want to beat him to a pulp as embrace him. I admired and liked him a great deal, but I suppose it was understandable that anyone wanting to shape a different organisation that was less raucous and more predictable would want to see the back of him.'

Hancock had thought that his generous use of ITN's money to – as he would see it – enthuse and reward ITN staff was justified by the results. But that argument no longer carried weight. A new financial discipline meant that never again must anyone at ITN be unable to account for the last farthing for which they were responsible. As Stewart Purvis says today of Hancock's departure: 'If we were going to change the culture, there was the question of leading by example, and after a number of attempts Nigel still didn't seem to get the point.'

'Nigel's departure,' says Pollard, 'definitely marked a symbolic moment in the passing of the old regime, from a philosophy of "work hard, play hard!" to one of "work hard, work harder!"'

CHAPTER 35

A REALLY BAD MISTAKE

In 1992 *News at Ten* celebrated its twenty-fifth anniversary. Over that quarter-century the programme had established itself as of fundamental importance to British television viewers. Through the seventies and eighties *News at Ten* was a fixture in the nation's life, a real alternative to what would otherwise have been BBC dominance. It gave commercial television class, and it brought in the money too. The ITV companies had been aware of that and, despite their earlier opposition, had generally accepted that *News at Ten* was a jewel, if not *the* jewel, in their crown. Certainly the IBA thought so, for ITN had been, after all, the regulator's creation.

But in the nineties, things changed. The beginning of 1993 saw the entire television system finally replaced with a new model that had already, like a tidal wave, swept some long-established companies and programmes off the air and into oblivion. Under this new system contractors for the different regional franchises had no longer been chosen by the IBA on the basis of their prospectus, their undertaking to make better programmes than their rivals. Instead, once they had reached a basic quality threshold, they had won their licence simply because they had been prepared to pay more money than anyone else for the chance to profit from their local monopoly.

By and large the new contractors could only offer more because they were cutting the cost of the programmes they planned to make – and the programmes they had to buy in, like ITN's news bulletins. More than that, having made the programmes as cheaply as possible, they now felt impelled to extract the last possible penny of profit from them. So where programmes played in the schedule to maximise the target audience had become central to the new ITV strategy.

Over the years, the companies, while grudgingly proud of *News at Ten*, had complained from time to time that it got in the way of other programmes they wanted to broadcast. The 'watershed', the time by which it was assumed that all good children were in bed and ITV was allowed to start showing more grown-up material, was fixed at 9 p.m. But that left only an hour of programming before *News at Ten*. The audience was unhappy when a feature film had to take a half-hour break to accommodate the news, and tended to switch off – or, worse still, over. Now that audience share and the battle to attract every single person 'available to view' was becoming so vitally important, the companies thought the time had come to shift ITN's main news bulletin later – or much earlier – in the evening.

Under new ownership ITN was climbing out of the 'black hole' into which its finances had fallen. Redundancies and budget cuts were now the order of the day, but the dynamic new chairman, Michael Green, had begun to sort out the desperate situation of the Gray's Inn Road building and ITN had embarked on a new life under more professional management. Or so it seemed.

Bob Phillis had worked for Green at Central Television and Carlton Communications, and had not the slightest wish to work for him again at ITN. Moreover, his plans to get an American broadcaster to take a stake in ITN and help it develop into a truly international company found no favour with Green's consortium. So Phillis took up a job offer he had been made, and left to become deputy director general of the BBC. To replace him as the new chief executive of ITN, Michael Green hired David Gordon.

For the previous twelve years Gordon had been chief executive of *The Economist*, credited with turning a respected but small-circulation magazine into an international success. 'What Green wanted,' says Gordon, 'was a good businessman who would respect journalistic values, someone whom he could use as a counterweight to the way he knew that he and the other ITV barons were perceived. Having done twelve years making *The*

Economist global, credible and profitable there was a good chance I could do the same for ITN.'

Says Green: 'I thought he was good. I thought David was very bright, very able, he'd been at *The Economist* twenty-five years, but – as somebody said to me afterwards – when somebody's been somewhere for twenty-five years, there's probably a reason. I remember in an interview – and David Gordon will back this up – before he came, when I said, "David, this is not going to work." He said, "It is." He's very persuasive; he convinced me and himself that it *was* going to work.'

Gordon knew he was leaving *The Economist*'s calm waters for commercial television's exciting but dangerous rapids. If he was to go white-water rafting he wanted to be rewarded. 'During contract negotiations,' he says, 'I told Green that I wanted the chance to make a million pounds within five years. But Green would not define terms. "Trust me," he said. I hesitated, and he who hesitates is lost. The fact is that I failed to do "due diligence" on Green.'

Gordon was charming, friendly and eager to learn, but more of an eccentric than ITN was used to. 'I don't know much about television,' he said, on his arrival at ITN in May 1993, 'but I know a man who does.' Such a blithe admission of ignorance did not endear him to ITN people, already 'walking wounded' after the battering the company had taken in the previous few years. Staff numbers had been almost halved, the *ITV News* budget dramatically cut. Whole floors in the new building in Gray's Inn Road still stood empty. Gordon's reputation sank still further when it was rumoured that he was an admirer of the theory of 'chaos management', then much in vogue. Trade-union officials who tried to negotiate with him came away convinced that he was 'totally bloody mad', a reputation Gordon rather enjoyed.

But from ITN's point of view he soon acquired one inestimable quality: although a complete stranger to ITN and television, he became passionate in ITN's defence. In short, David Gordon went native.

'One Monday evening,' he says, 'I had been out at a meeting when I happened to see an evening paper headline – "*News at Ten* To Be Moved". The following morning I got a call from Andrew Quinn, at the ITV Network Centre, who told me, "Yes, it's true." I said, "This is serious."' Gordon summoned his executive committee, which included editor-in-chief Stewart Purvis, editor of Channel 4 Programmes Richard Tait, editor of *ITN News* on ITV David Mannion, and associate editor Sue Tinson.

Purvis was upset: 'The ITV people had all gone off to a meeting somewhere up north. I'd asked them, "Is this the moment you're going to decide on moving the *News at Ten*?" I'd been given a categorical "No", and that was what I'd told David. So I was embarrassed.'

'I was worried about staff morale,' says Gordon. 'Some development man said, "They're the owners, they control where they play the news." Others were spoiling for a fight, and others, like Dave Mannion, thought that ITN could persuade ITV to back off because they'd got their sums wrong.'

Gordon had already come to the view that, at that moment, ITN did not have any assets other than a fixed-time programme with a regular presenter – Trevor McDonald. To abandon *News at Ten*, he felt, put the future of ITN itself at risk. 'I felt I had to stand for maintaining the value of ITN for all its shareholders, as well as for good journalism, so I issued a statement saying we'd heard of this plan and would like time to consider it.'

Gordon also wrote to ITN's directors to say that Quinn's confirmation of rumours that *News at Ten* was to be moved 'has caused tremendous anxieties and worries amongst the staff that their flagship is to be torpedoed'.

Green was on holiday, but when he heard what Gordon had done he made a furious phone call to ITN. Says Gordon, 'When Michael Green rang I could have heard him from where he was in Spain: "Who the f—k do you think you f—g well are?" he screamed, like a banshee. I think he was in a rather telephonically challenged hotel.'

Green agrees he was furious that Gordon, whom he had appointed to run ITN as its chief executive, was now publicly criticising what he and other ITV company bosses were planning to do to *News at Ten*.

Gordon realised he had acted wrongly in issuing a press release that blew cold air on ITV's plans before he had consulted his ITN board. 'You were quite justified in being angry over the *News at Ten* press release: I landed you in it,' he wrote to Green.[1] Nevertheless he continued to argue strongly to the ITV Network Centre[2] that moving *News at Ten* would be wrong: it was the ITV schedule before ten o'clock that was failing, said Gordon, not *News at Ten*.

For example, looking at the month of May 1993, the ITV share of the audience at 9 p.m. was 48 per cent. By 9.45 it had already fallen six percentage points to 42 per cent. At the end of *News at Ten*, at 10.30, the audience was only two per cent lower, at 40 per cent. The fall in the audience was not, therefore, ITN's fault.

At an ITN board meeting editor-in-chief Stewart Purvis reported that *News at Ten* had 6.3 million viewers, compared with the BBC's 5.6 million for their *Nine O'Clock News*, and *News at Ten* a 35 per cent share as opposed to the BBC's 28 per cent. He complained that ITN had been deliberately excluded from discussion of the *News at Ten* issue: 'The announcement about the *News at Ten* from the [ITV]strategy conference came without warning. ITN was told specifically by senior Network Centre staff that we were not being invited because "the scheduling of news is not on the agenda."'[3]

On the day it became known that ITV was going to move *News at Ten*, Sir David Nicholas was taken to hospital with a heart-attack. There, in intensive care, he was rung up by the *Daily Mail*, who asked him to write an article about the proposal. Nicholas – in his hospital bed, not at all well and unable to write anything – nonetheless gave the paper a powerful telephone interview in which he attacked the idea: 'If they moved *News at Ten* it would show that ITV was no longer serious about news on television.' *– can't find it in my heart eh,*

At ITN David Gordon embarked on a dangerous, clandestine campaign in which his special forces were sent secretly to sabotage ITV's plans. Says Sue Tinson: 'David Gordon felt it quite wrong that ITN had not even been consulted by ITV on their decision to move *News at Ten*. "Let's see what we can do to stop it," he said. It was a ten-day campaign. We felt we were saving ITV from itself.' As ITN's operation got under way, Tinson ran into Michael Green. 'Nobody seems to be objecting much,' he told her. 'Stay tuned,' she replied.

Mark Wood, representing Reuters, had joined the ITN board when Green's consortium took over ITN in 1993. He was not impressed by David Gordon's instant rejection of ITV's plans to move *News at Ten*. 'I think taking up cudgels against your biggest customer – and, indeed, your biggest group of shareholders – is not wise. It was not listening to any arguments, it was immediately on the attack – "*News at Ten* is our flagship, this is a threat to everything ITN stands for" – without any dialogue, immediate recourse to lobbying . . . It comes back to "What is ITN?" ITN was by this time, and is now, a commercial organisation. It's not a sort of state utility. It's a commercial organisation that serves customers. There are other issues around shareholder equity and branding, and so on, which are important, but at the end of the day the schedule was ITV's schedule, and ITN provided a service to the customer and at the very least needed to listen to the arguments, which ITV were never given a chance to utter.

'I think that the ITN reaction did a lot of lasting damage. And the reason is that for many years there had been a perception within ITV, enunciated by the great diehards on many occasions, that ITN was an arrogant organ-isation that was not sensitive to ITV's interests or needs and felt itself somewhat "above". I think that perception was not justified, but it had become entrenched. And it had created a gulf – and this deepened the gulf – between customer and ITN which lasted for years, and created a perception of ITN as arrogant and insensitive, particularly to ITV's needs.'

ITN management certainly paid no heed to considerations of this kind. It went straight into battle. David Gordon's war cabinet agreed that its campaign would begin with the politicians. 'We knew the politicians generally were keen on ITN,' says Tinson. 'There were no rows with ITN as there were with the BBC.' Michael Brunson got hold of Labour leader John Smith and his press secretary David Hill. Together they drafted a letter of protest to Sir George Russell, the chairman of the Independent Television Commission, successor to the IBA, and the body charged with ensuring that news standards were maintained: 'Were this plan to go ahead,' said Smith's letter, 'it would be a major blow to the coverage of news and current affairs on British television.'[4] At the same time, Brunson, in a long interview in *The Times*, set out some of the political arguments in detail. 'We couldn't use the same arguments today that we used then,' says Brunson, 'because the parliamentary day has shifted, and the politicians all go home early. But then Westminster was abuzz and working late. It had to be properly covered. Without *News at Ten* there would have been a democratic deficit. If we hadn't pushed for it on those grounds we would have been derelict.'

Gus O'Donnell, prime minister John Major's press secretary, met Sue Tinson for lunch and arranged for her to speak directly to the prime minister at home in his constituency. In a forty-minute phone conversation she laid out the arguments and ITN's worries. But then there was a hiatus: Major seemed to have accepted the points she had made but, after a few days, had made no public statement. Speaking to Nick Lloyd, the editor of the *Daily Express*, Tinson discovered that he was dining with the prime minister that night: he volunteered to raise the issue. Lloyd told Major: 'Say something about it and I'll make it a front-page story.' Then, at last, the prime minister came out with the words ITN wanted in a letter to the ITC: 'I am concerned that one of the strengths of the independent television network may be seriously impaired if the main evening news is not a central part of the schedule.'

Keeping *News at Ten* where it was turned out to be a popular rallying cry. 'The issue took off like a rocket,' says David Gordon. 'There was a public wave of anger that something dear was being removed from them. It was not really our lobbying that was important: that simply channelled the public pressure.'

At ITN Gordon had got hold of all the contracts the ITV companies had entered into before they had been given their licences by the Independent Television Commission, and at the ITC they had done the same thing. They found that half the companies had expressly undertaken to continue with *News at Ten* if they got the contract. Says Sarah Thane, then the ITC's director of public affairs, 'We were absolutely horrified to think that when the ink was scarcely dry on the new licences they could be thinking of getting rid of *News at Ten*. When you've been through a licence award process and people have made commitments in significant areas, you don't expect them to toss them out of the window.'

This was the ITC's first real test as the new 'light touch' regulator, with which the Thatcher government had replaced the IBA, and chairman Sir George Russell moved fast. 'Before I learned anything from them officially,' he says, 'I wrote to all the companies reminding them of their contracts, and that it was an obligation on all of them to put the news out at the same time. Then Margaret Thatcher, John Smith and Paddy Ashdown, for the Lib Dems, came out with their letters. I was just pleased I took the decision to warn the companies before they did – it meant I couldn't be accused of giving in to political pressure. All the same, when all the political parties take the same view you have to take it seriously.'

So even before the ITV companies had made a formal approach to the ITC telling them of their proposal to move *News at Ten*, even before they had lined up their forces for the charge, they were routed, and in the most ignominious way. Michael Green was furious at what had happened – and still is.

'Look, a schedule moves!' he says. 'If George Russell thinks he's a scheduler, he should have been running a television station. I don't believe that was his career, that was Marley Tiles, that was Alcan, and then he was chairman of Channel Four.[5] Chairmen shouldn't be schedulers.'

Though Russell firmly denies it, Green still insists that the ITC would have allowed *News at Ten* to be moved if it had not been for political pressure: 'We didn't go into it casually, we knew exactly what we were doing. We were right to do it, we did do it in the end. The fact that the prime minister of the day came out with a statement as to when the news should be, on a commercial channel owned by pension funds that need their money in order to pay their pensioners, that the prime minister of the day decides what time news is on! That definitely floored me! And the fact that our regulator listened when that happened floored me again! Anyway, we did move it, it just took longer and, boy, we did not go into it half-heartedly, and we were surprised at how perception can be all – because the prime minister decided it shouldn't be moved!'

The ITV companies thought about taking the ITC to judicial review – and backed away from the prospect. At ITN it was regarded as a famous victory. Their greedy new Philistine owners had been seen off in no uncertain terms. Television professionals, politicians and, yes, even ordinary viewers had united to repel this new breed of rapacious businessmen. This was natural but unwise; it was also premature. ITN had won a battle, not the war, and the way the system had now been set up meant that they could not win in the long run.

Sensing a popular cause, the politicians had come running to support ITN, but how often could they be relied upon to do that? More, was it even a good idea to involve them? Broadcasters should try to keep the politicians out of their hair, not look to them for aid in scheduling a programme. What will they say when the government wants a favour in return, say, a party political broadcast transmitted at a particular time?

Since ITN chairman Michael Green had failed to stand up for *News at Ten* against Michael Green (the owner of Carlton and Central Television),

ITN's David Gordon felt it right that, as chief executive, *he* should have done so. But, as he recognised, it was the end of his relationship with Green. In May the following year there was a series of acrimonious exchanges as they quarrelled over Gordon's terms and conditions of employment. 'Dear Michael,' wrote Gordon, after one such encounter. 'Last Wednesday's meeting was deeply upsetting, and while I am glad that you took the trouble to phone this afternoon the shock has not yet worn off.'[6]

They agreed a three-month 'cooling off' period in their quarrel, but by October Gordon was writing to protest that he was being shut out of crucial negotiations on the supply of news to ITV: 'Dear Michael, I must ask you to reconsider your view that the chief executive should not be present at a meeting to redo the company's most important contract. The argument that I am not "commercial" is unfair and unjust . . . '[7]

By January 1995 it was all over. David Gordon agreed a sum of £350,000 to be paid to him in compensation for loss of office, and it was announced that he would be leaving.[8] 'I have enjoyed nearly every aspect of the job,' he was reported as saying, in a somewhat pointed way, 'I leave it in good hands and I will always remain a fan of the *News at Ten*.'[9]

Gordon is still bitter about his dismissal: 'Green thinks that anyone prepared to work for Michael Green is not worth listening to; he thinks his is the only view, and that is why he has failed. It's taken ten years for the world to realise the kind of person Michael Green is – seeing how he treated people you could see that he would always be surrounded by toadies. He either emasculates people or he throws them out. I am not a trimmer.'

On 3 April 1995 Stewart Purvis was appointed to succeed David Gordon as chief executive of ITN, and found a letter of advice from his predecessor awaiting him: 'Focus on the long-term. As an ex-deadline-meeter, you are trained to be effective by 5.40 or 10.00 p.m. This is valuable. But someone has to think about where the company is going long-term.' There followed some personal advice from Gordon to the man who had taken his job: 'Open up more. Show your human-ness. Now that you are at the top of the greasy pole, you can afford to be a little less careful, diplomatic and restrained. Take more risks.' And finally – no prizes for guessing who Gordon had in mind: 'Always stand up to bullies.'[10]

It was not long before *News at Ten* again came under attack.

ITV had been going through a bad patch; losing market share, without direction. But in 1997 Richard Eyre, from advertising and commercial radio, took over the Network Centre, and hired David Liddiment, from Granada Television, as his director of programmes. Their brief from the ITV companies was simple: revamp the schedules so that ITV made more money. 'It was clear,' says Liddiment, 'that as part of that package news was back on the agenda. I had the responsibility to deliver the best possible mix of audiences with the best possible programmes – and news was an essential part of that. The issues were all about the importance of getting young people to watch, and *News at Ten* meant we were losing those young people at ten p.m. So the question was "How could the network attract and retain a younger demographic which Channel 4 in particular was now making hay with?"' Liddiment and Eyre came to the conclusion that they had to get rid of *News at Ten*.

Not all the ITV companies agreed. Granada now owned London Weekend Television. On Saturdays and Sundays, when there was no *News at Ten* to get in the way, LWT was doing very well in attracting a young audience and the lucrative advertising that went with it. Why should Granada/LWT want to see *News at Ten* moved, and programmes more appealing to young people replace it on weekdays? That would only mean that their weekday rivals, Carlton, would be in a better position to pitch for the same pot of advertising money in the London area that was, for the moment, exclusively theirs.

But Granada finally came round, and now Eyre and Liddiment were free to approach the ITC to get their approval to moving *News at Ten*.

At the Authority, now that the ITC had replaced the IBA, it was a different world. Under the new regime introduced by the 1990 Broadcasting Act, the ITC no longer attended ITN's board meetings to ensure that the quality of the news was safeguarded. David Glencross had been succeeded as the ITC's chief executive by Peter Rogers, not a programme man but formerly director of finance. Sarah Thane had become the ITC's director of programmes.

In 1993 Thane had been indignant when the ITV companies wanted to get rid of *News at Ten*, but now she and Rogers took a different view. Uppermost in their minds was the need to stop the slide in ITV's share of the audience, and they made it clear that if ITV came up with changes in the schedule involving the news they would be prepared to listen. 'All we were trying to signal there,' says Thane, 'was that over the four or five years that had elapsed since the first attempt to change the timing of News at Ten, ITV had lost market share. One of the strong arguments was that by moving it you could bring in good programmes earlier. Some research did show that News at Ten, for an increasing number of viewers, was something to view if there was nothing else. News at Ten was no longer an automatic appointment to view. In our research the sentimentality of attachment to News at Ten fell away under questioning.

'I felt we were on the horns of a real dilemma. I knew there would be devoted viewers who would be angry, but I agreed with Peter Rogers that there was no value in our simply saying to ITV, "Go away." I felt this would not be in tune with the times. The regulator is there not to duck, but you can't just slam the door in the licensees' faces. As long as they delivered the commitment of a thirty-minute news in peak-time, it was debatable whether we should dictate to them where it went in the schedule.'

Unlike his predecessor David Glencross, Peter Rogers didn't feel particularly strongly about ensuring that ITN's main peak-time news programme went on being broadcast at ten o'clock. 'I thought the whole spirit of the 1990 Act made it more difficult to become involved in detailed scheduling decisions. As time went by, the idea that you should try to hold the licensees to anything they had said in their proposals seemed less and less credible. You had to have some latitude about promises they had made – as time went by.'

So much for contracts, then. But this was a difficult decision for the ITC. It had to take account of the free-market forces that had swept away the old IBA while at the same time trying to demonstrate that, as the new regulator, it still had clout. Rogers and his team did not feel that it was any longer their job to tell the companies when to play the news – as long as it ran a half-hour programme somewhere in peak-time.

'We'd known the ITV proposal to get rid of News at Ten was coming,' Rogers explains, 'and there was quite a bit of contact between their staff and ours as to whether it was a runner. The essential message the ITC was putting out was that "it's not an article of faith with us any more". The proposal was not out of the question, but they had to make a case that could be argued through. At the absolute minimum viewers must not be worse off. The evening news service could be different, but as a whole, it should be better. You could say that it must be as good or better than, but not insist it be the same. Later we agreed we would only say no to the proposals if they looked like a worse service.'

What ITV proposed was to scrap *News at Ten* and substitute in its place a half-hour news at six thirty, near the beginning of peak-time. There would be a shorter late-night news at eleven o'clock. A stronger television regulator would have said, without further ado, that this was unacceptable. How could such an early-evening news possibly deal with the events of the day in the coherent and considered way that *News at Ten* had tried to do? How could it cope honestly with war, sex and violence when so many young children were watching? How could it bring news from the United States, where the day had scarcely begun? How could it hope to beat the next day's papers as it had always aspired to do?

Stewart Purvis, now ITN's chief executive recalls talking to Peter Rogers to get a sense of how he and senior ITC officials would look on ITV's proposal to get rid of *News at Ten*. 'Peter Rogers sold the pass right at the beginning,' says Purvis. 'He told me that ITV had been to see him about an eleven o'clock news, and he told me, "I think it's a great idea" – eleven o'clock news: a great idea!" So the chief executive of the ITC effectively approved the plan before it went anywhere. Sarah Thane? Well, Peter was her boss: she had to follow. The ITC's handling of the whole thing was pathetic.'

ITN made the best representations it could to ITV. Stewart Purvis wrote to Richard Eyre:

> *News at Ten* is a national institution – highly regarded, cost-effective and award-winning. It is a landmark in the schedules and in the nation's viewing habits. Its strong brand image, one of the best-known names on ITV, helps ITV's identity, which is crucial in an increasingly multi-channel environment.
>
> The breaks around *News at Ten* have been valued by independent experts at more than £100 million per year. Research has found that ABC1 men[11] are more loyal viewers of *News at Ten* than other people. These men are mostly not available to you early in the evening.[12]

Purvis proposed a compromise deal to ITV that would allow *News at Ten* to be moved to a later hour on some evenings to accommodate longer-running programmes that could not be fitted in between nine and ten o'clock. He suggested that these occasions could include a once-a-month blockbuster movie and perhaps one series of six ninety-minute programmes like *Cracker*. He also offered to cut a minute and a half off *News at Ten*'s running time to help clear up the 'clutter problem' – all the bits of local news and weather that got between the end of *News at Ten* and the beginning of the next programme and turned the viewers off.

But ITN's attempts at compromise were met with a cold eye at ITV. Says Purvis: 'There was a presentation which I made to Richard Eyre, David Liddiment and Steve Anderson [ITV's controller of news], in which I went through my previous pitch and then put forward a ratings-based argument. I showed them the audiences the BBC was getting at ten p.m. for non-news programmes. And even with some quite big shows they were not getting big audiences – there wasn't this great audience just waiting to be scooped up by ITV at ten o'clock. And I also pointed out that the moment you took one of the two equally well-regarded news programmes away – BBC at nine and ITV at ten – then the audience for the one that was left would undoubtedly go up. I could see the first seeds of doubt about his plans forming in Richard Eyre's mind, and I could see Liddiment getting angrier and angrier and angrier. At the end Liddiment just walked out, with Anderson behind him. I never got a proper reply to my argument.'

Says Steve Anderson: 'The drive for a change in the time of the late evening news was coming from the Carlton [advertising] sales house. Being as competitive as it was, Carlton felt that with *News at Ten* in its weekday schedule four nights a week[13] it was having to bear an unfair burden. They just wanted to make more money. The power of ITN's brand was not recognised by ITV – and Michael Green's Carlton sales house forced the issue. The reputation that ITN brought to ITV was being pitted against revenue, "if it doesn't make money it has no reputation", but *News at Ten*'s totemic value was underestimated.'

Bearing in mind the effective – and victorious – campaign that ITN had conducted in 1993, ITV now instructed Purvis and his colleagues that this time round they were not to lobby in any way against the proposals to get rid of *News at Ten*. One of ITV's concerns was that David English, representing Associated Newspapers on the ITN board, was a strong supporter of *News at Ten*. ITV were fearful that he might use the *Daily Mail* to whip up a campaign to keep the programme where it was. But here fate intervened: David English suddenly died.

Says Stewart Purvis, 'The question was, who would be the next chairman of ITN. It was more or less Reuters' turn, and the Reuters director on the board, Mark Wood, really went for the job. One of his major planks was "I won't give you any trouble over *News at Ten*." He got the job, and it really all flowed from that.'

Mark Wood denies that his support for moving *News at Ten* was the reason he was appointed chairman, insisting that the issue was not discussed in that context. But everyone knew where he stood. As he says, 'I'd made it quite clear that I had no objection to ITV moving *News at Ten*, if that's what they wished to do. I did have issues – as had David English – about damage to the brand, and whether this affected losing our flagship position, and we discussed that long and hard, but David Liddiment took great pains to explain the logic of his new schedule. He argued reasonably convincingly that he would deliver a larger audience. His argument was "You've got a fall-off in the audience at ten o'clock, which is disastrous, but if we change the schedule around you'll actually get an inheritance which is stronger, and you'll be fine." At the time, those arguments were coherent. I said I was aware that Stewart had assembled very strong arguments suggesting that the data were wrong, and they were working on them and it was pretty convincing stuff.

'But I was also aware that by that time they [ITV] weren't even listening, and that was what really bothered me – and it bothered the other non-ITV shareholders I have to say . . . there was an element of determination just to go ahead and do this, and I think a lot of it goes back to the David Gordon decision in 1993, which, frankly, had them spoiling for a fight anyway over this. I think there was an element here of some ITV people saying, "We're not going to be pushed around for ever by ITN, and when the news goes out is our decision."'

With even their own chairman now on ITV's side it was more difficult than ever for senior ITN managers like chief executive Stewart Purvis and editor-in-chief Richard Tait to keep lobbying for *News at Ten*. Of course lobbying did go on, but it did not always go well. Tait assumed that Michael Checkland, a former director general of the BBC and now deputy chairman of the ITC, would be on *News at Ten*'s side: the programme was, after all, a clear example of public service broadcasting. Lunching with him, Tait came away with the impression that Checkland was supportive of ITN's position. That turned out to be wrong. In general Checkland took the view that the regulator should not try to schedule, and when he had heard the arguments put forward by ITV he voted in favour of allowing them to move *News at Ten*.

Co-ordinating ITV's campaign to consign *News at Ten* to television history was ITV's artful and able head of public affairs, Mark Gallagher. At the ITN party during the Labour Party Conference in 1998 he was so worried about ITN's lobbying of the politicians that he had the now Dame Sue Tinson, his opposite number at ITN, shadowed throughout the evening. He wanted to see that she didn't telephone people, to note the people she spoke to, and try to overhear what she said. 'That's how paranoid we were about the power of the Dame,' says Gallagher.

A great many MPs were concerned about ITV's proposal to do away with *News at Ten*, and the House of Commons Select Committee on Culture, Media and Sport summoned ITN's top management to give evidence. But whatever they whispered privately they could not say publicly without ruining their relationship with ITV – and putting their main news contract at risk. Reminded in no uncertain terms by ITV that it was ITN's job to support whatever the customer wanted, the ITN men sang the ITV tune.

Each in turn was asked by the committee whether, speaking personally, they wanted to keep *News at Ten*. 'First of all,' asked chief executive Stewart Purvis, rhetorically, 'does the new schedule threaten the quality of what we do? I do not believe it does. . . We decided it was not right for us to try to stand in the way of ITV on their new schedule.'

'On balance,' said chairman Mark Wood, 'I am convinced by the arguments for change. I think it is in the commercial interest of ITN to work with ITV to make that change and, therefore, yes, I support the proposals.'

And finally editor-in-chief Richard Tait: 'Personally I regret its passing, but professionally I am convinced that we have the resources and talent in ITN to produce high-quality news programmes for ITV for whatever schedules they and the regulator determine.'

Did ITN's senior management – Mark Wood, Stewart Purvis and Richard Tait – fight hard enough to hold on to *News at Ten*? Some thought not. Says Sir Alastair Burnet: 'Well, you see, editors should be prepared to resign, but it ill-becomes me to be rude about Stewart Purvis, and I would simply say that he may have campaigned behind the scenes, but I'm completely unaware of it. I wasn't aware of any campaign.'

Purvis feels he pushed his luck on *News at Ten* as far as he could without endangering ITN's existence. After all, he says, 'Does ITV really want to carry news at all? From what I had witnessed over the years I knew that ITV was much more cavalier in its attitude to news than anyone could ever have imagined. I thought, If I run a public campaign for *News at Ten* there are going to be such levels of hostility that – come the contract – there probably won't be an ITN. On the other hand you can say that if *News at Ten* went then there wasn't going to be an ITN anyway. It's a very fine balance whether you risk saying, "I'm going to piss off my biggest customer so much by telling them when to transmit their news that I will risk that there will never be another contract." To have campaigned against the end of *News at Ten* would seriously have risked the end of ITN. "They'll get you for this", if you like.'

Sir George Russell thought ITN should have been bolder. 'I was astonished to find ITN itself was arguing to the select committee that the *News at Ten* should be moved,' he says. Former chairman both of ITN and the ITC, Russell had repelled ITV's attempts to shift *News at Ten* when they tried it on in 1993. He knew all about the relationship between ITN and ITV but, unlike Purvis, Wood and Tait, he was now free to speak his mind. He did. In his evidence to the committee he said firmly, 'I believe that *News at Ten* should stay where it is . . . I believe that *News at Ten* is one of the biggest things of quality that ITV can state publicly, and I think they are rather rash to throw it away on assertion [that they can do better].'

The new schedule, he pointed out, was inevitably untried, untested. Why not experiment first with a pilot, leaving *News at Ten* where it was and extending the early-evening news to half an hour to see if it really could attract a similar upmarket audience? Russell pointed out that the companies were making good profits that would not be much affected either way by scrapping *News at Ten*. 'I see no proven commercial reason for this move,' he concluded. 'I do not see any significant reason for moving it on quality grounds either . . . '[14]

Following its inquiry in 1998 the select committee 'recommended that the ITC reject the application from ITV to, in effect, abolish *News at Ten*'. Their recommendation was ignored.

In Russell's view the ITC had missed an opportunity. When the companies had come in to renegotiate their contracts in the mid-nineties the ITC had not made it a condition that they sign up again to keep *News at Ten*. So when a couple of years later ITV renewed its proposals to abolish the programme, the ITC had nothing much to fight with, even if it had had the courage for a confrontation. 'The second time around, the ITC didn't have a leg to stand on,' says Russell.

But Sarah Thane doesn't agree that there was ever a chance of using the renegotiation of a licence to force the companies to renew their commitment to *News at Ten*. 'Renewal of a licence,' she says, 'is essentially a financial issue. The ITC was looking at the companies' costs and revenues – there was no provision in the 1990 legislation for the ITC to demand particular programme formats. In the end, the debate within the ITC coalesced around audience behaviour, and whether ITV would be able to sustain news audiences with news at six thirty and eleven o'clock. The Commission wanted ITV to guarantee they could deliver the same size total news audience. The question was "How big a risk are we taking here?" ITV gave us lots of figures, saying they could make them all add up.' Eyre and Liddiment told the ITC that the total number of viewers for news on ITV would not fall.

'There was only one audience for this campaign,' says Mark Gallagher, 'the ITC officers and members. Sarah Thane was a target. When I started working for ITV, ITN was seen as a very useful ally. ITN delivered the credibility ITV needed. If you were meeting civil servants at the Home Office you could never underestimate the importance of having ITN with you round the table. So ITN was "good news". But the whole thing turned around as soon as Richard Eyre was appointed to run ITV. He was an outstanding leader but unfortunately for ITN he saw *News at Ten* as an impediment, and it became a whipping boy for ITV's failure to win bigger audiences. The feeling was "Shift *News at Ten* and all will be well." With David Liddiment's arrival as director of programmes there was a rare moment of self-confidence at the centre of ITV. The idea was that if *News at Ten* could be moved then ITV could deliver popular quality programmes like *A Touch of Frost*, and that was the proposition I took on the campaign trail. We told the ITC that what they needed first and foremost was a healthy ITV. It was no good hanging on to the jewel in the crown of *News at Ten* if no one was looking at ITV. We also promised terrific programmes to put in *News at Ten*'s place – a new documentary strand, *Inspector Morse* as opposed to *Holiday Airport*. We would continue to serve the ABC1 audience, but with more viewers.'

In 1993, the political party leaders had intervened directly in the *News at Ten* debate by writing to the chairman of the ITC. This time they were more reticent. Alastair Campbell, Tony Blair's press secretary, announced: 'The prime minister supports *News at Ten* staying where it is because it has got a deserved reputation for reporting often complex political, international and other issues in a very digestible and even-handed way.' But Tony Blair did not write to the ITC as his predecessor John Major had done.

In November 1998 the ITC decided by seven votes to three to give 'qualified approval' to ITV's proposals for a main half-hour news at six thirty, and a later twenty-minute bulletin at eleven o'clock. There were conditions, among them that 'There will be no diminution in the funding, or in the range and quality of national and international news.' The ITC's press statement said:

> The proposals made by ITV offer a wide range of choice of programming between the watershed at 21.00 and 23.00; in particular, they open up oppor- tunities for more adult comedy, for documentaries and current affairs programmes as well as long-form drama and film. It is clear from audience research that such programming has a strong appeal. The ITC will ensure that ITV delivers the proposed enhancements to diversity.

The statement made it plain that after twelve months there would be a review of the changes, and that if the conditions the ITC had set were not being met then there would have to be 'remedial action'.[15] What that remedial action would look like was left conveniently unexplained.

ITN and ITV now shared the building in Gray's Inn Road. On the morning of the announcement both sides in the battle awaited the ITC's decision with anxiety. From the ITC Sarah Thane telephoned ITV's Richard Eyre. 'You are not to go public on this with comments yourself,' she told him. 'We, the ITC, are going to carry the can for this decision. And remember, it's a year's trial. Don't let us down.'

As ITV staff waited nervously for the ITC to announce its decision Richard Eyre called Mark Gallagher, David Liddiment and ITV's controller of news Steve Anderson into his glass-walled office. 'He told us, "I don't want you to let anybody see you reacting to this news, but we have won,"' says Gallagher. 'For forty-five minutes or so we were walking around trying to look neutral. But when the announcement was made, absolute mayhem broke out. This was, after all, the first policy debate that ITV had won in a decade. In the ITN offices directly opposite us across the atrium they were looking really glum as the evening wore on. And then, in our offices, with the champagne flowing, I remember saying, "What are we going to do next?"

'ITV had won the battle but was now about to lose the war. Because it had not been sufficiently confident that it would win, ITV just didn't have the promised high-quality replacement programmes ready. Where was the two-hour *Inspector Morse*? Where were the *Cutting Edge* documentaries?'

The last *News at Ten* was on Friday, 5 March 1999. 'That was it,' wrote Michael Brunson, who, as political editor, was shortly to resign from ITN. 'After thirty-two years it was all over. Straight commercial pressure, unrestrained by the official regulatory body, the ITC, had killed off Britain's favourite and most successful news programme.'[16] Three days later, on Monday, 8 March, came the first transmission of the new *ITV Evening News*, watched by distinguished guests at a lavish party held in a hotel just across Westminster Bridge opposite the Houses of Parliament. There were brave speeches about the future, but the occasion was suffused with an angry sadness that something so worthwhile as *News at Ten* had been discarded, and consigned to history. Former prime minister Margaret Thatcher harangued fellow-guests on the folly of letting the programme go. 'I'm going to make a fuss,' she assured Michael Brunson. As he says, it was too late for that. He did not remind her that her 1990 Broadcasting Act had encouraged ITV to schedule the news for profit rather than for public good. He thought she would not have listened anyway.

'The thing that shocked me about the way the ITC handled it,' says ITN's Richard Tait, 'was that they *did* have the authority to insist on strategic changes as the price for moving *News at Ten*. It was a fiasco for everybody.

ITN lost its best-known brand – *News at Ten* – and the reputation of its own company brand was seriously eroded.'

At the ITC, Sarah Thane denied that public service broadcasting would suffer as a result of the Commission's decision. She told the *Guardian*: 'All of us here try to serve the public interest. I realise on this occasion that, because of the enormous affection for *News at Ten* – which I share – it's painful to see a programme such as that disappear. But I believe the decision we've made will give viewers a better service – not just on news terms, but across the schedule.'[17]

Sarah Thane's hopes were cruelly disappointed: 'I did feel that the degree of trust I had placed in them was betrayed, at least to some extent. Because we felt confidence in Eyre and Liddiment and their determination to strengthen ITV – David always had high creative ambitions – the ITC felt they would grasp the opportunity to do great things. So why didn't they? Did the owners put pressure on them not to spend the money? They got rid of *News at Ten* so quickly they didn't have much to put in its place – the new eleven o'clock bulletin got such little support from the programmes that came before it. If I've learned a lesson it's that commercial animals like these want to get their gains under their belts as fast as possible. But the row that followed must have done them commercial damage.'

Because ITV had not been at all confident that it would get approval to abandon *News at Ten*, it had not yet made the programmes it had promised to put in its place. 'In the event,' says David Liddiment, 'we launched the new schedule too early. Had we waited till September we would have had more programmes ready.'

Viewing figures for the first few weeks without *News at Ten* didn't look bad, but by June 1999 the audience for the news had fallen away. The figure for the two bulletins combined was 7.8 million, compared with 10.8 million in the same period of the previous year. The eleven o'clock news in particular was doing badly – just too late at night for most people. At the beginning of 2000, up to late February, the average reduction of the total news audience was 1.7 million.

The Select Committee on Culture, Media and Sport, had been furious that its recommendation to keep *News at Ten* was ignored. Now it reconvened to say, "We told you so," and conduct an inquiry, 'Whatever Happened to *News at Ten*?' In March 2000 the Committee's report concluded that: 'This Committee has received clear and compelling evidence that the evening news audience on ITV has fallen significantly in direct contradiction to the confident predictions made by ITV when it was seeking to justify its request to move its news bulletins as part of a new schedule . . . We recommend that the ITC require ITV to reinstate *News at Ten*.'[18]

When the members of the ITC met to review the new schedule, a year after they had issued *News at Ten*'s death warrant, they were distinctly unhappy. 'They know they are handling the hottest of hot political potatoes,' wrote the *Guardian*'s media commentator Maggie Brown, 'and that their role in protecting ITV from folly has hardly been heroic. Research before them outlined the substantial collapse in ITV's news audiences, down 13.9 per cent in a year for national bulletins, and an "unacceptable" 22 per cent on average for regional news.'[19]

When they had agreed to ITV's plan to scrap *News at Ten* the members of the ITC had acted on the advice of their senior officials, Peter Rogers and Sarah Thane. 'Clearly,' Rogers now admits, 'the whole thing did not go right. We had been watching the viewing figures, holding off the critics. Now the Commission members decided it wasn't working. But we never insisted that ITV should put *News at Ten* back – that would have been "scheduling", and that was not our job. We didn't want to rub their noses in it so we said, "Give us some new proposals, just give us something to get us there, and then we'll try and sell them", but they couldn't. The staff at the ITC certainly looked for some middle ground – there could have been a deal – but the companies thought they could get away with it. The lawyers were getting involved and ITV decided to go for a judicial review on the grounds that they had the right to determine the schedule, and that the promises they had made about it to us were not binding.'

Rogers gave an affidavit as to what had happened, in preparation for the judicial review, and then took his retirement. At ITV, chief executive Richard Eyre had left without a successor in place, while Carlton and Granada were fighting between themselves as they struggled to save their unhappy enterprise, ITV Digital. ITV had no time to think sensibly about news programmes – even if it had cared to. And so things drifted towards what looked likely to be a bloody fight to the death between two badly wounded organisations, the broadcaster and the regulator, ITV and the ITC.

ITN could only look on in silent misery. But worse was to come. Under the guise of a solution that would solve the problem, a plan was devised that made ITN a laughing-stock. — *Sleely intellect*

When Patricia Hodgson was appointed chief executive of the ITC in succession to Peter Rogers, she was, understandably, determined not to be saddled with failures that were none of her making. She wanted the argument with ITV about the news settled – and fast. 'I was looking for a compromise, but ITV couldn't or wouldn't meet me half-way. We could have let the process go on, and I thought we would win if it came to judicial review, but I felt a compromise would lead to a better relationship.'

At the BBC, the commercially astute director general Greg Dyke (no great friend of ITN) had seized his opportunity. In October 2000 he moved the main BBC news from 9 p.m. to 10 p.m. Now that ITN's flagship programme had been scuttled, its BBC rival sailed in to take up station where *News at Ten* had once ruled the waves.

'We had told David Liddiment,' says Richard Tait, 'that if he moved *News at Ten* then the BBC would take that slot. We could see the car crash coming: we could see that the BBC would move. It wasn't that we were just journalists who didn't understand businessmen. The fact is, ITV was wrong.'

In September 2000 it was agreed that *News at Ten* would return – but much shorter and on only four nights a week, or three if there was football or a long drama, as there was virtually every week. As a sweetener ITV would be given another minute of advertising time. 'The ITC would have agreed to ten thirty, but ITV went for ten o'clock,' says Patricia Hodgson 'The deal got a good press but it soon became clear that ITV's heart was not in it. The first few weeks were OK, but it became obvious over time that there was a lack of commitment – I used to plot it every week. It was so depressing.'

The truncated, occasional *News at Ten* came back on the screen in January 2001 but, as Richard Tait wrote, 'ITV resented the deal and it is hard to find much evidence of a serious attempt to make it work. Rather like Sherlock Holmes climbing out of the Reichenbach Falls, *News at Ten* returned from the dead but was never quite the same.'[20]

When Stewart Purvis had come down to the newsroom to announce to ITN's journalists that *News at Ten* was returning it had been received as a triumph, a major ITN win over the ITV vandals in the building. There was cheering and shouting – but it was soon apparent that this was the most hollow of victories. If there is one thing that should be sacrosanct about news programmes it is that they be regular fixtures in the schedule, there when you turn on for them. But ITV kicked the new ten o'clock news around as if it was worthless. On some evenings it was there, on others it was not; and even when it was billed to start at ten o'clock it was often several minutes late. Soon the programme became popularly known, in the most humiliating way, as News at When? This was a disgrace.

In early 2003 ITN began to lobby hard for a fixed time for the late bulletin on every weekday evening, and in May ITV's Steve Anderson, its controller of news, said that ITV now wanted to go for ten thirty. At the beginning of October the ITC, in one of its last acts before it was itself abolished to make way for yet another regulator, Ofcom, agreed.

David Liddiment, the former director of programmes for ITV, who had been a leader in the campaign to kill off *News at Ten,* now made an extraordinary admission. 'Here's a startling piece of hindsight:' he wrote in his *Guardian* column, 'ITV would be better off today if it had never tried to move *News at Ten.*' But Liddiment did not accept that he was to blame for what had gone wrong; he still believed that a six thirty and eleven news pattern was the best for a modern ITV, and that, given more time, it would ultimately have proved itself. He had not wanted ITV to compromise with the ITC but instead to go to judicial review to establish ITV's right to schedule news wherever it thought best: 'I thought scheduling was *my* job,' he says. But both sides had backed away from a showdown, ITV frightened it might lose, the ITC worried that a courtroom battle would damage the relationship between them. Instead there had been the 'fudge' of the three-days-a-week *News at Ten.* 'A very bad deal was concocted,' says Liddiment. 'The owners of ITV were focused not on news but on ITV Digital, and at the ITC Patricia Hodgson agreed to a deal that did dishonour to ITV, to the ITC, and sold viewers short.' Says Hodgson: 'If I had not agreed to the compromise, if I'd agreed they could go on with the eleven o'clock bulletin, then I think ITV viewers would never again have had a chance of getting a late evening news at a reasonable hour.'

As it was, ITV's relaunch schedule, when it began on 2 February 2004, included a regular half-hour news programme presented by Trevor McDonald at ten thirty, five days a week.

It had been an instructive experience. ITV's owners had been exposed as never before to be no more than businessmen, first and last. Worse, they had been revealed as bad businessmen, doing terrible damage to their most prestigious brand, ITN, and its highly successful programme *News at Ten*. The regulator, the ITC, had been shown up as a busted flush unable any longer to defend the news on commercial television as it had done for the previous forty years.

That did not augur well for the new regulator Ofcom. After the *News at Ten* débâcle, would Ofcom have the stomach to intervene in *any* issue affecting news on ITV? Speaking at the Royal Television Society's Cambridge convention in the summer of 2003, Michael Grade (who was the following year to become chairman of the BBC) said that, in his opinion, the decision to scrap *News at Ten* had signalled the end of public service broadcasting on ITV.

& so he brought it back.

CHAPTER 36
ANY OTHER BUSINESS?

In the 1980s, Alastair Burnet, with support from David Nicholas, had argued that only new faces round the boardroom table, people who were not just ITV broadcasters but outside investors, would be interested in ITN's expansion. Only they would be able to see the possibilities and be ready to invest in them, setting ITN free of the shackles that bound it so slavishly to ITV and Channel 4 and stopped it going out into the world to make its fortune. Others, like Stewart Purvis, saw no reason in theory why the ITV directors on ITN's board should not want to support ITN's expansion themselves.

As the 1990 Broadcasting Act came into force at the beginning of 1993, the new consortium headed by Michael Green had taken over ITN. The new owners included ITV broadcasters Carlton, Central, Granada and London Weekend Television, but also a non-broadcaster, Reuters. To replace Bob Phillis, a new chief executive, David Gordon, had come bounding in. It was his success at *The Economist* in greatly increasing sales of the magazine, particularly overseas, that had chiefly recommended him to Green. Now it was his job to do the same for ITN. Once again ITN was going for gold.

Gordon quickly commissioned a series of research reports to help the board decide the right strategy for ITN, and in June consultant Richard

Hooper produced 'An Audit of ITN's Strengths and Weaknesses'. The 'core businesses', he said, were of course 'the two profitable long-term contracts with ITV and Channel 4'. These were definite assets, and there were others, including the *ITN World News*, and 'reporter packages'. But when Hooper listed ITN's 'Weaknesses and Liabilities' he concluded that 'regrettably the list is much longer. Some of the assets listed above are simultaneously weaknesses. For example, ITN's reliance on just two customers for 87 per cent of revenue . . . must be a cause for concern in the turbulent seas of UK broadcasting.'

But expansion abroad was going to be difficult: 'ITN is a small company . . . Deriving from its size, ITN suffers from a lack of global coverage.' Hooper quoted comments from some of its customers and partners:

> News gathering is a world occupation and ITN is too narrow (customer). Whilst ITN has a reputation for being fast of foot and good at reading the tea leaves of breaking news (Jeremy Thompson being in Somalia in June at the right time), it cannot physically cover the ground in the way that the BBC or Reuters do. It is below critical mass. 'Size is a weakness'. Only £2million out of £79 million turnover is generated outside the UK . . . This must be a starting weakness for any international strategy.

But, said Hooper, in his 'Conclusion – Threats and Opportunities', 'ITN, like so many national players in a liberalised market full of technology surprises, has little prospect of significant growth in the UK. If there is to be expansion, it has to happen beyond UK borders.'[1]

There seemed no alternative but to boldly go about the world looking for new business. As David Gordon told his board: 'This is a business crying out for higher volume. Given the inherent limitations of getting more work out of the two broadcast channels in Britain, the obvious avenue is international broadcast and cable.'[2]

David Gordon and Mervyn Hall, who had been appointed ITN's sales director in January 1994, set about seeing what the world would buy from ITN. In July 1994 Gordon reported that they had visited Singapore, Hong Kong, Japan, Australia and New Zealand, offering a service of customised reporter packages exclusive to an individual country – ITN reporters would do extra camera pieces or commentary so they could sign off with 'This is Joe Bloggs, for Channel 9 Television', or whatever it might be.

While accepting that 'the international news market is over-supplied', Gordon had argued that 'the superior programming of ITN will assuredly find a profitable niche'. But news is a pretty local sort of thing. Viewers want to hear about issues that concern them and, on the whole, in their language, with their accent. There were deals to be done, as there had always been, to buy (or swap) material from other news producers like CNN or Reuters, but no real chance to develop a major new market. After all, ITN was not even a broadcaster, and it had little recognition abroad as a brand except among television professionals. And when the BBC began to expand on its own account it had the huge advantage of being able to offer a range of programmes of all kinds, where ITN could offer only news.

In November 1994 Gordon had to report that the international sales drive was making only slow progress. He 'agreed that it was a problem for the company that it had not been able to identify a major new business', and in the following January conceded that 'it had now become clear that international sales would never be a huge pillar of the business, but that it would produce a useful contribution.'³

In January 1995 Gordon summed up:

> ITN's competitive advantages are its quality, brand, price and the ability to customise its services for a wide variety of clients. These are the strengths on which to build, particularly editorial excellence and value. ITN's disadvantages are the lack of its own distribution channels – ITN is in effect a large independent producer – and the lack of established commercial relationships as yet with foreign broadcasters and non-traditional customers (cable, satellite, computer and telephone companies).⁴

The international sales drive ran out of steam. David Gordon quarrelled with Michael Green and resigned, and on 3 April 1995 Stewart Purvis became chief executive in his place.

On 1 June 1995 the board was told that ITN had won a contract to produce a wedding video for the Greek royal family. It was an indicator of the scale on which it could expect to find new business – at least at that time. By July that year the sales department had been disbanded.

When pressed, Michael Green admits the relative failure of ITN's strategic plan for international expansion – selling its news programmes abroad – during his time there: 'Well, OK, it didn't really work.' But he insists that other initiatives still could. 'We started the *ITV News Channel* – you'll see how that will grow. [Rupert] Murdoch spends *years* developing products – you know how old Sky News is now? And I guarantee it lost money last year! Look at ITN's library now. Look at the value. They've got a mini-Reuters there! ITN has some very exciting things!'

In 1996 ITN had signed a new contract with ITV that cut £15 million from the £56 million price it was currently charging. Costs were pared, but not, Purvis insists, in way that caused serious damage to ITN. 'I negotiated a price reduction with ITV which left us enough money to do the job properly,' he says, 'then I set about building up other revenues to cover the gap. Every time the profits went down, they went down by less than the cut in the ITV contract price. But "the tender" was completely different in scale.'

Since it had come into being in 1955 ITV had been able to take its national and international news from only one source: ITN. Set up at the insistence of the regulator, it had been the only company allowed to do the news on ITV. The Broadcasting Act 1990 had been intended to create a free market in commercial television, but ITN had hung on to its monopoly. It had remained the sole 'nominated news provider', alone in having the regulator's permission to supply news to ITV. This had given it a breathing space in which to adjust to the new and highly commercial world introduced by the Broadcasting Act, but such a monopoly was difficult to defend in the long run. Sure enough, in May 2001 it was announced that the ITC had decided to give nominated-news-provider status to a consortium (confusingly called Channel 3), led by Sky Television. So now there was a challenger to ITN.

Of course, the nominated-news-provider idea had never been perfect, as Stewart Purvis points out: 'The hole in the system was that when you went to the regulator, the ITC, and showed them your budget – what you intended to spend on your news programmes – it meant nothing at all because you hadn't yet had to sell that budget to the customer, the broadcaster. You passed the test without any kind of reality. I'm told the Sky application for nominated news provider was first class. Well, so it should have been, because it didn't have to be grounded in reality.'

However flawed the nominated-news-provider system was, ITN, for the first time in its existence, now knew that it had to negotiate with ITV not just about the price of the next contract but whether it would continue to have the contract at all. Competition would force it to reduce its price to ITV still further, and if it didn't reduce it far enough ITV could instead contract with the Sky consortium. This put ITV in a win/win situation, but was terrible news for ITN, which had always known that without the ITV contract, without a deal with the original and still by far its biggest customer, it was unlikely to survive.

'ITN,' reported the *Guardian*, 'Britain's largest commercial news provider, has covered countless wars, floods, famines and whatever else the world can throw at it but is now facing perhaps its sternest test. For the first time in its 45-year history, ITN faces competition for the contract to supply news to ITV, a process which would rip the guts from the company should it lose.'[5]

It was hard to understand why ITV should entertain a bid from Sky. Surely it would not want to give a contract to by far its most dangerous rival for the control of commercial broadcasting in Britain? In the *Scotsman* Andrew Neil – a former Sky executive – explained:

> So why, the casual observer might understandably ask, does ITV bother to go through the motions with Channel 3 News? The answer, dear reader, is simple: in order to beat down the price of ITN. That is no bad thing in principle: ITV owes it to its shareholders to get the best broadcast news at the best possible price. The danger for viewers – and for healthy competition in broadcast news (essential, in turn, for the health of our democracy) – is that ITN is about to be squeezed so tight by its ungrateful ITV masters that it will no longer be able to compete, in breadth and quality, with BBC News.[6]

But Neil's analysis did not tell quite the whole story of how the contract tender had come about. As ever, it was all tied up with the issue of ownership.

On many occasions in the nineties ITN's owners had discussed the idea of 'floating' ITN, in the hope that investors would be prepared to buy shares in it at a price that would put a high value on their own stakes in the company. In 1993 they had investigated the possibilities but concluded that before any float went ahead 'the need to be able to demonstrate clear business projects outside the main news contracts area is very important.'[7] 'Project ICE' had come to nothing, but at the beginning of the new century, as the 'dotcom' boom saw countless media businesses go to market and find eager buyers for the shares offered, there was another attempt. ITN had been making profits – 'You've made me lots of money, Stewart,' Michael Green told his chief executive Stewart Purvis – so ITN's owners, now led by Charles Allen of Granada, wondered whether this really was the time to float the company and, hopefully, see the stockmarket recognise what a valuable item ITN was. A *Financial Times* article inspired by Allen pointed out that when the *Daily Mail* group had bought a stake in ITN in 1996, the price it paid valued the company at about £100 million. 'Shareholders', the article reported, were saying that a flotation would show that ITN was now worth 'hundreds of millions'.[8]

All the different ITV companies were now clearly heading towards consolidation. With a lot of infighting Granada and Carlton were coming together as the majority shareholder, preparing to take over the whole show. If that happened, what should be their attitude to ITN? How were they to make the most money out of it? Charles Allen, the driving force at Granada, summoned Stewart Purvis to discuss ITN's future with him.

'There was this air of unreality about flotation,' says Purvis. 'I had a meeting with Charles Allen where he actually spelt out his strategy, I was really surprised he would do that to me. Allen had invited me round to tell him what ITN could become. And I made my presentation on what we could do in a float. He seemed quite interested in all that, but then he said to me, "Of course, I do have an alternative, to go the cost-cutting route."'

Purvis was later to call this the 'float it or f—k it strategy'. Allen, he says, was telling him that ITV could either build up ITN's value through floating it or get value out of it in a different way – one which would benefit only the ITV shareholders. If, wearing his ITV hat, Allen could drive down the price of the news contract, he could save ITV money while at the same time making it difficult for ITN to make a profit, and so reduce ITN's value. As a result, it would be much easier for ITV to buy out the other, non-ITV shareholders in ITN – Reuters, the *Daily Mail* and General Trust, and United Business Media – at a rock-bottom price.

'I thought at the time that this was a pretty odd way of incentifying the ITN management to do a float!' says Purvis. Nevertheless, at Allen's request he laid out ITN's future plans for the benefit of prospective investors if the float went ahead: 'A report came back from the "fan club" – that's the group of people that the bank is used to doing business with – saying that they liked the look of ITN's management, and liked the ideas for developing the company. But, they said, where is the new long-term ITV contract? If ITN is such a good idea, where is the contract?

'Then I was offered a job elsewhere so I said, pushing my luck, to the ITN board, Look, there seems to be so much indecision about the future of the company. I do need to know whether you are going to float the company or not. The board did not like me pointing a gun at their heads. But they had a private meeting afterwards and then they called me up and said we're going for a float, and on that basis I did not take the job I was offered.'

But before ITN's owners could agree on the terms of a flotation, the financial atmosphere changed. There was a hiss of hot air escaping as the 'dotcom' balloon began to collapse.

'It was only a matter of weeks before it became clear that they were not going to float,' says Purvis. 'I dare say a float might have given me share options worth millions of pounds, but who knows if they would ever have been worth anything in the real market? So I'm not the bitter and twisted guy thinking I could have been a millionaire, because who knows what the shares of ITN are worth to this day? We're still not clear about that.

'But it was quite clear to me that when ITV went out to tender on the news contract, with Sky involved, they were going down the cost-cutting, "cut ITN down" route. The tender document actually stipulated that this was to be a bid for the *ITV News* contract – not *ITN News* any more.'

As anticipated, ITV used Sky to drive down the price of the ITV news contract. Stewart Purvis and his editor-in-chief Richard Tait got to the point of calculating what ITV would have to pay if they pushed ITN to the wall and into a state of collapse. 'Richard and I worked out what the close-out value costs of ITN were, so that we knew that if ITN lost, the shareholders would have to pay a certain amount of money, and we worked out what ITV's share of those closure costs would be,' says Purvis. But finally ITV gave the contract to ITN. The price was now £35 million, roughly half what the ITC had expected the companies to pay for news when they were first awarded their licences back in 1991.

Says Purvis: 'Why ITV went for us in the end, though our bid was still higher the Sky's, I do not know, but a couple of ITV people involved did say to me, "Do you seriously think we would have given one of our major programme contracts to a competitor like Sky?" . . . People will say, "They'd always have ITN." Well, I've seen it, I've had the conversations with the [Clive] Hollicks and the [Michael] Greens of the world. I knew their attitude to ITN. When it came to *News at Ten* they just chopped all mention of the ITN brand altogether. If they could do that to a company that they owned a great chunk of, it showed really how reckless they could be towards ITN itself.'

In the amalgamation of Carlton and Granada, Michael Green lost out to Granada's Charles Allen. Green's initial – and very valuable – contribution as chairman of the consortium that bought ITN in 1993 had been to free the company from the great millstone of Gray's Inn Road, to do a property deal that let ITN get on with its real business of doing the news. Green liked being chairman of ITN, liked bringing his friends to watch *News at Ten* go out from the studio gallery. But he had gone into ITN as a business opportunity. He had immediately tried to kill off *News at Ten*, and finally succeeded in doing so; he had presided over a series of deep cuts in the *ITV News* contract budget; and for the best part of a decade he had taken profits out of a company that was growing ever more threadbare. How much did he really care about ITN and its future? A lot, Green insists: 'I always believed that news was an integral part of a rich schedule, and we needed to have a good, well-funded news programme.'

But, he says, the people running commercial television who have come after him are now endangering ITN's survival: 'The brand ITN is being destroyed. That it is now called *ITV News* means that ITN is going to disappear as a name if we are not very careful. I think that the *owners* of ITN are making a mistake in allowing that to happen, that *ITN* is making a mistake in allowing that to happen, and that the *customer* is making a mistake in allowing that to happen! I think the brand ITN is a *good* brand, that it added to ITV. It didn't detract . . . And one of my few arguments with Stewart Purvis was that in offering our services to our customers — like Channel 4, like ITV — I would have *insisted*, and it would have been a deal-breaker, that the brand remained! And as you can see, it's been a chip-chip-chip, you know, a *Channel 4 News* end title, and ITN gets a credit of half a second! The brand's being destroyed.'

As for the strategy for ITN that ITV is now pursuing: 'I hate to say it, but everything that I feared was going to happen at ITN is now happening. I believe that the value of ITN when those shares are eventually sold will be minimal. And the stupid thing is, it's the shareholders themselves who are destroying the value. Penny wise and pound foolish. That is the danger. It is absolutely tragic . . . And I think what's happening is that ITN is disappearing as an organisation.'

CHAPTER 37
A THREADBARE EXISTENCE

At reunions and anniversaries it is always tempting for old ITN hacks to look back and agree that things ain't what they used to be, to bemoan a golden age now turned to dross, to remember a time when the sun always shone that is now for ever clouded over, and to recall a happy hour that seemed to go on for ever while today you can't get a drink and, anyway, someone is always about to call 'Time' on the whole thing.

And, of course, it is equally tempting for today's ITN team to rubbish what has gone before. The old ITN, it is argued, was a self-indulgent amateur dramatic society compared with today's superbly professional media company; a company that today simultaneously makes money for its owners, provides a quality news service for its viewers, sells that service at an unbelievably low cost to its customers, while all the while offering more job satisfaction to its employees than anyone could reasonably ask. So what are the real differences between now and then, past and present?

I started work at ITN in the mid-1960s as a relatively young reporter, and recall a news organisation that was at last adequately, though not extravagantly, funded and full of self-confidence, ready to back its own journalism to the hilt. Given that BBC News was still relatively dull and sluggish it was easier for ITN to report interestingly and often excitingly in a way that more than made up for any shortage of funds or people. Very importantly, ITN's second editor, Geoffrey Cox, though himself a cautious, careful man, was prepared to hire talented people who would be regarded in today's television industry as unemployable.

For example, it could be said of Antony Rouse – and indeed it was – that he was not much more than a bundle of neuroses held together by a salary. He was always individual and independent, irritatingly unconcerned by others' opinion of him. As a young man he had sold advertising space in Canada and worked for the news agency UPI in Washington and London. Rouse was recommended to Cox for a job at ITN by his friend Nigel Ryan, who decribed him as 'the second most intelligent man in Europe'. This was slightly overstating the case but Rouse certainly brought a fresh eye to ITN's still rather conventional coverage. 'In the sixties a national industrial dispute with the unions was typically covered with shots of trade-union leaders going into Number Ten Downing Street,' he says. 'That was our idea of a film story then.'

Rouse worked on *Dateline* and as a scriptwriter before becoming a most idiosyncratic output editor of the *News at Ten*. Early on he was a pioneer of presenting the programme from where the news was happening – from Belfast as Northern Ireland erupted in violence, or from Paris during the riots and revolutionary days of 1968. More importantly, he was not interested in what the opposition was up to but in whatever news ITN's journalists had discovered and reported. 'I never bothered to look at what the BBC were doing with their news running order,' he says, 'I knew our news-information people had taken a note of it in case I really needed to know.' Today that might seem irresponsible, or simply silly, but Rouse encouraged ITN's reporters, producers and scriptwriters to produce the best television news they could without worrying too much about what the opposition might be doing. If you delivered run-of-the-mill coverage – even on an important story – it was likely to be dropped in favour of something more interesting. Rouse's approach produced news programmes that were individual and engaging – even if sometimes just quirky. It meant that everyone was on the lookout for strong, original stories in the knowledge that, if one was found, the result was likely to be given all the space it deserved. Home and foreign news editors felt able to dispatch their teams on a story that was not necessarily obvious but that looked interesting and might possibly turn into something big. They were more eager for success than frightened of failure. This readiness to back its own judgement and invest in a story helped to give ITN great impact and to build up its authority. But by the turn of the century ITN was a different place, more cautious, more careful, and increasingly dull. *News at Ten* had been replaced by a shambolic succession of unsatisfactory scheduling solutions that were not of ITN's devising.

Nigel Dacre had been put in charge of that wobbly Portakabin where ITN's *World News* had first been produced for the satellite broadcaster Superchannel. There, with few resources, he had, as *World News* editor, managed to enthuse his small team with the sense that they were the first to be stepping into a new television universe. His presenter at the time, John Suchet, says: 'I've always been a great admirer of Nigel Dacre because he's very clever and a very good programme editor, incisive, someone who knew how to construct a running order. He had great management skills – I saw him inspire the *ITN World News* team: he was always able to spin some production disaster – we suddenly lost the rights to some vital source of film, for example – into good news. He'd make it a challenge.'

But when it came to the ITN news on ITV, Nigel Dacre had a more difficult job. Compared with an output editor from a much earlier age, like Antony Rouse, he was no longer a completely free agent. Where Rouse and the whole of ITN would have been outraged if anyone from ITV had dared to suggest what might be included in his running order, Dacre was often picking up the telephone to hear ITV's controller of news telling him just that. 'At the beginning it was hands off,' says Dacre, 'and we had some enormous successes, coverage of Diana's death and the school shooting tragedy at Dunblane, for example. But then the ITV Network Centre began to want more and more involvement. They were trying to make the news more in tune with the rest of the channel.'

Nigel Dacre himself had no problems with changing *ITN News* to *ITV News* – though others in and out of ITN certainly did. 'We were right to make the news customer-focused,' he says, 'and to tailor the programme to the needs of the channel. You have to work closely with the network and the controller. My job was to brief the network and consult them on the big strategic issues and to see that we had a close relationship.'

But Dacre became increasingly aware that he was dealing with a more interventionist ITV. 'The extent of the dealings between ITV and ITN grew dramatically,' he says. 'With Stuart Prebble as ITV controller of news we might have had perhaps two calls a week and a weekly meeting. With Steve Anderson we had daily discussion. The relationship with ITV is vital. The channel controllers have the final say on the choice of editors for the programmes ITN makes for them, but if there is a conflict over the running order of a bulletin then the ITN editor of that programme must retain control. I felt that the news had to be independent. I do think that the network has a right to say, "Let's have a different newscaster", for example, but it does not have the right to make on-the-day decisions.'

Steve Anderson – unlike some of his ITV colleagues – was not hostile to ITN. But while he never tried to impose his own preferred running order on *ITV News* programme editors, he made no secret of what he thought was important and sometimes even what should lead a bulletin. In April 2002, for instance, the star England footballer David Beckham broke a bone in his left foot, and an ITN team had a report on the aftermath of what was alleged to be a massacre by Israeli forces in the Palestinian refugee camp of Jenin. Which story should lead? In a number of calls Anderson made it plain that he thought Beckham's foot should be the top story, arguing that it was really news, not simply an update on something that had happened a few days before, however important it might be. In the end Beckham's foot kicked off the more populist *ITV Evening News*, and Jenin the *ITV News at 10.30*. ITN could say that it had hung on to its independence of judgement.

Nigel Dacre's concern was more about the level of ITV's involvement than specific attempts to influence the running order, but eventually relations between him and Steve Anderson reached a low point. ITV wanted a change, and so did Nigel Dacre. Some time previously he had told chief executive Stewart Purvis that he'd been editor of ITN's news programmes on ITV long enough. So now, after seven years, Nigel Dacre left the job, and when no new role could be found for him, left ITN. 'Nigel had basically run out of road with ITV,' says Stewart Purvis. 'I thought that Steve Anderson and David Liddiment at ITV weren't giving him due credit for his efforts in the unusual circumstances they had created. But I then carried out my own research inside the ITN building and found that, in footballers' parlance, Nigel had lost the dressing room. In fairness to ITV they did accept that Nigel had got them through an extraordinary period in reasonable shape. All I would add is that I kept Nigel in position a lot longer than ITV wanted.'

During Nigel Dacre's time, the ITN news on ITV – the *ITV News* – became more 'formulaic', – a word Dacre accepts as a fair description of the way he worked. Quite rightly he wanted to establish a way of doing things that gave *ITV News* a recognisable and consistent style and look. But some of his team at the time thought that this led to programmes where people went through their paces for the sake of form, rather than because the news demanded it. Michael Brunson, for example, who quit his job as political editor soon after *News at Ten* ended in 1999, was critical of the way in which Dacre tackled things: 'Under Nigel Dacre there was a preoccupation with what the bulletin felt and looked like. I was quite frequently asked to do live spots from Westminster. When I asked, "About what?", the answer came back, "Anything that's happened." It was all about "We feel threatened, we need to put our big-name reporters on every programme." In the past I would have had a chat with the output editors, people like Phil Moger or Nick Pollard, about what the story was. If all the programme editors care about is your presence on screen then you get lazy.'

Pollard, a former executive producer of *News at Ten* and now head of Sky News, says: 'Nigel Dacre was essentially systems; he was interested in types of story, not the story itself. That indefinable ITN swashbuckling spirit of journalistic enterprise went into eclipse.'

Naturally, Dacre resists the idea that 'formulaic' programmes meant ones that were dull. 'At the end of the day,' he says, 'my job was to make the best of things. I genuinely worked hard at trying to make it work. I think the last few years of *News at Ten* were strong years for ITN, and I think we had as much fun in them as had ever been had before at ITN. Every year we were beating the BBC, and ITV never did say that *News at Ten* had run out of steam – and that was easy ground for them, had it been true. It was ironic that *News at Ten* was moved at the time that it was strong again.'

Richard Tait argues that in the decade 1991–2001 ITN's news programmes for ITV remained successful and competitive. 'In that period,' he says, 'ITN won twenty-five Royal Television Society news awards as against BBC1's twenty-four, and of the other major prizes – from BAFTA, Monte Carlo and the American Emmys – ITN's news on ITV won twelve awards, while BBC1's news won five.'

Despite that success, not everyone at ITN then would agree that those tough years in the late nineties, which included the demise of *News at Ten*, were much fun. In the newsroom at Gray's Inn Road I recall a rather grim atmosphere, and an increasingly threadbare existence, as ITN staff tried to cope with round after round of efficiency savings. Understandably Nigel Dacre then seemed a rather careworn boss. He deserves credit for his determined struggle to maintain standards within the constraints of tighter budgets, but inside ITN there is a strong division of opinion about the way he ran ITN's news on ITV: 'Under Dacre,' says Jon Snow, 'the *ITV News* was just a centrally manufactured thing. I think he came close to destroying the product he was in charge of.'

But Richard Tait, ITN's editor-in-chief for much of the time Dacre was trying to defend ITN territory against ITV intervention, is much more sympathetic: 'I think Nigel Dacre was treated appallingly by ITV at a time of sharply diminishing resources,' he says. 'He's a great producer, and a great loss to ITN. I've got a lot of time for him.'

CHAPTER 38

THE WAY WE LIVE NOW

'When I arrived at ITN in 1987,' says Richard Tait, 'it was at the end of the party. And it had clearly been a marvellous party. But that world had come to an end.' After the Broadcasting Act took effect at the beginning of 1993 the need to make a profit had put ITN's budget under real pressure, year on year. But that was as nothing to the result of the tender process which in 2001 left ITN signing up to an ITV contract of £35 million – essentially half what it had been able to spend ten years earlier. The prime task of Nigel Dacre and Richard Tait was to stop those deep cuts being visible on the screen. 'We were able to maintain the quality largely because we went digital,' Tait says, referring to the system that now allows all video material to be handled digitally, on computer screens in the ITN newsroom. 'We could take the money out without it hitting the sharp end. The budget cuts should have crippled ITN but they did not. We managed that sharp decline in resources by changing working practices. And the fact that the talent in the company hasn't gone suggests to me that ITN is not putting out a crap service.'

Back in 1995, David Mannion, who had been in charge of ITN news on ITV, had resigned because Tait, not he, had been made ITN's editor-in-chief. As the ITN minutes record: 'Mr Mannion had been unable to understand why he could not get the job, and could not be consoled.' For

most of the next decade Mannion was, frankly, well out of it. As Tait and
Dacre struggled to cut ITN's coat according to the thinner, even threadbare,
cloth they now had to work with, Mannion was earning his living elsewhere
in commercial television. He was not at ITN when the savage cuts required
by the new contract came in. But now that he is back, with the title of
editor-in-chief, ITV News, he has had to pick up the pieces and live with
the deal. 'Nobody,' he says, 'comes out of it smelling of roses. ITV did put a
gun to ITN's head and that wasn't the right thing to do. It was a purely
arbitrary cut to the budget. The fault was in the negotiating system itself:
had there been a better relationship between ITN and ITV it wouldn't have
happened, and it's a crying shame it did. What was going on was quite
arbitrary machete-ing.'

But just how damaging have the cuts really been? In its *Programmes
Review* of 2003, just before it was replaced as commercial television
regulator by Ofcom, the ITC noted that: 'During the year to date ITV's
news programmes have seemed more confident and assured, especially on
consumer and health issues, and in tune with their market. But the new
and leaner contract with ITN makes it more difficult for them always to
compare in depth with their competitors.'

It was in January 2004 that David Mannion returned to what he had
previously shown he was so good at – running the news on ITV. It was a
popular choice, rather like Greg Dyke arriving to take over the BBC after
the gloomy days of John Birt. The following month morale rose again
when the newly consolidated ITV relaunched the *ITV News*, along with the
rest of their schedule.

By May 2004, writing in the Royal Television Society's magazine
Television, Clive Jones, the ITV News Group's chief executive, was arguing
that things at ITN were now looking up, after a period when its
programmes had seemed tired:

> Viewers had begun to notice and vote with their feet. Focus groups revealed
> a strong residue of belief that *ITV News* delivered strong and authoritative
> programming, but it was losing its trademark 'zest and edge', and it was
> beginning to feel old-fashioned compared with its competitors. Our tradi-
> tional roles of being pioneers and innovators had been usurped. Inside ITN,
> morale was low in the wake of the contract negotiations which had resulted

in severe cutbacks and the *News at When?* saga. A number of the key correspondents and senior reporters had become so disillusioned that *ITV News*
faced a potentially very damaging haemorrhage of major talent.[1]

But now, Jones wrote, all was well:

> Today *ITV News* is off its knees, and not only on its feet, it has a spring in its
> step under the inspired leadership of editor-in-chief David Mannion ... *ITV*
> *News* is now self-confident, innovative, bold, and it has also leapfrogged both
> the BBC and Sky in its production values. The £1.3 million revamp of the
> *ITV News* set and the *ITV News* Channel has created a 'video theatre of news'
> from which all ITV's news output is now presented.

The new set is essentially a smart, glass-topped desk in an otherwise empty
studio space in ITN's basement. Several remotely controlled cameras, plus
another on a boom, cover the newscasters as they walk and talk on a sort
of narrow, curved walkway in front of a giant cyclorama, or on the spur
that leads from it to the desk at which they can sit. On the backdrop they
can see dim monochrome video images which technical wizardry brings to
the viewer in colour of unprecedented brilliance. But modern and technically impressive though it is, the new set has its critics – many of them, no
doubt, grumpy old men like me.

It may be state-of-the-art, but somehow there is about it a touch of Fred
Astaire and Ginger Rogers and 'the big white set' of their 1930s musicals.
Somehow as they stride or stroll along their raised walkways, you half
expect the two presenters of the *ITV Evening News*, that attractive couple
Mark Austin and Mary Nightingale, for example, to go into their dance at
any moment. The new set, with big, strong pictures on the cyclorama and
electronic graphics spread across the floor, is visually impressive: it's well
calculated to make a family preoccupied with getting supper ready look up
and pay attention for a moment. But pay attention to what? To the story, or
to 'high production values'? There's a danger that the look of the news has
become more important than what's in it. ITN's able newscasters seem to
have become rather distant figures in a virtual landscape, dwarfed by the
giant images behind them, no longer the warm, close-up, authoritative
people with a good story to tell that they used to be. There was some point

to seeing Fred Astaire's feet – he could, after all, dance a little – but why is it important to see the feet of a newscaster? The ability to walk and talk at the same time should surely come second to the ability to deliver the news in a convincing way – and, as any presenter knows, it's hard to feel you're being really effective in long-shot. ITN is in danger of allowing good news-casting to take second place to flashy presentation.

Deborah Turness is now editor of ITV Network News – appointed to revamp the programmes when ITV relaunched itself in February 2004. She was not slow to criticise the past: 'I was brought in to turn around the production values,' Turness told the *Observer*. 'The programmes had become very turgid, very predictable, very formulaic. In television terms they were quite dull. They didn't exploit pictures. They didn't use the personality of the reporters. They really weren't delivering to the audience. There was no sense of energy, of endeavour, of enthusiasm, of drama or excitement. Every television news programme should contain all those things every day. Otherwise, what the hell are we doing?'[2]

No one but a figure from the earliest days of television news – like the BBC's lugubrious Tahu Hole – would deny the importance of presenting a news story as effectively as possible; and it's fair to say that in recent years ITN's news programmes had become rather unexciting. But has the right remedy been found? 'There is now an unprecedented amount of news out there,' says Turness. 'I want people to watch *our* news. It must be distinctive – watch *us*, not the BBC, not Sky, not Bloomberg.' But is Turness right to think it's the 'look' of her news programmes, rather than the content, that will make them distinctive and encourage people to watch them?

As Chris Shaw, a former ITN editor of *Five News* and now senior programme controller at Channel 5, pointed out soon after the *ITV News* relaunch: 'News is about real events at real locations. Once you have such a fantastic set of technical kit there must be a temptation to divert more of *ITV News*'s resources into production and less into the basic but more costly activity of newsgathering.'[3]

Well, what about the newsgathering? How do those who see their reports presented in this 'theatre of news' feel about the show they're now appearing in?

'Frankly, I wouldn't watch it if I didn't work for it,' says one seasoned ITN journalist, bluntly. 'Some reporters tell me that they now go into the building with a sense of dread, wondering what silly idea for a story they've dreamt up this time.'

When presentation is so important there is always a strong temptation to decide how to handle a story before anyone has gone and reported it. Rather than ask the journalists on the ground what they think the story is, there has been a tendency for the planning meeting that Deborah Turness takes at 9.15 a.m. at ITN to decide for them. Then the reporting team will be told 'the way we see this story is so and so'.

An ITN insider gives an example of this particular problem: 'We sent Tim Ewart, ITN's sports editor, to Portugal to cover the European Cup in 2004 – he's now our longest surviving reporter, and very, very experienced. Of course, he was alert to the possible misbehaviour of England football fans, just like we were in London. When the fans rioted in Albufeira, Ewart interviewed a UEFA official as to whether England would be excluded from the competition if this bad behaviour continued. The UEFA man told him that the fans would have to be the cause of really major violence, actually at the scene of some match, before UEFA was likely to do anything. Tim thought that was the interesting story to report, and he told us so, but the planning meeting decided that they much preferred the familiar, 'fans may get England thrown out of the competition' line. The result on the *ITV News* that night was rather confused – not the clear effective story it should have been.'

Says Turness: 'When we started doing this we needed to change everything quickly, so there was a very top-down approach – within days we changed the way we were doing stories. But you do get into the habit of overprescribing. So, while the top will keep pushing ideas down to the people doing the story, the next step is to encourage more reporters to come forward with creative ideas of their own.'

Some reporters feel that to fit with some clever idea of how a story should be presented they are being asked to do silly things, even to make fools of themselves, in the way they report a story. At ITN there has always been an emphasis – quite rightly – on getting the arresting picture that helps summarise the essence of the story, or drive home its drama, but that is different from making the material the reporter has delivered jump about just to catch attention. Is it a good idea for a news programme suddenly to turn colour pictures into black-and-white negative for dramatic effect, or to take a Commons statement from the prime minister and, for emphasis, replay what he has just said while the picture jumps into tighter and tighter close-up? When there is no real news about the latest sex scandal from the FA does it really help to go into 'reconstructions' of what might have happened? Surely this is not so much covering the news as 'sexing it up'.

One of the reasons why presentation may sometimes take precedence over reporting is that it's cheaper. The more you can plan – virtually script – the story in advance, the less money you waste on things that don't work out. ITN is now on a diet that contains no fat at all, and this is not healthy. 'We have been cut not just to the bone, but into the bone,' says Bill Neely, who, back in 1989, took a pay cut in order to come to work at ITN. Experienced reporter though he is, Neely is no Neanderthal, pining for the past but, like a poorly equipped British soldier, he knows what it's like trying to win a battle with inadequate resources.

'It was win-win for Sky in the last contract round,' he says. 'Either they would win the *ITV News* contract or they would damage us by knocking the price down, and they *have* damaged us. Now we are struggling. There are stories every day that the home and foreign desks have to say no to. Nothing galls me more than to hear BBC colleagues say, "Missed you at that." It's very, very hard. Is there equipment we'd like? "Yes, please – yes please. We want and need that. Can we have it?" "No." There are things that have been missed. How can you run a national and international news service on £35 million a year? We are a small player now. It's the big boys' game and we don't have the money to join in.'

What about another foreign affairs reporter, and now presenter, Andrea Catherwood? She is less gloomy. 'Cost reductions have had an effect,' she says, 'but I think the quality of the journalism remains. Sometimes it can even have positive results – as it did in the very early cash-strapped days of ITN. But we are all extremely stretched; we're all multi-skillers instead of dedicated teams with separate skills. It's harder work, less fun.'

ITN always denies that it has 'dumbed down' *ITV News*. Instead it prefers to say that the programme's news agenda has broadened to embrace more consumer, health, lifestyle and show-business stories – which it has. As one cynical ITN journalist puts it, 'Our popular quality journalism used to mean the front page of the *Daily Mail*; now it means the *Daily Mail's* back pages.' But even if that's not true, more about the Beckhams must mean less about 'abroad'.

Says one of ITN's reporters who frequently travels abroad: 'If it's a really big story like the Iraq War, then ITN takes it very seriously and we are a major competitor. But when you are not dealing with a big story, interest falls away very quickly. ITN on ITV is not very interested in foreign news – I've noticed a fairly dramatic change. Some of my colleagues who are based in foreign bureaux have been commissioned to work on very few stories in the area they're based in. What's the point of having senior people in a bureau when they can't get on the air?

'I hope that as the *ITV News at 10.30* really gets established it will be different, because its aimed at the AB upmarket men who watch at that time and who take more interest in foreign affairs. But the fact is that the six thirty *ITV Evening News* is the flagship now; that's where the money is targeted, and that's the problem. The danger is that we may not do enough "foreign" because on the whole it's not wanted at six thirty. And if the six thirty doesn't want it then it's obviously less likely that ITN will send a crew to cover it just for the "late" – particularly since the "late" is now so short.

A beneficiary of ITN's graduate training programme – a scheme now defunct, as a result of the cutbacks – Alex Bolton is a young ITN bulletin editor. He agrees that the twenty-minute ten thirty programme is no longer the focus for ITN, as *News at Ten* once was. 'Things are very stretched, and at the moment the lion's share of the resources go on the six thirty news, the half-hour programme. A decision has been taken that the six thirty programme is the priority. This makes it difficult for the editor of *ITV News at 10.30* to come up with something different – we don't always have the option of a completely fresh take on the news of the day.'

So *ITV News at 10.30* – even though it is broadcast four long hours after the *ITV Evening News* – is usually similar in content to the earlier programme, although it is shorter. The contrast with a decade ago, when the 'early' was something of a rehearsal for the 'late', and every activity in the newsroom built up towards the flagship *News at Ten*, is marked. And indeed, although the *ITV News at 10.30* is presented by Trevor McDonald, it is no longer described as 'the flagship'. It is, after all, the *ITV Evening News*, not the *ITV News at 10.30*, that is now in peak time.

It's hard, looking at the screen, not to feel that, while great ingenuity and considerable investment have gone into the presentation of these ITN news programmes for ITV, the journalism on which they depend is not sufficiently well funded. Talented reporters already mentioned in this book, and many others, like Tom Bradby, Juliet Bremner, John Irvine, Julian Manyon, James Mates, Robert Moore, Sue Saville and Mark Webster, are being wasted. All of them know how to produce authoritative, interesting, original stories, yet the viewer sees relatively little of them. Compared with the way the BBC and Sky News are now funded, the contract with ITV just doesn't give ITN the money to produce all the good journalism – and particularly the good reporting – of which they are capable.

Says Alex Bolton: 'We are all flabbergasted when we look at what the BBC is spending. They can get a live satellite from anywhere in the world whenever they want it. In terms of resources we obviously can't compete with that. Not much is ever commissioned at ITN now without it getting on air. With us every frame has to count, and we don't have the luxury of sending off reporters and crews on fishing expeditions. Now, more than ever, we have to rely on the quick reactions and sense of purpose which allow us to punch above our weight.

'The cuts in resources make it more challenging for the specialist correspondents to pursue "off-diary" ideas – potential stories that need researching. Paradoxically, though, we are now doing more to generate news ourselves. The *ITV Evening News* will look for a big issue, like MRSA or paedophile chat lines, and really go for it, even if doing so is labour intensive. What we're trying to do is cover fewer stories better.'

When it comes to pay, many junior ITN people today work much harder for less money. As Bolton says, 'Any younger journalist is aware of just how much times have changed at ITN. Salaries were really forced down in the early nineties. Add to that the axing of the graduate training scheme and it's meant that it's harder now for us to recruit at junior levels.

'Some of the things that went on at Channel 5 in the late nineties really were a bit shocking. To save money, inexperienced youngsters were recruited instead of skilled journalists and technicians. There was a lot of talk about multi-skilling but it was really about saving money. In many cases they were doing things like basic vision mixing with only a few days' training. Along with my fellow trainees I was offered just sixteen thousand pounds to join the Channel 5 News team, a big cut on previous starting salaries. In many ways it wasn't ITN's fault: that was all Channel 5 was prepared to pay.'[4]

For many years now money has not been any sort of problem for the man who, in the public's mind, *is* ITN. And he deserves his handsome salary. Through all the turmoil in the boardroom, the resignations of senior managers and redundancies in the newsroom, through all the highs and lows of the last twelve years, it has been Trevor McDonald's presence on the screen that has brought reassurance and comfort to the viewer, a sense of continuity and constancy that has been invaluable both to ITN and to ITV. No wonder that they both cling to him.

As Clive Jones, chief executive of the ITV News Group, says, 'Trevor McDonald is one of the iconic figures of ITV. I want to bring to the channel gravitas and authority that can create trust and bond viewers to it. ITN and ITV should both take enormous pride in that Trevor McDonald is the most trusted newscaster in Britain. ITN had the guts and the foresight to take a black Caribbean immigrant and make him their front-man.'

Not since Alastair Burnet has a newscaster played such an important role in the ITN story. In October 2003 Trevor McDonald's contribution to British broadcasting was recognised yet again when the prime minister, Tony Blair, made a surprise appearance at the National Television Awards ceremony to present him with a special prize, the final gong of the evening.

McDonald joined ITN on New Year's Day in 1972. He had worked in Trinidad for radio and television, and come to London in response to an offer from the BBC's World Service. When he applied for a job at ITN, he and editor Nigel Ryan agreed that he would not be a 'black' reporter, specialising in race issues, and indeed it seems that McDonald's colour has never been a problem for him in his chosen profession. Four years after he joined ITN he told an interviewer that the only racial rebuff he had ever been conscious of was when a Republican woman in Belfast shouted at him, 'Get out of here, you dirty British!'

Over the next decade McDonald reported from around the world and established himself as an effective journalist, as the ITN board minutes often record. But in the mid-eighties he began newscasting too, and in 1992, after the departure of Alastair Burnet and Sandy Gall, he was one of three in contention for the top job of presenting *News at Ten*. It had been decided – once again following the American trend – that only one news-caster was now needed. The choice lay between Trevor McDonald, Alastair Stewart and Julia Somerville.

Dave Mannion, then in charge of *ITN News* on ITV, remembers sitting in a second-class railway carriage (no doubt senior managers were all doing their bit to help the economy drive) with editor-in-chief Stewart Purvis and chief executive Bob Phillis, mulling over the problem. He says, 'Suddenly Phillis slapped the table and said, "Right, who's it gonna be?" I said, "In my view it has to be Trevor. He has the natural warmth coupled with real authority that I want to see and I can't in the other candidates. It's got to be someone you don't mind bringing you bad news. Trevor has Cronkite-like qualities.", But what about the fact that Trevor McDonald was black? 'Quite honestly,' says Mannion, 'Trevor's race had not crossed my mind. Then I thought, Will Trevor lose us viewers? The answer was no. Trevor is simply more English than any of us.'

The others agreed, and Trevor McDonald got the job. Whatever Mannion says, it was daring to appoint as presenter of Britain's most popular news programme someone so obviously from an ethnic-minority background – such a small section of the British population. And if it had never occurred to Mannion that McDonald was black it certainly had to others at ITN. Noting favourable press reaction to the announcement, the board minutes record that 'The decision on McDonald's appointment had been made after extensive research, and in full consultation with ITV.' Yet even after that, says Stewart Purvis now, he still had the greatest difficulty finding anyone in the ITV network ready to say either 'yes' or 'no' to McDonald.

ITN's choice was certainly a good one. While he might not have the detailed political knowledge of an Alastair Burnet to make him the obvious choice to present an election-night programme, McDonald, now of course Sir Trevor McDonald, has long been the most popular, most trusted, tele-vision newscaster in Britain. As for the question of his colour, that is no longer – if it ever was – an issue for him. 'I don't think about being black,' he says, 'though I certainly don't feel I'm anything else. I'd done a lot by the time I came to present *News at Ten* so all my concerns about it had disap-peared. If I do think about it at all it's with a sense of immense pride.'

McDonald's opposite number on *Channel 4 News*, Jon Snow, is firmly of the opinion that no working journalist should accept an honour and, indeed, when he was offered one, he politely refused.[5] McDonald says that he hesitated when in 1999 he was offered a knighthood. Would he be taken seriously – particularly back home in Trinidad? He phoned his sister there for her advice. 'She told me, "Of course you should accept, because of what it means to others."'

When *News at Ten* finally died in 1999, ITN's late news was at first shifted very much later, to eleven o'clock: Trevor McDonald at first moved to present the new early-evening peak-time programme at six thirty. 'Don't worry,' he recalls the prime minister saying to him at the party to welcome in the new schedule, 'we'll soon have you back at ten o'clock.' Some hope: *News at Ten* had gone for good – Margaret Thatcher's reforms of the commercial television system had seen to that. True, after the shambles that followed the failure of the new ITV schedule to hold news audiences, the late news was temporarily restored for some of the week to a notional ten o'clock spot. But in February 2004 things changed again, and McDonald moved to present the *ITV News at 10.30*, even though it is transmitted outside peak time when there are fewer people available to view. Leaving aside the lateness of its transmission time, *News at 10.30* was not at first a resounding success, not a patch on the old *News at Ten*. When a programme supposed to bring us the most important national and inter-national stories of the day could lead on a footballer's expensive divorce settlement it was not surprising that the critics were scornful. Here is Jasper Gerard in the *Sunday Times*:

> Has Britain fallen out of love with the Kit Kat?' No, this was not from John Craven's *Newsround*, which used to meld seamlessly with *The Magic Roundabout*. This was the main headline last week on ITN's flagship news programme. The *Beano*'s got more bottom than the relaunched *ITV News* … It can't be long before dear Sir Trevor McDonald, in an ignominious end to a fine career, finds himself presenting with a moonlighting Teletubby.

There was more.

> … after endless cuts ITV's news coverage is just typing pool chitchat about chocolate bars. You scream at the screen: 'Sir Trevor, we don't really care.' …

On the rare occasions when ITN's flagship plunges into anything meatier than some starlet's neckline, it misses the point, because it sees stories as mere merriment. If thousands die in an earthquake it will focus on the miracle baby that makes it . . . *ITV News* is an apology of a show and may as well be axed. And, Clever Trevor, mate, have a break. Have a flaming Kit Kat.[7]

It is fair to say that the *ITV News at 10.30* is now much improved. With a more substantial news agenda, more foreign coverage in particular and more new stories generally it is no longer just a cut-down, rehashed version of the *ITV Evening News*. But in fact Sir Trevor will 'have a break'. Though he breathes no public word of critisism of his programme he has announced that he will stop presenting the *ITV News at 10.30* at the end of 2005, ITN's fiftieth anniversary year. Although he expects to continue working on ITV, particularly its current affairs programme *Tonight*, it will be, for Trevor McDonald, the dignified end of a long and distinguished career with ITN.

But is the end of the road for ITN itself now in sight?

CHAPTER 39
AND FINALLY . . . ?

'In a period in which just about everything else about British commercial television has changed', writes former ITN editor-in-chief Richard Tait, 'ITN has been a point of (relative) stability . . . It is still a hugely important part of British public service broadcasting: its news bulletins for ITV, C4 and (until the end of 2004) Five reach nearly ten million people a night, only just behind the news audiences on BBC1 and BBC2. Its enterprising and accessible journalism is still admired by its competitors. But at present it is not hard to find people who wonder whether it will survive much longer as a separate entity.'[1]

Fifty years after it began, ITN is again uncomfortably close to the situation it was in then, its survival in a new television environment uncertain. Can it continue, or will Sir Trevor McDonald's successor soon be saying, 'And finally . . . ' for ITN itself?

When ITN was created, its owners were all ITV contractors. They wanted ITN to be, first and foremost, their news supplier, and they were reluctant to invest in any expansion beyond its core activity. Alhough ITN won contracts to supply news to other British channels, beginning with Channel 4, some of its senior managers and journalists wanted the company to go much further and make its mark in the world. Convinced that its ITV directors would never back their ambitions for ITN, Alastair

Burnet and David Nicholas supported the idea of bringing in outside investors, non-ITV broadcasters, who might help them make ITN a truly international news company, genuinely independent of ITV.

But their hopes were not realised. Not only did the plan to become a world-class television news company never quite materialise, but the introduction of non-broadcaster owners didn't help at all: indeed, it left ITN in a worse state than before. At least in the past all its directors had been in the same boat, however ragged their rowing, all owners of ITV companies. Now, while some were ITV broadcasters, others were not. Some simply wanted to maximise profits, while others, the ITV companies, were just as interested in holding down – or reducing – the contract price for the news programmes that ITN was selling them.

Perhaps it might have been better for ITN if the plans to 'float' the company during the 'dotcom' era had come to something. Says Charles Allen, now chief executive of ITV, and the largest shareholder in ITN: 'I advocated then that it should have been floated. No single party would own it – it would be owned by the City, with shareholders; it could have been a completely separate business. At the time I was advocating that idea, in early 2000, the market was very hot. If we could have floated ITN then it could have been quite interesting. So none of us would have had ownership of it; it would have been a separate entity. I think my view is you have two realistic options: ITN is either wholly owned as a division within a single broadcaster, or basically it could have been floated on the market. But we ended up right in the middle, with five people each owning 20 per cent, and three of them certainly with different agendas.'

While the awkwardness of its ownership structure remains, it is unrealistic to suppose that the ITN board will approve the investment needed for major expansion and diversification. Unusual among media companies, ITN has no non-executive directors who have no stake of their own in the company and can therefore take an unbiased and independent view of how to proceed. Despite that, ITN is doing its best to develop businesses that are complementary to what, after fifty years, remains its core function – providing news to ITV. In 1993 the ITV contract made up 67 per cent of ITN's revenue; but in 2004 the value of that contract was only 40 per cent of ITN's income. That partly reflects the drastically reduced value of the ITV deal, but it also suggests that other sources of income are becoming more important.

One subsidiary business in particular, the ITN Archive, now accounts for 8 per cent of ITN's revenue. In addition to licensing material from its own library of film and television material, ITN is successfully marketing the British Pathé and Reuters collections, as well as the contents of Granada's programme archive. Under its youthful managing director Alwyn Lindsey, turnover in the ITN Archive business should grow to more than £10 million in 2004. Says ITN chairman Mark Wood: 'ITN Archive has achieved 30 per cent plus growth now for four years in succession, so this is a business which has got potential to be up in the twenty-, thirty-, forty-million-pound range before too long.'

Most of the archive's customers are television producers, but the idea is to mine the treasure buried there to supply material to the new generation of mobile phones. Nicholas Wheeler, managing director of ITN Multimedia Content, says that with more and more of the fifty million mobile phones in Britain capable of receiving and playing high-quality sound and pictures, this is another business with potential. You can now get ITN television news on your mobile for as little as 25 pence a bulletin.

ITN has long had an interest in commercial radio, and through Independent Radio News, in which it has a 20 per cent stake, ITN supplies news bulletins to nearly three hundred commercial radio stations around the country. That, too, makes a small but useful contribution to ITN's revenue. And if supplying news programmes round the world has not turned out to be a growth business, repackaging news material may well be. Says chairman Mark Wood: 'News is a core platform for the business, but new value comes from re-engineering the content, as well as from non-news areas. I think one of the most valuable bits of our daily news production is our entertainment news, for example. We are one of the world's best producers of showbiz news. We don't always realise it but we are. And showbiz news is very, very exportable. I think we've got a tremendous growth business here.'

ITN is now climbing out of another difficult financial situation. In 2001, says Wood, the company was losing money heavily. The cut in the *ITV News* contract price was a major factor in this gloomy picture, but just as important were the losses on the *ITN News Channel*, the round-the-clock digital news service, which began that year.

In the closing years of the twentieth century Stewart Purvis and Richard Tait, then chief executive and editor-in-chief, had become convinced that

ITN could no longer do without the kind of twenty-four-hour news channel that Sky and the BBC already operated. With ITV news audiences coming under increasing pressure from digital channels, they decided that ITN must get itself into that business while it still had the resources to do so. More specifically, a news channel was needed to cover and broadcast dramatic news developments when ITN was otherwise virtually unstaffed and off the air; it would also keep news flowing, between the existing bulletins, to IRN and the new mobile-phone ventures. And, of course, who could say how important a news channel might be in the future, as the whole of television began preparing to switch off existing terrestrial analogue services and go digital? But even though the *ITN News Channel* was run on a minute budget, around £3 million a year, it attracted virtually no advertising – and therefore no income. The *News Channel* was losing money – and was projected to do so for some time ahead. Here, inevitably, the divisions on the ITN board between the broadcasters and the non-broadcasters surfaced again.

'To me the *News Channel* is the whole news issue in microcosm,' says ITV's Charles Allen. 'All the owners of ITN got the *News Channel* started, and then, when it continued to lose money, the non-broadcasters said they weren't prepared to go on supporting it. Because they weren't broadcasters they had no interest beyond profit and loss. This is a channel which, in the short term, won't make any money – that could be three years plus. They weren't prepared to suffer the losses as we, the broadcasters, were, so we ended up buying them out – ITV now owns 100 per cent of it. I think that using the *News Channel* example demonstrates what has been happening in every aspect of ITN, because of the divisions in the ownership.'

Clearly ITN cannot hope to expand in any major way while the ownership remains divided; and while it is doing its best to make money from the businesses it has developed on the fringes of its news operation, the ITV contract is still by far the largest single contract it has. To lose that would probably mean the end of ITN. So what are ITV's intentions?

In 2003 Charles Allen emerged as the victor of his struggle with Michael Green, and the consolidation of all the ITV companies into one ITV plc came another step closer. Allen now owns 92 per cent of what was the old ITV network – all the ITV regional franchises except those in Scotland, Northern Ireland and the Channel Isles; and as a result of the Granada/Carlton amalgamation Allen now has a bigger stake in ITN than anyone else. Because he can decide whether or not to renew that all-important *ITV News* contract at the end of 2008, he is theoretically in a position to put ITN out of business if that is what he wants to do. So does he?

'Basically we – ITV plc – currently own 40 per cent of ITN. Either, in the remaining years of the contract, I will be able to buy the other 60 per cent and then will own the company in its entirety, or at the end of the licence we will not contract our news with ITN. We will undertake to produce our own news in-house.'

Whatever happens, Allen says, he will not give ITN another contract to provide the news: 'No, we won't renew the contract at the end of the licence.' What if this meant that ITN, without its ITV contract, could not survive? To Allen, that is not important: 'The whole purpose of this is to provide, either way, a strong news operation for ITV. I think there are very talented people in ITN who would be part of that, whatever happens.' So the fact that there would no longer be an independent ITN is not relevant? 'I think in the future it isn't, but I do think I would like to see within ITV a news operation which is not only a provider to ITV but could be a provider to others. I see opportunities to grow the news operation, which under multi-ownership has not been the case.'

So that's it, then. If Charles Allen's plan prevails, ITN will either become a wholly owned subsidiary (or a division) of a single broadcaster, ITV plc, or it will most likely go out of business. And which of these scenarios turns out to be correct will depend on whether Allen can strike a deal with the other shareholders to buy their stakes.

As former editor and chief executive Stewart Purvis puts it: 'I suspect the race between survival and oblivion [for ITN] will be a close-run thing . . . The key factor is that the existing ITN national news contract runs until the end of 2008. As that date approaches, ITV plc – the merger of Carlton and Granada, which owns 40 per cent of ITN – will regularly point out to the three non-ITV shareholders, Reuters, United Business Media and the Daily Mail Group, each with 20 per cent, that ITV has the power to make ITN relatively worthless by not renewing the contract. ITV's alternative, it will emphasise, is to provide its own news output, having already brought the expertise of ITV's and ITN's key news managers in-house with the creation of the ITV News Group, covering both national and regional news.'

'It's up to the other shareholders in ITN,' says Charles Allen. 'They can look at what the business is generating for them in dividends versus what they would be prepared to sell me their stakes for. I think it's a financial calculation. There are four years of the ITV contract with ITN left so you can calculate what money's going to come in, and therefore it's a simple arithmetic calculation.' So why can't they all agree on a price? 'Well, inevitably, in arithmetic calculations, there are some people who want more and other people who want to pay less. My point is, frankly, because we're getting on with it, it doesn't really matter. We're already getting on and running the news, whether I own ITN or not.'

As that last point suggests, it is really no longer a matter of whether ITN can remain an independent news supplier to ITV: that absolute independence has already been lost. In January 2004 David Mannion became editor-in-chief, ITV News. As the joint ITV/ITN press release said:

> David will be responsible for managing and developing ITV News at both national and regional level. His primary objective will be to build on the structural relationships that exist between ITV News and ITN, the ITV regional newsrooms and the ITV News Channel to ensure that the ITV News Group operates as a fully integrated unit, benefiting from maximum news-gathering and editorial co-operation.

In plainer language, ITN and ITV are now inextricably entangled.

Mannion is paid by ITN and, as an ITN employee, reports to his chief executive and chairman, Mark Wood. But at the same time, as editor-in-chief of ITV News, he also reports to Clive Jones, the ITV News Group chief executive. This dual loyalty is a sensitive issue at ITN, where tempers fray at suggestions that ITN is losing its independence. But the fact is that ITN and ITV, if not yet one, are moving closer together all the time.

Assuming it survives at all, then, as a provider of national and international news, ITN is likely to be folded within the ITV embrace. And why not, when, as Charles Allen and many others quite reasonably point out, every other major broadcaster in the world owns its own news? In America CBS, NBC and ABC would find it bizarre if they had to take their news programmes from some independent company. Here in Britain, BBC News is at the heart of the Corporation, not some independent supplier. But then, of course, the BBC is not a commercial broadcaster. It may get beaten up by politicians from time to time, but its news programmes are not directly subject to commercial pressures.

ITN was set up as a separate independent company partly because it made economic sense for the different contractors to share the cost of a news service, but also to minimise the likelihood that ITV's news would ever be leaned on by a single owner. Over fifty years, it is hard to find examples where pressure has been applied, let alone applied successfully.

Sitting in the newsroom in Television House one day, soon after ITV first went on air, news editor Arthur Clifford took a call from Val Parnell, a director of ATV and the producer of one of the early ITV's most successful entertainment programmes, *Sunday Night at the London Palladium*. Parnell wanted to know why ITN had not carried a story – as the newspapers often did – about the prize a contestant had won on *Beat the Clock* in the previous night's programme ('You'll have the time of your life, beating time to big prizes'). Clifford told Parnell that ITN had not thought it a real story, just a puff for his programme. 'We are an independent news company,' he said loftily. 'There's no more to be said.' 'You're going to find yourself out of a job, Mr Clifford,' shouted the angry Parnell. 'In that case I'll call a press conference to explain the situation,' said Clifford. No more, apparently, came of the matter. It was a small-scale affair, but none the less showed how an ITV company director could somehow assume that ITN's job was not to report the news as its editor and his staff saw fit, but as the owners wanted it to be.

Similarly, in 2002 ITN found itself under pressure to include in the *ITV News* mention of other ITV programmes, as if they were real stories, instead of advertisements. So it was that *ITV News* found itself promoting the ITV talent-spotting show *Pop Idol*. Said ITV's controller of news Steve Anderson: '*Pop Idol* was the biggest TV story of the year . . . It would have been a rare failure of editorial judgement for *ITV News* to ignore a story everyone was talking about.'[2]

Putting pressure on an independent ITN to include ITV programme promotions in its bulletins as if they were news stories is one thing, but scarcely as serious as what has been happening in America. There, it seems, commercial pressures are now keeping *off* the air important stories that a broadcaster's owners don't like. Professor Steven Barnett, of

Middlesex University, relates what he calls 'a particularly stark example of corporate censorship' at ABC Television, a part of the Disney Corporation, which is often talked of as a possible buyer of British television companies.

Investigative reporting by ABC News revealed that Disney was employing a number of sex offenders at the Disney World theme park in Florida. According to credible witnesses, Disney was not running adequate checks on job applicants because the process was too expensive. Disney's chairman, Michael Eisner, said in a radio interview, 'I would prefer ABC not to cover Disney.' While denying that it had been 'leaned on' by the mighty mouse, ABC did not run its report. Says Professor Barnett, 'It is difficult to avoid the conclusion that, had the ABC network remained outside the Disney sphere of influence, it would have aired a very damaging story about recruitment practices at Disney theme parks.'[3]

Over the years, ITN has retained its reputation for independent reporting – and its owners have generally resisted the urge to grab hold of the editorial lever. But what would happen if a single owner of ITV wanted to influence editorial policy for commercial reasons?

Just in case you hadn't noticed, there is now, remarkably, no overall editor, or editor-in-chief of ITN. Mark Wood, the ITN chairman, is there to be consulted, but all the weight of ITV (and, indeed, of Channel 4 and any other broadcaster with whom ITN does business) now falls directly on the editor of each particular ITN news programme. Without the ultimate back-up of an editor-in-chief of ITN, how could the editor of ITV Network News, currently Deborah Turness, be expected to resist any pressure that ITV might bring to bear? Without its own editor-in-chief, how can ITN be editorially independent?

Perhaps this is unnecessary nit-picking. If ITN's editorial independence in the past fifty years has not been subject to serious commercial pressures, do we really need to worry that it may happen in future? As Sir David Nicholas says: 'Most television in Europe had been state-owned; but as commercial television opened up there, we got an absolute deluge of companies coming to see us and asking how a commercial company could do high-quality news. And I was always able to say that in our system no one had ever leaned on me to bend the news this way or that. A commercial attitude, a commercial environment, isn't necessarily detrimental to good news.'

No doubt he is right, but his ITN answered to many different broad-casting companies. For ITN there were disadvantages in that, but there was also safety in numbers. A glance at Italy shows what can happen if media power becomes concentrated. There the prime minister, Silvio Berlusconi, receives television coverage that is almost universally positive. It just happens, of course, that he controls over 90 per cent of state and commercial television. But it's not really the risk that powerful owners or politicians will insist on particular stories being put in or taken out of the running order, or will require them to be slanted in a particular way, that is the real concern.

Ever since ITN's managers decided that it was for their 'customers' – ITV, Channel 4, Five, and anybody else they could sell their news to – to dictate the kind of news programme they wanted, there has been a problem. Making news programmes fit seamlessly into a particular broadcaster's schedule means abandoning some of that independence of judgement that was once ITN's trademark. What was once the *ITN News* is now the *ITV News* or *Channel 4 News*. Once, the news stood apart, separate, inde-pendent. Now it tries to conform to the rest of the individual channel's output. This is much more than a matter of news appearing in the livery of the particular channel – the same on-screen colours, lettering and so on. This is trying as hard as possible to provide a news that will attract exactly the type of audience that the broadcaster is after.

Of course it would be absurd – and ITN never tried – to ignore the kind of audience that would be watching news programmes at different times of the day. But the important thing was that ITN used its own judgement about what to include in its bulletins, and in what style and tone to present it. It did not rely on research from the broadcaster to tailor its news programmes to some specific audience but ran its own show. When a voice signalled the news – 'Over now to the news from ITN' – it was a hand-over to a different and independent organisation that brought its own editorial values and judgements to the viewer. Indeed, it could be argued that it was valued by the viewers not for being *part* of the broadcaster's schedule but for being *apart* from it, for being different.

As its editor, Geoffrey Cox guarded ITN's independence jealously. It was, he says, 'absolutely cardinal'. And yet, as we have seen, ITN does not now feel the need for its own editor-in-chief. So will ITN finally lose its independence if it is wrapped within the comforting embrace of ITV? 'I don't say it will,' says Cox today, 'but the fight will be very hard. A tough editor in there could still do it but, my goodness, you are adding an enormous extra burden for him.'

It was in 1982 that Channel 4 asked ITN to supply a news programme that was completely different from what it did for ITV. But 'different' then was defined more in terms of agenda – no royalty, no natural disasters – than by demographics, focusing on particular socio-economic groups within the population.

Since those days the idea of news programmes closely tailored to what a particular group of people is thought to want to watch has become standard practice. ITN's editorial independence has been formally retained, but ITN's independence of mind in deciding what's in a bulletin has been more strictly circumscribed. Mark Wood, now ITN's full-time chairman, finds that sensible: 'Being an independent supplier is one thing, but you don't project news into a void: you project news into a schedule. And I always took the view that ITN's role was to be a successful part of a successful schedule, which meant that you had to work with the schedule and the schedulers to achieve the highest viewership.'

Charles Allen defends his pursuit of demographics on the grounds that he wants *ITV News* to attract an upmarket audience – better off, better educated: 'The point is, we don't get paid on ratings, we get paid on commercial impacts. So more recent discussions with David Mannion [editor-in-chief, ITV News] have been about the fact that I am actually more interested in ABC1s, and therefore I might get fewer viewers but I'll get more valuable viewers. To give an example of that: ABC1s are worth eighty pounds a thousand, and C2s and Ds are worth eight pounds a thousand. So I'd rather have a few more ABC1s than tens or hundreds of C2s, Ds and Es; and I think that is now influencing the new vision for ITV under David Mannion . . . You're seeing a touch on the tiller that says, "We're moving it slightly more upmarket." We're changing the positioning, and what I'm delighted to say is that peak-time news, the six p.m. to seven hour, is up for the first time in the twelve years I've been in the industry.'

Some people are, indeed, more equal than others. For Charles Allen, As, Bs and C1s are the priority, while C2s, Ds and poor old Es are not. Well, what's wrong with that? Shouldn't we thank our lucky stars that Allen sees a built-in incentive, a financial motive, for telling ITN to provide a more upmarket news? Well, it would certainly be dismal indeed if he saw ITV's future – and with it ITN's – as scrabbling around at the bottom of the 'red-top' newspaper market for viewers. All the same, something has been lost, some element of public service broadcasting has disappeared, when ITV is more interested in attracting viewers to the news as consumers rather than citizens. Nearly fifty years ago, editor Geoffrey Cox told his reporters that their job was to inform the nation in order to sustain democracy. Today it is essentially about giving people what they say they want.

In the 1970s and 1980s, for example, ITN stuck with the Northern Ireland story week after week, year after year – even though it wasn't popular. Would Charles Allen say today, 'The viewers don't like it. Let's not do it'? '*I* wouldn't say that at all,' Allen responds. 'But Dave Mannion would say that. His job, as editor-in-chief, is to deliver the news that my viewers want to watch. It's not his job to try and force-feed people on things they don't want to watch, and I think that is an attitudinal change, not only for ITV but for broadcasting generally. You cannot force people now, in a series of four hundred channels, to watch things they don't want to watch.'

But you *can* try to persuade them – as long as you have the will, and the resources required to do the job. Just because a news programme is 'upmarket' doesn't mean that it is necessarily of 'high quality'. It may be accurately pointed at the target audience, it may even score plenty of 'commercial impacts', but it may still be not as good as it should be if it's not sufficiently well funded to do the job. As we have seen, *ITV News* is now a rather threadbare creature, a television Oliver Twist in need of more financial nourishment. Even ITV News Group chief executive Clive Jones seems to agree that the cuts in ITN's budget have gone too far: 'I think we have achieved enough savings with ITN, if not too many,' he says. Yet his boss Charles Allen believes there may be scope for yet further belt-tight-ening.

How can ITN possibly do a high-quality news for half what it cost in real terms twelve years ago? 'Oh, easily,' Allen replies. 'We're making programmes across every sector that cost half what they cost twelve years ago. The whole industry has changed. We're now in an industry of talent and technology, whereas we were in an industry of bricks and mortar and engineers. So the game has changed dramatically.' But *half* the cost? 'Easily half, easily half. And it will get more effective going forward.' Does Allen really believe that ITN can produce a higher-quality news for ITV on the budget it has now? 'Absolutely.'

Given the cuts in the budget, and the progressive loss of independence, what is the future for ITN?

The evidence is that Charles Allen wants his news provider under his control, whether within his ITV News Group, or as a company that ITV controls absolutely. Either way means the end of ITN as we have known it, as an independent company in the ITV system. Of course, it might be that one of ITN's present shareholders – Reuters, say – might strike a deal to play a bigger role in partnership with ITV, but it still seems more likely that ITV will want total control of its own news, whether or not Charles Allen remains as chief executive.

And yet the irony is that even as ITN's separate and independent identity disappears, its name may re-emerge more strongly. For some years now the emphasis has been on branding ITN's news on ITV as the *ITV News*, and letting ITN's name and reputation fade away. This wilful erosion of one of Britain's most respected brands continues, and Charles Allen says it will remain his policy until the final consolidation of ITV. For the moment, it seems, it is not in his interest to promote ITN's virtues or its value. But once it's all over, once all of ITV and ITN are within Allen's grasp then, para-doxically, the ITN name will apparently be polished up to shine again. Why? Because Allen recognises that the ITN brand still carries weight, at home and abroad, and that other customers for the news – like Channel 4 – will find it easier to buy it from an organisation called ITN than one called ITV.

Says Allen: 'My vision for ITN would be as an integral part of ITV. If we owned it in total, I would use the ITN brand, and the whole operation – though it was wholly owned by ITV – would be branded ITN. My vision for it is that the ITN brand is a strong brand, and I think I would see it as a news provider not only to ITV but to others . . . If you look at our structure in ITV, we really have three businesses. We have our broadcasting business, which is called ITV Broadcasting; we have our production business, which is called Granada; and the reason it's called Granada is that it provides programming not only to ITV but to other players – like

Channel 4 for instance; I would call the third division ITN, if I owned the entity in its entirety. And therefore what I would do then is build the ITN brand.'

When I have total control of ITN, Allen seems to be saying, and given my belief in news at the heart of the schedule, you can rely on me – not to keep the old, independent ITN alive but to give it a new life as a thriving, expanding division of ITV.

Does that amount to 'And finally . . .?' Yes, it probably does. An ITN that belongs body and soul to a single broadcaster must be quite different from the company that stood proudly alone in Britain's commercial television system, its independence specifically protected by a powerful television regulator. The name ITN may remain but Independent Television News will not be the same.

Of all the factors affecting ITN that have changed in importance since the birth of commercial television fifty years ago, the power of the television regulator is probably the most significant. It was the ITA that first established ITN and then, with its successor the IBA, protected its infant creation from mean-spirited ITV owners. But the ITC showed itself powerless to protect its protégé, and now the new regulator Ofcom has no professional interest whatsoever in whether ITN lives or dies. Its only concern – quite rightly, perhaps, from the public's point of view – is the news on the screen. To Ofcom, who provides that news is irrelevant, a matter of complete indifference. ITN no longer has a champion in the television regulator.

So, for its survival in any shape or form, ITN is dependent on ITV and whoever owns ITV – whether it's Charles Allen, his successor or some American corporation. Of course, safe in ITV's arms, a new kind of ITN might indeed thrive, even expand. 'I believe passionately that news needs to be at the heart of what we're doing,' Charles Allen says. 'I want to provide content to others. I think we missed an opportunity with ITN because ITN should have been CNN [the American Cable News Network], and we haven't driven that, and I hope there might be opportunities still in the future for ITN – our news business, let's call it that – to also be an international provider.'

So Allen holds out the prospect of making good that dream of ITN becoming a world player. At the same time he insists that ITV is perfectly placed to shoulder the public service broadcasting responsibilities for providing high-quality news programmes on British commercial television: 'I fundamentally believe that it would be wrong for the BBC to be the only player that provides public service broadcasting, and I think that ITV is incredibly well placed to do regional, national and international news of a quality that can compete with the BBC,' he says.

Provided that ITV is prepared to fund this responsibility, that is good news for viewers and for those who may be working for this new ITN. But Allen is already negotiating with the government about his price for providing public service programmes of other kinds. Sooner or later ITV will want compensation for the cost of providing news of high quality; without it ITV may abandon that obligation, get out of broadcasting and into the digital world instead.

Says Tim Suter, Ofcom's executive board member responsible for content and standards: 'In this extraordinary construct, a commercial public service broadcaster, news will be the last obligation to go, and at the moment that is not being discussed. But there will come a point when the value of the remaining years of analogue, non-digital broadcasting is so low and the cost of public service obligations like the news so great that broadcasters like ITV will simply hand back their licences and go digital.' Ofcom has already conceded that in a digital world ITV would only be required to provide regional news 'if financially sustainable'.

That's the worry for the longer term, but what happens in the immediate future?

At the end of 2005 new licences will be issued by Ofcom that will commit broadcasters like ITV to carry out their public service obligations. Ofcom does have the power to decide what is an 'appropriate' level of funding for the news. While it seems unlikely that ITV will be made to pay ITN any more for its news programmes than it does now, it will nevertheless be required to give undertakings about the scheduling and quality of the news it intends to broadcast. But Ofcom is no powerful Independent Television Authority: it is a communications-industry regulator rather than a body dedicated to encouraging good broadcasting – as interested in mobile-phone ring tones as in the quality of television content. What confidence can we have that ITV will live up to its undertakings under the 'lite, lite' touch of Ofcom?

Says Richard Tait, ITN's last editor-in-chief: 'I'm not sure that the public service aspects of what ITN was doing have been sufficiently recognised by the regulator or anyone else. Only if public service broadcasters like ITV are held to their obligations can you have a company like ITN that aims at excellence. That has been ITN's aim all its life. Successive governments and regulators have said that news is special and can't be left to the market to decide its fate. But only if the regulator insists on high quality will ITN survive in recognisable shape. ITN is now in a perilous situation. It's the last really important bit in an experiment that is being sadly abandoned – that you can have high-quality programming operating in a commercial environment.'

After the damage ITV did to ITN in killing off *News at Ten,* why on earth should Charles Allen or any other owner of ITV be trusted to look after ITN's interests? 'I think that's fair, I think that's the issue,' Allen admits, agreeing that the decision to end *News at Ten* was short-sighted. But didn't it demonstrate conclusively that ITV knew the price of everything, and the value of nothing? 'I completely agree,' says Allen. 'I think it was a mistake. I think we should never have done it.' But will ITV be any better behaved this time round, or will it simply provide the cheapest news it can get away with, and push it to the margins of the schedule?

All traditional terrestrial broadcasters are under pressure, but while the BBC has its governors, newly galvanised to insist on high standards, ITV is governed by a far less potent regulator in Ofcom. High-quality news depends on good programming around it, but commercial television seems to be in decline, original, high-quality programmes of nearly every kind increasingly rare. Watching that decline is a little like the experience that the great Victorian Matthew Arnold described in his poem 'Dover Beach', as he saw the tide retreating and heard the 'melancholy, long withdrawing roar' of the 'sea of faith' that had sustained him. Yet we continue to need a commercial television service of real quality, because only in that situation do we have much chance of getting good television news on ITV.

To leave it once again to the BBC – or now Rupert Murdoch's Sky – to provide us with high-quality news would be to admit we could not match the vision and determination of the founders of commercial television. It would be a betrayal of those, like Norman Collins and Kenneth Clark, who thought that the nation deserved a real alternative to the BBC; to pioneers like Aidan Crawley and Arthur Clifford, who wanted *ITN News* to be the best; to Geoffrey Cox, who believed ITN's job was to sustain democracy; to news editors like Don Horobin and John Mahoney; to producers like David Phillips and John Toker; to thoughtful journalists like Julian Havilland and John Whale; to rumbustious reporters like Alan Hart, Michael Nicholson and Bill Neely; to trusted newscasters like Alastair Burnet, Jon Snow and Trevor McDonald; to editors Nigel Ryan and David Nicholas, who made *News at Ten* Britain's best news programme, and to their successors Stewart Purvis and Richard Tait, who kept the show on the road when it grew bumpy; and to all those who have worked at ITN, whether in front of the camera or behind the scenes, trying to make the best news programmes.

It was not at all obvious, when ITV began, how a commercial television system could provide high-quality news. But at the ITA Robert Fraser found a way that both the owners of ITV and the government were prepared to support: in return for a good chance of making good money, companies undertook to fund a good independent news service. Are we really content now, after the achievements of the past half-century, to abandon television news entirely to the market? Do we really want to treat today's viewers as mere consumers of a commodity, in which the news they get is no more important than the products advertised in the commercial breaks or, worse still, through sponsorship, or 'product placement'?

ITV's viewers still want and deserve the accurate, impartial information about the world that it has long been ITN's business to bring them. We owe it not just to the past but to the future to see that even if the ITN we have known is reaching the end of its remarkable run then something at least as good replaces it. If we found it possible fifty years ago to ensure a high-quality news service on commercial television then surely we can do so again. Let us make sure that such a system is in place before we say, 'And finally . . .' to the news from ITN.

NOTES

1 FOR LOVE AND MONEY

1. Peter Black, *The Mirror in the Corner: People's Television,* Hutchinson, 1972.
2. Quoted in Black, *ibid.*
3. George Barnes, then BBC director of the spoken word.
4. Quoted in Geoffrey Cox, *Pioneering Television News,* John Libbey, 1995.
5. Black, *The Mirror in the Corner.*

2 'WONDERFULLY GOOD'

1. IBA, 01204, 23 September 1954.
2. ITA board minutes, ITA/ITC, 16 November 1954.
3. IBA, 01204, 5 October 1954.
4. IBA, 01204, 13 January 1955.
5. IBA, 01204, 28 January 1955.

3 GENTLEMAN AMONG THE PLAYERS

1. Aidan Crawley, *Leap Before You Look,* Collins, 1988.
2. Arthur Eperon, *Daily Herald,* 25 February 1955.
3. Independent Television News Ltd was incorporated on 4 May 1955.
4. *Manchester Guardian,* 24 May 1955.

4 SIGNING ON

1. The *Amethyst* incident came at the end of the Chinese civil war in 1949.
2. Alexandra Palace in north London was the base for BBC television – but not radio – news.
3. Present were: Capt. Tom Brownrigg; John McMillan; Norman Collins; Harry Towers; Sidney Bernstein; Victor Peers and Aidan Crawley.
4. Robin Day, *Television: A Personal Report,* Hutchinson, 1961.
5. ITN board minutes, 14 June 1955.
6. There was no videotape recording at this time. Telerecordings, made by filming a television screen, were of relatively poor quality.
7. Day, *Television.*
8. Chataway was elected to Parliament in 1959 as MP for Lewisham North.

5 THE WOODEN SQUARE

1. Aidan Crawley, *Leap Before You Look,* Collins, 1988.
2. ITN paper 41, ITA/ITC, G9/68, 7 September 1955.
3. It had been leaked to Pye by Norman Collins, at ABC.

6 OPENING NIGHT – ON AIR

1. Its title was 'Non-Stop'.
2. Geoffrey Cox, *Pioneering Television News*, John Libbey, 1995.
3. Writers usually allow one second for every three words of commentary.
4. Bernard Levin, *Manchester Guardian*, October 1955.
5. £1,000.

7 ALMOST ALL OVER

1. IBA/ITC, 6, 14 June 1955.
2. Peter Black, *The Mirror in the Corner: People's Television*, Hutchinson, 1972.
3. IBA/ITC, 01204, 1 November 1955.
4. The address of the ITA's London HQ.
5. IBA/ITC, 01204, 24 November 1955.
6. ABC finally became a member of ITN on 1 March 1956.
7. Deputy chairman, *The Economist*; director, Reuters; vice-chairman, Daily News Ltd.
8. IBA/ITC, 01204, 6 December 1955.
9. ITN paper 47.
10. Letter, 31 October 1955, ITN paper 49.
11. ITN paper 53.
12. The other was his great friend John Cotter, ITN's film manager.
13. Aidan Crawley, *Leap Before You Look*, Collins, 1988.
14. IBA/ITC, 01204, 21 December 1955.
15. IBA/ITC, 128/147, 27 December 1955.
16. Aidan Crawley's figures.
17. ITN board minutes, 15 January 1956.
18. *Broadcast*, 22 September 1980.
19. ITA/ITC, M6, 8 March 1956.
20. ITA/ITC, M6, 9 March 1956.

8 THE OTHER NEW ZEALANDER

1. Public Record Office, PREM 11/1212, 109280, 22 June 1956.
2. Geoffrey Cox, *Pioneering Television News*, John Libbey, 1995.

9 'AWAY WE GO AGAIN'

1. Kenneth Adam became BBC controller of television programmes in 1957.

2. ITA/ITC, M6, 9 February 1956.
3. Granada's London headquarters.
4. ITA/ITC, 128/147, 11 February 1956.
5. The title editor-in-chief was dropped.
6. ITN paper 88, ITA/ITC, G9/68, 22 October 1956.
7. *Panorama*.
8. ITN paper 87A, 23 October 1956.
9. ITA/ITC, 69/100, 1 November 1956.
10. ITA/ITC, G9/68, 26 March 1957.
11. ITA/ITC, 98/67, 16 March 1957.
12. ITA/ITC, 98/67, 18 March 1957.
13. ITA/ITC, 69/100, 8 April 1957.
14. ITA/ITC, 69/100, April 1957.

10 SOMETHING NEW IN NEWS

1. Robin Day, *Television: A Personal Report*, Hutchinson, 1961.
2. James Cameron, *News Chronicle*, 1 July, 1957.
3. ITA/ITC, 69/70, 2 July 1957.
4. ITA/ITC, 69/70, 3 July 1957.
5. Day, *Television*.
6. *ibid*.
7. *Daily Express*, 24 February 1958.
8. *Observer*, 2 March 1958.
9. Robin Day, *Grand Inquisitor*, Weidenfeld and Nicolson, 1989.
10. 22 January 1956.
11. Kenneth McDonald, *Evening News*, 26 March 1956.
12. At 2004 values Robin Day's fee would then have been about £39,000 and Ludovic Kennedy's £35,000.
13. The studio director.
14. Anne Sebba, *Battling For News: The Rise of the Woman Reporter*, Hodder and Stoughton, 1994.
15. Geoffrey Cox, *See It Happen: The Making of ITN*, Bodley Head, 1983.
16. Reginald Bosanquet with Wallace Reyburn, *Let's Get Through Wednesday*, Michael Joseph, 1980.
17. ITA/ITC, 69/100, 7 December 1956.
18. Cox, *See it Happen*.
19. *ibid*.
20. A BBC *Panorama* sound crew did well in Hungary, but did not make it to Budapest.

21. Cox, *See it Happen*.
22. Bernard Levin, *The Times*, 19 September 1957.

11 BIG IDEAS

1. ITN paper 57, 3 January 1956.
2. ITN paper 93, 29 March 1957.
3. 19 March 1957.
4. Geoffrey Cox, *See it Happen: The Making of ITN*, Bodley Head, 1983.
5. John Boorman, *Adventures of a Suburban Boy*, Faber and Faber, 2003.
6. 3 February 1960.
7. ITN paper 181, 27 June 1960.
8. ITA/ITC, 69/70, 19 March 1964.
9. John McMillan and Lord (David) Windlesham, respectively general manager and his deputy at Rediffusion Television.
10. ITA/ITC, 69/70, 3 April 1964.
11. ITN paper 285, 16 April 1964.
12. ITA/ITC, 67/98, 19 February 1965
13. *The Future Scope of ITN*, ITN paper 264, 28 June 1963.
14. Cox, *See it Happen*.
15. ITN paper 285, 16 April 1964.

12 JEWEL IN THE CROWN

1. ITA/ITC, 67/98, 26 March 1965.
2. ITA Consultation on News and Current Affairs, 25/26 January 1966.
3. ITA/ITC, M70, 1 September 1966.
4. ITA/ITC, 67/98, 30 January 1967.
5. 13 March 1967.
6. ITN board minutes, 8 March 1967.
7. *Guardian*, 5 June 1967.
8. ITA/ITC, 67/98, 15 June 1957.
9. Pan Am then offered a seven-minute helicopter service from JFK airport to the roof of the Pan Am building in central New York. The service ended after a spectacular accident killed 5 people.
10. Geoffrey Cox, *See It Happen: The Making of ITN*, Bodley Head, 1983.
11. *ibid*.
12. *ibid*.
13. 18 August 1967.
14. ITA/ITC, 67/98, August 1967.

15. ITA/ITC, 67/98, 31 October 1967.
16. ITA/ITC, 67/98, 15 December 1967.
17. ITA/ITC, 67/98, 5 January 1968.
18. PPC minutes 16(68), ITA/ITC, 14 February 1968.
19. Second Report from Select Committees, Session I, 1971.
20. ITN board minutes, 3 July 1968.
21. *Daily Mirror*, 23 August 1969.

13 THE SECRET OF SUCCESS

1. A Steenbeck was a machine on which film could be viewed with its soundtrack as it was run rapidly backwards and forwards.
2. David Phillips, *The Half Hour Bulletin*, ITN paper, 26 April 1967.

14 THE REPORTERS

1. John Whale, *The Half-Shut Eye*, Macmillan, 1969.
2. Maurice Wiggin, *Sunday Times*, 13 August 1967
3. The Lord Chief Justice Lord Widgery was later appointed to enquire into the events of Bloody Sunday.
4. ITN paper 786, 13 December 1977.
5. Michael Nicholson, *A Measure of Danger*, HarperCollins, 1991.
6. *ibid*.
7. *ibid*.
8. *ibid*.
9. David Alford, *Sunday People*, 23 March 1986.
10. Sandy Gall, *News from the Front*, Heinemann, 1994.
11. Sandy Gall, *Don't Worry About the Money Now*, Hamish Hamilton, 1983.
12. ITN paper 490, 11 March 1970; Nigel Ryan said Sandy Gall would alternate with Leonard Parkin in the newscaster/reporter role.

15 A FORCE FOR GOOD

1. ITA/ITC, 98/67, 20 April 1956.
2. Jeremy Potter, *Independent Television in Britain*, vol. 4, Macmillan, 1990.

3. 22 May 1967.
4. An outside broadcast as Chichester sailed triumphantly into Plymouth harbour.
5. ITA/ITC, 67/98, 26 May 1967.
6. 31 July 1969.
7. 16 October 1969.

16 FIRSTBORN GIRL CHILDREN

1. ITN paper 165, 1959.
2. ITN paper 663, 1974.

17 TUSSLE AT THE TOP

1. 12 June 1967.

18 AN EDITOR WITH STYLE

1. ITN paper, 12 January 1968.
2. After leaving the ITA Fraser became even more important to Nigel Ryan as chairman of ITN from 1971 to 1974.
3. The ITA became the IBA, the Independent Broadcasting Authority, in 1973.
4. ITN paper 537, 17 June 1971.
5. 21 June 1971.
6. 12 July 1971.
7. Jeremy Potter, *Independent Television in Britain*, vol. 4, Macmillan, 1990.
8. ITA/ITC, 69/70, ITN paper, April 1971.
9. Jeremy Potter, *Independent Television in Britain*, vol. 3, Macmillan, 1989.
10. ITA/ITC, 58/134, 20 April 1972.
11. *Stage and Television Today*, 25 January, 1973.
12. IBA/ITC, 108/135, 17 August 1973.
13. IBA/ITC, 108/135, 26 October 1973.
14. IBA/ITC, 108/135, 8 November 1973.
15. IBA/ITC, 110/137, 15 July 1974.
16. ITA/ITC, 69/70, February 1971.
17. ITA/ITC, 69/70, 18 May 1971.
18. ITA/ITC, 69/70, 21 May 1971.
19. Tim Ewbank, *Daily Mail*, 3 October 1974.
20. Basic pay was increased by 19 per cent. Other payments made the deal worth an estimated 28 per cent.

21. ITN board minutes, 21 October 1974.
22. *Broadcast*, 8 November 1976.
23. John Pearson, Industrial Society Report, 20 April 1977.
24. Jean Rook, *Daily Express*, 20 September 1977.
25. Martin Jackson, *Daily Mail*, 24 September 1977.

19 OUT OF THIS WORLD

1. ITA/ITC, M70, 9 June 1969.
2. Jeremy Potter, *Independent Television in Britain*, vol. 4, Macmillan, 1990.
3. Stanley Reynolds, *Guardian*, 22 July 1969.
4. ITA/ITC, M70, 21 July 1969.
5. L. Marsland Gander, *Daily Telegraph*, 21 July 1969.
6. *UK Press Gazette*, 28 July 1969.
7. William Hardcastle, *Listener*, 24 July 1969.

21 ITN AT WAR

1. ITN board minutes, 20 September 1971.
2. Andrea Catherwood gave birth to a boy, Finn Catherwood Smith, on 9 February 2004.
3. Mark Wood, *Broadcast*, 26 September 2003.
4. *Tonight with Trevor McDonald*, ITV, 22 March 2004.
5. Obituary, *Guardian*, 24 March 2003.
6. *The Role of Embedded Reporting During the 2003 Iraq War: Summary Report*, 6 November 2003.
7. *ibid.*

22 REGGIE

1. Wilfred De'Ath, *Observer* magazine, 8 June 1975.
2. John Sandilands, *Woman*, 1978.
3. Jilly Cooper, September 1980.
4. Reginald Bosanquet with Wallace Reyburn, *Let's Get Through Wednesday*, Michael Joseph, 1980.
5. *Ibid.*

6. *Daily Mail*, 1 May 1976.
7. *Daily Mail*, 15 May 1976.
8. *Sunday People*, 23 May 1976.
9. ITN board minutes, 17 January 1977.
10. ITN paper 874, November 1979.

23 TURNING OVER

1. Martyn Pedrick, *In the Front Line*, Robson Books, 1983.
2. John Pilger, *Heroes*, Jonathan Cape, 1986.

24 LOSING CONTACT

1. 8 June 1972. Despite her terrible burns, Kim Phuc made a good recovery.
2. Michael Nicholson, *A Measure of Danger*, HarperCollins, 1991.
3. *Ibid*.
4. South Africa's Bureau of State Security.
5. Nicholson, *A Measure of Danger*.
6. The British Secret Intelligence Service.
7. Nicholson, *A Measure of Danger*.

25 THE AGENCY GAME

1. *Manchester Guardian*, 24 May 1955.
2. ITN board minutes, 17 May 1955.
3. ITN paper, 8 June 1955.
4. ITN board minutes, 21 October 1959.
5. Nigel Ryan, draft for Jeremy Potter, *Independent Television in Britain*, vol. 4, Macmillan, 1990.
6. IBA/ITC, 110/137, 9 April 1975.
7. ITN board minutes, 19 March 1979.
8. *Guardian*, 30 March 1979.
9. ITN board minutes, 21 May 1979.
10. Letter, 25 May 1979.
11. Eschel Rhoodie, *The Real Information Scandal*, Orbis SA, Pretoria, 1983.
12. Elaine Potter, *New Statesman*, 15 June 1979.
13. David Nicholas, letter to Charles Denton, Central Television, 1 October 1984.

26 SCOOP!

1. Nicholson, *A Measure of Danger*.
2. Peter Snow believes he told Nicholson

the landing would be at Kyrenia – in the north.
3. London *Evening Standard*, 23 July 1974.
4. Nicholson, *A Measure of Danger*.

27 COMING INDOORS

1. David Phillips, ITN memo, 19 August 1976.
2. Paul McKee, ITN memo, 9 September 1976.

28 A DIFFERENT NEWS

1. ITN paper 934, February 1981.
2. Jeremy Isaacs, *Storm Over Four: A Personal Account*, Weidenfeld and Nicolson, 1989.
3. *Observer*, 8 January 1981.
4. *Observer*, 15 January 1981.
5. Isaacs, *Storm Over Four*.
6. Letter, 15 February 1983.
7. ITN paper 1058, July 1983.
8. Isaacs, *Storm Over Four*.
9. Letter, 23 September 1983.
10. ITN paper 1094, September 1984.
11. ITN paper 1097, October 1984.
12. *Television Weekly*, 20 July 1984.

29 TELLING THE TRUTH

1. Ian Hargreaves and James Thomas, *New News, Old News*, ITC, 2002.
2. Anthony Smith, *The Shadow in the Cave*, George Allen & Unwin, London, 1973.
3. Adrian Monck, *Press Gazette*, 23 July 2004.
4. Glasgow University Media Group, *Bad News*, Routledge and Kegan Paul, London, 1976.
5. *Daily Telegraph*, 9 November 1978.
6. Martin Harrison, *TV News: Whose Bias?*, Policy Journals, 1985.
7. ITN board minutes, January 1983.
8. Jeremy Isaacs, *Storm Over Four: A Personal Account*, Weidenfeld and Nicolson, 1989.
9. ITN board minutes, 28 January 1983.
10. ITN had submitted its own bid but had been unsuccessful.

11. Paul Bonner with Lesley Aston, *Independent Television in Britain*, vol. 6, Macmillan, 2003.
12. ITN paper 941, April 1981.
13. ITN paper 948A, June 1981.
14. Julia Hartley-Brewer, *Guardian*, 15 March 2000.
15. Tim Jones, *The Times*, 29 February 2000.
16. Richard Tait, *Daily Telegraph*, 17 March 2000.
17. Caroline Davies, *Daily Telegraph*, 15 March 2000.
18. LM eventually paid £50,000 of the damages awarded by the High Court.

30 EXPAND OR DIE
1. Bill Dorran and Jane Owen, *Sunday People*, 17 October 1982.
2. Profile, *Observer*, 8 January 1984.
3. Letter, *Observer*, 15 January 1984.
4. Peacock Committee Report, cmnd 9824, HMSO, 1986.
5. *Death on the Rock*, *This Week*, Thames Television, 28 April 1988.
6. In 1990 Sue Tinson was appointed DBE.
7. ITN board minutes, 19 September 1988.
8. Andrew Lycett, *The Times*, 18 March 1988.
9. ITN board minutes, 18 September 1989.
10. Peter Monteith, *Television Week*, 1 February 1990.
11. ITN board minutes, 19 February 1990.
12. This last requirement was ultimately dropped.

31 TOMORROW THE WORLD
1. ITN paper 1026, 9 February 1987.
2. IBA memo, 2 April 1987, quoted in Paul Bonner with Lesley Aston, *Independent Television in Britain*, vol. 5, Macmillan, 1998.
3. IBA paper 136(87), 1987.
4. Bonner with Aston, *Independent Television*, vol. 5.
5. ITN board minutes, 16 February 1987.
6. *ibid.*, 16 February 1987.

32 OUT OF CONTROL
1. ITN board minutes, 15 January 1990.
2. *ibid.*, 19 February 1990.
3. *ibid.*, 9 March 1990.
4. *ibid.*, 21 May 1990.
5. Georgina Henry, *Guardian*, 12 October 1990.
6. Steve Clarke, *Sunday Times*, 14 October 1990.
7. ITN board minutes, 18 February 1991.
8. *ibid.*, 20 May 1991.
9. Maggie Brown, *Independent*, 27 March 1991.
10. *Broadcast*, 7 June 1991.
11. ITN board minutes, 17 June 1991.

33 THE DOOMED BID
1. Letter, 22 August 1991.
2. Letter, 27 August 1991.

34 LEANER, FITTER
1. ITN paper 1339, 11 April 1988.
2. Desmond Hamill, *Guardian*, 29 July 1991.
3. Sue Summers, *Daily Telegraph*, 7 August 1991.
4. ITN board minutes, 19 October 1992.
5. Melinda Wittstock, *The Times*, 13 October 1992.
6. *The Times*, 31 March 1993.
7. ITN board minutes, 11 January 1994.
8. *ibid.*, 16 March 1992.
9. Lester Middlehurst, *Daily Mail*, 16 March 1992.

35 A REALLY BAD MISTAKE
1. 13 July 1993.
2. 7 July 1993.
3. ITN board minutes, 19 July 1993.
4. Quoted in Michael Brunson, *A Ringside Seat*, Hodder and Stoughton, 2000.
5. Sir George Russell had chaired these companies before becoming chairman of ITN, and then of the IBA and its successor, the ITC.
6. 20 May 1994.

7. 5 October 1994.
8. ITN press release, 27 January 1995.
9. Quoted in Raymond Snoddy, *Greenfinger: The Rise of Michael Green and Carlton Communications*, Faber and Faber, 1996.
10. 31 March 1995.
11. That is, men from the upper socio-economic classes; better educated, better-off.
12. *The Future of Prime Time News on ITV*, 8 October 1997.
13. On Friday night *News at Ten* was part of LWT's London weekend schedule.
14. Select Committee on Culture, Media and Sport, Evidence, 22 October 1998.
15. ITC press release, 105/98, 19 November 1998.
16. Brunson, *A Ringside Seat*.
17. Janine Gibson, *Guardian*, 23 November 1998.
18. Fifth Report, Select Committee on Culture, Media and Sport, 22 March 2000.
19. Maggie Brown, *Guardian*, 1 May 2000.
20. Richard Tait, *Financial Times*, 7 October 2003.

36 ANY OTHER BUSINESS

1. Richard Hooper and Mark Friend, *Audit of ITN's Strengths and Weaknesses*, 16 July 1993.
2. ITN board minutes, October 1993.
3. *ibid.*, 23 January 1995.

4. ITN paper, January 1995.
5. David Teather and Maggie Brown, *Guardian*, 25 June 2001.
6. Andrew Neil, *Scotsman*, 23 July 2001.
7. ITN board minutes, 19 July 1993.
8. James Harding, *Financial Times*, 7 June 2000.

38 THE WAY WE LIVE NOW

1. Clive Jones, *Television*, vol. 41:5, May 2004.
2. James Robinson, *Observer*, 6 June 2004.
3. Chris Shaw, *Press Gazette*, 20 February 2004.
4. In June 2004 it was announced that ITN had lost the Channel 5 News contract to Sky News.
5. Strangely, Snow's name had been put forward by his local council, Camden, for his charitable work – not for his journalism.
6. *ITV News at 10.30*, 7 July 2004.
7. Jasper Gerard, *Sunday Times*, 22 February, 2004.

39 AND FINALLY ... ?

1. Richard Tait, *Financial Times*, 8 June 2004.
2. Letter, *Broadcast*, 22 February 2002.
3. Steven Barnett, 'Impartiality redefined: protecting news on commercial television in Britain', IPPR, 2002.

INDEX